Cultural and Linguistic Considerations in Forensic Mental Health Assessment

Cultural and Linguistic Considerations in Forensic Mental Health Assessment

A Guide for Clinicians

BARRY ROSENFELD
ALICIA NIJDAM-JONES

OXFORD
UNIVERSITY PRESS

OXFORD
UNIVERSITY PRESS

Oxford University Press is a department of the University of Oxford.
It furthers the University's objective of excellence in research, scholarship,
and education by publishing worldwide. Oxford is a registered trade mark of
Oxford University Press in the UK and in certain other countries.

Published in the United States of America by Oxford University Press
198 Madison Avenue, New York, NY 10016, United States of America.

CIP data is on file at the Library of Congress

ISBN 9780190900960

DOI: 10.1093/9780190900991.001.0001

The manufacturer's authorized representative in the EU for product safety is
Oxford University Press España S.A. of Parque Empresarial San Fernando de Henares,
Avenida de Castilla, 2 – 28830 Madrid (www.oup.es/en or product.safety@oup.com).
OUP España S.A. also acts as importer into Spain of products made by the manufacturer.

For Cara, Jane, Kate, and Anna - my Fab Four - Barry Rosenfeld

For Byron and Hugo, who remind me to see differently, question deeply, and always do better - Alicia Nijdam-Jones

Contents

List of Figures

List of Tables

Preface

Forensic mental health professionals grapple with a wide array of challenges, from ambiguous legal standards and complex ethical dilemmas to heterogeneous (and sometimes disingenuous) symptom presentations, all while providing expert opinions under highly stressful conditions. An increasingly common challenge for virtually all forensic clinicians is evaluating people from cultural and linguistic backgrounds different from their own in ways that are respectful and contextually informed. As practicing clinicians and researchers working within our complex and evolving field, we have endeavored to grapple directly with these thorny issues, often learning through reflection on our own mistakes and those we've observed in others. This book evolved from our clinical and research experiences, as well as our desire to support others in approaching these challenges with greater sensitivity and cultural responsiveness.

Although cultural competence has become a frequent focus in mental health circles, the shifting landscape of practice has raised important questions about what that term actually means in applied work. Our goals for this book are modest: to offer practical, actionable suggestions that a) help clinicians feel more confident working in diverse and dynamic contexts, and b) improve the fairness and accuracy of forensic evaluations. Along the way, we emphasize cultural humility and reflexivity, recognizing the systemic inequities and power dynamics that impact the forensic assessment process.

We have tried to provide a balanced review of the growing scientific literature interspersed with real-world examples. Of course, new research emerges almost weekly, and no book or resource can keep pace (even if it was a blog updated daily)! Still, we hope the ideas and principles outlined here will offer a steady guide as our field continues to move toward more equitable and culturally responsive forensic practice.

1
The Importance of Culture in Forensic Assessment

Summary

With Western societies becoming increasingly multicultural, mental health professionals are frequently called upon to evaluate and treat individuals from diverse backgrounds and intersecting identities, including but not limited to cultural, linguistic, ethnic, and religious identities. Countless challenges arise when conducting a forensic evaluation of individuals from diverse backgrounds, and this book attempts to tackle many of these challenges. We do so by identifying fundamental problems, offering possible solutions, and reviewing the existing research that supports what we hope to be the current state of "best practices." Although some of the challenges forensic evaluators face may seem (and can be) unresolvable, others can and should be met with the knowledge and skills that can be acquired. This book is intended to provide some of that knowledge by addressing a wide range of topics that may confront the forensic evaluator. We begin with chapters addressing core elements that cut across most types of forensic evaluation, such as clinical and diagnostic interviewing (Chapter 2), the assessment of response style and malingering (Chapter 3), and the use of multiscale inventories–primarily the Minnesota Multiphasic Personality Inventory (MMPI) and Personality Assessment Inventory (PAI) instruments (Chapter 4). Subsequent chapters focus on more specialized forms of assessment, either in terms of the focus of inquiry, such as the assessment of cognitive and intellectual functioning (Chapter 5) and the risk of violence or reoffending in adults and children (Chapter 6), or on the context for the evaluation, such as the evaluation of children and families (Chapter 7) and asylum/international human rights evaluations (Chapter 8). Finally, we conclude with an outline for a culturally informed research agenda that identifies gaps in our existing knowledge base and topic areas that need more innovative or rigorous investigation (Chapter 9). Because this book is intended to provide hands-on guidance for

Cultural and Linguistic Considerations in Forensic Mental Health Assessment. Barry Rosenfeld and Alicia Nijdam-Jones, Oxford University Press. © Oxford University Press (2026).
DOI: 10.1093/9780190900991.003.0001

practicing clinicians and researchers, we begin each chapter with a case vignette that illustrates some of the problems/issues addressed and close each chapter with specific take-home points to consider.

Case Vignette

Mr. M, a 47-year-old Pakistani immigrant, was referred for an evaluation of his mental state at the time of the offense, following an incident in which he stabbed and killed his wife of 28 years. The homicide occurred inside the family's suburban home in the late evening, after Mr. M had returned from work as a deliveryman. There was no evidence of prior violence within the family, nor had Mr. M displayed any history of behavioral or mental health problems. Instead, he was known to be a quiet, hardworking man who was helpful to his neighbors and a good father to his four children. However, he had recently sought treatment for worsening gastrointestinal problems and difficulty sleeping that began after he was assaulted and stabbed several months earlier. His attorney requested an evaluation to assess whether his sudden violent outburst could be related to posttraumatic stress disorder. Although Mr. M was able to communicate effectively with his attorney in English and had lived in the US for the past 18 years, he preferred to speak in his primary language of Urdu. The evaluation raised several important questions, including when an interpreter is necessary for evaluations in which the person is only partially fluent in a language spoken by the evaluator and what, if any, psychological testing can be used. Perhaps more importantly, is it ethically appropriate for a mental health professional to evaluate an individual from a culture they have little knowledge or familiarity with, or should one seek a Pakistani psychologist or psychiatrist to conduct the evaluation? The following chapters address these and many other issues, highlighting the challenges that arise in the evaluation of culturally and linguistically diverse individuals.

Decisions about how to evaluate individuals from backgrounds that differ from the evaluator or dominant cultural context can challenge even the most experienced forensic mental health professional. Although many of the concerns raised in the opening vignette may be obvious to the skilled clinician, the vignettes in this book are drawn from actual cases we have encountered (altered to ensure confidentiality). And while some of these vignettes describe seemingly egregious mistakes (which will be addressed in the chapters that follow each vignette, with the exception of this chapter), they reflect real decisions made by experienced clinicians who were retained to conduct a forensic mental health evaluation. Fortunately, many of our colleagues have become increasingly aware of the most common issues in cross-cultural forensic evaluations (i.e., evaluations of culturally or linguistically diverse individuals). Topics such as the use of interpreters, how and when to use psychological testing (and how to interpret the results), and the integration of culturally specific information into the diagnostic and assessment process have become familiar points of discussion in both the research literature and clinical forums (e.g., Fanniff et al., 2022). This book summarizes the current state of the field in order to expand the knowledge, sophistication, and overall cultural competence of mental health professionals who work in forensic settings.

For the past several decades, mental health professionals have had ample opportunity to receive training in how to adjust typical clinical evaluation procedures to the requirements of forensic evaluations. The increased availability of forensically oriented master's- and doctoral-level training programs, postdoctoral fellowships, and specialized workshops and texts have raised the bar for forensic practice. There is a much greater awareness of the unique needs and demands required of forensic work. For instance, almost all forensic clinicians understand the need to seek and consider collateral sources of information, the importance of formally evaluating response bias, and the focused nature of forensic inquiry (i.e., addressing one or more specific psycho-legal issues). However, far less attention has been paid to the adjustments that may be required to evaluate individuals from culturally and linguistically diverse backgrounds. When the examinee does not speak the same language as the evaluator or is from a markedly different culture, the evaluator must adapt their assessment approach to account for a wide range of unique considerations. These adaptations pertain not only to the interview itself, such as the best practices for using an interpreter, but also to how the individual's cultural background may impact the interpretation of the behaviors observed and responses elicited.

The Importance of Culture

The American Psychological Association's (APA) Specialty Guidelines for Forensic Psychology (2013) highlights the need for evaluators to consider "linguistic and cultural differences that might affect their judgments or reduce the accuracy of their interpretations" (p. 15). This principle is grounded in the APA Ethics Code, which cites the importance of understanding possible sources of bias, including an individual's race, culture, and ethnicity (APA, 2017a). Clearly, there is a strong consensus among psychologists that understanding an individual's culture, along with possible sources of bias on the part of the evaluator, is necessary for conducting culturally sensitive evaluations.

Understanding the differences between our own experience and those of the individuals we are asked to evaluate is particularly important for forensic mental health professionals because cultural differences are not simply a product of immigration and language. Mental health professionals often have little in common with those they evaluate or treat, even when they are born and raised in close proximity to one another (Ponterotto, 1998; Sue, 2004). Educational, socioeconomic, and religious differences are among the many factors that can impede the evaluation process, hindering the development of rapport and leading to misunderstandings and perhaps even incorrect conclusions about important questions. How can an evaluator assessing competence to stand trial distinguish whether a criminal defendant's resistance to working with an attorney is based on their prior experiences, rather than a mental disorder, without understanding the nature of that person's previous encounters with attorneys or the criminal legal system?[1] What about determining the extent of psychological damages attributable to a report of workplace discrimination or harassment? Differentiating genuine from fabricated or exaggerated symptoms often depends on understanding how the person's responses differ from those typical of their peers. However, the forensic mental health professional is rarely a "peer" of the person they evaluate.

The need to appreciate differences between ourselves and those we evaluate impacts all aspects of clinical work but has particular importance during a forensic interview. As in any clinical setting, the development of rapport is critical to a successful forensic evaluation, as it can impact a wide range of interactions. For example, accurately interpreting an individual's verbal responses (i.e., both the evaluator's questions and the examinee's answers) and non-verbal behaviors (e.g., eye contact, tangential speech) often requires understanding the individual's unique cultural and experiential background. The myriad ways that cultural influences can impede effective forensic interviewing, along with steps that can be taken to minimize the impact of these challenges are addressed in more detail in Chapter 2. However, the importance of these influences is at the center of calls for cultural competence. Gauging when—or more accurately, to what extent—cultural considerations must be reckoned with is a task for every clinician in virtually every evaluation. When a forensic mental health professional shares some of the same background and life experiences as an individual they are evaluating, it may raise an entirely different set of issues, perhaps even compromising their objectivity. In sum, the goal of cultural competence is to truly understand the examinee's perspective to assist the evaluator in seeing the world through the same lens that the examinee does.

Understanding and addressing cultural and linguistic differences is an increasingly important element of all types of clinical practice, as evidenced by the emphasis on cultural competence and responsiveness in clinical and

[1] We use the term *criminal legal system* rather than *criminal justice system* throughout this book due to the growing recognition that justice or fairness is not necessarily characteristic of the legal systems in which forensic mental health professionals operate (e.g., Dolovich & Natapoff, 2017).

ethical guidelines (e.g., APA, 2017a, 2019a, 2019b). The APA's Ethics Code offers the following guidance on diversity as it applies to fairness, impartiality, and respecting people's rights and dignity:

> *Psychologists are aware of and respect cultural, individual, and role differences, including those based on age, gender, gender identity, race, ethnicity, culture, national origin, religion, sexual orientation, disability, language, and socioeconomic status, and consider these factors when working with members of such groups. Psychologists try to eliminate the effect on their work of biases based on those factors, and they do not knowingly participate in or condone activities of others based upon such prejudices.*
>
> (APA, 2017a, p. 3)

Regarding the practice of psychological assessment (which encompasses forensic assessment), the Ethics Code provides even more tangible guidance:

> *Psychologists use assessment instruments whose validity and reliability have been established for use with members of the population tested. When such validity or reliability has not been established, psychologists describe the strengths and limitations of test results and interpretation.*
>
> (Standard, 9.02)

These standards provide an essential starting point but offer little detail and few potential solutions. Indeed, the extent to which culture complicates forensic assessment is varied and often profound. For example, cultural knowledge is critical to accurately differentiating pathological from normative behaviors or beliefs and identifying culturally unique considerations that might impact the evaluation process. These considerations can be particularly important in forensic evaluations, where deviations from normative behaviors often have direct relevance for the legal and clinical questions at issue. Should the seemingly bizarre beliefs expressed by an examinee be considered evidence of delusional thinking, or should they be understood as culturally normative beliefs common among the individual's peers? Likewise, while the assessment of possible feigning is central to many forensic evaluations, the applicability of specific tools or techniques for identifying symptom exaggeration may be questionable when applied to someone from a markedly different culture. In short, implementing the goal of cultural competence into practice is often a challenging task, particularly for those working in forensic mental health settings.

When we began writing this book, our intent was to address primarily "international" forms of diversity, focusing mainly on the cultural and linguistic challenges faced by practitioners in the US, Canada, and other Western countries where immigration is common (e.g., Australia, the United Kingdom). The level of cultural and ethnic diversity present in legal settings is steadily increasing across these regions. Individuals from immigrant communities account for roughly 16% of persons incarcerated in US Federal prisons, 12% of those imprisoned in the United Kingdom (UK), and roughly comparable (if not higher) percentages are found in Australia and many European prisons (Australian Bureau of Statistics, 2024; Bureau of Prisons Statistics, 2022; Institute for Crime and Justice Policy Research, 2021; Ministry of Justice, 2022). As a result, forensic mental health professionals are frequently tasked with evaluating individuals who speak a different language or have different customs and expectations.

Although this book focuses on the challenges posed when evaluating immigrants from markedly different cultural and linguistic backgrounds than the evaluators, the principles addressed in this book will have relevance beyond immigrant populations; integrating these considerations into practice will hopefully promote better forensic evaluation methods among diverse populations generally, including diversity within the broader population based on race, gender, ethnicity, and Indigeneity. Although fluency in the majority language may not be an issue in many of these cases, the need to understand an individual's unique cultural and experiential background is no less important. The growing emphasis on social justice, particularly in relation to the structural racism embedded within the criminal legal system, has placed racial and ethnic differences at the forefront of many debates in the US and other Western countries. While the history and colonial contexts differ, Canada and Australia's treatment of Indigenous peoples has raised concerns that parallel those expressed in the US and UK regarding systemic inequities affecting Black citizens. Similar issues have been raised in many Western European countries, where immigration has increasingly diversified societies that were once relatively homogenous.

The need for an antiracist approach to clinical practice generally, and forensic mental health assessment in particular, demands that evaluators understand and consider the impact of race, ethnicity, and culture, as well as all other forms of identity—including sexual orientation and identity, differing physical and mental abilities, age, religion, and others. Any of these domains can impact the accuracy of forensic evaluations and may necessitate adaptations to what would otherwise be construed as standard forensic practice. Arguably, each of these topics might form the basis for an entire book (or at least separate chapters). Instead, we will attempt to highlight overarching issues, drawing attention to what is known (and unknown) regarding the specific topics that form the structure of this book.

One exception to this statement is age; while some attention will be paid to issues related to youth in the forensic mental health system, the issues raised by age (at both ends of the spectrum) are often distinct from other forms of diversity. Because of the different legal processes that apply to adolescents and the unique clinical issues that often apply to older adults, a thorough analysis of the challenges posed by age is beyond the scope of this book. Instead, we focus primarily on culture, taking a broad lens as to what this term means, but focusing heavily on the issues that arise when evaluations involve those who have immigrated from another country or culture.

In short, our primary goal for this book is to help enhance the cultural competence and responsiveness of forensic mental health professionals by providing concrete examples and recommendations. We do not claim to be the final authority on these issues, particularly given our positionality as White, North American clinical psychologists who divide our time between academia and independent practice. However, we have encountered enough challenges in our own work and have made enough mistakes along the way to have identified many of the pitfalls that arise in the forensic evaluation of culturally and linguistically diverse individuals. Given this experience, we believe we can offer some valuable insights for readers of this book.

Prior to exploring the many issues and adaptations that arise in cross-cultural forensic evaluations, we begin by reviewing several key constructs, starting with culture, ethnicity, and race. These distinct yet overlapping constructs represent a range of influences that are central to the themes of this book. Subsequent sections in this chapter address the concepts of cultural competence and acculturation more generally, highlighting the relevance of these constructs for forensic mental health professionals.

Culture, Ethnicity, and Race

Culture

Before we begin, it is crucial to recognize that culture, ethnicity, and race are distinct concepts, each with unique challenges. These terms often reify and reduce complex, overlapping experiences into singular categories that fail to reflect the complexity of lived experience. Culture, ethnicity, and race are distinct but often intertwined concepts. For example, culture, unlike race, is learned rather than attributed. Yet despite over a century of research, *culture* remains an imprecise term with no agreed-upon formal definition (Burke, 2017). In fact, some scholars have recommended avoiding the word altogether, instead focusing discussions on the specific beliefs, art, technology, or ideology referenced (Kuper, 1999). Despite the ongoing controversy over the definition (or utility) of the term culture, there is consensus regarding the complexity of culture and widespread recognition that culture can influence the cognitions and behaviors of both individuals and groups (Spencer-Oatey, 2012). However, modern understandings of culture acknowledge its fluidity and variability. Culture is not a neat "box" or a fixed entity but a process that evolves over time and through interaction.

Individuals learn culture through their social and physical environments, which can manifest in creating observable artifacts, values, basic underlying assumptions, behaviors, and the interpretations of behaviors (Shein, 1990). Essentially, culture is something shared among two or more individuals that reflects their experiences, customs, and internalized social norms. However, boundaries between cultures are not well defined, as there are no clear lines between the features of one culture and another. Cultures vary over time and are not uniformly distributed across individuals or groups (Spencer-Oatey, 2012). This is particularly true in complex societies, where cultural influences overlap, mix, and evolve.

Culture has both universal (etic) and unique (emic) features, meaning that observable behaviors may appear culturally distinctive (e.g., differences in gaze patterns, such as avoiding or making eye contact), but the motivations behind such behaviors could be universal (e.g., demonstrating politeness, deference, and respect; Matsumoto, 1996). However, experts agree that culture should not serve as an evaluative or value-laden function (Spencer-Oatey, 2012). Instead, it is simply descriptive, describing the similarities and differences between one cultural group and another.

The APA's Multicultural Guidelines (2017b) provides a relatively succinct definition of culture:

> *... belief systems and value orientations that influence customs, norms, practices, and social institutions, including psychological processes (language, care-taking practices...) and organizations (media, educational systems). Culture has been described as the embodiment of a worldview through learned and transmitted beliefs, values, and practices, including religious and spiritual traditions. It also encompasses a way of living informed by the historical, economic, ecological, and political forces on a group.*
>
> (APA, 2017b, p. 165)

Consistent with these descriptions, we define culture as a learned belief system and value orientation that can impact cognitions and behaviors by influencing one's worldview, practices, customs, and norms. However, as previously noted, culture is also a complex and variable concept, and how one internalizes a shared culture varies from one person to the next. Thus, although group members may share a culture, culture is a broad categorization with considerable variability in whether, or to what extent it influences any particular individual. Acknowledging this variability is essential to avoiding essentialist assumptions, such as framing entire groups as homogenous (e.g., Asian cultures or Hispanic cultures). Instead, culture should be understood as dynamic and situated within specific social, historical, and ecological contexts.

The relationship between culture and an individual's personality and behavior has also been extensively studied. According to Hofstede's dimensional model of culture (Hofstede et al., 2010), cultures differ across six dimensions: Power distance (the extent to which a culture expects equality, with higher power distance reflecting an acceptance of inequality), uncertainty avoidance (societal levels of stress as they relate to ambiguity and unknown futures), individualism versus collectivism (the extent to which individuals are integrated into primary groups), masculinity versus femininity (the division of emotional roles and values based on gender), long-term versus short-term orientation (whether one's efforts focus on the future, the present, or the past), and indulgence versus restraint (one's focus on feelings of fulfillment related to gratification versus control of basic human desires).

There are significant associations between Hofstede's model of cultural dimensions and personality traits commonly observed in individuals who share certain cultural experiences in specific geographic regions. For example, in a study examining data from 33 countries, Hofstede and McCrae (2004) found several significant correlations between cultural dimension scores and the personality traits that comprise the 5-factor model. Specifically, individualism was positively correlated with extroversion (r = .64), while power distance was negatively associated with extroversion (r = −.57) and positively associated with conscientiousness (r = .52). In addition, masculinity was positively associated with neuroticism (r = .57) but negatively associated with agreeableness (r = −.36). Uncertainty avoidance was positively correlated with neuroticism (r = .58) and negatively associated with agreeableness (r = −.55). These findings indicate the conceptual overlap between models of culture and core elements of personality, demonstrating the impact of culture on an individual's perceptions and behaviors. However, while these observed associations reveal general tendencies, they should not be used to stereotype individuals. Instead, these models highlight the importance of understanding culture as a contextual factor that interacts with individual experiences. This approach encourages evaluators to consider cultural influences while avoiding assumptions based on group-level characteristics.

Ethnicity and Race

The term *ethnicity* is sometimes used interchangeably with *culture*; however, ethnicity specifically refers to an affiliation among individuals who may share a common language, historical origin, religion, and/or nationality (Lustig & Koester, 1999). Such commonalities are not universal but relate to specific group affiliations. For example, Hispanic is a term commonly used to describe individuals from Spanish-speaking countries (e.g., those in Latin America) based on shared historical origins and religious affiliations (albeit largely shaped by colonization). However, the term obscures vast and potentially important historical, ethnic, and other societal differences among groups and individuals from these culturally diverse countries. Understanding an individual who identifies as Hispanic[2] requires more than simply assuming that their language, religious beliefs, and customs are shared or homogenous, as this may or may not be true.

Conversely, race differs from both culture and ethnicity. Race is a problematic concept, as it emerged in colonial Europe as a tool to classify and dominate "others." Although often confused with culture, *race* is considered an arbitrary political and social construct (Lustig & Koester, 1999). It is important to note that racial categories are not biologically determined but rather reflect sociopolitical processes that shape shared experiences and perceptions. In fact, there is no genetic or biological basis for race, as evidenced by the fact that all humans are 99.9% genetically identical (National Academies of Science, Engineering, and Medicine, 2025). Moreover, there is far more genetic variability within commonly identified "racial" groups than between them. Hence, cultural characteristics and practices associated with racial categories stem from shared historical and sociopolitical experiences, rather than genetic or biological similarities (Betancourt & López, 1993).

What is Cultural Competence?

Cultural competence is another construct important for addressing cultural diversity in our clinical practice. The goal of cultural competence is to understand, appreciate, and appropriately integrate information about a person's broader cultural context into the analysis of the individual. Increasingly, this term has served as a benchmark, admittedly aspirational, for clinicians seeking to enhance their comfort with and understanding of cultural influences that might impact their work. The principles underlying this construct should be second nature to mental health professionals, given that a primary focus of clinical work is understanding the *individual* we are tasked with evaluating or treating. Understanding the individual requires a frame of reference—including seeing that individual within the cultural or other circumstances in which they have lived (past and present). This frame of reference is precisely what is needed to differentiate whether observed behaviors or traits are characteristic of the individual or if they are shared by others from their same cultural (or subcultural) background.

[2] As explained later in this chapter, with the exception of this example, quotations, and description of specific research findings, we utilize the term Latine instead of Hispanic.

Many researchers have developed working definitions of cultural competence, each of which helps set the stage for improved practice. Betancourt et al. (2003), for example, defined cultural competence as acknowledging and incorporating "the importance of culture, assessment of cross-cultural relations, vigilance toward the dynamics that result from cultural differences, expansion of cultural knowledge, and adaptation of services to meet culturally unique needs" (p. 294). Some further discussion of this construct is warranted in order to set the stage for thinking more broadly about the impact of diversity on forensic analysis, as well as developing steps that can be taken to enhance one's skills (i.e., increase competence).

To begin with, some critics argue that cultural competence can be misleadingly framed as an end product or static goal, rather than as an ongoing and dynamic process. In response, many formulations of cultural competence encourage clinicians to engage in a continuous, ongoing learning process. The goal is not to gain mastery of one or more specific cultures but to understand the extent of one's limitations, knowledge, and experiences. This awareness, often referred to as "cultural humility," should remind the clinician of their own limitations and hopefully foster a desire for growth and learning (rather than assuming one already possesses sufficient expertise). Indeed, the belief that one can fully understand any culture is naïve, as even one's dominant cultural context is likely to be diverse and multifaceted (as evidenced by the political and racial climate in the US—and countless other countries). We believe that an essential part of good clinical practice, whether forensic or otherwise, is the consistent engagement in an ongoing learning process. This learning process pertains not only to developments within the field but also to expanding our knowledge about cultures and subcultures different from our own and that often exist within our own countries (and even neighborhoods).

In our practice, *cultural competence* relates to understanding, appreciating, and effectively engaging with individuals whose cultural contexts differ from one's own. The term encompasses several interconnected concepts, including but not limited to cultural sensitivity, cultural literacy, cultural humility, cultural responsiveness, antiracist practice, (avoiding) microaggressions, language competence, and intersectionality (Fontes, 2022). Mental health services have increasingly moved beyond merely emphasizing the importance of cultural competence to the goal of developing a clinical practice that is culturally fair, responsive, and safe. Key concepts that underpin cross-cultural practice include:

- **Cultural Literacy**: Developing knowledge of the circumstances, cultures, and histories of people from specific groups, and understanding how this history influences their values, beliefs, and behaviors.
- **Cultural Sensitivity**: Being aware of how cultural differences may require clinicians to adjust their own behavior, such as adapting communication

approaches or interactions to accommodate individuals from specific groups (a process described in more detail in Chapter 2). This involves rejecting ethnocentrism—the assumption that the values, beliefs, and behaviors of the dominant cultural group or context represent the standard by which others are evaluated.

- **Cultural Humility**: Recognizing that clinicians cannot know everything about different cultures and must remain respectfully curious, self-aware, and open to learning from others, including those they evaluate or treat.
- **Cultural Safety**: Creating environments where individuals feel respected and valued by addressing and challenging colonial power imbalances in healthcare systems that historically benefit certain groups at the expense of others.
- **Antiracist Practice**: Actively working to identify and eliminate racism and race privilege by addressing inequities in systems, organizational structures, policies, and attitudes (Fontes, 2022). Antiracist practice is especially important in forensic mental health assessment, where systemic racism is interwoven into the criminal legal and health systems, creating disparities in privilege and access (Came & Griffith, 2018).

Increasing Cultural Competence

Working cross-culturally requires a range of skills and attitudes, such as culturally fair and appropriate clinical practices, cultural sensitivity and humility, and the development of cultural safety and antiracist practices (APA, 2017b; APA, 2019b; Council of Chairs of Training Councils, 2021). As previously mentioned, the term *cultural competence* has been critiqued for being perceived as an end product. Hence, it is critical to remember that part of the ongoing development of cultural competence is the continuing movement toward cultural humility and practices that support cultural safety and antiracist work. For clinicians working with individuals from culturally and linguistically diverse backgrounds, this means adopting a lifelong commitment to learning about the cultural contexts that shape the experiences of those they evaluate. A strong commitment to continuously developing one's cultural competence is crucial to becoming a culturally responsive practitioner.

Several scholars have offered recommendations for enhancing cultural competence. Derald Sue, one of the early proponents of cultural competence, identified three central domains to the construct: Attitudes and beliefs, knowledge, and skills (Sue, 2001). These domains are not only central to a theoretical understanding of what cultural competence means, but they give rise to several tangible steps that can enhance the ability of clinicians to effectively engage with individuals who are different from themselves. Several underlying assumptions guide this theory and its interventions, including the most obvious: All mental health professionals have biases that are learned but not innate or inevitable. While Sue's framework was primarily focused on race and ethnicity, its core principles are equally relevant when working with culturally and linguistically diverse individuals, including but not limited to immigrants. In forensic settings, evaluators must navigate cultural and linguistic differences in communication, behavior, and expectations. Here we adapt Sue's framework to target the challenges and considerations specific to individuals from diverse cultural and linguistic backgrounds, emphasizing heritage, linguistic practices, and systemic barriers (see Table 1.1).

Are any of us free of biases? While the answer is certainly "no," a range of factors, both internal and external, may inhibit us from recognizing or acknowledging these biases, even to ourselves. Hence, a critical starting point in enhancing cultural competence is the willingness to examine ourselves, our culture and personal background, our attitudes, and our beliefs. This examination includes recognizing the limits of our competence and expertise as well as how our personal background and experiences influence our thinking. Thus, the starting point for minimizing the impact of biases is to understand our own values and beliefs, and how they are rooted in our own lived experiences. This process is essential for identifying the stereotypes and biases we hold about others, whether positive or negative, and recognizing that not all individuals are equally represented by those stereotypes. Once we can identify reactions that we may have toward specific racial, ethnic, or social groups, we can minimize the risk of these biases influencing our clinical judgments.

The second domain Sue (2001) highlighted involves gaining relevant knowledge. This domain is intertwined with attitudes and beliefs, as it includes gaining knowledge of one's own background and biases. However, the emphasis here is on extending our knowledge about those we evaluate. Understanding how our background and attitudes might impact other people's reactions to our behavior is no less important than understanding the influence their backgrounds have on our behavior. When working with culturally and linguistically diverse individuals, clinicians require knowledge of acculturation processes, cultural norms, systemic barriers (e.g., immigration policies, access to health care), and linguistic dynamics. For example, many Guantanamo Bay military prison defendants had understandable concerns about the fairness and objectivity of American evaluators and the attorneys that represented them, particularly when the US government paid for those evaluators and attorneys (and interpreters).[3] Whether expressed openly or not, these concerns are clearly logical and are similar to the

[3] Many criminal defendants who are born and raised in the US express similar concerns about their court-appointed defense attorneys, citing the fact that court-appointed attorneys are paid by ("work for") the government and often appear to be familiar, or even friendly with the judge and/or prosecuting attorney.

Table 1.1 Adapted framework for components of cultural competence in forensic settings with culturally and linguistically diverse individuals

Belief/Attitude	Knowledge	Skill
Aware of and sensitive to one's own cultural heritage, and values/respects differences.	Understands how one's cultural heritage affects perceptions and professional interactions.	Seeks out educational, consultative, and multicultural training experiences.
Aware of own background/ experiences and biases and how they influence psychological processes.	Possesses knowledge about how cultural and linguistic biases shape perceptions and behaviors.	Seeks to understand self as cultural being.
Recognizes limits of competencies and expertise when working with culturally and linguistically diverse groups.	Knowledgeable about cultural heritage, systemic barriers (e.g., immigration policies), and linguistic challenges faced by diverse communities.	Familiarizes self with relevant research on cross-cultural and linguistic practices.
Comfortable and respectful of differences that exist between themselves and others.	Knowledgeable about communication norms, family dynamics, and acculturation processes in those one evaluates or works with.	Involved with culturally and linguistically diverse community organizations, networks, and events.
In touch with negative emotional reactions to cultural or linguistic differences, and can be nonjudgmental.	Understands how cultural heritage, linguistic practices, and systemic factors shape identity and behavior.	Able to engage in culturally appropriate and linguistically inclusive verbal/nonverbal interactions.
Aware of stereotypes and preconceived notions.	Understands the impact of systemic inequalities, language barriers, acculturation stress, and cultural norms.	Can intervene effectively in institutional settings to address inequities for culturally and linguistically diverse individuals.
Respects religious and/or spiritual beliefs of others.	Understands culture-bound values and beliefs, linguistic preferences, and their impact on mental health practices.	Willing to seek consultation with cultural mediators, interpreters, or community leaders.
Respects diverse cultural and linguistic practices, community networks, and traditions.	Knows the effects of systemic barriers and institutional discrimination on culturally and linguistically diverse communities.	Can take responsibility to provide linguistic accommodations (e.g., interpreter use) and culturally appropriate evaluation techniques.

Belief/Attitude	Knowledge	Skill
Values multilingualism and respects linguistic diversity.	Can identify potential sources of bias in assessment tools and techniques.	Has expertise in culturally responsive and linguistically informed forensic assessment practices.
Appreciates cultural differences in family and community structures.	Understands how cultural and linguistic heritage influences social, educational, and vocational opportunities.	Works to eliminate bias, prejudice, and discrimination.
Acknowledges the impact of systemic discrimination and language-related barriers.	Knows how racist and discriminatory practices operate at a community and institutional level.	Educates examinees about how cultural and linguistic considerations can shape clinical processes.

Adapted from Sue (2001)

concerns often expressed (and perhaps more often felt but unspoken) by Black defendants in the criminal legal system when approached by a White forensic evaluator. Another potential source of bias or misinterpretation is the different roles that family may play in decision-making, and even who is considered "family," as this, too, varies across cultures and subcultures.

These are perhaps obvious examples of situations where the culturally responsive evaluator should be mindful of the role race, ethnicity, and culture might play in the evaluation process, but countless other examples also exist. The broad range of issues that require attention further highlights an obvious reality: While achieving adequate knowledge about any particular culture (or subculture) *may* be possible, it is impossible to become an expert in all domains across all (or even many) different cultures. The point of highlighting a few of these domains is to help guide the evaluator who is faced with an evaluation of someone they do not fully understand, to provide a starting point for filling some of those knowledge gaps.

The final domain that Sue (2001) highlighted is the need to develop specific skills in order to improve an evaluator's ability to accurately assess an individual who differs from them. The process of improving culturally sensitive assessment skills includes taking steps to minimize the impact of evaluator bias on clinical findings and developing expertise in culturally sound assessment techniques more generally (discussed in Chapters 3 through 6). This includes seeking consultation with potentially relevant informants such as traditional healers and community-based organizations that have the potential to provide context for the evaluation and case-conceptualization process. Such culturally relevant information can be integral to developing a culturally informed (and hopefully more accurate) understanding of an individual. Finally, as discussed in Chapter 2, specific skills around educating individuals on the nature of the procedures (e.g., informed consent) and working with interpreters will often enhance the evaluation process. However, as noted previously (and will be reiterated frequently), none of these steps are intended to be "accomplished." Instead, they reflect ongoing challenges that require frequent attention, regardless of how much experience a clinician has with any specific cultural group.

Considering Acculturation

Although the degree to which culture and diversity impact the evaluation process varies across cases, settings, and individuals, a key consideration is the pattern, in which an individual enages with and or is acculturated to the dominant cultural context. Acculturation has been defined as "the dual process of cultural and psychological change that takes place as a result of contact between two or more cultural groups and their individual members" (Berry, 2005, p. 698). When applied to the context of immigration, this definition implies that immigrants will assimilate to the dominant cultural context, though not necessarily by abandoning their original culture (sometimes referred to as *cultural maintenance*; Berry, 1997).

One of the most well established theories of acculturation is Berry et al.'s (1989) two-dimensional model, which attempts to describe how an individual reconciles the norms and values of their heritage culture with those of the dominant or receiving cultural context. Although acculturation is an ongoing process and is not stagnant, Berry's model categorizes individuals into one of four groups depending on how they identify with (or reject) their own heritage and the majority culture: Integration (Bicultural), Assimilation, Separation, and Marginalization. Individuals who maintain their unique cultural identity while still integrating some of the norms and expectations of the dominant context are often considered *bicultural.* An assimilationist would identify with the dominant context and reject their heritage culture by adopting the values and norms of their dominant cultural context. In contrast, a separationist would strive to maintain the norms and values of their heritage culture and reject those of the dominant culture. Lastly, a marginalist would reject both their heritage culture and the majority culture, and therefore, they would not maintain or adapt to the values of either group. In the context of a forensic mental health evaluation, understanding how an individual maintains or integrates their heritage within the dominant cultural context can impact a range of decisions, such as what tests and normative data are used or how assessment results are interpreted. Perhaps not surprisingly, in an ever-changing, multicultural society such as the US and most Western countries, acculturation is primarily perceived in terms of linguistic fluency and cultural integration, both of which facilitate knowledge and familiarity with the norms and expectations of the dominant cultural context.

When applied to the legal system, understanding an individual's degree of cultural integration can help the forensic evaluator gauge the extent to which behaviors are likely to reflect cultural norms with which they are unfamiliar versus distinctive aspects of the individual. Similarly, acculturation may guide decisions about whether an interpreter is necessary, the adequacy of existing normative data for psychological tests, and other tangible decisions in the forensic assessment process (as highlighted by the opening case vignette). These considerations are relevant not only for individuals from different cultures but also for those who identify with one or more cultural minoritized groups in their country of origin (e.g., based on racial/ethnic background, sexual orientation or identity, or even differences in physical abilities such as language or hearing impairments). It is essential to recognize that each individual's experience with acculturation is unique, regardless of whether they belong to a culturally dominant context or minoritized group. While this book primarily focuses on acculturation in the context of individuals from different countries, we address related issues for minoritized groups where they arise.

Determining the extent to which an individual is familiar with the mainstream culture (i.e., is *assimilated*) can be challenging. Several scales have been developed to measure acculturation, and cross-cultural research has occasionally relied on these instruments or approaches, but there is no widely accepted or gold standard approach. Moreover, the nature and complexity of acculturation measures are often disappointing, and the resulting research has been largely uninformative. For example, most measures of acculturation focus on simplistic indicators such as the number of years living in the adopted country, degree of fluency with (or percentage of time speaking) the local language and, for individuals who immigrated as children, years of education in the new country. Given the dynamic nature of acculturation and the likelihood (and often preferability) of maintaining a bicultural identity, these indicators are far from ideal. In fact, some measures of acculturation assume unidirectional *assimilation*, treating acculturation as synonymous with assimilation, and essentially ignoring the possibility of maintaining a bicultural identity. Although some instruments measure orientation to both heritage and dominant cultural contexts simultaneously, such as The Bidirectional Acculturation Scale for Hispanics (Marin & Gamba, 1996), formal measures of acculturation have limited utility for the forensic evaluator when considering whether adjustments are appropriate for a given situation or individual.

Of course, adjustments based on acculturation—or the lack thereof—are also influenced by the nature of the procedures and the specific psycho-legal question at issue. Whereas a comparison to culturally relevant norms (including, but not limited to, formal normative data compiled for a particular instrument) is critical to many aspects of assessment, such as psychological or neurocognitive testing, other questions may be less dependent on an understanding of what is "typical" of a person's culture. For example, an evaluation of an individual's competence to stand trial (discussed in Chapter 2) is based on a comparison of the defendant to a specified *criterion* (i.e., the *Dusky* standard[4]), not to any established norms or scores on an instrument (although an instrument may help gauge the extent of any impairment in this ability). Conversely, determining whether scores on a test reflect feigned cognitive impairment or genuine abilities typically requires a comparison to appropriate normative data, not necessarily an absolute threshold in terms of the number of errors made. This distinction between *norm-referenced* and *criterion-referenced* testing is crucial when evaluating individuals from diverse cultural and linguistic backgrounds (and is discussed in greater length in subsequent chapters). The following chapters provide guidance around many of these issues and highlight gaps in our current knowledge and expertise that may limit the conclusiveness of the opinions offered by forensic mental health evaluators.

Applying a Cross-Cultural Lens to Research

Cross-cultural research, whether focused on the identification of culturally unique issues or qualities (e.g., expressions of a mental disorder) or adaptation of tools or techniques developed in one culture but applied in another, typically involves one of two approaches based on the *etic* and *emic* distinction previously described (Helfrich, 1999). The *etic* perspective is based on the principle of universality. It examines the generalizability of underlying constructs across cultures, emphasizing similarities and identifying differences by studying similar objects (e.g., aggression) and comparison standards (e.g., measurable levels of aggression using specific tools). This approach largely ignores the role of culturally specific norms, values, practices, or beliefs that could influence the object of study. By contrast, the *emic* approach considers culture as an "integral part of human behavior" (Helfrich, 1999, p. 133) and examines how one's cognitions and assumptions are influenced by their culture. Although different,

[4] In *Dusky v. US (1960)*, the US Supreme Court held that an individual is competent to stand trial if they have "sufficient present ability to consult with his lawyer with a reasonable degree of rational understanding—and whether he has a rational as well as factual understanding of the proceedings against him."

neither perspective is superior to the other, and both have advantages and disadvantages for particular lines of inquiry. Indeed, many cross-cultural researchers integrate these two approaches, as both etic and emic perspectives have strengths and limitations when employed individually.

The vast majority of cross-cultural research addressing forensic assessment topics, particularly those focused on applying specific assessment instruments, have used an etic approach. This approach typically involves translating a measure (or its instructions) into another language or simply examining the properties of the instrument when applied to individuals from a culture other than the one in which it was developed, often to evaluate whether it has comparable or adequate psychometric properties (Cook & Hart, 2017). This etic approach has been the primary mechanism by which tools such as the Minnesota Multiphasic Personality Inventory (MMPI) have been examined when applied to non-English speaking samples. Likewise, translated versions of violence risk assessment tools and scales to measure feigning, cognitive effort, intellectual functioning, and psychopathy have routinely used an etic approach.

However, inherent in etic research methodologies is the possibility that the construct (e.g., intelligence, violence risk factors, manifestations of psychopathy) may not catch emic, or culturally specific expressions, of possible diagnoses, which may result in decreased validity. Take, for example, the process of clinical diagnosis. Translating existing diagnostic criteria into another language (i.e., the etic approach) presumes that the underlying construct (e.g., depression or panic disorder) is expressed in the same way across all cultures, despite ample evidence to the contrary (e.g., see Rasmussen et al., 2014, for an example of culturally distinct manifestations of trauma). While one may be confident that a translated version of a diagnostic interview enables the evaluator to gauge the presence or absence of the existing diagnostic criteria, one cannot be equally confident that the established diagnostic criteria adequately capture the underlying mental disorder (or phenomenon) that the evaluator hopes to understand. Moreover, even the assertion that etic approaches focus on the same criterion (e.g., established diagnostic criteria) presumes that the evaluator's interpretations of observed behaviors or statements are accurate (e.g., that diminished interest in activities reflects anhedonia), which may or may not be justified. At its essence, the etic perspective assumes universality in the underlying construct by simply assessing the psychometric properties of a specific instrument in another language or culture. It emphasizes similarities across cultures rather than considering the possibility of culturally specific norms, values, practices, and beliefs that may influence the assessment of, or engagement in, the behavior or trait.

In contrast, the emic approach would begin by exploring how the underlying construct of depression is manifest in a particular culture and would seek to identify culturally relevant signs and symptoms that correspond to its presence. Many cross-cultural researchers have identified culturally specific symptoms or mental disorders that may or may not map closely onto phenomena recognized by the standard diagnostic manuals (i.e., the Diagnostic and Statistical Manual of Mental Disorders, now in its fifth edition, text revision [DSM-5-TR]; American Psychiatric Association, 2022; the International Classification of Diseases, now in its eleventh edition [ICD-11]; World Health Organization, 2022). Indeed, the development of instruments and criteria to identify culturally specific symptoms or syndromes has grown over the past quarter-century. However, these tools are rarely utilized in forensic assessment, in large part because they typically target idiosyncratic populations and/or symptoms, often using face-valid tools that are vulnerable to distorted responding. Nevertheless, cross-cultural researchers typically recommend considering culturally specific adaptations to maximize the utility and accuracy of assessment tools used with unique cultural groups (Cook & Hart, 2017).

Although the typical reader of this book will probably not develop or adapt specific forensic or psychological assessment instruments for their practice, understanding the distinctions between etic and emic approaches can help illuminate the strengths and limitations of the different tools and techniques that are available. Furthermore, this process can help the practicing clinician decide when deviations from the standard application of a tool or procedure may be justified (or justifiable), as opposed to assumptions based on the existence (or absence) of published research. Perhaps most importantly, when an evaluator has decided to utilize an instrument developed for assessing culturally specific symptoms or phenomena, understanding the research underlying such instruments can be essential to ensuring accuracy in expert opinions or testimony, and even navigating challenges to the admissibility of these instruments.

A Note about Language and Terminology

The way we talk about cultural groups and identities is constantly evolving, and we acknowledge that the terminology we are using at the time of this book's publication may not align with current practices when it is read in the future. At the time of writing, we have adopted the APA's (2023) Inclusive Language Guidelines to inform our language choices. We strive to use precise and respectful terminology when referencing research samples and research findings, aiming to describe individuals and communities as specifically as possible rather than relying on broad, homogenizing terms. For instance, as noted previously, the term "Hispanic" is rooted in colonial history, originating from Spanish colonization in the Americas. We recognize that this term has been the subject of extensive discussion and critique within the communities it seeks to describe. Therefore, unless we can accurately identify the specific identities of individuals or groups referenced as Hispanic (e.g., Mexican, Argentinian), we use the term Latine to acknowledge the diverse identities within the Latine community and to respect the complex history and ongoing conversations about the use of these terms.

We also understand that identity is multidimensional, and that intersectionality—the interconnected nature of race, gender, socioeconomic status, and other aspects of identity—plays a crucial role in shaping individual experiences, which are influenced by intersecting dynamics of oppression and privilege. Throughout this book, we strive to reflect on and represent these intersections in our language and analysis, recognizing that they contribute to the complexity of each person's lived experience.

We also recognize that language is more than a tool for communication; it reflects and reinforces power dynamics. Our goal is to use language that empowers and respects the communities involved, rather than marginalizing them. In writing this book, we have made efforts to engage with and listen to members of the communities we discuss, seeking to ensure that our terminology is respectful and aligned with the preferences and experiences of those we reference. Despite our best efforts, however, the terminology we use may still have limitations or may not fully capture the richness and diversity of the identities and experiences discussed. We encourage readers to approach this text with a critical eye, understanding the inherent complexities of cross-cultural and forensic assessment. As scholars and clinicians, we remain committed to continuous learning and to adapting our language, terminology, and practices as new insights and understandings emerge.

A Roadmap for the Book

Forensic mental health evaluations are inherently challenging, and the complications that arise when evaluating culturally and linguistically diverse individuals magnify those complications tremendously. Although there is a growing awareness of the importance of cultural competence, relatively little guidance exists as to what tangible steps are needed to enhance one's competence. This book is intended to provide some of that guidance by addressing a wide range of topics that confront the forensic evaluator evaluating an individual from a different cultural background than themselves. Although far from exhaustive, particularly given the rapidly expanding research base, this book summarizes a range of critical issues and settings common to many, if not all, forensic mental health assessments.

We begin with chapters addressing the core elements that cut across most types of forensic evaluation, such as clinical and diagnostic interviewing (Chapter 2), the assessment of response style and malingering (Chapter 3), and the use of multiscale inventories more broadly (e.g., the MMPI and PAI instruments (Chapter 4). Subsequent chapters focus on more specialized forms of assessment, either in terms of the focus of inquiry, such as the assessment of neurocognitive and intellectual functioning (Chapter 5) and violence risk assessment (Chapter 6), or the context for the evaluation, such as the evaluation of culturally and linguistically diverse children and families (Chapter 7) and asylum/international human rights evaluations (Chapter 8). Finally, we conclude with an outline for a culturally informed research agenda (Chapter 9) that attempts to identify gaps in our existing knowledge base and topic areas that need more innovative or rigorous investigation. Because this book is intended to provide hands-on guidance for practicing clinicians and researchers, we begin each chapter with a case vignette that illustrates some of the problems/issues addressed and close each of the remaining chapters with specific take-home points to consider.

2

Diagnostic and Forensic Interviewing

Summary

This chapter reviews a range of factors that can impact the process of interviewing an individual from a cultural or linguistic background different from that of the evaluator. Forensic mental health professionals are frequently asked to evaluate individuals who do not speak the primary language of the legal setting or come from cultural backgrounds unfamiliar to the evaluator. Such individuals may manifest symptoms or problems differently than what is typical in the evaluator's culture and may behave in ways that are prone to misunderstanding or misinterpretation. This chapter reviews the many ways that cultural differences and linguistic barriers can impede the forensic interview, including influences that arise even before the interview begins, barriers that impact the interview itself, and issues related to the use of interpreters. We conclude with several recommendations for minimizing the impact of these challenges on the forensic interview.

Case Vignette

Petrovic R, a 61-year-old Serbian man, was referred for an evaluation in conjunction with alleged war crimes brought forth by the United Nations International Criminal Tribunal for the former Yugoslavia. Mr. R was alleged to have ordered the execution of more than 40 men, women, and children during the 1990s war between the former Yugoslavian states. Before trial, Mr. R's defense attorneys submitted a psychological evaluation opining that their client's cognitive functioning was so severely impaired that he was unable to participate meaningfully in the proceedings (i.e., he was incompetent to stand trial) and therefore should not be prosecuted. The psychologist who evaluated Mr. R relied solely on a clinical interview conducted through an interpreter, arguing that no other tests or procedures were valid for a Serbian-speaking defendant. Moreover, because the evaluation

Cultural and Linguistic Considerations in Forensic Mental Health Assessment. Barry Rosenfeld and Alicia Nijdam-Jones, Oxford University Press. © Oxford University Press (2026).
DOI: 10.1093/9780190900991.003.0002

was conducted ex parte *and no funds were available to provide for an independent interpreter, the psychologist relied on a Serbian paralegal employed by the attorneys who represented Mr. R. Although this paralegal had routinely helped translate interviews for the defendant's English-speaking attorneys, the evaluator questioned the appropriateness of relying on an employee to provide interpretation services for the forensic interview. Are there any concerns with relying on this person to translate the forensic evaluation? Are there legal, ethical, or pragmatic requirements that guide the selection of an interpreter in forensic settings? Are there cultural considerations that might impact the nature or accuracy of the evaluation? Does the venue for this case (The Hague, Netherlands) impact the legality or appropriateness of these decisions?*

Conducting a forensic interview is a challenging endeavor under the best of circumstances.[1] These challenges are magnified, often substantially, when cultural or linguistic diversity complicates the evaluation process. A lack of familiarity with the examinee's culture or an inability to speak that person's dominant language can necessitate a range of different accommodations. The most obvious of these is the need to rely on an interpreter,[2] but it might also necessitate efforts to develop an understanding of culturally specific norms and expectations, as well as behaviors and attitudes that may be prone to misunderstanding or misinterpretation. Likewise, an awareness of psychological symptoms that may be unique to the individual's culture can be critical to an accurate assessment. The importance of understanding the many ways that culture and language can impact the accuracy of forensic evaluations cannot be overemphasized, particularly given the life-altering consequences that can follow from many forensic evaluations. This chapter is intended to provide a thorough but user-friendly review of the many issues that arise in "cross-cultural" forensic assessments. In addition, we provide concrete recommendations that, while not meant to be exhaustive, will hopefully facilitate reflection and consideration.

Although critical in many aspects of psychology, the need to consider language and culture is a frequent complication in forensic mental health evaluations. Most Western countries have become increasingly diverse over the past few decades, and the impact of ever-growing ethnic and cultural diversity is even more pronounced in criminal legal settings. In addition to the racial

[1] Some of the content contained in this chapter was previously included in a publication by V. Barber-Rioja & B. Rosenfeld (2018): Addressing linguistic and cultural differences in the forensic interview. *International Journal of Forensic Mental Health, 17*(4), 377–386, https://doi.org/10.1080/14999013.2018.1495280.

[2] We prefer the term translator to interpreter given the importance of word-for-word translation of the examinee's responses; many interpreters are trained to make sense of the individual's responses, often at the expense of faithful "word-for-word" interpretations that preserve both the content and expressions so that the evaluator – not the inteperter – can properly determine the significance of the examinee's language. Nevertheless, because these terms are used differently in the field of linguistics (with translation referring to written material and interpretation being used for spoken word), we have utilized the terms traditionally used to avoid confusion.

and ethnic diversity that characterizes US citizens (e.g., the high rate of Black and Latine individuals in the criminal legal system), foreign-born individuals[3] represent roughly 20% of people incarcerated in the US (Government Accountability Office, 2018). Even among individuals born and raised in the US (or UK, Canada, Australia, etc.), English may not be the only, or even primary language spoken in the household, and the extent of acculturation is variable, particularly among adolescents and young adults. Equally dramatic rates of culturally diverse individuals, including immigrants and foreign-born individuals, are evident in criminal legal systems worldwide. For example, roughly 20% of people incarcerated in Australia are foreign-born and another 25% are identified as Aboriginal or Torres Strait Islanders (Australian Bureau of Statistics, 2024). Many European countries have similarly high rates of immigrants in their criminal legal systems, forcing evaluators to consider the impact of the individual's unique culture and language on the evaluation process. In short, forensic mental health professionals often evaluate individuals who communicate in a different language, follow different cultural norms, and manifest symptoms in ways unfamiliar to the evaluator.

The importance of addressing cultural and linguistic differences in the process of a forensic evaluation is not simply advisable; it is an ethical mandate. As noted in the previous chapter, the American Psychological Association's (APA) Specialty Guidelines for Forensic Psychology (2013) encourage evaluators to consider "situational, personal, linguistic, and cultural differences that might affect their judgments or reduce the accuracy of their interpretations" (p. 15). This principle is grounded in the APA's Ethics Code, which also highlights the need to understand potential sources of bias, including an individual's race, culture, and ethnicity (APA, 2017a).[4] In short, there is a strong consensus that an understanding of the examinee's cultural background and an awareness of the potential for cultural differences to inject bias into the evaluation process are required for conducting culturally sensitive evaluations.

Understanding the differences between our own experiences and those we are asked to evaluate is particularly important for forensic psychologists, in part

[3] Similarly, we have prioritized the use of the term immigrant whenever possible, but we recognize that some individuals involved in legal proceedings, whether facing criminal prosecution or participating in civil or family court matters, may not fit the definition of having immigrated to the country in which their proceedings occur (e.g., a criminal defendant may be extradited to the US following arrest in another country). As such, we will occasionally use the term foreign-born to encompass individuals with varied migration experiences, including refugees, asylum seekers, and those on temporary visas.

[4] The APA Ethics Code specifies, in Principle E (Respect for People's Rights and Dignity): "Psychologists are aware of and respect cultural, individual, and role differences, including those based on age, gender, gender identity, race, ethnicity, culture, national origin, religion, sexual orientation, disability, language, and socioeconomic status, and consider these factors when working with members of such groups. Psychologists try to eliminate the effect on their work of biases based on those factors, and they do not knowingly participate or condone activities of others based upon such prejudices."

because cultural differences are not simply due to immigration or language. Mental health professionals often have little in common with those they evaluate, even when they have been born and raised in close geographic proximity to one another (Sue & Sue, 2016). Differences in educational opportunities, socioeconomic status, and religious background are just a few of the factors that can impede the evaluation process, often hindering the ability to develop rapport with the examinee and potentially leading to misunderstandings. At worst, evaluators may reach incorrect conclusions about important psycho-legal questions that can adversely impact individuals or entire communities. These issues are particularly pronounced during the clinical interview, as the development of rapport is critical to eliciting the necessary information and accurately interpreting the individual's statements and behaviors. Although there are numerous ways in which cultural, social, and sociopolitical differences can impede the forensic interview, we divide these issues temporally, separating those that may (or should) arise even before the interview begins from those that typically impact the interview itself. In addition, we address issues related to the use and training of interpreters, who are often an essential component of the interview process. These challenges are detailed in this chapter, culminating in several recommendations for minimizing the impact of these challenges on the evaluation process.

Before the Interview Begins

Understanding the Individual's Culture

Given the potential importance of cultural and language barriers in the forensic interview, it may seem obvious that an evaluator should have some knowledge of the individual's culture prior to meeting with them. While it might seem preferable to identify an evaluator from the same country or cultural background as the person being evaluated, this approach is often not feasible and, in some cases, may be counterproductive. For example, individuals from regions affected by violence or persecution may mistrust those from their broad cultural group due to internal prejudices or regional conflicts between, for example, different religious, caste, or ethnic groups. Refugees, in particular, may feel vulnerable in such situations. Furthermore, finding evaluators who share cultural or linguistic backgrounds can be challenging due to the significant differences in ethnic, linguistic, and socioeconomic characteristics between psychologists and the individuals they evaluate. Indeed, in New York City, where one of the authors works and lives, an estimated 800 different languages are spoken. Additionally, while approximately 25% of the 8.4 million city residents speak Spanish, even finding a Spanish-speaking psychologist can be challenging—let alone one with expertise in forensic assessment. Of course, merely finding a Spanish-speaking psychologist does little to guarantee an understanding of the individual's culture, as there are numerous cultures in which some variation of Spanish is spoken. Moreover, many (if not most) forensic mental health evaluations require specific expertise to adequately address the psycho-legal issues at hand, which is even less likely to be present in a psychologist who happens to be fluent in the examinee's primary language and culture.

Although it is often possible for the evaluator to learn a great deal about an individual's culture and lived experience during the clinical interview itself, the ability to do so hinges on both the development of an adequate level of rapport with the examinee and the extent to which the person's mental state permits a rational, informative conversation (which is by no means assured in any mental health evaluation). However, the variability in how much information can be elicited from the examinee and the reliability of the information that is elicited during the interview highlights the importance of adequate preparation in advance of the evaluation. Ideally, this process will include systematic efforts to learn about the individual's cultural background prior to the interview.

There are no definitive guidelines on how one should gather information or how much information to gather about the cultural and sociopolitical history of a person referred for a forensic evaluation. Likewise, the methods used to obtain this background information may vary across clinicians and cultures, partly based on the accessibility of useful information and the broader sociopolitical context in which the individual's experiences have unfolded. Therefore, any suggested guidelines should probably be prefaced with the caveat "it depends," since case-by-case (and culture-by-culture) differences will impact these decisions. For example, some forensic evaluations, such as child custody or termination of parental rights, require a thorough understanding of an individual's or family's cultural background and social norms since behaviors that appear unusual or inappropriate from one cultural lens may be understood quite differently within another (see Chapter 7). This does not suggest that culturally grounded behaviors are always legally acceptable. Certain harmful practices, such as female genital mutilation and child marriage, are recognized as human rights violations and illegal in most countries, even where they are still occasionally practiced (UNICEF, 2024). Notably, efforts to end these practices are often led by advocates and survivors within affected communities. Nonetheless, understanding cultural norms and values are essential in forensic contexts to distinguish the motives and degree of the pathology underlying an individual's behavior. These factors may vary significantly depending on whether the behaviors and attitudes are culturally explicable. In general, familiarity with cultural norms is crucial to determining whether an individual's expressed beliefs suggest the presence of a mental disorder (e.g., psychosis). Such an understanding can directly influence assessments of criminal responsibility, violence risk, and the need for pharmacological intervention.

As a starting point, we recommend that the evaluator seek information about the primary language(s) spoken by the examinee (and perhaps immediate family members), as well as whether regional dialects might impact the selection of an appropriate interpreter. For example, in conducting a research study of Tibetan refugees arriving in Dharamsala, India, our research coordinator quickly discovered that the three different dialects of Tibetan required recruiting a diverse set of local research assistants to ensure adequate translation and interpretation of the data elicited. Additional topics that may warrant some attention before the interview include the educational system(s) in place in the individual's country of origin, the broader economic and sociopolitical climate, and any historical or structural factors (e.g., colonization, migration patterns, or conflict) that may shape the individual's experiences or worldview. Of course, these may also vary dramatically across regions, particularly in countries where the level of economic and social development differs radically between urban and rural areas.

Religious and spiritual traditions can also be critical to understanding an individual's clinical presentation, particularly as they relate to traditional explanations or interventions to address problems that the individual has experienced. This information can be crucial to recognizing mental health symptoms that may be masked by cultural norms or, conversely, normative reactions that might be mistakenly interpreted as symptoms of a mental disorder. Even knowing the questions to ask to elicit culturally bound syndromes or symptoms can be greatly facilitated by a bit of background research into the individual's culture. The Afghan Symptom Checklist (Miller et al., 2006) presents an excellent example of symptoms of psychological distress that would often be missed or misunderstood by the clinician who is not very familiar with Afghani culture. Hinton et al. (2013) created a similar self-report scale for use with Cambodian immigrants, who often manifest psychological distress in the form of unique somatic symptoms. Note that we do not necessarily advocate for the use of the scales themselves, as relying on a self-report checklist in the context of a forensic evaluation has obvious limitations. Still, familiarity with the content of these instruments would be invaluable in assessing an Afghani or Cambodian immigrant. While only a handful of scholarly investigations have identified culturally specific mental health symptoms, other examples certainly exist (e.g., Bayles & Katerndahl, 2009; Krause, 1989; Rasmussen et al., 2014, 2015).

Cultural norms regarding the role of one's family or community in decision-making can also be essential to understand in advance of the forensic interview. As discussed further below, even expectations about who might be present during the interview or who can have input into legal decisions vary by culture. For example, some individuals may rely heavily on the opinions of family members or community elders in making important decisions, even when those individuals may be motivated by broader concerns (e.g., the impact on the community or a family's reputation). Decisions that appear irrational to the evaluator may be understood quite differently after considering the influence of unseen or unidentified individuals from the individual's family or community.

Another important consideration in many cross-cultural forensic evaluations is the potential impact of gender roles, social class and related sociocultural expectations. For example, in some contexts, strict norms may limit the interactions between men and women who are not married to one another. The clothing worn by an evaluator (particularly a woman) may also violate cultural norms and, if not recognized in advance, may even prevent the interview from occurring. Likewise, when cross-gender interactions are constrained by an individual's religion or culture, including a third person in the interview room may be necessary. Although the degree of adherence to cultural norms will no doubt vary across individuals from any particular culture or country, knowledge of these cultural considerations in advance of the evaluation can be critical to ensuring that the interview proceeds respectfully and effectively.

Social class and class-bound values may also impact the development of rapport, particularly among individuals who have experienced significant oppression or discrimination and who may carry understandable mistrust shaped by historical and institutional harms. These experiences can foster understandable wariness toward those in positions of authority but often extending to anyone perceived as having higher social standing (e.g., an attorney or forensic evaluator). Whaley (1997) described this phenomenon as *cultural mistrust*, characterizing it as an adaptive response to experiences of racial injustice, discrimination, and systemic inequity. While this mistrust may be protective in many contexts, it may also complicate the development of rapport and open communication in the clinical interview. Of course, some degree of caution is a common and reasonable reaction to any forensic evaluation; however, it may be especially pronounced among individuals who have experienced discrimination and institutional harm. Recognizing and, when appropriate, explicitly addressing these dynamics during the interview process can reduce guardedness and support more accurate and respectful assessment.

Research conducted prior to the evaluation may also reveal topics considered taboo within the examinee's cultural or religious context. For example, the use of alcohol and expressions of suicidal ideation are considered sinful by many Muslim communities. Awareness of the sensitive nature of these topics should guide how the clinician introduce and explore these topics, ensuring that inquiries are framed in a respectful and culturally appropriate manner. Moreover, when alcohol use or suicidal ideation are acknowledged, it may be evidence of a level of distress that is far more severe than would typically be assumed in an individual born and raised in a culture where the use of alcohol or acknowledging thoughts of suicide are more common and culturally accepted. Conversely, clinicians may be tempted to dismiss practices that appear to be culturally sanctioned (e.g., the use of khat, a stimulant popular in Yemen and East Africa), yet research indicates that this substance is often abused by individuals who devote so much time to chewing khat that it interferes with work or family obligations (Mihretu et al., 2017). Given the importance of accurately assessing substance abuse and suicidal ideation, evaluators should not avoid these topics but instead approach them with awareness, sensitivity, and respect for the individual's culture and religious context, in order to facilitate more open and honest conversations.

Although a substantial amount of information can be obtained through internet search engines, more detailed information can often be obtained from official government websites or independent agencies (e.g., Amnesty International). When in-depth knowledge is needed or readily available sources generate limited useful information, consultation with someone with lived or professional expertise related to the particular region or subculture in question may be invaluable. For example, when a community of immigrants from a particular region or culture exists, community service agencies or scholars (e.g., anthropologists, sociologists) may be willing to provide information or formal consultation. Even when the individual being evaluated is from a small community or unique subculture, it is often possible to identify persons with deep knowledge about the values, traditions, norms, and sociopolitical context associated with that culture. Regardless of the cultural consultant's background, it is essential to distinguish the general information that an independent third party can provide from the case-specific information typically sought from collateral informants, since the cultural consultant will not (and should not) have access to privileged or identifying information about the person being evaluated.

The preceding discussion should also be qualified by the fact that "culture" is not a static characteristic that applies homogeneously to all individuals from a region, country, or ethnic group. Nor does it remain consistent across an individual's lifetime. Culture changes historically, and it is experienced variably depending on intersecting factors such as age, gender, status, and other roles and positionings. Further, as discussed in Chapter 1, when an individual has migrated from another country (as is often, but not always the case in forensic evaluations that involve culturally or linguistically diverse individuals), some degree of adaptation or acculturation will likely have occurred as the individual learns the customs and language of their adopted country and learns to live "between worlds." Some research has suggested that one's degree of acculturation may, in some cases, be more important than the individual's culture of origin when navigating the forensic mental health examination (Weiss & Rosenfeld, 2012). Recognizing the variability within cultural, racial, and ethnic groups is no less important than identifying the unique elements of these broader groups, but may be less readily apparent to the naïve forensic examiner.

Optimizing the Use of Interpreters

The ability to communicate effectively in a shared language is essential to any clinical interview. Therefore, whether or not to use an interpreter is a critical decision made before the interview. Language fluency often varies dramatically among both recent migrants and those who have lived in their new country for many years, but the ability to communicate effectively in a common language is essential to any mental health interview. Recent surveys estimate that roughly 25,000,000 people living in the US (approximately 8% of the total population) have limited English proficiency and rely primarily on a non-English language (Migration Policy Institute, 2015). This linguistic diversity reflects the multicultural reality of most societies and should be regarded as a normal feature of contemporary forensic practice, not a deficit. Thus, forensic mental health clinicians frequently need to rely on an interpreter to conduct a clinical interview. When a recent migrant to the US speaks little or no English, identifying whether an interpreter is necessary is straightforward. However, attorneys may not recognize the magnitude of their own communication gaps with clients who have partial or limited English fluency because the content of their discussions has been superficial or one-sided. Thus, it is often advisable not only to inquire about language fluency in advance of the interview but also to have an interpreter available for any evaluation where language issues *may* exist, even if the interpreter is ultimately deemed unnecessary (few interpreters will object to having been paid to sit idly during the assessment).

Even in cases where the individual appears relatively fluent in the language(s) spoken by the evaluator, forensic mental health interviews often require nuanced communication about complex issues. Having an interpreter available for particularly challenging or essential discussions (e.g., querying about unusual beliefs or eliciting symptoms to establish a diagnosis) is often critical to conducting a thorough and accurate evaluation. Of course, when an interpreter is present, the evaluator should adjust the time allotted for the interview accordingly, as reliance on an interpreter invariably increases the length of time needed for the interview (discussed in more detail later in this chapter).

The opening vignette to this chapter demonstrates how determining an appropriate interpreter is not always straightforward. For one, the availability of interpreters for a given region or for less commonly spoken languages is limited. In the ideal case, the interpreter would share a similar linguistic and cultural background, and perhaps even the same regional dialect, as the person being evaluated. However, even then, one must carefully evaluate the interpreter's suitability. Significant sociopolitical, cultural, or religious differences may exist that impact the interpreter's ability to provide an unbiased or sympathetic translation. For example, important differences often exist within broad cultures or countries, resulting in regional dialects that can be challenging to translate accurately or obscuring potentially relevant cultural differences. These challenges were highlighted in an evaluation of a Kurdish-Iraqi criminal defendant conducted by one of the authors. Substantial regional differences in word use (according to the highly skilled interpreter) and key cultural and religious differences (Sunni Kurd versus Shia Arab) emerged between the examinee and interpreter. Moreover, the examinee's experiences, having been subject to marginalization and abuse by the ruling Ba'ath party (particularly under the Hussein regime), were no less foreign to the interpreter than they were to the evaluator. These issues demonstrate the potential benefits of using an interpreter who not only shares linguistic competence but also the cultural awareness, impartiality, and ethical grounding required for equitable and effective forensic communication.

Even if an interpreter can be identified who shares the same language and cultural background as the person being evaluated, the skill of the interpreter will undoubtedly vary. For example, in our experience, relatively few "court-approved" interpreters are trained in simultaneous interpretation (where translation follows the speaker almost immediately, throughout the interview), rather than consecutive interpretation (where the interpreter listens to the speaker and translates after the speaker has finished). Consecutive interpretation typically takes more time, and research suggests that simultaneous interpretation may yield greater accuracy in clinical and legal settings.

Gany et al. (2007) found that clinically significant errors occurred 5 to 10 times more often with consecutive interpretation compared to simultaneous interpretation. Moreover, many of these errors were classified as having high levels of clinical significance, including some errors that were potentially life-threatening (e.g., an expression of serious suicidal ideation that was translated as seemingly benign regret). Interpreters with less than one year of experience also made nearly three times as many errors as those with more than one year of experience. Not surprisingly, consecutive interpretation also required roughly 50% more time for each encounter, demonstrating the need to allot extra time for the interview. Unfortunately, careful selection of an ideal interpreter is not always possible due to logistical constraints and a limited availability of qualified professionals. When interpretation concerns are evident during the evaluation, it is advisable to document those concerns (e.g., phrases or portions of the interview where confusion arose), as those concerns may have relevance for understanding or contextualizing the examinee's responses.

Even when a skilled interpreter can be identified, the nuances of a forensic mental health interview are often unfamiliar to someone without mental health training. Symptoms such as auditory hallucinations, flashbacks, and thoughts of suicide may be unfamiliar to the interpreter. Ensuring that the interpreter understands the intent behind these symptoms can be facilitated by a brief discussion in advance of the evaluation. We often find it helpful to meet with the interpreter immediately before beginning the interview (e.g., asking the interpreter to arrive 15–20 minutes before the evaluation is scheduled to start) in order to provide adequate time to explain the nature of the evaluation and review key terms and concepts that might be expected to arise. A skilled interpreter will often take notes during these meetings (and should be encouraged to do so), ideally clarifying or determining how to translate complex words or concepts in advance of the interview. In order for this meeting to be useful, the clinician needs to make a habit of thinking through the questions and topics likely to be raised in the forensic interview.[5]

When preparing an interpreter for a forensic interview, it is crucial to emphasize the importance of an accurate, complete and impartial interpretation that preserves meaning, register, and clinically relevant features of speech. Forensic interpreting prioritizes these elements because word choice, phrasing, and tone often carry diagnostic significance. Recourse to a literal, or "word-for-word" translation is often necessary to achieve this level of fidelity, although it should not be taken to extremes (e.g., translating *tengo calor* as "I have heat" rather than "I'm hot"). The goal is a complete, faithful interpretation that maintains both the content and expressive qualities of the examinee's language so that the evaluator – not the interpreter – can determine its clinical significance. This approach differs from many community or court interpreter practices, which prioritize semantic equivalence and overall comprehensibility, but is essential in forensic contexts, where word choice often carries diagnostic relevance. Particularly in the forensic interview, the precise wording, word order, and flow of an individual's speech can be of critical importance to identifying disordered thought processes or unusual beliefs (e.g., delusions, paranoia). Thus, we encourage evaluators to work collaboratively with interpreters to maintain these standards, clarifying expectations in advance, and preventing unsanctioned "clarifications" or side conversations. Best practice is to instruct interpreters to render every utterance in the first person, ask for repetition when needed, explicitly flag ambiguities, idioms, or culture-bound terms, and refrain from summarizing unless explicitly directed to do so by the evaluator. This collaborative process

[5] While ideal, we readily acknowledge that this practice is often not feasible.

enables the evaluator to assess any communication difficulties and ensures the interpreter does not inadvertently filter or retinterpret clinically meaningful language.

Many interpreters are reluctant to interrupt the examinee, which impacts the interpreter's ability to preserve detail. This can lead to long, uninterrupted responses that the interpreter then summarizes, risking loss of important details. This problem can be readily observed by the evaluator, as the discrepancy between the volume of words (or length of time) spoken by the examinee will be markedly different than the interpretation provided. The memory capacity of even a skilled interpreter is no different than anyone else's, and lengthy responses will likely result in content being omitted or simplified unless turn-taking is actively managed. If the interpreter is not willing to slow down the responses by interrupting, we strongly encourage the evaluator to establish short "chunks" and give explicit permission to pause or request repetition, both by interrupting the examinee once a response appears to become too long and by explaining to the examinee that answers need to be short enough to be accurately interpreted. Accompanying these verbal interruptions with hand gestures can be useful (e.g., a hand raised as if to "stop" the person), as the examinee will begin to recognize that a raised hand means they need to allow the interpreter the opportunity to interpret a portion of the response before they continue speaking. When available, simultaneous interpretation can improve efficiency. If using consecutive interpretation, build in frequent pauses to ensure accuracy and completeness, particularly when responses are lengthy or complex. The examinee's mental state also affects how much information can be conveyed in accurately interpreted "chunks." Some mental health symptoms may impede the person's ability to regulate their speech, as is evident to anyone who has ever evaluated someone having a manic episode!

A final consideration in interpreter selection is an awareness of who should NOT serve in this capacity. For example, the opening vignette described a scenario in which a defense team member served as an interpreter. While having some familiarity with the person being evaluated may seem advantageous and may increase that examinee's level of comfort during the interview, the defense team is required to serve the client's best interest, which might be compromised by a true and accurate interpretation (e.g., if a criminal defendant disclosed information that conflicted with the legal strategy or previous statements). Similarly, family or friends of the person being evaluated may volunteer their services (and typically have the advantage of being free of charge), but the person being evaluated may not feel comfortable revealing sensitive information in front of someone they know—and may not even be willing to acknowledge this discomfort. Of course, family members also have a vested interest in the outcome of the evaluation, and their interpretation skills (even if they are fluent in the requisite languages) may be inadequate for complete and impartial interpretation. Instead, to minimize the risk of any conflict of interest, one should make every effort to use an independent, professionally trained interpreter who has no personal or professional relationship with the person being evaluated. This may not always be possible, particularly in a small or close-knit community where interpreters may be familiar with the examinee, but minimizing the potential for any conflict of interest, whether real or perceived, is critical. Ideally, the interpreter would also be certified by a court or other administrative body, assuming such certification exists for the language and in the region where the evaluation will be conducted. If repeated evaluations are needed, it is often preferable to use the same interpreter, provided the examinee (and evaluator) feels comfortable with that interpreter. Examinees may fear that information could reach the community or authorities and may perceive an interpreter (rightly or wrongly) as posing a risk due to dual allegiance. Inquiring about the individual's comfort with the interpreter (e.g., through the attorney or a different interpreter) can reveal and perhaps offer an opportunity to alleviate some of these concerns, though any concens should also be documented.

The Forensic Interview Process

Eliciting Informed Consent

The first step in any forensic interview usually involves explaining the nature of the evaluation and seeking the individual's consent (or willingness, if informed consent is not required) to participate. The expectation of informed consent is grounded in both case law and disciplinary ethics codes (e.g., American Academy of Psychiatry and the Law, 2005; APA, 2017a; National Association of Social Workers, 2008) and requires that the "professional communicates sufficient information to the other individual so that she or he may make an informed decision about participation in the professional relationship" (Barnett et al., 2007, p. 179). The nature of the information disclosed and the clinician's response to a refusal will necessarily vary across settings (e.g., the clinician may be expected to complete an evaluation even if the individual refuses to participate) but typically involves explaining the nature and purpose of the assessment, anticipated use of the information elicited, limits of confidentiality, the voluntary nature of participation, and possible consequences of a refusal to participate (APA, 2013; Heilbrun, 2009).

Although informed consent is widely recognized in the US and many other countries, there are many cultures in which this process is either unfamiliar or even contrary to cultural norms. Indeed, the concepts of autonomy and self-determination in medical treatment decisions are relatively recent developments even in the US and may be virtually incomprehensible to an individual from a country or culture where these principles are neither common nor valued. Hence, disclosing information about the purpose of the evaluation, let alone eliciting the individual's "consent" to participate, may be confusing, particularly when the individual feels compelled to obey the wishes of their attorney or is in a custodial setting. Concepts of voluntariness, while critical to informed consent, are even more confusing in the context of a forensic evaluation, where the individual may perceive (rightly or wrongly) negative consequences for refusing to participate (e.g., transfer to a psychiatric hospital for observation).

Given the importance of informed consent in many forensic evaluations, some clinicians utilize written documents to ensure (and memorialize) the examinee's understanding. However, individuals unfamiliar with Euro-American standards for informed consent may find the use of documents, even if they are written in a language and manner that can easily be comprehended, even more confusing and potentially threatening. Gostin (1995) warned that formal informed consent procedures that are typically required in the US (e.g., standardized disclosures, written informed consent forms) might seem "alienating and dehumanizing" to many individuals who are unfamiliar with this practice. He recommended that the clinician "obtain the consent of patients in ways that are comprehensible and consistent with the person's language, custom and culture" (p. 844). If the use of a written informed consent document is the clinician's standard practice, the document must be written at an accessible reading level, given the diverse literacy and educational backgrounds of many forensic examinees. Such forms will also need to be translated into the examinee's dominant language prior to the evaluation. As with any translation, back-translation is necessary to ensure the accuracy of any translated documents and resolve any discrepancies that might arise in the initial translation process. In short, forensic mental health professionals need to be aware of and respect cultural differences while adhering to their own culture's expectations regarding informed consent.

Conducting the Interview

A cornerstone of any forensic mental health evaluation is the clinical interview. Although similar to a clinical interview conducted for other mental health evaluations, forensic interviews have unique elements that create several added complications. For example, while establishing rapport is critical to any clinical interview, this process is far more challenging in forensic settings. First, the consequences of a "negative" outcome may be particularly detrimental for the examinee, ranging from loss of anticipated financial compensation or access to one's children to deportation or lengthy incarceration—and possibly even death. Moreover, regardless of the nature of the legal proceedings, examinees are often forced to undergo the evaluation. While they can always refuse to answer questions, they may anticipate an even worse outcome if they are viewed as uncooperative. Even when the evaluation has been requested by the individual or their attorney (rather than court-ordered or necessitated by the legal issue at hand), the forensic interview is often perceived as coercive. Many individuals also enter the evaluation with an expectation that the clinician is inclined to judge them negatively—an expectation that is often warranted. Although these assumptions may be hard to negate, a relaxed pace and conversational interview process can help develop a more neutral, if not outright positive, rapport. Conversely, rushed evaluations where the interviewer is perceived as "interrogating" rather than "inquiring" are almost certain to impede the development of any meaningful rapport.

The challenges inherent in forensic interviews compound substantially when the individual does not share the evalator's cultural framework around time, scheduling, or other interpersonal formality. Although such differences may be uncomfortable for evaluators accustomed to rigid time structures, beginning the evaluation by offering (or sharing together in) a small snack or drink can communicate respect, reciprocity, and genuine regard for the individual, helping to offset any perception that the clinician is adversarial or impersonal. In one evaluation conducted by one of the authors, an Imam who was highly respected in his community vividly illustrated how cultural expectations and social position can shape the evaluation process. The individual, a plaintiff in civil litigation, arrived for an evaluation three hours early and requested to be seen immediately, even though the evaluator was already in the midst of another scheduled interview. The Imam's expectation, informed by his culture and position of authority, was that his time should be prioritized over the person who was in the midst of his scheduled interview. When this expectation was not met, he left the building and refused to participate in the evaluation that had been requested and arranged by his own attorney (he was eventually convinced by his attorney into giving the evaluator a "second chance"). Idiosyncratic expectations such as this one may be difficult to anticipate (although a similar response might be elicited from a wealthy or famous individual in the US), but a greater awareness of the importance of the Imam's position might have helped navigate the situation and avoid the challenges that ensued. For example, this individual could have been scheduled first or perhaps as the only evaluation scheduled for the day. Finally, there may also be culturally specific factors to consider to promote both respect and accurate assessment results, such as breaks at prayer times or scheduling the evaluation to avoid holidays or fasting days, particularly if these concerns might impact the individual's concentration or energy level.

Requiring an interpreter also complicates the process of rapport building for the forensic evaluator. Because the interpreter mediates virtually all communication, we strongly discourage a seating arrangement where the interpreter and examinee face one another. Instead, the clinician and examinee should face one another, enabling direct eye contact, while the interpreter should sit to the side of the examinee (if possible). This arrangement also helps the interpreter maintain a neutral posture and may provide a greater opportunity for the evaluator to directly observe the person being evaluated.

Reliance on an interpreter also requires clinicians to adjust their questioning style. Clinicians who have limited experience working with interpreters often pose lengthy, complex questions, only to hear the interpreter simplify the paragraph-length question into just a few words. It can sometimes be hard to gauge whether this problem is due to the interpreter only understanding part of the evaluator's lengthy question or because the interpreter simply decided (or needed) to simplify the question. Regardless of the interpreter's motive, the practice is problematic. The clinician can minimize this problem by using brief, plain-language questions one concept at a time, and avoiding jargon. When changes in the wording of a query are suspected (or obvious), we recommend interrupting the question-and-answer process to restate expectations for the interpreter: interpret in the first person, convey everything said without summarizing, and ask the evaluator to clarify or rephrase a question rather than rephrasing on your own. Invite interpreters to explain cultural context explicitly (e.g., "the examinee used an idiom that may imply ...") after conveying the content, to support cultural safety and transparency.

A similar problem often arises when the interpreter does not know how to translate an examinee's response. This is often obvious because the interpreter will respond directly to an examinee, essentially engaging in a back-and-forth discussion without translating any of the content to the interviewer. When interrupted by the evaluator (which is the appropriate response—ideally as soon as the interpreter responds to the examinee without translating the original response), interpreters will often assert that there are multiple possible interpretations of the language used. However, interrupting this exchange to clarify what portions of the examinee's response were not understood allows the *evaluator* to rephrase or clarify a question rather than allowing the interpreter to inject their own judgment. This approach should decrease the likelihood of important information being "lost in translation."

Another challenge to the clinical interview may arise when evaluating individuals from cultural contexts in which shame or "loss of face" places a central role (Hall et al., 2016). Individuals from such backgrounds may withhold important information out of concern for how others will perceive them or out of fear that their thoughts or actions could reflect negatively on their family or community. The risk of withholding information is particularly high when questions pertain to thoughts and behaviors that are considered taboo in the individual's culture. For example, asking about sexual behavior or suicidal ideation may be especially sensitive when evaluating an individual from a conservative religious or cultural background. Of course, a thorough evaluation often requires that such questions be asked, and disclosures that these taboos have been violated may have important clinical relevance. Acknowledging one's awareness of the social norms surrounding sensitive topics may, in itself, increase the individual's comfort in responding honestly to these and other questions.

Even when an individual appears fluent in the English language, cultural differences may impact how they respond to questions. For example, when working with Indigenous individuals from some communities, the evaluator should be aware that examinees may be inclined to say yes rather than no to direct yes-or-no questions, reflecting relational or conversational norms rather than literal agreement. Similarly, in several Southeast Asian cultural contexts, individuals may nod or respond affirmatively out of politeness rather than agreement, particularly when interacting with authority figures. Among Vietnamese Americans, for instance, the term "*da*" (yes) can indicate both agreement and "I am politely listening to you," especially when speaking with someone they respect or in a position of authority (Nguyen & Kehmeier, 1980; Wong & Fujii, 2004). Conversely, to show respect when interacting with authority figures, Vietnamese Americans may respond with a silent smile when they disagree or do not understand what is being said. These culturally grounded forms of communication can be easily misinterpreted in forensic settings, where accuracy and nuance are essential. Equivocal responses require clinicians to probe with more open-ended questions, especially if they elicit ambiguous responses to questions that have particular significance for the forensic issues at hand (e.g., responses regarding unusual or clinically significant symptoms or behaviors). Likewise, avoiding excessive interpretation of both verbal and non-verbal behaviors (such as smiling or nodding in response to a question) should be approached as potentially culturally situated expressions and lead to further inquiry rather than assuming that the intent or emotion underlying the response is universal.

Finally, as noted previously, an awareness of culturally specific symptoms and healing practices is critical when evaluating an individual whose cultural background differs markedly from the evaluator's. Such culturally grounded expressions of distress may not become apparent until conducting background research prior to the evaluation (as described earlier in this chapter), yet they can be essential for adequately understanding the nature and meaning of the individual's difficulties they may be experiencing. For example, individuals from non-Western contexts may experience or describe their difficulties primarily in physiological terms rather than as evidence of a mental health problem, or as a common response to loss or trauma. Without an awareness of these culturally specific manifestations that the person might experience, the evaluator risks overlooking potentially important clinical information. Inquiring whether the individual has sought assistance from a traditional or non-allopathic healer may also help the clinician recognize problems or symptoms specific to the individual's cultural context. The DSM-5 Text Revision (DSM-5-TR) Cultural Formulation Interview (American Psychiatric Association, 2022) provides several useful questions to elicit culturally unique symptom presentations and understand the individual's interpretation of those symptoms. Although the Cultural Formulation Interview is not specific to any one culture, these guidelines serve as a helpful framework for thinking about cultural influences, particularly as they pertain to the diagnostic interview.

The Mental Status Examination

A critical element of any clinical interview is the Mental Status Examination (MSE). The MSE aims to identify any mental disorders that might be present by asking a series of questions targeting specific psychiatric symptoms and integrating behavioral observations into the responses elicited. Although numerous guidelines exist for conducting the MSE, most clinicians develop their own individualized approach to this task, using questions that target the behaviors, cognitions, and symptoms relevant to the evaluation at hand (Golden & Hutchings, 1998). However, the MSE is vulnerable to multiple sources of bias or distortion when applied to individuals from a cultural background other than that of the evaluator and can lead to significant inaccuracies and misinterpretations (Mezzich et al., 2009; Shepherd & Lewis-Fernandez, 2016). Furthermore, these biases are not limited to cultural or linguistic differences but can also reflect broader sociopolitical dynamics (e.g., the effects of colonization, systemic racism, or historical trauma) that shape how distress is expressed, how evaluators interpret behavior, and whose norms are considered "standard" within forensic evaluations.

Several domains of the MSE are particularly vulnerable to distortions, beginning with the assessment of the examinee's attitude, emotions, and insight. First, attitude refers to the level of cooperation and engagement with the interview process that the individual demonstrates. Yet, culture and sociopolitical contexts impact how an individual's attitude is perceived, beginning with the person's willingness to disclose information. In some cases, reluctance to share personal information may reflect cultural expectations surrounding family loyalty or modesty, whereas in others it may be informed by sociopolitical histories of surveillance, discrimination, or coercive systems that continue to shape interactions with authority. Many forensic evaluations require obtaining a thorough psychosocial history from the individual being evaluated, but as noted previously, individuals from some cultural backgrounds may emphasize loyalty to the family over individual interests, and therefore may be reluctant to answer questions that could reflect negatively on the entire family (Sue & Sue, 2016). If not understood by the evaluator, this reluctance may be misinterpreted as an attempt to influence the outcome of the evaluation or an attempt to minimize or exaggerate symptoms, rather than an effort to avoid bringing shame upon family members. Individuals from a culture with clearly defined roles that guide dominance and deference may also be uncomfortable when these roles are more ambiguous (as is often the case in a clinical interview) and may therefore be less likely to self-disclose information (Sue & Sue, 2016). Shepherd and Lewis-Fernandez (2016) observed that Australian Aboriginal individuals often respond to questions through "a trading of narratives," but cautioned that some clinicians might perceive this response style as evasive or tangential, despite it being normative and appropriate within the individual's cultural context.

Evaluating an individual's emotional expression is a second aspect of the MSE that can be particularly important in a forensic interview. For example, the absence of guilt or remorse may be relevant to the assessment of psychopathy and thereby impact an assessment of risk for future violence or criminal recidivism. Accurately gauging emotional expression is also relevant to diagnosing many other mental disorders, such as depression, borderline personality disorder, and schizophrenia. However, many cultural groups emphasize the restraint of strong feelings rather than the free expression of emotions (Shepherd & Lewis-Fernandez, 2016; Sue & Sue, 2016), which can be misinterpreted as callousness, dysphoria, or inappropriate affect when the influence of culture is not recognized.

A related issue may arise with examinees who have sufficient English fluency as to be effectively bilingual. Bamford (1991) described the *detachment effect*, which occurs when parallel encoding systems for each language comprise unique sets of associations. Because abstract terms (e.g., freedom, love) often have more variations in connotations and affective associations than more concrete terms (e.g., dog, chair), bilingual individuals may have more difficulty understanding questions and communicating emotions and feelings in their non-dominant language. This can lead clinicians to perceive more defensiveness or intellectualization than when interviews are conducted in the individual's dominant language. The detachment effect is also associated with less effective communication as well as less effective expressions of emotion, psychological symptoms, and self-disclosure.

The third aspect of the MSE that warrants attention is the assessment of the individual's insight into their behaviors or symptoms. Insight is typically relevant to the assessment of violence risk, amenability to treatment or intervention, and competence to make treatment decisions. Moreover, concerns about treatment compliance, which are often linked to insight, may impact compliance with the conditions of supervised release (e.g., parole or probation) or release from a psychiatric facility (e.g., for individuals involuntarily committed after being found not guilty by reason of insanity or under sexually violent predator statutes). However, the assessment of insight is impacted by the individual's beliefs about the causes and meaning of their symptoms. Because many cultures conceptualize mental health problems as having physical, spiritual, or religious origins, they may also believe that the appropriate treatment should be grounded in these same beliefs. A preference for seeking treatment with a religious or traditional healer may reflect a culturally normative perception rather than treatment resistance or lack of insight into the presence of a symptom or disorder. Insight may also pertain to emotions such as frustration or anger, yet there are some cultures in which individuals will disavow feelings perceived as detrimental (Sue & Sue, 2016). Thus, a lack of insight into the existence of negative emotions may be culturally normative rather than a reflection of a mental disorder. In sum, an understanding of how people within a given culture conceptualize and manifest symptoms is necessary to accurately evaluate the nature and extent of the individual's insight.

Assessing Functional Legal Capacities

Many forensic evaluations require tailoring the clinical interview to address specific legally relevant functional abilities, such as competence or fitness to stand trial (CST) or competence to waive constitutional rights. Although several forensic assessment instruments exist to supplement these evaluations, the forensic interview plays a crucial role, particularly when cultural and linguistic factors complicate the assessment of knowledge and understanding of the legal process. Despite the importance of culture and language in assessing decisional competencies, little research or case law guidance exists to guide these evaluations.

One critical issue that frequently arises, particularly with regard to competence to stand trial, is whether language or culture can be a sufficient basis for deeming an individual incompetent to stand trial (or "unfit," depending on the jurisdiction). In most jurisdictions, language or cultural considerations are not a sufficient basis for a finding of incompetence, as the legal criteria typically require the presence of a mental disorder, disease, or defect. However, anecdotal evidence has suggested that findings of incompetence may occasionally occur, particularly when adequate interpretation services are not available (e.g., Vernon & Miller, 2001).

One case that directly addressed the issue of linguistic challenges as a basis for incompetence is *State v. Ortiz-Abrego (2017)*. In this case, a Washington state court concluded that the defendant, whose primary language was Spanish and who had limited formal education and auditory comprehension difficulties, was not able to adequately understand the proceedings, even with interpreters present during the trial. Although a Spanish-speaking neuropsychologist evaluated him mid-trial and recommended accommodations, including simplified Spanish-language explanations and comprehension checks, these measures were not implemented, and the trial court ultimately found him incompetent. In its ruling, the court criticized the state experts for failing to evaluate Ortiz-Abrego in a culturally and linguistically appropriate manner. The court emphasized that competence evaluations must account for cultural and linguistic factors to meet minimum standards of adequacy. Nevertheless, absent an affirmative finding of some sort of mental health or cognitive disorder, there is often little basis for concluding that an individual is unable to learn the information needed in order to participate meaningfully in their trial.

Of course, one need not be a legal scholar, or even a high school graduate, to be considered competent to stand trial, given that the "bar" for competence has typically been set quite low (Melton et al., 2018). Moreover, common practice among forensic evaluators conducting a CST evaluation is to attempt to "teach" the defendant any information that they were initially unaware of (Melton et al., 2018). In fact, this practice is embedded in many of the more widely used CST instruments, such as the MacArthur Competence Assessment Tool, Criminal Adjudication (MacCAT-CA Poythress et al., 1999), the Evaluation of Competence to Stand Trial, Revised (ECST-R; Rogers et al., 2004), and the Fitness Interview Test, Revised (FIT-R; Zapf et al., 2001). However, it is unclear whether this process is sufficient to address the needs of a culturally and linguistically diverse defendant who is unfamiliar with US legal proceedings, as little research has addressed this question.

Other aspects of language and culture may also impact the CST evaluation process, beginning with the attorney's decision to refer their client. For example, Varela et al. (2011) found that attorneys were significantly less likely to refer a Spanish-speaking client for a competence evaluation compared to English-speaking clients. Gardner et al. (2020) also found a disproportionately low rate of interpreter use in competence evaluations relative to the frequency of criminal defendants with limited English proficiency. However, this discrepancy may partly reflect the failure of some evaluators to indicate that an interpreter was used, as required by the APA Ethics code. While these findings might indicate biases in the competence evaluation process, we could not locate any systematic research examining cultural or linguistic influences on either CST findings or any of the instruments used to gauge impaired competence.

Despite the apparent dearth of cross-cultural research on competence to stand trial, one study examined CST-related abilities (based on the MacCAT-CR) among a racially diverse group of youths (11–17 years old) and young adults (18–24 years old) living in the US. Viljoen et al. (2007) found significantly greater deficits among minoritized participants compared to White, non-Latine participants, even though all were fluent in English. However, minoritized participants also demonstrated significantly greater improvement following the "teaching" portion of the MacCAT-R (even after controlling for socio-economic status), indicating that these initial deficits are often resolved with brief education. Nevertheless, in the absence of any systematic research with non-English-speaking samples to support the MacCAT-CR or similar CST instruments (e.g., ECST-R), evaluators are encouraged to utilize idiographic instruments (e.g., the FIT-R) that guide the evaluation process but do not generate scores or permit comparison to normative samples (Anderson et al., 2022).

Similar challenges arise in understanding and waiving constitutional rights, such as those outlined in the *Miranda* warning, which also involve comprehension of legal processes. These concerns are particularly noteworthy given that Rogers et al. (2009) found that over 70% of Spanish-language *Miranda* disclosures omitted critical information such as the right to remain silent or the right to counsel. One recent study found that native Arabic and Chinese speakers who were attending US colleges had far poorer comprehension of *Miranda* warnings than native English speakers (Pavlenko et al., 2019). Interestingly, the degree of English proficiency was not associated with *Miranda* comprehension in this study, suggesting that cultural factors other than language may impact the ability to understand these warnings.

In response to concerns about the adequacy of existing Miranda comprehension measures, Seaborn et al. (2010) developed a measure specifically intended for deaf criminal defendants who were able to use sign language. Although performance was stronger among those with higher levels of education, the authors concluded that most individuals who function below an eighth-grade reading level would be unable to adequately understand Miranda warning, regardless of whether it was presented in writing, through sign language, or both. Ironically, courts have typically overlooked problematic translations of the *Miranda* warning (Einesman, 1999), concluding that even flawed translations are adequate to protect the rights of criminal defendants with low English proficiency. Hence, like the analysis of CST above, norm-referenced measures of *Miranda* comprehension should be avoided in the absence of more substantial empirical data than currently exists.

Revisiting the Vignette

The opening vignette raised several important issues, some of which will be addressed in greater detail in subsequent chapters. The most obvious, already discussed in this chapter, is the evaluator's decision to rely on a paralegal for interpretation services. As noted previously in this chapter, this approach has several problems, including but not limited to the potential for deliberate misrepresentation of the defendant's responses (e.g., if the defendant disclosed potentially damaging information). Even if the interpreter's objectivity was not in question (which is hard to imagine), the absence of formal training or the use of a certified interpreter raises questions about their level of skill, since interpretation is a uniquely different skill from simply speaking the language.

A second question raised in the vignette is whether any form of psychological testing is appropriate. As will be discussed in the next two chapters, the answer to this question is usually yes, provided that interpretation is appropriately cautious, and limitations are acknowledged in any report and/or testimony. In this case, the Croatian version of the MMPI would likely be appropriate for a Serbian national, given the similarities in both language and culture (Ramet, 2011).

Finally, the vignette indicated that a primary referral question was competence to stand trial. While most forensic evaluators have a clear and easily accessible standard upon which to base their evaluation (e.g., the *Dusky* standard, in the US), the vignette (and actual case) was set in the United Nations' International Criminal Court (ICC). There is a standard for competence (or "fitness") in the ICC, and it is similar to standards used in other jurisdictions, but also includes elements that might not be readily known to the evaluator (see Freckelton & Karagiannakis, 2014). This highlights the importance of having an adequate knowledge of the underlying legal standards, a fact that is understood by every well-trained forensic evaluator. Moreover, while not mentioned in the vignette, but relevant to those working in international settings (addressed in Chapter 8), it is equally important for evaluators to determine whether any unique set of credentials or licensure is required for testimony outside the jurisdictions where they typically practice. In this case, the ICC typically permits testimony by individuals from a wide range of countries and professional backgrounds, provided they are adequately credentialed in their home country (Appazov, 2016).

Summary and Recommendations

Mental health professionals are frequently asked to evaluate individuals from culturally and linguistically diverse backgrounds. However, despite a growing body of research on a range of topics related to cross-cultural assessment, there is relatively little guidance available as to how one should incorporate culturally responsive and safe procedures into a forensic mental health assessment. Moreover, there is surprisingly little research to guide clinical procedures. For example, no published research (to date) has systematically addressed the impact of interpreters on the forensic interview process or how much knowledge of the individual's culture context is needed to conduct an effective interview (a threshold that likely varies with the culture and forensic issue at hand). Given the importance of culture in the assessment process, clinicians working in forensic mental health settings should continuously work on increasing their cultural competence and humility through attending workshops, seeking consultation, or doing independent study, and by incorporating tools such as the DSM-5-TR Cultural Formulation Interview into their assessments (see also Lewis-Fernandez et al., 2016). Although the benefit of these different approaches to enhancing culturally responsive practice have not been rigorously tested, any efforts to increase one's awareness are likely to be valuable for improving one's practice.

To close this chapter, we offer a number of recommendations, based on our own clinical experience and research, that have strengthened our own practices when working with individuals from diverse cultural and linguistic backgrounds:

- **Evaluate your cultural competence**: Assess your ability to provide a culturally and linguistically appropriate evaluation tailored to the examinee's background.
    - If this ability is lacking, determine whether an evaluator with comparable (or sufficient) expertise who is more fluent in the language or culture is available.
    - Recognize that linguistic fluency alone is insufficient; an evaluator born and raised in Spain may speak the same language as an examinee from Honduras but may lack familiarity with the issues related to immigration, acculturation, and cultural differences.
- **Conduct background research**: Some background research prior to the evaluation is usually necessary to identify culturally specific considerations that may impact communication and cross-cultural understanding.

- Identify the examinee's primary language(s), regional dialects, and cultural subgroup(s), as variations can significantly impact the evaluation and the interpreter's accuracy or relevance.
- Consider the sociopolitical context of the examinee's culture, such as caste systems, ethnic conflicts, colonization, or histories of persecution, to better understand how systemic inequities may shape their experiences and identify potential biases in interpretation.
- Determine whether the complexity of the case requires formal consultation with cultural or linguistic experts.

• **Use a skilled, independent interpreter**: Employ a professional interpreter with expertise in forensic contexts to ensure accurate communication, particularly when the examinee has limited English proficiency.

- When possible, provide interpreters with some training specific to forensic mental health contexts to enhance their understanding of nuanced terminology (e.g., symptoms of mental illness).
- Clarify that requests for 'word-for-word' translation refer to the complete and faithful rendering of all speech and not to overly literal translation of each individual word (e.g., translating *tengo calor* as "I have heat" rather than "I'm hot"), with the goal to preserve the examinee's precise wording, word order, tone, and clinically relevant language.
- Monitor interpreters carefully to prevent oversimplifications or unsanctioned "clarifications" during back-and-forth communication.
- Interrupt lengthy or ambiguous responses to facilitate accurate, word-for-word translations and avoid losing critical information.
- Avoid interpreters with personal or professional ties to the examinee to ensure neutrality and prevent conflicts of interest.

• **Adapt the informed consent process**: Ensure that informed consent is culturally and linguistically appropriate for the examinee.

- When feasible, provide consent documents translated into the examinee's primary language and ensure accuracy through back-translation.
- Use simplified, low-literacy versions of consent materials when needed to improve comprehension.
- Review the informed consent verbally with the examinee, using an interpreter if necessary, to confirm understanding.
- Adapt formalities to align with cultural norms without undermining ethical standards or legal requirements.

- **Account for cultural norms in the evaluation**: Recognize how cultural norms might influence the individual's responses and engagement during the evaluation.

  - Avoid making assumptions about nonverbal behaviors (e.g., eye contact, smiling, body language), as their meanings may vary significantly across cultures.
  - Use open-ended questions to clarify ambiguous verbal or nonverbal responses and avoid misinterpreting intent or emotion.
  - Recognize that cultural norms may discourage disclosure of sensitive information, particularly when discussing taboo topics (e.g., substance use, sexuality, suicidal ideation).

- **Tailor the forensic interview**: Adapt the interview to reflect the examinee's cultural and linguistic background for a more accurate understanding of their experiences and behaviors.

  - Allow for extended interview times when an interpreter is required, as consecutive interpretation always increases the length of the evaluation.
  - Identify culturally specific symptoms (e.g., somatic symptoms or culturally bound syndromes) and adjust questions accordingly.
  - Integrate collateral information from culturally relevant sources (e.g., family members, community leaders) to contextualize the examinee's responses.
  - Consider structured tools, such as the DSM-5 Cultural Formulation Interview, to systematically explore cultural influences on the examinee's symptoms and behavior.

3
Assessment of Malingering and Defensiveness

Summary

Few topics are as central to forensic mental health evaluations as the assessment of response style and, in particular, the potential for malingering or defensiveness. However, there is growing recognition of the potential impact of culture and language on the assessment process, and the potential for elevated error rates when well-established tests are studied in culturally and linguistically diverse samples. This chapter provides an overview of the current approaches to assessing feigning, symptom exaggeration, or defensive responding in culturally and linguistically diverse samples. The chapter will outline potential influences on the assessment of response style as well as review the available research on the impact of these influences on test accuracy, focusing on both psychiatric symptom validity measures and cognitive effort tests. We conclude with a number of recommendations for navigating these challenges in clinical practice.

Case Vignette

Baldo J, a 37-year-old single male born, raised, and living in Greece, was referred for an evaluation by a US-based insurance carrier following his claim for vocational disability benefits. Mr. J had been employed by a US military contractor, living and working on a military base in Afghanistan for approximately 36 months, when he returned to his home country at the onset of the COVID-19 pandemic. Several months later, after learning that his employment had been terminated, Mr. J filed for disability benefits, citing symptoms of depression and posttraumatic stress disorder (PTSD) as the basis for his purported inability to resume work in his

Cultural and Linguistic Considerations in Forensic Mental Health Assessment. Barry Rosenfeld and Alicia Nijdam-Jones, Oxford University Press. © Oxford University Press (2026).
DOI: 10.1093/9780190900991.003.0003

country of origin. Although he had never sought or received any medical or mental health treatment while working on the military base, he provided a mental health evaluation from a Greek psychiatrist (translated into English) that supported his application for disability benefits. Mr. J provided a seemingly credible account of exposure to periodic shelling on the military base where he worked and reported experiencing considerable distress upon learning of the death and dismemberment of a close friend (on another military base). However, he denied suffering any physical injuries himself. His insurance carrier requested a comprehensive evaluation of Mr. J's current symptoms and functional abilities and specifically requested an evaluation for the possibility of malingering (given the timing of his report of psychological symptoms). However, Mr. J indicated that he spoke very little English and required an interpreter for all interviews and testing. Are there any tests for malingering or cognitive effort that can be reliably used with a non-English speaking individual, or is the evaluator forced to rely solely on clinical judgment? Is it ever appropriate to translate test questions and/or instructions into another language? If testing is administered, how confident can the evaluator be in any test interpretations or conclusions?

Few topics are as central to forensic mental health evaluations as the assessment of response style, and more specifically, malingering. Response style refers to the systematic way individuals respond to psychological testing. An ever-growing number of tools have been created to identify whether an individual's response style is impacted by intentional negative or positive impression management. Malingering, perhaps the most important form of negative impression management occurs when an individual intentionally exaggerates or fabricates psychological or cognitive symptoms in order to obtain some type of external gain, such as receiving financial compensation, evading criminal responsibility, or accessing prescription medication.

Malingering is not a diagnosis. It differs from psychiatric disorders like factitious or conversion disorders because it: (1) involves the *intentional* production of symptoms, and (2) the individual is motivated by external incentives (rather than, for example, attention-seeking or a desire to be seen as "ill"). Because the term is highly stigmatizing, and there can be significant consequences for an individual labeled as malingering, clinicians are advised to be particularly cautious when using the term to describe an examinee's symptom presentation or motivation. For example, the label of malingering can lead to a loss of access to needed medical or mental health services and/or compensation for genuine injuries. In criminal legal settings, labeling an individual as malingering can have severe legal consequences ranging from decreased legal protections (e.g., for an individual who is genuinely impaired) to enhanced criminal sanctions. Hence, clinicians are encouraged to be particularly cautious when characterizing symptoms as feigned or exaggerated, regardless of whether the term malingering (which presumes an external motivation) is used. Given the importance of these determinations, reliance on well-validated tests has become standard practice (Heilbrun et al., 2008; Melton et al., 2018).

There are many forensic settings where there is an increased risk of feigned psychopathology or exaggerated cognitive impairment due to the presence of strong external incentives. In civil law settings, this includes personal injury litigation and individuals seeking vocational disability benefits or workers' compensation. In criminal legal settings, the insanity defense, competence to stand trial, and eligibility for capital punishment can all be powerful incentives to feign serious mental or cognitive impairments. On the other hand, there are some forensic settings where minimization of symptoms (i.e., positive impression management) is far more likely. For individuals involuntarily committed pursuant to sexually violent predator statutes or after a finding of not guilty by reason of insanity, release from a secure treatment facility may hinge on the perceived absence of symptoms or problematic behaviors. Likewise, evaluations of fitness for duty, child custody determinations, or termination of parental rights provide a clear incentive to present as having few or no psychological difficulties. Within these and other forensic contexts, clinicians need to be particularly cautious as there are numerous factors that could influence response styles and symptom presentation, some of which are external and others that pertain to cultural differences in responding and symptom endorsement. This chapter begins by describing cultural considerations in feigning assessment in general, followed by a review of the current literature on assessing feigning, symptom exaggeration, or defensive responding in culturally and linguistically diverse samples. The chapter culminates with a set of recommendations for assessing whether an individual's symptom presentation has been purposefully distorted.

Cultural Considerations in Feigning Assessment

When evaluating individuals from diverse cultural or linguistic backgrounds, there are several key considerations that a clinician must be mindful of during and after the assessment. These include the impact of language on the assessment process, the utility of non-verbal tests, and specific cultural characteristics that may impact test-taking skills or response styles. The following sections review these considerations within the context of feigning assessments.

Linguistic Influences on Psychological Assessment

Considering an examinee's language proficiency and preference is key to any psychological evaluation. However, in the context of a feigning assessment, where the clinician's conclusions can have significant impacts on the individual being evaluated, clinicians must be particularly mindful of how they proceed and what testing they use. As noted in the previous chapter, when there is a mismatch between the evaluator and examinee in language fluency, errors in communication may arise that can lead to misunderstandings or misdiagnosis (Altarriba & Santiago-Rivera, 1994). At its essence, language impacts what information is conveyed to the evaluator and how (accurately) that information is presented and perceived.

When working with a bilingual individual, assessing that person's language preference at work, home, and socially will help the evaluator better understand their fluency. Although formal tools can be used to evaluate English proficiency, many are not feasible in the context of a forensic evaluation (e.g., the Test of English as a Foreign Language or TOEFL). Moreover, even if formal testing is possible, performance on these tests may be vulnerable to the same incentives to distort one's responses that apply to other types of testing that might be administered. When an examinee cannot communicate effectively, it may also cause them considerable stress (Cofresí & Gorman, 2004), which could impact their response style and lead to distorted responding (e.g., over- or underreporting of psychological symptoms).

Response style may also differ depending on language fluency and the language in which the test is administered. For example, Guttfreund (1990) found that bilingual Spanish-speaking Americans reported higher levels of anxiety and depression when administered tests in their dominant language than when English-language tests were used, suggesting that Spanish-speaking individuals may underreport symptoms in English-language assessments. In another study of bilingual adults, López et al. (2016) found that performance on a short-term memory test (Digit Span) was significantly better when tested in English than in Spanish. The authors attributed this finding to the number of syllables recalled (most digits have one more syllable in Spanish than in English), resulting in different cognitive strategies used to complete this test in the two languages. This finding has particular relevance for the assessment of feigning as an index derived from the Digit Span test (i.e., the Reliable Digit Span index), which is often used as an indicator of cognitive effort (Greiffenstein et al., 1994). Given these differences in test performance across languages, evaluators must carefully determine which language is most appropriate for administering tests to fully bilingual individuals. Regardless of language or bilingualism, evaluators should only rely on well-validated assessment measures that have been officially translated into the examinee's language in order to maximize the accuracy of the information elicited.

Translating Assessment Tools

A simple response to the question of "when should I translate an assessment into another language?" would be "never." And while there are many circumstances where translation is clearly inappropriate, we would suggest that there are *some* (very limited) circumstances in which translation of test instructions is acceptable and may even be advisable. The central distinction in this regard is whether test interpretation is norm-referenced or criterion-referenced. Norm-referenced tests refer to those tools where an individual's score or performance is compared to a normative sample (such as the multiscale inventories discussed in Chapter 4), in order to determine the extent to which their score deviates from "typical" respondents.[1] Criterion-referenced tests, on the other hand, systematically assess the presence or absence of a predetermined set of symptoms or characteristics (e.g., diagnostic criteria for a specific disorder). Because almost all the instruments relied upon in the assessment of feigning or minimization are best conceptualized as norm-referenced tests, translating test questions for use in a specific evaluation (i.e., when no prior translation is available, or a translation exists but lacks adequate normative data) is never justified. What *may* be justified, however, is translating test instructions, particularly for tests that are either primarily or entirely non-verbal. For example, instruments such as the Dot Counting Test (Boone et al., 2002) or the Test of Memory Malingering (TOMM; Tombaugh, 1996), both of which are discussed later in this chapter, require a brief explanation of the test and relatively simple instructions. These tests have been studied in a range of settings and samples, including a number of cross-cultural applications. While results have varied as to the effectiveness of these tools, there are data addressing their effectiveness that the evaluator can rely on to assist in interpreting test results (addressing a key requirement of *Daubert*, that tests have known error rates).

In many cases, the evaluator will simply ask the interpreter to translate the instructions into the examinee's dominant language. Although practical, a preferable approach is to obtain a formal translation of test instructions in advance, either using a professional translation service or through a standard translation/back-translation process. Of course, translating the instructions does not eliminate the possibility of bias in the test administration or interpretation; these issues are discussed later in this chapter. Following a pre-determined

[1] A thorough review of what comprises an appropriate normative sample is beyond the scope of this chapter. In brief, this decision depends on a wide range of factors and is a function of the type of test and the nature of the planned interpretation. In some instances, test interpretation requires a comparison to the typical person without any history of mental illness of cognitive impairment. However, in many settings normative data might be comprised of individuals with a serious mental disorder or cognitive impairment in order to determine whether an individual's performance is consistent with—or atypical for—someone with a genuine disorder.

script for test instructions may be preferable, but it is not necessarily a requirement, particularly given that many evaluators paraphrase test instructions when they administer tests in English. Nevertheless, evaluators should document their administration process (including any translation) and be prepared to answer questions about where translated tests were acquired, who conducted the translation, and what (if any) evidence exists to support the utility of the tests administered.

Non-Verbal Tests are Not Culture-Free

Given the obvious potential for cultural and linguistic biases when using verbal stimuli in psychological assessments, many clinical resources recommend non-verbal measures with non-English speaking individuals in an attempt to "provide a fair and less biased assessment" (McCallum, 2017, p. 3). Although non-verbal tools may be less overtly problematic than verbal stimuli, the potential for bias certainly still exists. Therefore, it is critical to recognize the impact of culture on test performance and how these influences may influence feigning assessment beyond the obvious language-based concerns. These cultural considerations apply to a range of issues, including speed-based tests, images or references unfamiliar to examinees from different cultural backgrounds, assumptions about organizational processes, and the impact of education on testing experience and performance. These issues are discussed in more detail in Chapter 5 (Cognitive and Neuropsychological Assessments), but are summarized briefly here.

Several studies have found that speed-based tasks are poor predictors of psychological constructs in non-Western cultures. Speed-based testing relies on the assumption that there is value in responding quickly. This assumption is clearly justified in most Western cultures and more economically developed countries, where rapid task completion is prioritized, often at the expense of accuracy. However, many cultural groups may not share this norm. For example, Sternberg and Grigorenko (2008) have noted that in many cultures, depth of processing is prioritized over processing speed. Therefore, asking clients to work as quickly as possible or applying a time limit for responding may not motivate all test-takers to respond quickly. For instance, one individual from rural India informed the evaluator that he could work fast or he could make no mistakes, but he could not do both, perceiving the two requests as mutually exclusive.

Another concern with non-verbal feigning assessment instruments is the use of images or references that may be unfamiliar to examinees from different cultural and linguistic backgrounds, particularly if they have limited exposure to Western culture. For example, an item-level analysis to determine which visual items on the TOMM, a cognitive effort test that is widely used in both criminal and civil forensic evaluations, examined errors in a sample of adults from Colombia (tested in their country of origin), many of whom were illiterate (Nijdam-Jones et al., 2019a). That study found that items uncommon within their communities (e.g., toaster, pennant, maple leaf) were the most difficult for individuals to correctly identify. Thus, differences in accuracy for measures that rely on visual stimuli demonstrate that even though a test may be non-verbal, cultural biases in the non-verbal stimuli may impact performance.

A growing body of research also highlights the importance of considering literacy and education as mediating factors when interpreting performance on non-verbal cognitive tasks (e.g., Rosselli & Ardila, 2003). Although many feigning assessment tools developed with Western samples report no association between performance and level of education (i.e., suggesting that "passing" a feigning assessment should not be impacted by level of education), research in some countries has contradicted these findings. Several non-verbal tools used to assess feigning have demonstrated a strong association between test performance and both level of education and literacy (described in more detail later in this chapter). These findings are not surprising given extensive research demonstrating that literacy is associated with stronger visual perception skills, logical reasoning, phonological processing, and working memory (Ardila et al., 2010; Kosmidis et al., 2011).

Culture and experience can shape one's cognitive functioning in many ways that impact test performance. For example, matrix-based cognitive testing (used in tests such as the non-verbal subtest of the Validity Indicator Profile; Frederick, 2003) assumes familiarity with the organization of images into rows and columns, making such tasks easier for some cultural groups than others. In short, while many non-verbal tests are used to assess cognitive effort and feigned cognitive impairment, they are not free from potential sources of bias.

Culturally Specific Response Styles

When assessing feigning and minimization with examinees from culturally and linguistically diverse backgrounds, it is crucial to consider how culture may impact symptom presentation, particularly in response to self-report inventories. Correa (2018) highlighted several influences common to Latine cultures that may impact validity testing, including *machismo*, extreme response styles, and culturally related stressors. For example, the term *machismo* refers to a culturally positive value of masculine pride and dominance common among Latin American men, and coupled with an emphasis on traditional gender roles. Correa suggested that high levels of machismo increase the likelihood that an individual will underreport or minimize some symptoms due to a culturally sanctioned hesitation around disclosing psychological distress.

Response style can also influence responses to standardized test items, such as those used on the Personality Assessment Inventory (PAI; described in more detail in Chapter 4). Systematic response styles can be divided into four broad categories: acquiescence (consistently agreeing with test items regardless of content), disacquiescence (consistently disagreeing with test items), extreme responses (consistently endorsing extreme ratings such as always or never), or middle response styles (consistently choosing moderate ratings such as sometimes or somewhat agree). Research suggests that Latine and African American individuals in the US are more likely to use extreme response styles, and to endorse items in a positive direction more generally (acquiescence) in comparison to European Americans (Bachman & O'Malley, 1984; Clarke, 2000; Hui & Triandis, 1989; Marin et al., 1992). On the other hand, Asian respondents may more often opt for middle responses when compared to North American respondents (Chen et al., 1995; Shiomi & Loo, 1999).

In a large international study across 26 countries, Harzing (2006) found significant differences in response styles associated with country-level characteristics. Specifically, respondents from countries with high power distance (an acceptance of inequality among citizens) engaged in more positive extreme response styles than middle and negative extreme response styles, whereas individuals from countries with high levels of collectivism demonstrated a preference for acquiescence and middle response styles. Harzing also found that participants who completed the tests in English provided more middle responses than when they were administered the test in their dominant language, which generated more extreme response styles. Because some tests intended to detect response bias rely on extreme responses, these tendencies may increase the risk of erroneous conclusions and highlight the need to consider the potential impact of cultural norms on response style.

Assessment Approaches for Detecting Symptom Exaggeration

Due to the serious consequences for an individual labeled as feigning or malingering, clinicians must consider multiple sources to inform their decision-making in this area, including self-report, collateral information, and psychological testing data. Slick et al. (1999) created a framework that has become widely accepted for identifying malingered neurocognitive deficits and distinguishing the degree of confidence that should be accorded (definite, probable, and possible). Simply put, the Slick criteria originally encompassed three main components: (1) the presence of significant financial or external incentive,

(2) evidence of fabrication or exaggeration using psychological testing, and (3) evidence of discrepancies from self-report. However, with the rapid growth in the number and type of available assessment tools and the research underlying these tools, the need to revise these criteria was evident.

The Multidimensional Criteria for Neurocognitive, Somatic, and Psychiatric Malingering (Sherman et al., 2020) provided this much-needed revision, proposing that clinicians consider four key components and distinguish between four "types" of malingering: (a) malingering of neurocognitive dysfunction, (b) malingering of somatic symptoms, (c) malingering of psychiatric symptoms, and (d) malingering with mixed presentation. The updated criteria require (a) the presence of a substantial external incentive, (b) invalid presentation indicative of feigning or exaggeration ("compelling inconsistencies"), (c) marked discrepancies between obtained test data/symptom report and other kinds of evidence, and (d) that the invalid presentation cannot be fully accounted for by another developmental, medical, or neurological condition. Given the importance of "objective" data in the assessment of malingering, it is not surprising that clinicians have increasingly relied on psychological assessment tools to provide data that can be systematically generated and evaluated.

A Short Primer on Classification Accuracy

An important metric for gauging the utility of feigning assessment measures is the instrument's classification accuracy, that is, the extent to which a measure accurately distinguishes genuine symptom presentations from those feigning or exaggerating symptoms (see Table 3.1). There are four primary indices of classification accuracy: sensitivity, specificity, positive predictive accuracy (PPA), and negative predictive accuracy (NPA), though many other indices can be derived from these simple statistics (e.g., overall hit rate, Youden's J). Sensitivity is often referred to as the "true positive rate" and reflects the proportion of feigning individuals that a tool accurately identifies as feigning. On the other hand, specificity refers to the proportion of honest responders that the test accurately identifies as not feigning (the "false positive rate" is 1-specificity). Importantly, sensitivity and specificity are independent of the base rate (proportion of feigners in a sample or population) and therefore can be directly compared across measures, studies, and samples. In other words, a higher sensitivity rate always means that a greater proportion of feigners will be identified, whereas a lower specificity rate equates to a greater proportion of honest responders being incorrectly identified as feigning (i.e., false positives). Because many instruments utilize one or more cut scores on an ordinal scale (e.g., number of correct or incorrect responses),

Table 3.1 Classification accuracy

Test Results	Reality	
	Feigning Symptoms	**Genuine Responding**
Classified as Feigning	True Positive (TP)	False Positive (FP)
Classified as Genuine	False Negative (FN)	True Negative (TN)

Note: Sensitivity = TP/(TP+FN); Specificity = TN/(TN+FP); PPA = TP/(TP+FP); NPA = TN/(TN+FN)

the Area Under the Curve (AUC) statistic, derived from the Receiver Operating Characteristic (ROC) curve, integrates sensitivity and specificity into a single index that can also be directly compared across samples and studies. The ROC curve can also help researchers identify the optimal cut-score for a given measure or sample depending on the relative importance of sensitivity and specificity, since the two operate in opposition to one another (i.e., as sensitivity increases, specificity decreases and vice versa).

PPA and NPA are also important indices for clinical decision-making but are less often reported, in part because they are heavily influenced by the base rate of feigning in the sample (Rosenfeld et al., 2000). The PPA reflects the proportion of individuals identified as feigning by a test result who are actually feigning, while NPA is the proportion of correct predictions of honest responding. However, because PPA and NPA cannot be compared across studies, and the "true" base rate of feigning in any given evaluation setting cannot be known, these statistics primarily serve as aids for interpreting sensitivity and specificity. Nevertheless, they serve as an important reminder of the potential for incorrectly identifying a genuinely impaired individual as feigning or, conversely, the likelihood that a test will fail to identify an individual who is feigning symptoms. Before choosing a specific test or cut-score to use when assessing feigning with individuals from diverse backgrounds, it is important to consider the available evidence based on the relevant indicators of classification accuracy.

Cross-Cultural Validity of Feigning Assessment Instruments

When deciding which psychological assessment tools to use with culturally and linguistically diverse populations, it is important to recognize that the vast majority of standardized assessment tools were developed and evaluated with English-speaking North American samples. Hence, clinicians must consider the appropriateness of the stimuli, translation, interpretative norms, and validation studies to determine if they are appropriate to use with the examinee. Fortunately, the past decade has witnessed a growing focus on studies examining the validity of feigning assessment tools with culturally diverse samples. While many of those studies still take place in highly developed countries in North America, Western Europe, and Australasia, others have increasingly utilized samples from countries in Asia, Latin America, and Africa. The following sections review the evidence for common symptom validity tests.

This review is divided across the different types of symptoms targeted, distinguishing those intended to detect feigned psychopathology (e.g., psychosis, depression) from those intended to identify feigned cognitive impairment. The former are typically referred to as symptom validity tests (SVTs), whereas the latter are considered performance validity tests (PVTs) or tests of cognitive effort. However, it should be noted that some overlap exists across these tests, as some SVTs include scales or indices intended to identify feigned cognitive disorders, and some PVTs aid in the assessment of feigned psychopathology. In addition, some scales and indices are intended to identify feigned medical conditions or feigning specific to psycho-legal abilities (e.g., competence to stand trial). Because no research to date has examined the utility of the latter instruments or indices in culturally or linguistically diverse samples, this chapter focuses only on SVTs and PVTs.

Detection Strategies for Feigned Psychopathology

When considering psychological assessment tools to identify feigned psychopathology (SVTs), it is important to consider the strategies used to detect feigning (Rogers, 2018). Understanding the detection strategies is particularly important in cross-cultural forensic assessments, as cultural factors (e.g., acquiescing to authority and culturally normative defensiveness) can impact an individual's responses in both clinical interview and assessment settings. Rogers (2018) described multiple detection strategies for identifying feigned mental disorders but collapsed these into two overarching approaches: those based on an unlikely symptom presentation and those based on "amplified" symptoms.

Unlikely symptom presentation strategies include: identifying rare or improbable symptoms, such as those that are infrequently reported by genuine patients with a given type of mental disorder; and implausible symptom combinations, such as reporting the co-occurrence of symptoms that may be common in isolation but rarely co-occur. Of course, symptoms that appear uncommon in some cultures may be relatively common in others, potentially impinging on the accuracy of unlikely symptom presentation strategies in evaluations involving individuals with culturally diverse backgrounds. Likewise, translation may also impact the phrasing of questions purporting to gauge implausible symptom combinations, leading to responses that reflect wording problems rather than deliberate symptom exaggeration.

Amplified symptom detection strategies involve the range and severity of reported symptoms. For example, many feigners endorse symptoms indiscriminately or report an excessive number of symptoms as extremely intense or distressing. Likewise, feigners may endorse only the most obvious or blatant symptoms of a mental disorder (e.g., thoughts of suicide when feigning depression) rather than those that are common but somewhat more subtle (e.g., feeling hopeless or excessive guilt). Identifying discrepancies between reported symptoms and observed behaviors is another detection strategy that is encompassed with "amplified" detection approaches. However, these strategies may also be impacted by linguistic and cultural factors, as confusion about the questions asked (e.g., to elicit symptom severity) can lead to acquiescence that gives the appearance of feigning. Some or all of the detection strategies described above are utilized by the growing bank of tests and assessment techniques available to the forensic mental health professional (see Table 3.2). The following pages address the potential for cultural influences in general, followed by a summary of the existing empirical support for the most common SVTs used for identifying feigned or malingered symptom presentation.

Minnesota Multiphasic Personality Inventory (MMPI)

The MMPI measures (MMPI-2, MMPI-2-RF, and MMPI-3) are the leading tools used to assess psychopathology and personality functioning in both clinical and forensic settings with adults 18 years and older.[2] A true-false self-report measure, the MMPI has multiple embedded "validity" scales that have been developed to identify both symptom exaggeration and the underreporting of psychopathology. First developed in the 1940s, the Minnesota Multiphasic Personality Inventory (MMPI; Hathaway & McKinley, 1943) has gone through several updates beginning with the first revision that created the 567-item MMPI-2 (Butcher et al., 1989) and was subsequently shortened and restructured (using the same 1980's normative sample) into the 338-item MMPI-2-RF (MMPI-2-RF; Ben-Porath & Tellegen, 2008). The most recent revision, the MMPI-3 (Ben-Porath & Tellegen, 2020), uses a new, nationally representative normative sample designed to match the US Census Bureau demographic projections for 2020. Because of the important role these scales play in forensic assessment, cross-cultural validity is addressed in detail in the following chapter, but the specific role of the MMPI in assessing feigned symptoms is addressed briefly here.

[2] Versions of these tests have also been developed for adolescents (the MMPI-A and MMPI-A-RF) but are used less often in forensic settings.

Table 3.2 Detection strategies for feigned mental disorders

Measures	Unlikely Presentation Detection Strategies	Amplified Detection Strategies
MMPI-2-RF / MMPI-3	F (Infrequent Responses) Fp (Infrequent Psychopathology Responses) Fs (Infrequent Somatic Responses)	FBS (Symptom Validity) RBS (Response Bias Scale)
SIRS/SIRS-2	IA (Improbable and Absurd Symptoms) RS (Rare Symptoms) SC (Symptom Combinations)	BL (Blatant Symptoms) SEL (Symptom Selectivity) OS (Overly Specified Symptoms) RO (Reported vs. Observed) SEV (Symptom Severity)
SIMS	Total Score	
M-FAST	RC (Rare Combinations) UH (Unusual Hallucinations)	ES (Extreme Symptomatology) RO (Reported vs. Observed)
PAI	MAL (Malingering Index) NDS (Negative Distortion Scale) NIM (Negative Impression Management) RDF (Rogers Discriminant Function)	MFI (Multiscale Feigning Index)
IOP-29	FDS (False Disorder Probability Score)	

Note: Adapted from Rogers, R. (2018). Detection strategies for malingering and defensiveness. In R. Rogers & S. D. Bender (Eds.), *Clinical assessment of malingering and deception* (4 ed., pp. 18–41). Guilford Press. MMPI-2-RF scale names typically include an "-r" suffix; this has been omitted here for clarity.

Each version of the MMPI measures includes multiple scales to identify over-reporting of symptoms, some of which are included in each version and others that are not. These validity scales utilize several detection strategies, including endorsement of rare symptoms (Fp, Fs), excessive breadth of symptoms (F, FBS), and obvious versus subtle symptoms (O–S; developed with the original MMPI but also available with the MMPI-2). Research on the MMPI-2 and MMPI-2-RF has demonstrated mean effect sizes for the detection of feigning that range from moderate ($g = 1.0$)[3] to very large ($g > 1.75$), corresponding to AUC estimates between .75 and .90 (Aparcero et al., 2023). It should be noted that individual studies of the MMPI have varied by setting, population, methodology, and test version, but very few effect sizes differed significantly between the MMPI-2

[3] *g* and *d* effect sizes are interpreted similarly but *g* is considered a more accurate estimate of mean effect sizes for meta-analyses that rely on small samples.

and MMPI-2-RF. Further, since item content has not changed significantly for most of the MMPI validity scales (particularly between the MMPI-2-RF and MMPI-3), these effect sizes are unlikely to differ markedly for the MMPI-3.

A central advantage of the MMPI instruments in evaluating individuals from diverse backgrounds is the availability of multiple translated versions. Although the MMPI-3 is only available in Dutch/Flemish, French (Canada), Greek, Italian, Japanese, and Spanish (US) at the time of this printing,[4] the MMPI-2-RF is available in Croatian, Czech, Danish, French (France), German, Hebrew, Korean, Norwegian, Portuguese (Portugal), Spanish (Spain & Mexico), and Swedish; and the MMPI-2 is available in Bulgarian, Chinese, Greek, Hmong, Polish, Romanian, Russian, Slovak, Turkish, and Ukrainian. However, only a handful of these translations have been utilized in research on feigned mental disorders.

A meta-analysis by Bopp et al. (2022) examined research focusing on the MMPI validity scales, using translated versions of the MMPI-2 and MMPI-2-RF. They identified 26 studies in seven languages: 12 in Spanish, seven in Italian, two in Norwegian, two in Croatian, and one each in German, Korean, and Chinese. When comparing the effect sizes between genuine responders and feigners, the authors found considerable variability across studies and languages, but most translations reported effect sizes in the same range as those found for the English-language version. Thus, while it is impossible to accurately gauge the classification accuracy of any specific translation, the pattern of findings supports the utility of the MMPI scales in assessing feigning in a range of cultures, countries, and languages.

Structured Interview of Reported Symptoms (SIRS)

Like the MMPI instruments, the Structured Interview of Reported Symptoms, currently in its second edition (SIRS-2; Rogers et al., 2010), is also widely used for assessing feigned psychopathology. This 172-item structured interview schedule assesses feigning using multiple response styles captured by eight primary scales that draw on both unlikely and amplified presentations (e.g., Rare Symptoms, Blatant Symptoms, Reported versus Observed Symptoms). Responses to each subscale are scored in one of four classifications (honest, indeterminate, probable feigning, or definite feigning), and these classifications are integrated using a flow chart to generate the decisions that include feigning, indeterminate, or genuine responding. A meta-analysis of the original SIRS (Green & Rosenfeld, 2011) found that the tool correctly identified 74% of individuals

[4] Additional translations are currently in development for Chinese, Danish, French (France), German, Hebrew, Korean, Norwegian, Spanish (Spain and Mexico), and Swedish.

suspected of simulating feigning (i.e., sensitivity) and correctly classified 89% of honest responders. Of note, these results were markedly different than the original validation studies, which reported 50% sensitivity and 99% specificity. Nevertheless, the eight primary scales comprising the SIRS generated effect sizes roughly comparable to the MMPI, ranging from d = 1.20 to 1.65. Although significantly less research has examined the SIRS-2, the studies that do exist have typically found lower sensitivity and higher specificity when compared to the original SIRS at the time of this writing.

Despite being frequently used in forensic mental health evaluations, only a handful of studies have examined the use of the SIRS/SIRS-2 cross-culturally. A Spanish version of the SIRS-2 is commercially available in the US, and a Chinese translation has also been developed and studied, but no other published translations are available for use by the forensic mental health evaluator. In the only published study utilizing the Spanish SIRS (at the time of this writing), Correa et al. (2010) found a sensitivity of 90% in detecting monolingual Hispanic outpatients in Texas who were instructed to feign vocational disability. However, they also found a false positive rate of 15%, indicating results roughly consistent with the meta-analysis by Green and Rosenfeld (2011). Despite its availability, at the time of this writing, no published research to date has examined the utility of the Spanish SIRS-2.

Research using the Chinese translation of the SIRS-2 has generated a more complicated picture. Liu and colleagues (2013) found widely discrepant results in two studies conducted in mainland China. Their first study used a simulation design, finding poor sensitivity (20%) but perfect specificity (100%) when comparing 40 college students instructed to feign mental illness to 40 psychiatric inpatients responding honestly. Using a sample of forensic psychiatric patients, their second study found 85% sensitivity in detecting patients suspected of malingering and perfect specificity (100%) in classifying those believed to be responding honestly. A more recent study from Northern Taiwan (Tam et al., 2023) found that the SIRS-2 demonstrated strong discriminative ability in identifying genuine responders from individuals instructed to feign. Aligned with the goal of the SIRS-2 developers to avoid false positives, the test generated lower sensitivity (56%) and high specificity (100%) in this sample. Only one study has examined the utility of the SIRS-2 in Mandarin-speaking Chinese immigrants living in the US (Chang et al., 2023). Although no honest responders were misclassified as feigning (i.e., perfect specificity), three were classified as "indeterminate." Sensitivity in detecting individuals asked to feign incompetence to stand trial was also very high (93%), as were effect sizes for the SIRS-2 subscales, as all eight scales generated d scores exceeding 2.0. These results provide some support for the utility of the SIRS with Spanish- and Mandarin-speaking individuals, but its utility in other cultural and linguistic groups is unknown. Given the complex wording of many SIRS/SIRS-2 items, the potential for confusion and inflated error rates when used with non-English speakers is a source of concern.

Structured Inventory of Malingered Symptomatology (SIMS)

Although not as widely used as other SVTs, translated versions of the Structured Inventory of Malingered Symptomatology (SIMS, Smith & Burger, 1997; Widows & Smith, 2005) have been the subject of several research studies, albeit primarily in developed, Western European countries. The SIMS is a 75-item true-false questionnaire developed as a screening instrument for identifying feigned psychiatric (psychosis, mood disorders) and cognitive symptoms (amnesia, intellectual deficits). The SIMS is much shorter than the MMPI, taking roughly 10 to 15 min to administer, and yields total summary score and five non-overlapping scales. A meta-analysis of 41 studies found that SIMS Total scores of ≥ 14 and ≥ 16 generate adequate sensitivity but low specificity, especially with genuine patients with schizophrenia, intellectual disability, or those with psychogenic non-epileptic seizures (van Impelen et al., 2014). These findings are consistent with its intended use as a screening instrument (in which sensitivity is prioritized over specificity), as elevated scores are intended to indicate the need for a more comprehensive evaluation. However, many researchers recommend higher cut scores, with some using >16 (Merckelbach & Smith, 2003) or >19 (Clegg et al., 2009), and others suggesting even higher cut scores of > 24 for use with forensic examinees (Wisdom et al., 2010). A recent review further clarified that SIMS scores above 16 should be viewed as "possibly invalid," with scores exceeding 19 ("probably invalid") or 23 ("very likely invalid") interpreted only within a screening context or as part of a broader assessment battery (Shura et al., 2022, p. 74).

The SIMS has been translated into German, Dutch, Italian, Portuguese, Spanish, and Turkish. A Spanish version of the SIMS intended for use in the US is also available, reportedly drawing on normative data collected in Spain and Latin America. In their meta-analysis, van Impelen et al. (2014) found a significant effect of language on SIMS performance when comparing total scores for non-clinical controls. Specifically, Dutch participants obtained lower total scores than participants who completed the SIMS in English, German, or Spanish. However, research on these translated versions has generally shown high levels of sensitivity and specificity. A systematic review of nine studies conducted in Western Europe (Germany, the Netherlands, and Spain) found that a SIMS cut-score of ≥ 16 found promising results, with a mean sensitivity of 89% (range: 82% to 100%) and specificity of 91% (range: 72% to 99%; Nijdam-Jones & Rosenfeld, 2017).

A more recent study, using a Turkish translation of the SIMS with 103 patients undergoing competence to stand trial evaluations (Ardic et al., 2019), also found strong results by comparing the total scores with another tool intended to screen for feigned psychosis (the M-FAST; Miller, 2001). However, a large simulation study of Italian psychiatric patients found much more modest results, with high sensitivity (> 90%) but poor specificity (< 50%; Giromini et al., 2018). These authors noted that a higher SIMS cut-off score (≥ 25) generated better classification accuracy (sensitivity = 78% and specificity = 73%). Although these studies show promise for the utility of the SIMS in detecting possible feigning, the variable specificity highlights the need for additional data to support any conclusions regarding possible malingering (consistent with its intended use as a screening tool). Moreover, the limited research on cultures and languages outside of Europe raises questions about its utility in markedly different settings (e.g., countries in Asia, Africa, and Latin America).

Miller Forensic Assessment of Symptoms Tests (M-FAST)

The M-FAST is another SVT intended to screen for feigned psychopathology. This 25-item instrument is verbally administered using a format similar to the SIRS/SIRS-2. Scale items were developed using detection strategies similar to those used by the SIRS. However, an elevated total score indicates a need for further evaluation using a more "definitive" method such as the SIRS or MMPI. Despite its intent as a screening tool, a meta-analysis found strong sensitivity (83%) and adequate specificity (85%) when the recommended cut-score was used (Detullio et al., 2019).

The M-FAST has also been translated into and studied in several languages, including Spanish, French, Farsi, Danish, Norwegian, Dutch, Korean, Turkish, Albanian, Armenian, and Bosnian. However, little to no published research has addressed the utility of these translated versions. Nevertheless, a systematic review of five international studies (Nijdam-Jones & Rosenfeld, 2017) found that the recommended M-FAST cut-score demonstrated adequate sensitivity (mean = 93%, range: 89% to 100%) but highly variable specificity (mean = 74%, range: 51% to 87%). With the use of this tool in translation across several languages and cultures, it appears to have adequate utility for its intended purpose: identifying individuals who may need further examination for feigned psychopathology (i.e., screening).

However, the wide range of specificity rates and correspondingly high rate of false positive classifications highlight the need for caution when interpreting elevated M-FAST scores. For example, Weiss and Rosenfeld (2017) found that some items (e.g., *I feel depressed most of the time*) were endorsed by over half of the individuals who had experienced severe trauma in West Africa and had immigrated to the US. They also found very high false positive rates in their sample, with 49% of honest responders with genuine or subthreshold PTSD symptoms, and an even greater proportion of those with clinically significant PTSD symptoms generating an M-FAST score indicative of possible feigned symptoms. Although a higher M-FAST cut-score ($\geq$ 13) decreased the rate of false positive findings to 17% (i.e., specificity = 83%), sensitivity also decreased with this increased cut-score (from 88% to 50%). Whether these findings reflect the influence of culture, language, context (trauma survivors with PTSD symptoms), or a combination of all three is unclear, but further research is clearly needed to address these possible influences. Nevertheless, low scores on the M-FAST may still provide some support for the credibility of an individual's symptom report, despite the need for considerable caution, as well as additional sources of information when interpreting elevated scores.

Personality Assessment Inventory (PAI)

The Personality Assessment Inventory (PAI; Morey, 1991) is a 344-item self-report multiscale personality inventory that utilizes Likert scale items to assess psychopathology among adults (18 years to 89 years).[5] Like the MMPI-2-RF and MMPI-3, the PAI takes approximately 60 min to administer and requires a fourth-grade reading level. The instrument generates 22 non-overlapping scales, including four validity scales: Inconsistency (INC), Infrequency (INF), Positive Impression Management (PIM), and Negative Impression Management (NIM). In addition, several additional scales and indices have been developed to enhance the detection of feigned and minimized symptoms, including the Malingering Index (MAL) and Rogers' Discriminant Function (RDF). As with other feigning assessment tools, elevations may indicate exaggeration but could also reflect genuine distress; therefore, only very high elevations on the scale intended to detect negative impression management are suggestive of intentional feigning. Cross-cultural applications of the PAI are described in more detail in the next chapter, but are summarized briefly here.

The PAI has been translated into several languages, including Spanish, German, Italian, Greek, Korean, and Chinese (see Table 4.1 for comprehensive list), but only the two Spanish-language versions (one developed for use in the US and one developed for use in Spain) appear to be commercially available. More importantly, limited research has examined the utility of the validity scales when

[5] Like the MMPI scales, an adolescent version of the PAI also exists (the PAI-A). We are unaware of any research examining the utility of scales intended to assess feigning on the PAI-A, let alone any research using a translation of this version.

using translated versions of the PAI. In our systematic review of cross-cultural feigning research, we identified only two translations that have been studied: the Spanish version developed for use in the US and an unpublished German translation (Nijdam-Jones & Rosenfeld, 2017). This limited research base has generated modest sensitivity (48%) and adequate sensitivity (90%) when using a t-score cut-off of ≥ 81 on the NIM scale, corresponding roughly to research with other feigning instruments (the MMPI and SIRS). However, research to date has not examined the cross-cultural utility of other PAI scales and indices developed to identify feigned symptoms, nor whether classification accuracy can be improved by integrating the PAI scales into a decision algorithm. Given the limited research examining the utility of translated versions of the PAI in detecting feigned psychopathology, reliance on this tool for clinical forensic evaluations appears questionable.

Inventory of Problems-29 (IOP-29)

The Inventory of Problems-29 (IOP-29; Viglione et al., 2017) is a 29-item self-administered test intended to detect both feigned psychiatric and cognitive disorders, such as psychosis, PTSD, depression, anxiety, cognitive impairment, and neuropsychological disorders. It takes approximately 5 to 10 min to complete and, given its format, is best characterized as an SVT, particularly given that 26 of the 29 items assess psychiatric symptoms and only three items assess feigned cognitive symptoms. The IOP-29 draws on both unlikely and amplified detection strategies, as well as focusing on how the examinee copes with their psychological or neuropsychological problems in the evaluation context. This approach differs from most other SVTs, which simply ask whether the examinee is experiencing symptoms that reportedly correspond to psychological or neuropsychological disorders.

Despite its recent publication, the IOP-29 has already been translated into multiple languages (in addition to English): Albanian, Bosnian, Chinese (Traditional & Simplified), Dutch, French, German, Italian, Lithuanian, Macedonian, Portuguese (European and Latin American), Romanian, Spanish (European and Latin American), Serbian, Slovene and Turkish. A review by Giromini and Viglione (2022) identified 15 studies using the IOP-29 and found that it produced roughly similar results to the MMPI-2, PAI, and SIMS, providing support for its utility as an SVT. However, the vast majority of the existing research has relied on simulation designs and only a handful have been conducted by independent research groups (i.e., did not include the test's authors). Hence, while the IOP-29 shows promise, particularly for cross-cultural forensic assessments, further research is clearly needed—particularly using clinical samples in genuine forensic settings.

Detection Strategies for Poor Cognitive Effort

An equally important focus in forensic mental health assessment, particularly in evaluations that hinge on cognitive functioning, is the evaluation of cognitive effort. Cognitive effort testing, also referred to as PVTs, is used to assess whether an individual put forth adequate effort when completing tests of cognitive functioning. Cognitive effort testing is particularly important when evaluating individuals for vocational disability and civil litigation (e.g., when allegations of head trauma may have occurred), but is also critical in many aspects of criminal law, such as evaluations for competence to stand trial or eligibility for possible capital punishment (in the US). Moreover, several studies have demonstrated that PVTs provide a useful complement to SVTs in identifying individuals who are seeking to feign or exaggerate psychiatric symptoms (e.g., Green et al., 2012; Rosenfeld et al., 2010).

Like SVTs, PVTs also utilize multiple detection strategies that can be broadly characterized as unlikely symptom presentations (e.g., magnitude of error and violation of performance curves or learning principles) and amplified symptom reports (e.g., floor effect, below chance performance; Rogers, 2018). Amplified detection strategies, such as the floor effect, are particularly common approaches to assessing poor cognitive effort, as they involve extremely simple tasks or questions that even individuals with limited cognitive functioning should be able to perform or answer correctly (see Table 3.3). The performance curve approach, on the other hand, is based on the assumption that the likelihood of a correct response should decrease as task difficulty increases. Similarly, violations of learning principles occur when individuals do not show expected response patterns, as evidenced by poorer performance on recognition memory versus free recall and stronger delayed recall versus immediate memory.

Another method of conceptualizing effort tests is through the testing process itself. For example, the strongest evidence for poor cognitive effort is the use of forced choice tasks that can elicit below-chance performance, since even an individual with severe memory impairment should be able to correctly answer or identify at least 50% of the test items. Because many cognitive effort tests are non-verbal, they are particularly appealing for cross-cultural forensic assessments. However, as noted earlier in this chapter, non-verbal administration does not mean that a test or task is "culture-free."

Test of Memory Malingering

The TOMM (Tombaugh, 1996) is one of the most widely used and frequently studied PVTs. The TOMM consists of two sets of learning trials (Trials 1 and 2)

Table 3.3 Detection strategies for feigned cognitive impairment

Measure	Detection Strategies
TOMM	Floor effect
DCT	Floor effect
Rey-15	Floor effect
VIP	Floor effect
	Violation of performance curve
	Consistency across comparable items
WMT	Floor effect
	Violation of learning principles

Note: Adapted from Rogers, R. (2018). Detection strategies for malingering and defensiveness. In R. Rogers & S. D. Bender (Eds.), *Clinical assessment of malingering and deception* (4 ed., pp. 18–41). Guilford Press.

in which the examinee is presented with 50 simple drawings for memorization and then presented with 50 pairs of drawings in a forced-choice recognition task. An optional Retention trial can be administered after a short delay, although most of the existing research has focused only on the two learning trials. As noted above, scores below chance provide extremely strong evidence of deliberate exaggeration of memory problems, but performance on Trial 2 that is poorer than expected can also be interpreted as evidence of inadequate cognitive effort or exaggerated memory deficits. Research has demonstrated strong support for the TOMM, with adequate sensitivity (46% to 56%) and excellent specificity (96% to 98%) using established cut-scores on Trial 2 and the Retention trial (Martin et al., 2020).

As a non-verbal cognitive effort test, the use of TOMM has been studied across a range of culturally and linguistically diverse samples. Our systematic review identified seven studies examining the TOMM with Spanish, German, and French-speaking samples (Nijdam-Jones & Rosenfeld, 2017). The TOMM produced a mean sensitivity of 60% and specificity of 91% across these studies. More recent studies in Portuguese, Mandarin, Romanian, and Arabic-speaking samples have shown similarly strong psychometric performance, with high specificity (91% to 100%) and moderate to strong sensitivity (50% to 94%; e.g., Bajjaleh et al., 2021; Chang et al., 2023; Crisan et al., 2023; Giromini et al., 2020). For instance, studies have found perfect specificity among Chinese-speaking immigrants tested in Mandarin (Chang et al., 2023), strong sensitivity in Portuguese samples feigning depression or mild traumatic brain injury (Giromini et al., 2020), and comparable accuracy in Romanian undergraduates (Crisan et al., 2023) and Arabic-speaking Israeli adults (Bajjaleh et al., 2021). Similarly, in Singaporean psychiatric samples, the TOMM demonstrated low false positives (97.7% specificity) and strong sensitivity (77.7%; Chan et al., 2020). Yet despite a consistently low rate of false positives across international contexts in detecting inadequate effort and exaggerated cognitive or psychiatric symptoms, research in the United States and Latin America has raised concerns about its cross-cultural applicability with Spanish-speaking adults. For example, in two American studies with clinical samples, the TOMM produced a 23.3% invalidity rate among Spanish-speaking mixed neuropsychiatric patients (Rhoads et al., 2021) and misclassified 20.9% of Spanish-speaking forensic inpatients as feigning (Aguilar et al., 2023).

Research has also demonstrated significant within-culture variability. Nijdam-Jones et al. (2017) found that performance on the TOMM varied substantially across eight Spanish-speaking Latin American countries. Participants from some countries demonstrated near-perfect levels of specificity (e.g., Argentina, Puerto Rico), whereas participants from other countries had much higher rates of false positives (e.g., Paraguay: 24%; Bolivia: 10%). That study also found that performance on the TOMM was negatively associated with age (i.e., older individuals typically obtained lower scores on the TOMM than younger participants; $r_s = -.30$). Moreover, performance on the TOMM was positively associated with education (i.e., those with more years of formal education typically performed better than those with less education; $r_s = .37$); both the age and education effects varied substantially across countries. When analyzed at the country level, TOMM performance was significantly associated with a country's level of economic development ($r_s = .91$). Another study by this research group (Nijdam-Jones et al., 2019b) found a significantly higher false positive rate in Colombian individuals who were illiterate (13% to 26%) compared to those with adequate literacy (< 5%).

In recognition of these cultural and educational disparities, the test publishers have developed the TOMM 2[6] (Tombaugh & McCaffrey, unpublished test manual) in consultation with an international team of experts in neuropsychology, cultural diversity, and fairness in testing. Only a few studies have examined performance on the TOMM 2, focusing on the measure's specificity with nonclinical samples. One study of a community sample in Spain demonstrated that the TOMM 2 T2 cut score produced 100% specificity; however, the authors also noted small correlations between levels of education with TOMM 2 performance across the different trials (Arango-Lasprilla et al., 2024). In another recent study of 188 Spanish-speaking individuals residing in the United States for a minimum of 12 consecutive months, performance on the TOMM T2 was exceptional, with 100% specificity, and there was no correlation with TOMM 2 performance based on levels of education or bilingualism (over 60% of their sample endorsed speaking English "very well"; Ramos Usuga et al., 2024).

[6] At the time of this writing, the TOMM 2 was not yet commercially available.

Together, these findings suggest that, although the TOMM and TOMM 2 appear to be an effective tool in assessing poor cognitive effort, individuals from less economically developed regions of the world, and those with low levels of education or serious mental illness may be at a much greater risk for poor performance on the TOMM despite adequate cognitive effort.

Dot Counting Test (DCT)

Another non-verbal cognitive effort test that has considerable appeal but far less empirical support for its cross-cultural utility is the Dot Counting Test (Boone et al., 2002). The DCT is a brief test that measures counting skills, which is an "overlearned" skill that typically remains intact even among individuals with severe traumatic brain injuries. Utilizing 12 cards with different numbers of dots in patterned (grouped) or scattered (ungrouped) positions, examinees are asked to count the dots as quickly as possible. Although multiple scoring approaches have been developed and utilized since the DCT was first developed (in the 1940s), the current approach used by most researchers is the Effort index or E-score (Boone et al., 2002). The DCT manual describes adequate sensitivity (62% to 68%, depending on the cut-score) and impressive specificity rates for the E-score (89% to 96%, depending on the clinical comparison sample), but subsequent studies have found more variable results.

Research with culturally and linguistically diverse samples has observed even more dramatic variability. In studies examining performance on the DCT among Punjabi Sikh civil litigants in India, monolingual Spanish speakers in Spain, French-speaking West African refugees living in the US, and Mandarin-speaking Chinese immigrants living in the US, the sensitivity ranged from 25% to 88%, while specificity ranged from 42% to 98% (Chang et al., 2023; Nijdam-Jones & Rosenfeld, 2017). Further, a simulation study of Singaporean adults found that the DCT was no better than chance, generating a sensitivity of .40 and specificity of 63%. However, a study of monolingual Spanish-speaking patients in a California forensic hospital (Aguilar et al., 2021) found more favorable results, with most genuine respondents obtaining scores indicating valid performance (i.e., specificity = 82%), which is similar to research using the tool with English-speaking forensic samples. Like the TOMM, for which little evidence exists for an association between education and DCT E-score in Western samples, Weiss and Rosenfeld (2010) found a strong negative association ($r = -.40$) between education and the DCT E-score in their sample of Punjabi Sikh adults involved in civil litigation. However, similar results have not been observed in studies of West African refugees (Weiss & Rosenfeld, 2017), Mandarin-speaking

Chinese immigrants living in the US (Chang et al., 2023), nor among Spanish-speaking patients residing in the US (Rhoads et al., 2021). A smaller study of community-dwelling adults in Kampala, Uganda (Baird et al., 2023) found that, using manual-based cut scores, the DCT incorrectly classified 71.4% (n = 35) of honest responders as invalid (i.e., feigning). The authors concluded that their "findings suggest that culturally mediated factors may contribute to differences in engagement or performance on the DCT" (p. 751). In summary, while the existing data are clearly equivocal, further research with the DCT may help identify settings, populations, or applications in which the tool has greater utility, particularly with individuals from diverse backgrounds.

Rey 15 Item Test (FIT)

The Rey 15 Item Test (FIT; Rey, 1964) is another PVT that has been used in the assessment of feigning and insufficient cognitive effort for many decades. This brief test also utilizes the floor effect approach to detect insufficient cognitive effort, as it appears more difficult (recalling 15 items) than it is due to the patterned data presented (a 3 by 5 matrix of letters, numbers and geometric shapes arranged in a logical pattern). A meta-analysis by Reznek (2005) demonstrated low sensitivity rates for the FIT (9% to 36%, depending on cut-scores used) but high specificity (90% to 95%). However, they found much less utility when used with individuals identified as genuinely intellectually disabled, suggesting that this tool may be less useful in differentiating genuine from feigned intellectual disability.[7] On the other hand, research with English-Arabic bilingual university students in Canada found the test displayed perfect specificity of 100% (Erdodi et al., 2017).

Due to the ease of accessibility and the non-verbal nature of the test, the FIT has been used in several cross-cultural studies, primarily with German and Spanish-speaking participants (Nijdam-Jones & Rosenfeld, 2017). However, similar to the research with English-speaking samples, the sensitivity of the FIT in these studies has been low, with a weighted mean sensitivity of 28% (range: 8% to 56%). While lower than in English-speaking samples, specificity for the FIT remains relatively strong, with a weighted mean of 89% (range: 84% to 92%). Other research has found similar results, with the FIT displaying low levels of sensitivity (33%) but fair specificity (89%) in Romanian patients using a cut-score adjusted to optimize discrimination (Crişan & Erdodi, 2022). In another simulation study conducted in Japan with a clinical control sample, Ryan et al.,

[7] Similar concerns have been raised for other PVTs, including the TOMM, DCT, and the VIP, all of which show elevated false positive rates in those with genuine intellectual disability.

(2019) found relatively low sensitivity (33%) and fair specificity (85%). However, among monolingual Spanish-speaking forensic inpatients, Aguilar et al. (2021) found that that the majority of participants with no known incentive to exaggerate symptoms "failed" the FIT, generating false positive rates ranging from 52% to 75.5%. Therefore, despite the ease of use, the FIT is infrequently utilized in forensic mental health assessments, particularly given the availability of other, more effective tools that assess feigned memory impairment (e.g., the TOMM).

Other Performance Validity Tests

A number of other PVTs have been evaluated in a range of cultures and languages other than English, but the literature on these is far less robust or extensive than the tools described above. In our systematic review of cross-cultural assessments of feigning, we identified several other PVTs that have been used in culturally and linguistically diverse samples (Nijdam-Jones & Rosenfeld, 2017). Most of these instruments also focus on memory, including the Word Memory Test (WMT), the Amsterdam Short-term Memory Test, the Reliable Digit Span, and the Digit Memory Test. Of these, only the WMT is commercially available in multiple languages, with published translations in Arabic, Farsi, German, Greek, Japanese, Chinese, Portuguese, Punjabi, Russian, Spanish, and Turkish, among others. However, despite assertions of strong empirical support on the publisher's website, little published research was identified to support these translations. Given the superior performance of the TOMM when compared to each of these alternatives, there appears to be little basis for recommending other PVTs that focus on memory.

Numerous other PVTs also exist, including both free-standing tools (e.g., the Coin-in-Hand test, Validity Indicator Profile) and embedded validity indicators derived from established neuropsychological tests (e.g., the Wechsler Memory Scales, Wisconsin Card Sorting Test). Although few of these have been utilized in samples outside of North America and Western Europe (primarily Germany and the Netherlands), one recent study examined the Coin-in-Hand (CIH) test in distinguishing older Taiwanese adults with genuine dementia from those instructed to simulate dementia (Yeh et al., 2019). Although the CIH generated better overall predictive accuracy than the TOMM (AUC = .79 vs. .69), the CIH also had poorer specificity, misclassifying 12% of honest participants as demonstrating insufficient cognitive effort, whereas the TOMM had perfect specificity (100%). Thus, while research examining non-verbal PVTs in culturally diverse samples will no doubt continue to grow, the TOMM currently appears to be the most well-supported instrument available—provided the evaluator considers the caveats described above.

Defensiveness and Socially Desirable Response Styles

In addition to the potential for feigned symptoms of mental disorder or cognitive impairment, forensic mental health evaluators must also consider the possibility that an individual will be motivated to simulate healthy psychological adjustment or deny the presence of genuine mental disorders. A subset of individuals intentionally engage in positive impression management, or "faking good," due to a concern that revealing symptoms or behavioral problems will adversely affect their chances of receiving a desired outcome (e.g., release from a psychiatric hospital or prison, custody of young children). In these situations, an individual may deliberately deny, conceal, or minimize undesirable personality characteristics, cognitive impairments, or psychological symptoms. Although positive impression management is less often researched than feigning, two primary detection strategies have been identified: denial of symptoms (or "patient characteristics") and socially desirable responding (e.g., denial of personal faults; Rogers, 2018).

The primary tools for detecting positive impression management are the MMPI and the PAI, both of which have robust research literatures to support their utility in this context. However, little research has addressed the use of these tools for detecting positive impression management in linguistically or culturally diverse samples. Moreover, scales to detect minimization typically generate weaker effect sizes than those used to detect feigned symptoms (Picard et al., 2023). Bopp et al. (2022) identified a handful of studies that used translated versions of the MMPI to detect positive impression management, including four studies that used the Italian translation, four that used a Spanish translation (conducted in Spain), two with the Norwegian translation, and one with the Korean translation. Most of these studies utilized the MMPI-2, but two examined the MMPI-2-RF (one in Italian and one in Spanish), and one, conducted in the US, used the Spanish translation of the MMPI-3. Mean effect sizes for the L (Lie) and K (Defensiveness) scales were g = 1.39 and 1.09 for Spanish translations and g = .98 and .89 for the Italian translations. Roughly comparable results were observed in the Norwegian samples, but the Korean translation generated much stronger effect sizes (this study also generated unusually strong effect sizes for the detection of feigned symptoms, raising questions about whether the study methodology resulted in inflated classification accuracy).

Given the recent publication of the MMPI-3 (Ben-Porath & Tellegen, 2020), it is not surprising that few translations are currently available and little cross-cultural research has been published. However, Whitman and colleagues (2022) described the psychometric properties of the MMPI-3 in a large sample of adults referred for an evaluation of parental fitness in Puerto Rico. The authors compared participants to the normative sample using the expanded item pool (433 items) used to develop the MMPI-3. Because this study utilized a differential prevalence design (i.e., comparing individuals at risk of minimization to those not deemed to be at risk), estimates of classification accuracy could not be generated, since it is not known which (if any) of the individuals engaged in a parental fitness evaluation actually engaged in positive impression management. Given that methodological approach, their finding of no significant differences in L or K scale elevations between their clinical sample and the MMPI-3 normative sample provides little guidance regarding the utility of the MMPI-3 in detecting positive impression management scales.

Even less empirical research has examined the utility of translated versions of the PAI in assessing defensiveness and minimization (Correa & Rogers, 2010). Although a handful of studies have examined differences in scale elevations and internal consistency between the Spanish and English versions of the PAI, no published research has focused on samples that have engaged in positive impression management (regardless of study design). However, research has indicated that Latine respondents typically endorse more items indicative of positive impression management, generating modest effect sizes when compared to non-Latine individuals ($d \leq .6$). This pattern suggests that some degree of defensiveness may be more common in Latine culture generally, making the distinction between defensiveness and culturally normative responding even more challenging. In sum, while there is some evidence to support the utility of the MMPI in detecting positive impression management, considerable caution should be used whenever administering translated versions of the MMPI, given the limited research literature support for only a handful of existing translations. This research is even more limited when using the PAI or the MMPI-3.

Revisiting the Vignette

Most of the issues raised by the opening vignette are likely clear by now, including that, yes, some type of assessment of feigned mental and/or cognitive disorders is almost always feasible. In this case, the MMPI-2 would be justifiable (and was used in this evaluation), given the availability of a standardized translation and normative data. It is noteworthy that the plaintiff in this case was a Greek national, which negates any question about whether Greek normative data would be appropriate (but see Chapter 4 for a more detailed discussion of this issue). In addition, cognitive effort measures such as the TOMM, WMT, or DCT may also be warranted, as research has provided some support for each of these instruments, albeit not with Greek nationals. Given the absence of Greek-language data for the majority of feigning assessment measures, the TOMM may be the most reliable option due to its non-verbal nature and broader range of published research across multiple languages and cultures. However, caution may be necessary when interpreting results, particularly for individuals with lower levels of education or literacy, as these factors have been shown to influence performance on non-verbal measures in some culturally and linguistically diverse populations, demonstrating that non-verbal tests are not free of cultural biases.

Although there is no published Greek translation of the TOMM or DCT, the instructions are sufficiently straightforward to justify having the instructions translated, either in advance or by the interpreter. We strongly recommend that these translated instructions be retained, in case of challenges to the administration procedures. However, in the absence of a standardized and commercially available translation, such as exists for the MMPI-2, test items should never be translated, either during or even before an evaluation—at least for norm-referenced tests. We have encountered too many instances in which an evaluator has asked an interpreter to translate test items, often during the evaluation, whether for the MMPI or other tools (SIRS, PAI, MCMI—even cognitive tests that involve vocabulary!). The absence of any mechanism for ensuring the accuracy of either the translation or the interpretation of resulting data clearly outweighs any possible benefits.

Unfortunately, the interpretation of test data regarding symptom validity cannot be so easily answered, as it hinges on multiple interconnected factors. Without question, some degree of caution is always necessary, though that statement applies to English-language tests administered to US or Canadian nationals upon whom the test(s) have been developed. In cross-cultural cases, clinicians must carefully consider the appropriateness of the measures used, how cultural and linguistic factors may impact performance, and the adequacy of established cut-scores for culturally diverse populations. For example, response styles such as acquiescence, extreme responding, or middle-response tendencies are influenced by cultural norms and may increase the risk of erroneous conclusions. Similarly, cultural norms around symptom reporting, such as tendencies to underreport emotional distress or endorse extreme symptoms in certain cultural groups, should also be factored into the interpretation. In short, the interpretation of tests administered cross-culturally will depend on (a) the extent of published research support, both for the tool itself as well as its application in other languages/cultures, (b) how closely the person being evaluated resembles the samples that have been used to evaluate the tool cross culturally, and (c) the magnitude of the findings (e.g., a TOMM performance significantly below chance should result in greater confidence than one that falls just below the established cut-off). Finally, transparency in the evaluation process and in any interpretation is crucial and should be evident in the expert's report.[8] One must clearly document deviations from standardized testing procedures as well as the potential impact such deviations may have on the test results and interpretations.

Summary and Recommendations

Over the past two decades, a growing body of research has focused on the cross-cultural utility of feigning assessment measures. Translated versions of feigning and cognitive effort tests are increasingly available; however, the mere availability of tests does not necessarily correspond to adequate validity when used with culturally and linguistically diverse samples. There is considerable support for several available measures of feigned symptoms and poor cognitive effort, but most of the research summarized in this chapter has been conducted with Spanish-speaking immigrants in the US or with Western European samples in Germany, Spain, and Italy. It is also essential to recognize the potential for language, cultural differences, and educational opportunities to impact performance, even on non-verbal measures.

Reliance on appropriately translated assessment measures and those that have adequate support for their validity is critical to the accuracy of forensic mental health evaluations. Nevertheless, because of the substantial risk of malingering or defensiveness that exists in virtually every forensic setting, the issue of response bias should not be ignored simply because of cultural considerations. Instead, feigning assessment measures can be administered and interpreted with cultural sensitivity when accompanied by an awareness of the strengths, limitations, and potential confounds that might impact interpretation. Prior to evaluating someone from a diverse cultural background or someone whose primary language differs from that of the evaluator, clinicians should review the existing research literature on the available measures, with particular attention to research that might have emerged since the publication of this book. Assessing the adequacy of established cut-scores and the potential for an elevated risk of

[8] The APA Ethics code (Standard 9.03 (c)) states "Psychologists using the services of an interpreter ... include in their recommendations, reports, and diagnostic or evaluative statements, including forensic testimony, discussion of any limitations on the data obtained" (p. 13).

false positives can improve the accuracy of evaluations. Although some instances may exist where little or no formal testing is possible, such circumstances are uncommon.

Regardless of which tests are used, cautious interpretation of test results is always warranted, particularly with results that might be equivocal. Using multiple sources and data points in the assessment of feigning will also aid in the evaluation, as will considering the potential role that culture and language may exert. Finally, no chapter on feigning would be complete without a reminder that evidence of feigning does not mean that no genuine symptoms or mental disorder exist, only that the clinical presentation does not appear to accurately represent the person's current mental state. Likewise, evidence of symptom minimization or defensive responding does not mean the person suffers from significant symptoms or a mental disorder. Feigning and minimization are often adaptive behaviors that are understandable responses to the circumstances, not evidence of the presence or absence of psychopathology.

- **Do not ignore feigning due to cultural or linguistic factors**: Avoid dismissing or overlooking the possibility of feigning simply because of linguistic or cultural factors that complicate the evaluation.
    - Consider how cultural and linguistic barriers may influence symptom presentation or response style and adjust your assessment procedures accordingly.
- **Use previously translated and well-validated measures when possible**: Identify tools that have been translated and have demonstrated adequate validity with populations similar to the examinee.
    - Instruments such as the MMPI are available in multiple languages, but clinicians should still be mindful as to whether there is sufficient research or appropriate normative data to justify their use in a given context.
- **Consider cultural and linguistic impacts on performance**: Evaluate how cultural or linguistic factors might impact performance on feigning assessment measures.
    - Linguistic mismatches between an evaluator and examinee can introduce stress that distorts responding, such as under- or over-reporting of symptoms.

  - Keep in mind that translation errors or cultural misunderstandings can lead to inflated error rates, which may result in inaccurate conclusions about malingering.

- **Assess acculturation levels before choosing norms**: Evaluate the examinee's level of acculturation to determine the appropriateness of testing and which tests and norms to use.

  - Consider how the examinee's level of exposure and integration with cultures similar to the normative group might affect symptom presentation or exaggeration.

- **Integrate multiple sources of information**: Use a combination of feigning assessment tools and collateral information to inform the assessment of feigning.

  - Incorporate data from medical records, employment history, and/or collateral interviews to corroborate claims or provide additional context.
  - When possible, rely on multiple assessment tools, including symptom validity tests (SVTs) and performance validity tests (PVTs), to ensure a comprehensive evaluation.

- **Recognize that non-verbal measures are not culture-free**: Non-verbal measures may be intuitively appealing as they bypass language barriers, but language-free measures are not necessarily free of cultural biases.

  - Speed-based tasks may conflict with norms for individuals whose culture emphasizes accuracy over processing speed.
  - Non-verbal tests may include culturally unfamiliar images or references, particularly for examinees from less economically developed regions.

- **Acknowledge within-culture variability**: Remember that individual differences within cultural groups can be as significant as differences across cultures.

  - Consider factors such as education, literacy, and regional dialects, which may significantly impact test performance.
  - Avoid overgeneralizing based on cultural group membership alone.

- **Be particularly cautious when interpreting ambiguous test results:** When findings are equivocal, err on the side of caution and use multiple data sources to reduce the risk of misclassification.
    - Integrate test results with clinical observations, collateral information, and cultural considerations to make informed decisions.
    - Clearly outline areas of ambiguity and the rationale for your interpretations in the evaluation report.

- **Ensure transparency in evaluation procedures:** Clearly document all decisions and adaptations made to ensure the evaluation is culturally and linguistically appropriate.
    - Document the use of translations, including their source and any limitations that might impact the evaluation results.
    - Record decisions about the selection of normative data and any adjustments made to standard procedures to accommodate the examinee's cultural or linguistic needs.
    - Explain how cultural, systemic, or linguistic factors influenced the interpretation of findings and how these considerations were addressed in the evaluation.
    - Provide sufficient detail to allow readers to evaluate the appropriateness of the evaluator's methods and conclusions.

4
Personality Assessment and Multiscale Inventories

Summary

This chapter provides an overview of the strengths and limitations of multiscale inventories when used with individuals from culturally or linguistically diverse backgrounds. The primary focus of this chapter is on the MMPI and PAI instruments, as these are the most widely used multiscale inventories in routine clinical practice and in forensic mental health assessment in particular. Other, less frequently used instruments are also reviewed. The chapter includes a discussion of the availability of translated versions of these instruments, including both commercially available translations and those developed by (and sometimes available from) independent researchers. Concerns that arise when considering the normative data upon which test interpretations are based are addressed, along with recommendations for negotiating the potential gaps in culturally specific normative data. Finally, issues related to test selection, remote administration, and the applicability of computerized interpretive reports are addressed.

Case Vignette

Maria J, a 31-year-old Mexican woman, was referred for an evaluation by her attorney in support of a civil lawsuit against the City of Newark, New Jersey. According to the Complaint, Ms. J and her 3 children (then ages 2, 5, and 6) were assaulted and terrorized by police officers who broke into her home, allegedly following an anonymous report that she was harboring a drug dealer. Her lawsuit alleged that the police officers broke down her front door in the middle of the night, waking her and her young children and forcing them all to lie partially clothed on the living room floor while they conducted an extensive search of the apartment. Photographic evidence supported her claim that the officers had destroyed

Cultural and Linguistic Considerations in Forensic Mental Health Assessment. Barry Rosenfeld and Alicia Nijdam-Jones, Oxford University Press. © Oxford University Press (2026).
DOI: 10.1093/9780190900991.003.0004

numerous objects in her home, tearing apart furniture and breaking some of her belongings while they searched (unsuccessfully) for evidence of drugs.

During the initial interview (conducted with the assistance of an experienced interpreter), Ms. J reported that she and her two older children had immigrated to the US approximately 4 years earlier, having fled her abusive ex-husband. Since moving to New Jersey, she has been working as a housekeeper. She reported having developed a number of psychological symptoms since the home invasion, including frequent nightmares about being physically assaulted, an exaggerated fear for the safety of her children (e.g., when they were at school), a pervasive sense of hopelessness about her future, and avoidance behaviors such as staying away from large stores or other public settings where she might encounter the police. Following the clinical interview, the evaluator sought to administer psychological testing to gauge the severity of her reported symptoms and the validity of Ms. J's self-report. The evaluator was in possession of a Spanish translation of the MMPI-2-RF but questioned the appropriateness of scoring (and interpreting) this test using the standard US normative data. Is the administration of this test appropriate, given the circumstances? If so, are there any adjustments that should be made to the standard test administration, scoring, and interpretation process? If Ms. J has questions about the meaning of an MMPI item, is it permissible to have the interpreter explain it?

In the context of forensic assessment, the appeal of multiscale inventories like the Minnesota Multiphasic Personality Inventories and the Personality Assessment Inventories is readily apparent to most forensic psychologists. This includes well-known variants such as the MMPI-2 (Butcher et al., 1989), MMPI-2-RF (Ben-Porath & Tellegen, 2008), MMPI-3 (Ben-Porath & Tellegen, 2020), and the PAI (Morey, 1991),[1] along with their corresponding adaptations for adolescents, the MMPI-A (Butcher et al., 1992), MMPI-A-RF (Archer et al., 2016), and the PAI-A (Morey, 2007). Indeed, surveys of forensic psychologists have routinely identified the MMPI as the single most frequently used "test" in forensic assessment, and multiscale inventories are generally used far more than any other type of instrument (e.g., Archer et al., 2006). There is, of course, an extensive array of multiscale inventories, but this chapter focuses primarily on four: the MMPI-2, the MMPI-2-RF, the more recently published MMPI-3, and the PAI. Other instruments, such as the Millon Clinical Multiaxial Inventory (MCMI), currently in its fourth edition (i.e., the MCMI-IV; Millon et al., 2015) and the adolescent versions of the MMPI and PAI, are also discussed briefly but are less widely used in forensic assessment. It should be noted that, at the time of this writing, a relatively limited research base supporting the

[1] At the time of writing, PAR is revising the PAI and collecting new clinical, community, and forensic data to support updated items and norms.

MMPI-3 has been published, particularly with regard to cross-cultural applications. Hence, the discussion of this test is also relatively limited. Nevertheless, many of the issues described in this chapter are applicable to most multiscale inventories.

To be sure, there are many obvious reasons to consider using a multiscale inventory when conducting an evaluation for forensic purposes. These instruments are intended to gauge the nature and extent of a range of psychopathology, personality characteristics, and test-taking styles. Test responses are plotted against normative data ("norms") that can identify deviations from typical response patterns. Thus, not only might the test profile help in establishing or differentiating between clinical diagnoses or conceptualizing the individual's clinical presentation more broadly, but these instruments can also provide useful information regarding the relative severity of symptoms such as depression, psychosis, anxiety, and aggression. Perhaps most importantly for forensic assessments, these instruments also include scales to measure the individual's response style. As described in Chapter 3, response style scales help the evaluating clinician ascertain the extent to which test responses might under- or over-estimate the respondent's actual problems or difficulties. Although never definitive, evidence of a distorted response style (e.g., deliberate symptom exaggeration or minimization) on the test might also raise concerns about the validity of the individual's responses during a clinical interview. Given the potential for deliberate symptom exaggeration in order to achieve an external goal (i.e., malingering) or minimization to mask genuine psychopathology (i.e., defensiveness), it is not surprising that many forensic evaluators view these tools as an invaluable resource in their forensic assessment practice.

The degree of comfort an evaluator feels with multiscale inventories is no doubt related to the nature and extent of their training and clinical experience. However, even evaluators without adequate training in the use of psychological testing may be tempted to use these tools given the ease of administration (essentially a simple self-report checklist) and the availability of computerized interpretive reports. In fact, it is not uncommon to find mental health professionals who utilize these tools even when they have little or no general training in psychological testing or in the use and interpretation of multiscale inventories. One psychiatrist, when asked on the witness stand about his training in using a multiscale inventory, replied that a psychologist had shown him the website where he could purchase the test and how to submit an answer sheet for scoring and computerized interpretation. His admitted lack of any training or expertise in psychological testing, let alone with this particular test, did not dissuade him from using multiscale inventories on a regular basis. Rather, the ready availability of these tools and their ease of administration likely encourage their use by insufficiently trained mental health professionals. Of course, inadequate training in the use of multiscale inventories is not limited to psychiatrists; psychologists, too, vary markedly in the extent and quality of their training and supervised experience in the use of multiscale inventories. Although ethical guidelines should discourage clinicians from utilizing tests or techniques for which they have insufficient training or expertise, our anecdotal evidence suggests precisely the opposite: many unskilled (or insufficiently skilled) clinicians rely on these tools, particularly when they are easy to administer and can be scored by a computer program that generates an interpretive report. Indeed, when used properly, testing with multiscale inventories is relatively simple, efficient, and can enhance the thoroughness of the forensic assessment process. But there are many settings where skill and training are needed to utilize psychological testing accurately, and the lack of these skills can result in inadequate or frankly incorrect interpretations. Cross-cultural forensic evaluation settings are a prime example of a setting where the potential for erroneous conclusions is particularly pronounced.

Even clinicians who are well trained in using and interpreting multiscale inventories may not have sufficient cultural competence to recognize the many problems that can arise when evaluating individuals from a background that differs from their own. For example, in our experience, it is not rare to encounter forensic evaluators who have asked an interpreter to translate the items on a self-report questionnaire into the examinee's dominant language, often during the interview itself. In other cases, a multiscale inventory may be administered in English to an individual with extremely limited English fluency and a cultural background that bears no resemblance to the test's normative sample. Perhaps obvious to many readers, both of these practices are fraught with problems, especially in forensic settings where the potential for erroneous conclusions can have severe implications on important legal outcomes. In fact, decisions about the appropriateness of testing can be quite complex when the individual being evaluated has some degree of English fluency, since cultural factors may still influence the interpretation of the test results, yet are often subtle or easily overlooked.

This chapter reviews a myriad of decisions, influences, and interpretive challenges that forensic evaluators should understand when considering the administration of a multiscale inventory to an individual from a cultural and linguistic background other than the one where the instrument was developed and/or "validated."[2] However, this chapter will not attempt to provide a

[2] We put the term "validated" in quotes to highlight the common misuse of the term. Tests are not "validated" (i.e., deemed valid or invalid), they are researched and demonstrate varying degrees of validity for one or more purposes. Because there are multiple types of validity (concurrent, predictive, construct, etc.), and the degree of empirical support will inevitably vary across studies and contexts, a test can never be deemed "valid." Rather, there may (or may not) be adequate support for a test's validity in a given context, for a specific purpose.

comprehensive overview of the administration and interpretation of the MMPI and PAI instruments more generally. Clinicians who use any of these scales in the context of a forensic assessment are expected to have an adequate background in psychological testing and in the specific applications (and interpretation) of these instruments. Understanding the strengths and weaknesses of multiscale inventories more broadly, as well as the advantages of one scale vis-à-vis the others is beyond the scope of this chapter (and is not the focus of this book). Instead, we identify the challenges that arise in utilizing multiscale inventories with individuals from culturally and linguistically diverse backgrounds and review their relative strengths and limitations when used in cross-cultural settings.

Do I Need a Translation?

One of the first questions an evaluator must confront, assuming that testing with a multiscale inventory would theoretically be useful, is whether a translated version of the instrument is needed. In many instances, the person referred for an evaluation has some degree of linguistic fluency in and acculturation to the dominant language and culture of the country where the evaluator practices (in our case, the US and Canada). Although not unheard of (particularly in evaluations conducted for immigration courts, such as asylum or deportation hearings, which are described in more detail in Chapter 8), it is less common to be asked to evaluate an individual who is a foreign national and has only recently immigrated, or to conduct an evaluation in another country altogether. Such occasions certainly can arise, and in those cases, the question of acculturation and/or familiarity with English (or the lack thereof) may be straightforward. However, when the person being evaluated has lived in the US or Canada for an extended period, the evaluator must determine whether an English-language version of the multiscale inventory is appropriate.

There are no simple solutions to this determination, particularly for the individual with some degree of acculturation and/or linguistic fluency (discussed in more detail in Chapter 5). One obvious approach is to ask the person being evaluated for their preferred or dominant language. Of course, that question implies a viable alternative exists if the answer is something other than English. Moreover, how this question is perceived by the person being evaluated can be influential yet often hard to gauge. Some individuals may feel pressured to acquiesce and complete testing in English—or may simply be overconfident in their ability to communicate in English. In contrast, others may request a translated version primarily in an effort to obstruct the process. Regardless of whether the individual is motivated to answer this question honestly, some assessment of the person's English fluency is often necessary. This can be done informally by asking the individual to read and paraphrase several test items, or it might be done systematically, such as by administering a reading comprehension test or a test specifically designed to gauge language acculturation (e.g., the Language Acculturation Meter; Trujillo et al., 2019). While the administration of an English-language reading test does not reflect the person's literacy in their dominant language, it can provide an estimate of their English fluency. However, gauging a person's reading comprehension ability is far more challenging when administering a multiscale inventory in a language other than English. Although some measures of literacy exist in languages other than English, such as the Word Accentuation Test (for Spanish; Del Ser et al., 1997), no cut-off scores have been established for identifying adequate reading comprehension abilities on any of these measures.

Regardless of the mechanism used to ascertain reading comprehension, the evaluator must carefully consider the extent of the individual's literacy, particularly given the tremendous variability in literacy across (and within) countries. What is *not* recommended, however, is a reliance on self-reported educational achievement as a proxy for literacy. Although most self-report inventories specify minimum grade-equivalent reading levels (e.g., fourth to sixth grade for the MMPI tests, fourth grade for the PAI), these are rough approximations based on standardized reading metrics such as the Flesch-Kincaid method. These metrics ignore the marked differences in educational systems worldwide and fail to reflect the substantial differences even within the US, where these literacy metrics were developed. In our experience, it is not unheard of to encounter individuals who have graduated from a US university yet struggle with their interpretation of the nuanced language common to multiscale inventories. Thus, careful consideration of the individual's level of literacy and comprehension, not simply their educational attainment, must precede any use of self-report psychological tests.

The opening vignette highlights a related, but equally important issue: clarification of confusing test items. Of course, this requires that the examinee first acknowledge their confusion (or need for input), which can be a common stumbling block for all the reasons stated (e.g., lack of awareness that the test item does not mean what they think, discomfort acknowledging limitations in their English-language fluency). But once raised, we strongly encourage the evaluator to explain the item as simply and clearly as possible (just as one would do with an English-speaking examinee who asks for clarification on the meaning of a test item), allowing the interpreter to translate that explanation into the examinee's dominant language. Despite their linguistic fluency, interpreters are not necessarily familiar with the nuanced language of a multiscale inventory; hence, they should never be asked to provide their own explanation of the item. It is also advisable to record the item numbers on which the examinee asks for clarification, to identify any possible patterns in their comprehension or test responses.[3]

Finally, no interpretation of comprehension would be complete without a post-testing assessment of the scales that reflect inconsistent responding (i.e., the VRIN, TRIN, and CRIN for the MMPI-3 and the INC scale for the PAI). Although elevations on these scales can reflect a range of issues (confusion, random responding, acquiescence bias, etc.), insufficient comprehension of the test items is certainly one of those possible explanations. Although it is likely pointless to administer an MMPI or PAI to an individual who does not have the requisite language skills to comprehend the test (in the language used and/or available), even individuals who appear to have adequate literacy and comprehension may display excessive confusion or inconsistency that essentially "invalidates" any interpretation of the test profile.

Translations of the MMPI and PAI

Once the clinician has determined that the administration of a multiscale inventory is feasible, a determination needs to be made as to whether it is worthwhile. This decision is not simply a question of whether the information gleaned could theoretically be useful, but usually reflects a cost-benefit analysis contrasting time spent on test administration and interpretation against other ways that time could be spent (not to mention the potential cost). To be sure, there are evaluations in which psychological testing does not appear necessary or even helpful. However, such cases are relatively uncommon in forensic settings, where the need for careful consideration of the individual's response style and psychological symptoms more generally is the norm. In such cases, there are notable advantages to using a well-established multiscale inventory in evaluating individuals from diverse backgrounds.

Unlike the clinical interview (discussed in Chapter 2), which is heavily influenced by the skill and competence of both the interpreter and the interviewer, a multiscale inventory that has already been translated into the dominant language of the person being evaluated can eliminate or minimize many of the most obvious challenges to the evaluation process. Indeed, at least some translated versions are available for most of the common multiscale inventories (see Table 4.1). Most of these translated versions are sold by commercial test publishers, although in our experience, some translations are more easily obtained than

[3] Given the frequent need for clarification of test items, the evaluator should always have an English-language version of the test available, in order to understand and adequately clarify any test items queried by the examinee.

Table 4.1 Available languages for commonly used multiscale assessment instruments

Language	MMPI-2	MMPI-2-RF	MMPI-3	MMPI-A	MMPI-A-RF	PAI	PAI-A
Arabic						X	
Bulgarian	X			X		X	
Chinese	X		*			X	
Croatian	X	X		X			
Czech	X	X					
Danish	X	X	*				
Dutch/Flemish	X	X	X	X			
Filipino						X	
French (Canada)	X	X	X			X	
French (France)		X	*	X			
German	X	X	*				
Greek	X		X			X	
Hebrew	X	X	*				
Hmong	X						
Hungarian	X			X			
Icelandic						X	
Italian	X	X	X	X			
Korean	X	X	*	X	X	X	
Japanese			X				
Norwegian	X	X	*				
Polish	X					X	
Portuguese (Brazil)						X	
Portuguese (Portugal)		X					
Romanian	X						
Russian	X						
Serbian						X	
Slovak	X						
Slovene						X	
Spanish (Mexico)	X	X	*	X			
Spanish (Spain)	X	X	*	X	X	X	
Spanish (US)	X	X	X	X	X	X	X
Swedish	X	X	*				
Turkish	X					X	
Ukrainian	X						
Vietnamese						X	

Note: Please contact the test publishers for the most up-to-date list of available translations. Only the PAI Spanish translations are commercially available; other translations may be obtainable through PAR. At the time of writing, the PAI is undergoing a major revision, with PAR collecting new data to update items, subscales, and norms.

*MMPI-3 versions were "in development" at the time of writing.

others. An important advantage of utilizing a commercially available translation is that a standardized version of the instrument exists and is often—though not always—accompanied by some sort of normative data (discussed in more detail later in this chapter).

Questions about the adequacy of a previously translated instrument can be addressed by having a skilled, independent interpreter or bilingual psychologist examine test items and responses that are unexpected or questionable. Poorly translated items (e.g., where multiple possible interpretations exist) can result in responses that appear out of sync with the individual's clinical presentation and may reflect a misunderstanding of the item's intended content. Although an aggressive attorney could challenge the adequacy of any translation used by the evaluator, it is hard to imagine many scenarios in which this would actually occur.[4] On the other hand, when asking an interpreter to translate a test during the clinical evaluation, the same question might be translated differently by different interpreters. More importantly, barring video or audio recording of the evaluation and test administration, there is no mechanism for determining whether interpreter error (e.g., failure to understand the item content or simply translating the item incorrectly) impinged upon the evaluation process. Hence, the advantages of having an existing and commercially available translation of a multiscale inventory available cannot be overstated.

Perhaps not surprisingly (given its popularity), the most frequently translated multiscale inventory is the MMPI (see Table 4.1).[5] At the time of this writing, the MMPI-2 was commercially available in more than twenty languages, including several of the languages that are commonly spoken by immigrants to North America, such as Mandarin,[6] Spanish,[7] French, and Korean. Other available versions are infrequently used in the US, either because English fluency is common in those countries/cultures or because rates of immigration are very low, such as Danish, Hebrew, Hmong, Norwegian, Romanian, and Swedish. Additional

[4] Of course, some risk of erroneous translation always exists, either because the translated question can be interpreted in multiple ways or because the test-taker has requested clarification. This risk, however, is no greater than the risk that any clinician will provide an idiosyncratic explanation for a confusing test item even when the scale is written and completed in English.

[5] The University of Minnesota Press maintains a webpage listing available translations of the MMPI-2, along with contact information for many of these versions, at https://www.upress.umn.edu/test-division/translations-permissions/available-translations.

[6] The "Chinese" version of the MMPI-2 utilizes traditional characters that are more commonly used in Taiwan, Hong Kong, and Macau but are often less readily understood by individuals from mainland China, and in particularly, those from rural areas or who have limited education.

[7] There are three versions of the MMPI-2 available in Spanish, one intended for the US, one for individuals from Mexico and Central America, and a third for individuals from Spain and South America. We are aware of no descriptions of the nature and/or importance of any differences between these three versions of the test.

("unofficial") translations of the MMPI-2 have also been developed (Butcher, 1996), but these translations are not commercially published and therefore are less easily accessible. However, many common and important languages are not represented in the pool of available translated MMPI versions, such as Arabic, Hindi, Russian, Urdu, and Vietnamese. Given the frequency of these languages in the US and other Western countries, the lack of reliable translations for the MMPI inventories in many languages represents a glaring absence from the toolbox of the forensic mental health evaluator.

Translated versions of the MMPI-2-RF, which was introduced in 2008, are also plentiful, though more limited than for the MMPI-2. Likewise, multiple translated versions of the adolescent version of the MMPI (the MMPI-A) also exist, as do a handful of versions of the MMPI-A-RF (e.g., Spanish, Korean). At the time of this writing, translated versions of the MMPI-3 (published in 2020) were available only in Spanish, French (for Canada), Dutch, Greek, Italian, and Japanese; however, the publisher's website lists several additional translations that are currently in development.

Commercially available translations of the PAI are far more limited than the MMPI, with only two Spanish versions (one intended for Spanish speakers in the US and another for Europeans) available through the publisher; no translations appear to exist for the adolescent version of the PAI (the PAI-A). Although published research has described findings based on more than a dozen translated versions of the PAI (e.g., Arabic, Chinese, German, Korean), these translations do not appear to be commercially available and are therefore of limited utility for the forensic evaluator. It should also be noted that while contact information for the publishers of translated instruments is typically available, the ease with which any given publisher can be contacted, the time required to obtain copies of the translated tests, and the costs associated with their purchase vary dramatically. Particularly when the evaluator faces time or financial constraints, the accessibility of these instruments may present challenges for the forensic evaluator.

Some translated versions of the MMPI and PAI can be purchased directly from the US publisher with just as much ease as the English language versions of the tests. Notably, the translated versions of the MMPI that are available directly from the US publisher (Pearson Assessments) are not limited to the Spanish translation intended for use in the US, but include the French Canadian and Hmong versions of the MMPI-2 and Dutch and Italian versions of the MMPI-3.[8]

[8] The Q-Global testing software utilized by Pearson, publisher of the MMPI-2, MMPI-2-RF and MMPI-3, also permits remote administration (both text-based and audio) of these tests in Spanish.

Of note, this process is even simpler when using an online administration, as the test-taker can simply select the audio administration when they begin completing the MMPI. Likewise, two Spanish-language versions of the PAI are available directly from the publisher (PAR Inc.), although no Spanish audio CD is available.

On the other hand, most international translations of the MMPI instruments are published in the country in which they were developed. Obtaining these instruments has often been remarkably easy, largely due to the collegiality and helpfulness of colleagues abroad. In other instances, however, the process has been quite frustrating and sometimes unsuccessful. Of course, accessing translated versions of the MMPI scales has improved substantially as internet-based purchasing has become more common, particularly with the growing availability of online administration and scoring. For example, the publisher of the Croatian MMPI-2-RF was very accommodating when asked about purchasing a copy of the test for use in a forensic evaluation. In fact, not only did the company facilitate the purchase and download of the Croatian-language online administration and scoring program, but they also provided technical support to (successfully) troubleshoot a problem that arose when the downloaded software did not initially function as expected. On the other hand, some of the contact information and links provided on the University of Minnesota website were not active at the time of this writing, and past efforts to contact publishers and authors directly have occasionally been challenging. In one instance, the publisher of a translated version of the MMPI-2 could not be contacted, but a researcher at a university in that country volunteered to fax a copy of the test questions (surprisingly, that psychologist recommended applying the US norms to score and interpret the test—a problematic suggestion that is discussed later in this chapter). However, on another occasion, a foreign test publisher refused to sell the test because the clinician was not legally authorized to practice psychology in that country—even though the evaluation was being conducted in the US. These experiences highlight the high degree of variability in the ease of access and extent of materials that are available across the different translated versions of multiscale inventories and the importance of having sufficient time to work through the logistical challenges involved in getting a foreign translation of any test. Finally, it is important to acknowledge that while ideally, the cost of test materials would not impede the use of appropriate testing, purchasing a foreign language version of a test may add a substantial cost to the evaluation that can be particularly frustrating when one does not anticipate using this test more than once.

Culturally Specific Normative Data

In addition to challenges associated with obtaining translated versions of a multiscale inventory, the extent and quality of culturally specific normative data is an even more critical concern. Although some translated versions of multiscale inventories are intended to be scored and interpreted based on US norms, others are accompanied by normative data that is specific to the population that the translated measure is intended to be used for. The extent and representativeness of culturally specific normative data vary considerably across the different translations, but are generally far less substantial than the normative dataset used to develop the MMPI instruments. In fact, even determining the nature and quality of culturally specific normative data can be challenging, particularly given that the test manuals that accompany translations (if they are available at all) are usually written in the language of the test. Thus, the forensic evaluator would need to translate substantial portions of the non-English language MMPI manual in order to understand the nature of any validation research that underlies the normative data and T-score conversions provided with that version of the test.[9] Of course, converting published normative data into conclusions about test validity is far more challenging than simply reading a test manual, but the test manual provides a useful starting point, just as it does with any English-language test that the forensic evaluator purchases and administers.

Further guidance is provided by the American Psychological Association's Ethical Standards, which specify that "psychologists use assessment instruments whose validity and reliability have been established for use with members of the population tested" (Standard 9.02b). This simple aspiration belies a number of complications, such as what constitutes "established" validity and reliability and who is considered "the population." For example, consider the MMPI-2 normative sample, which included more than 2600 men and women from the US. The representation of different ethnic groups was intended to approximate the 1980 US Census data. However, one might legitimately challenge whether the incorporation of 77 Indigenous American respondents into the normative dataset was sufficient to deem the MMPI-2 suitable for evaluating an individual who was brought up in an Indigenous culture, acquired fluency in their community's language, and was immersed in an environment deeply rooted in their ancestral cultural values and way of life. No simple answer to this question exists,

[9] The translation process can be greatly facilitated when the manual is in an electronic format (which is occasionally the case, and will no doubt become increasingly common), as on-line translations (e.g., Google Translate) may be sufficient for the evaluator to gain a reasonable understanding of the test manual.

but the adequacy of any normative data requires careful consideration, particularly when important clinical judgments, such as the genuineness or severity of an individual's reported symptoms, may hinge in part on the outcome of any psychological instrument.

There is, of course, no dispute that the normative dataset provided by the MMPI-2 authors was a vast improvement over the original MMPI normative sample, and the MMPI-3 appears to be a further improvement over the MMPI-2.[10] The original MMPI normative sample was widely criticized for its demographically narrow composition, as scale development was based on a comparison sample of 724 adults who were visiting friends or family members at the University of Minnesota hospital. This sample was predominantly White, non-Hispanic, married, and had less than a college education. The weaknesses of this sample were glaring by the 1980s, as it provided a poor representation of the US population (and always had!). Not surprisingly, important differences were often observed when scores on the original MMPI were compared across racial and ethnic groups within the US, including but not limited to Indigenous people in the US (Greene, 2000). Hence, the MMPI-2 normative sample was intentionally sampled to correspond roughly to the 1980 US Census with regard to ethnic diversity (i.e., the proportion of Black, Asian-American, non-Latine White, Latine, and Indigenous participants) and geography (recruiting roughly equal proportions from the Northeast, South, Midwest, and West). However, this approach still resulted in several very small subgroups within the normative sample, with only 73 Latine participants (3% of the total normative sample), 77 (3%) who identified as Indigenous, and 19 Asian-American participants (less than 1%). As is clear from these data, the Latine and Asian-American samples markedly under-represented the proportions of these individuals living in the US at the time and are even less reflective of the US now. These discrepancies raise questions about the extent to which group-based normative data are a meaningful basis for interpretation of test scores obtained from non-White, ethnically diverse individuals (discussed in more detail below).

A considerable body of research has focused on the extent to which racial and ethnic groups within the US produce different response patterns on the MMPI-2 (and the original MMPI before that; Hall et al., 1999). For example, research comparing Black and Latine samples to White/non-Latine samples with the MMPI-2 has generated relatively consistent findings, with modest differences on multiple scales (usually, but not always, generating higher scores). The scales most often affected include the validity scales (L and F), as well as

[10] The MMPI-3 technical manual describes a normative sample of 1620 adults (810 men and 810 women) intended to approximate the 2020 US census, including 82 (5.1%) individuals who identified as Asian-American and 227 (14.0%) who identify as Latine.

potentially important clinical scales (Schizophrenia and Hypomania). However, meta-analysis suggests that these differences are modest (Hall et al., 1999), rarely exceeding 0.5 standard deviations (i.e., roughly five T-score points). Thus, most experts have opined that the potential for glaring inaccuracies in test interpretation, while possible, is sufficiently modest to permit confident interpretation of the MMPI-2 when applied to marginalized individuals within the US. Moreover, these differences may reflect genuinely elevated rates of some symptoms or difficulties that are more commonly seen in particular racial or ethnic groups. For example, research with Indigenous American participants has demonstrated significant deviations from the US normative data on many validity and clinical scales. However, these differences have been characterized as an accurate reflection of both "historical oppression and present diversity... [and] an expression of a divergent worldview" (Pace et al., 2006, p. 320). In short, while there is little debate as to the appropriateness of the MMPI-2 when used with non-White individuals within the US, these findings say little about the validity of test interpretations when using translated versions.

Although the research quantifying differences between marginalized subgroups within the US is extensive (at least for some comparisons; relatively little research has examined Asian-Americans, for example), studies examining translated versions of the MMPI-2 are far more limited. This limitation is even more pronounced for the MMPI-2-RF, MMPI-3, and PAI, as the published research for these instruments lag far behind the MMPI-2. Some research may also exist in non-English language publications, including the test manuals that often accompany a published translation of the MMPI-2, but accessing (and understanding) these sources can be even more complicated than obtaining and utilizing the translated version of the test. Among the glaring absences from the research literature is a systematic analysis of differences within and across broad racial or ethnic categories. For example, research has often examined Latine (typically referred to as Hispanic or Latino in past research) samples, yet we are unaware of any research contrasting different subgroups within this broad label (e.g., Puerto Rican, Mexican, Argentinian, Cuban).

Linguistic differences between different Spanish-speaking populations are implicitly acknowledged by the presence of multiple different translations, but many researchers fail to even specify which Spanish-language version was used, let alone examine whether any meaningful differences emerge depending on the translation or normative data applied. Research has identified important regional and cultural differences between Latine subgroups, as evident from the marked differences found in the error rate of the TOMM described in the previous chapter, but we are unaware of any comparable research for MMPI or PAI scales. Although the MMPI-3 dramatically improved on the MMPI-2/RF normative sample by developing a diverse Latine normative sample for the

Spanish-language version (275 men and 275 women), the sample is described in broad categories (Mexico, Central America, Caribbean Islands, and South America) and no research to date has examined potential regional or cultural differences (Ben-Porath & Tellegen, 2020). This uncertainty should not be taken as an invitation to ignore the publisher's recommendations regarding which test is best suited to a particular individual. Rather, researchers should be examining multiple aspects of cross-cultural validity for multiscale inventories, and clinicians should take steps to familiarize themselves with the limited research that does exist.

When research can be identified and understood by the evaluator, it often provides little assurance that the interpretive conclusions of the test are valid. One recent meta-analysis examined research using translated versions of the MMPI-2 and MMPI-2-RF for the assessment of feigning and/or minimization (Bopp et al., 2022; described in more detail the Chapter 3). This study identified a total of 26 published studies, but only the Spanish and Italian translations had been studied often enough to calculate mean effect size estimates, and then only for the validity scales. However, the limited volume of research identified in this review forced the authors to ignore potential differences between the three Spanish translations and collapse MMPI-2 and MMPI-2-RF for the purpose of meta-analysis (a decision supported by a meta-analysis demonstrating comparable effectiveness of the English-language MMPI-2 and MMPI-2-RF for detection of feigning and minimization; Aparcero et al., 2023). Thus, while the small literature on the identification of feigning with the MMPI and PAI has generated results that provide some support for the utility of translated versions of the multiscale inventories with regard to response style, even this literature is limited to this handful of studies and languages. Hence, any conclusions based on these translations, particularly when extrapolated to a Polish, Hebrew, or Chinese version, require both a leap of faith (in the test's equivalence) as well as considerable caution in the interpretation.

Moreover, there is surprisingly little cross-cultural research using multiscale inventories outside of the assessment of feigning and minimization. For example, Selbom and colleagues (Laurinaitytė et al., 2017; Sellbom et al., 2018) have published several articles examining the MMPI-2-RF with incarcerated Lithuanian samples, focusing on psychopathy and risk of re-offense (both of which are addressed in Chapter 6). Whitman and her colleagues have described the psychometric properties of the MMPI-3 in samples of Puerto Rican adults undergoing a parental fitness evaluation (Whitman et al., 2022) and among candidates undergoing pre-employment screening for jobs as police and other public safety officers (Whitman et al., 2024). Similar studies have examined the Spanish version of the PAI in forensic settings (e.g., Burneo-Garcés et al., 2020);

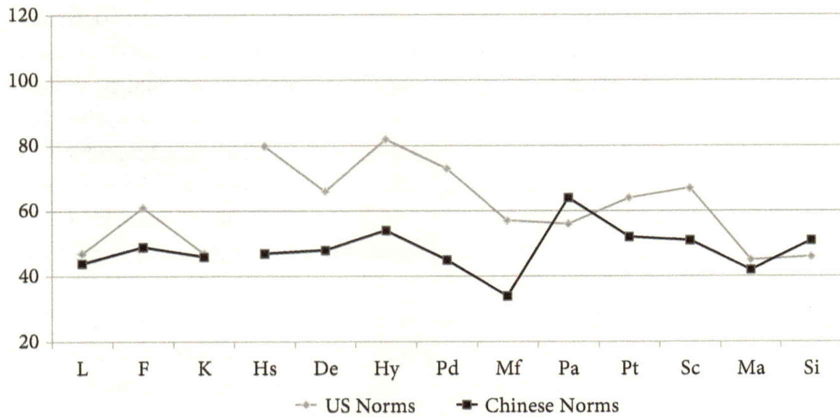

Figure 4.1 Comparison of Chinese and US MMPI-2 T-scores for a 43-year-old man

however, this literature, while growing, is still quite limited. Thus, the forensic evaluator needs to determine what, if any, empirical support exists for any clinical interpretations that go beyond response style.

That said, the existing research literature examining culturally specific normative samples shows modest mean differences in MMPI profiles (e.g., comparing English and Spanish-language versions) that would typically have little impact on test interpretation. However, there are notable exceptions to this general pattern. For example, the Chinese translation of the MMPI-2 relies on a normative sample that deviates considerably from the US norms and can result in T-score differences of ten to twenty points on some scales (most notably the F and Schizophrenia scales) that could certainly lead to dramatic differences in the interpretation of a given profile (see Figure 4.1). Hence, we recommend caution when interpreting translated versions of these multiscale inventories that go beyond response style. In addition, evaluators should review the available research specific to the examinee's language and culture to determine whether notable deviations have been observed in the published literature.

A further limitation in interpreting translated multiscale inventories pertains to the nature of the published research, as the vast majority of this research has focused simply on quantifying group differences in scale means. While a helpful starting point, this approach cannot determine whether any systematic bias exists in response patterns or scale interpretations. More informative approaches either (a) examine whether scale elevations have expected associations with personality characteristics, behavioral problems, or psychiatric symptoms (i.e., external criteria) in diverse cultural groups, or (b) examine whether these associations are comparable across different cultures or settings. For example, Ghamkhar Fard et al. (2022) found that several MMPI-2-RF scales demonstrated expected association with DSM-5 personality disorder symptoms in a sample of Iranian citizens. Similarly, Shumaker et al. (2024) found comparable associations for both Latine and non-Latine White college students between MMPI-3 scales and a self-report measure of personality. Of course, the failure to find group differences between two small samples provides relatively weak evidence of scale equivalence, but the accumulation of similar studies helps provide support for interpretations based on translated versions of multiscale inventories. Absent a substantial extension of studies like those noted above, we recommend a cautious approach to the interpretation of profiles generated by a translated version. For example, one might treat scale elevations as if they were bounded by a confidence interval of roughly 5–10 T-score points, given past findings that between-group differences often reach roughly 5 T-score points for a range of different ethnic and racial group comparisons (and the standard error of measurement for the English language versions of these tests is roughly 4–5 T-score points).

When some degree of acculturation to the dominant culture exists, another helpful method of gauging the impact of culturally specific normative data is to plot an individual's MMPI responses against more than one set of norms. For example, plotting test responses against both the US norms as well as norms derived from the individual's country of origin can facilitate an assessment of the extent to which the different normative samples might impact the interpretation of the test profile. In cases where an optimal set of norms may not exist (e.g., for a particular Latin American or Asian country and/or language), triangulating from the norms available from two or three countries may provide the most accurate basis for interpretation. Given the absence of clear guidelines for the appropriateness of different possible sets of normative data, contrasting profiles based on two or more sets of normative data can provide the clinician with a clearer sense of how much decisions regarding normative data might have impacted test interpretation.

Test Selection

Given the differing availability of translated instruments across the various multiscale inventories, many evaluators will, and should be, strongly inclined to utilize the MMPI-2 or MMPI-2-RF for evaluations of culturally diverse adults (and the MMPI-3, as translations become increasingly available).[11] These tools are commercially available in a greater range of languages than any other instrument, as many tools are only available in Spanish. Moreover, while the research supporting translated versions of these tools is still limited, it is far more substantial for the MMPI-2 and MMPI-2-RF than for other instruments. Of course, these tools also have significant empirical support for the English (US) versions, not only for assessing response style but also for critical diagnostic questions that often arise in forensic evaluations. Nevertheless, test selection is often based more on the availability of a translated version than on the test's characteristics.

For evaluations of Spanish-speaking individuals, on the other hand, the range of available options is substantial, including less frequently used instruments such as the MCMI-IV, the Trauma Symptom Inventory (TSI; currently in its second edition, Briere, 2011), and the Behavior Assessment System for Children (BASC; currently in its third edition, Reynolds & Kamphaus, 2015).[12] Like the MMPI and PAI instruments, the MCMI includes validity scales intended to gauge response style and target multiple diagnostic categories potentially relevant in forensic settings. However, the primary distinction of the MCMI is its focus on personality disorders, which are relevant to many types of forensic evaluations. Furthermore, unlike the MMPI and PAI, the MCMI has been widely criticized, both for the inadequacy of its validity scales and for the limited research base supporting even the English-language version of the test (Sellbom et al., 2022). Indeed, at the time of this writing, virtually no published research has addressed the reliability or validity of the MCMI-IV, raising questions about its appropriateness for forensic assessments. Thus, while theoretically useful in some limited circumstances (with English- or Spanish-speaking individuals), the potential for erroneous conclusions based on the MCMI-IV is substantial, as is the risk of placing the expert (and attorney) in a vulnerable position (e.g., during an aggressive cross-examination). Although our experience when testifying about psychological testing is that aggressive cross-examination on test data is rare, and successful challenges to admissibility are even less likely, an astute attorney could certainly emphasize (or even exaggerate) the test's limitations, and thereby diminish the expert's credibility.

[11] Given the rapid growth of translated versions of these tools, even during the time since we began working on this chapter, it is quite possible that additional translations will be available even before this book is printed!

[12] Published research has also described Danish, Dutch/Flemish, Farsi, Italian and Portuguese (Brazilian) translations of earlier versions of the MCMI, as well as a Chinese translation of the BASC-3 and a Korean version of the BASC-2, but we are unaware of commercially available versions for any of these translations.

The Trauma Symptom Inventory (TSI-2) is another multiscale instrument occasionally used in forensic evaluations, particularly when a detailed assessment of posttraumatic stress disorder (PTSD) is a principal concern. The TSI-2, which is also available in Spanish, Bosnian, Dutch, French, German, Malay, and Polish, and has been studied in several other languages (e.g., Arabic), also includes two scales to assess response validity: one assessing defensiveness and another focused on atypical responses. Although the research literature is more robust than for the MCMI, studies examining the TSI-2 validity scales have also demonstrated weak results, particularly when using genuine psychiatric patients rather than simulation studies with non-clinical control samples. In one of the few studies to examine the cross-cultural utility of the TSI-2, Weiss and Rosenfeld (2017) administered either a French translation or the English-language version to trauma-exposed West African immigrants. Although they found no differences in response patterns based on language of administration, the scale showed poor accuracy in differentiating those who had been instructed to feign PTSD from individuals classified as having genuine PTSD symptoms. Perhaps more importantly, very few individuals with clinically significant PTSD symptoms generated elevations on the clinical scales that would correspond to a PTSD diagnosis. These findings are consistent with a review of US case law regarding the TSI-2 that concluded that the instrument was sufficiently well-supported to be useful in forensic settings but should be used only in the context of a more comprehensive assessment battery (Roberts et al., 2022).

Forensic evaluators who work with adolescents and young adults may also consider the Behavior Assessment System for Children (BASC-3). This tool's youth self-report and parent versions are also available in Spanish and include multiple scales that can help assess response style and differential diagnosis. Moreover, cross-cultural research supporting the BASC-3 appears far more substantial compared to other tools available for use with adolescents, including the MMPI-A/MMPI-2-RF-A, the PAI-A, or the adolescent version of the MCMI (the MACI-II; Millon et al., 2020). For example, Edyburn and colleagues (2020) found a moderate degree of measurement invariance between the Spanish and English versions of the BASC-3. However, the BASC-3 also suffers from some of the same limitations as other instruments, including the limited evidence to support scales used to identify distorted responding. Hence, as with the interpretation of the MCMI-IV and TSI-2, evaluators administering the BASC-3 should consider accompanying it with a concurrently administered Spanish translation of an adolescent version of the MMPI or PAI.

Another option available to forensic evaluators when faced with an individual who speaks a language other than English or Spanish is the Rorschach Inkblot Test. While not a multiscale inventory per se, and often controversial in forensic circles (despite rare challenges to its admissibility; Viglione et al., 2022), there are also situations where the Rorschach has potential utility in the context of forensic assessment. For example, there is considerable evidence for the ability to detect psychotic thought processes using the Rorschach, even when the individual may be motivated to mask these symptoms (Lilienfeld et al., 2000). Ironically, among all the psychological tests available to the forensic evaluator, the Rorschach has what appears to be the strongest set of international normative data of any psychological test, with an international dataset compiled from 21 adult samples in 17 different countries and 31 youth samples from five countries (Meyer et al., 2007). Comparisons among these culturally distinct samples support the cross-cultural equivalence for many Rorschach scores and indices. Of course, unlike the self-report multiscale inventories, administration of the Rorschach requires that the clinician be fluent in the language spoken by the individual being evaluated, as the nuances of word choice and phrasing are almost certainly lost in the translation process. Hence, administration of the Rorschach through an interpreter (even when highly skilled) is not considered appropriate.

When an interpreter is needed and the evaluation centers on an individual whose dominant language is something other than Spanish, deciding between official translations of the MMPI-2 and MMPI-2-RF is more challenging, as the strengths and weaknesses (and similarities) between these instruments are more extensive. At the broadest level, the longer length of the MMPI-2 provides for more scales and greater reliability for some of those scales (since scale length is associated with some forms of reliability). Because the MMPI-2-RF was developed using the same normative database used to develop the MMPI-2, there is considerable overlap between these two versions—and they share the same limitations in the underlying normative data (previously discussed). However, the MMPI-2-RF was developed to improve the psychometric properties of its predecessor, such as reducing the item overlap across scales that often confounds the interpretation of the MMPI-2.

These advantages were also retained in the MMPI-3, despite the limited availability of translated versions. Although the overlapping item content between the MMPI-2-RF and MMPI-3 validity scales suggests that these scales will likely retain their utility when translated versions of the MMPI-3 begin to appear, little research has examined whether any differences in clinical utility exist between the different versions of the MMPI. Hence, resolving this debate as to which version is "stronger"—let alone more appropriate for forensic applications—is probably more a matter of opinion than science (at this time, at least). Suffice it to say that the stronger psychometric properties of the test and the shorter time required to complete the test have increasingly led evaluators to utilize the MMPI-2-RF over the MMPI-2, and will no doubt fuel the transition to the MMPI-3. The exception to this trend may be the availability of specific translations that are not yet available with the more recent iterations of the MMPI.

Nevertheless, as noted previously, the extent and quality of normative data continue to evolve and require attention from the evaluator prior to making any decisions about which scale(s) to administer, what normative data to rely on, and what interpretations are justified.

Computerized Interpretive Reports

The availability of computerized interpretive reports is perhaps one of the greatest temptations for unskilled evaluators who seek to utilize multiscale inventories. Moreover, this temptation, particularly for those with limited expertise in test interpretation, does not diminish when using a translated version of a multiscale inventory. As noted previously, it is all too common to see untrained clinicians, whether psychologists or other mental health professionals (e.g., psychiatrists, social workers), utilize these tools with little or no understanding of the psychometric properties of the instruments. This practice is facilitated by the ready availability of computerized interpretive reports. Although the appeal of objectivity (and speed) in test interpretation can be compelling, multiple problems arise in the application of computerized interpretive reports. These problems are greatly exaggerated when the test is used with individuals from culturally and linguistically diverse backgrounds, and the use of such reports does not appear appropriate (in our opinion) for forensic settings where erroneous conclusions can have substantial repercussions.

In the context of cultural and linguistic diversity, the inability to contextualize a computer-interpretive report makes these reports even more problematic than in the typical forensic assessment settings. For example, because some scale elevations might have different implications depending on contextual factors, knowledge of the individual's background (e.g., education, English fluency, acculturation) and circumstances (e.g., setting and context for the evaluation) will—and should—impact scale interpretations. In the case of cultural and linguistic differences, the potential for an individual to misunderstand test items, or for problems in the translation of some test items, might result in elevations on scales intended to identify feigning (e.g., endorsement of highly unusual items). Likewise, atypical symptoms in most Western cultures may either be relatively common or have a different meaning altogether in another culture or language.

Of course, contextual influences are not limited to cultural and linguistic issues, as a scale elevation may be interpreted differently when an individual is known to have a serious mental disorder that has required repeated hospitalizations versus no known history of psychiatric treatment. However, this distinction may also be harder to gauge in an individual from a markedly different cultural context, where barriers to mental health care and differing beliefs about mental illness may result in symptoms being misattributed, stigmatized, or untreated. Because these considerations are not incorporated into computerized interpretive reports, the potential for incorrect interpretations is heightened when applied to individuals from culturally diverse backgrounds. In short, reliance on computerized interpretive reports does not seem appropriate when using a translated version of the multiscale inventory or even when applying the English version to an individual whose background renders "standard" test interpretation questionable.

Revisiting the Vignette

Although forensic mental health evaluators relied on the Spanish translation of the MMPI-2 and MMPI-2-RF for many years, the adequacy of the available normative data was questionable at best (even before it became outdated). With the publication of the MMPI-3 and the availability of a large Spanish-speaking normative sample against which to compare an individual's responses, it is hard to imagine a scenario in which one could justify using the MMPI-2 or RF with a Spanish-speaking individual. However, there are many languages for which translations of the MMPI-3, let alone adequate normative data, are unavailable. In those instances, a strong argument could be made for relying on older versions of the MMPI.[13]

When navigating confusion or comprehension problems in the course of test administration, evaluators are responsible for ensuring that any explanation of the test items maintains the integrity of the original content. For Ms. J, any potential confusion over test items should be addressed by the evaluator by providing a paraphrase or simplified explanation of the item's intended meaning to ensure it does not get "lost in translation." The interpreter can then translate this explanation into Spanish. This way, the process mirrors what would be done with individuals whose dominant language is English and ensures that the evaluator, as opposed to the interpreter, remains accountable for the accuracy of the explanation. Ideally, the evaluator should also note the item number and explanation provided, which would allow for later review and documentation of patterns in her comprehension.

Further, the appropriateness of the normative data must be carefully examined. While the MMPI-3's Spanish-speaking normative sample represents a

[13] It should be noted that while the normative sample for the MMPI-2 and MMPI-2-RF were collected in the 1980's, many translated versions of these tools utilize more recent normative samples.

significant improvement over prior versions, it is still normed on Spanish-speakers in the US. When available, the forthcoming Mexican version of the MMPI-3 may be more appropriate. In cases where normative data are less representative, evaluators may consider plotting test responses against multiple sets of norms.

As with any psychological testing, careful analysis of the validity scales intended to gauge confusion or random responding (e.g., VRIN, TRIN, CRIN for the MMPI-3, or the INC scale for the PAI) is also critical. Elevations on these scales might be due to random responding, acquiescence, or other issues that may result from comprehension challenges or cultural influences, rather than deliberate distortion. These factors must be thoughtfully interpreted in light of Ms. J's specific circumstances, including her language proficiency, cultural background, and potential trauma-related symptoms.

Finally, transparency in reporting is essential to ensure the evaluation withstands potential scrutiny in a forensic context. For Ms. J, the evaluator should document any deviations from standardized administration procedures, such as the use of an interpreter, paraphrased explanations of test items, or adjustments made to account for normative sample limitations.

Summary and Recommendations

Multiscale inventories can be an invaluable resource for the forensic evaluator, particularly when considering potential symptom exaggeration or minimization, weighing alternative diagnoses, and gauging the severity of psychiatric symptoms. The availability of multiple translations for the two most commonly used multiscale inventories (MMPI and PAI) makes these instruments particularly useful in the evaluation of individuals from culturally and linguistically diverse backgrounds. However, important decisions exist regarding when or if one should administer a translated version and how to consider alternative sets of normative data. The interpretation of test profiles requires expertise in both the instruments generally and in the specific translations and normative data that apply to a given individual. In short, the variability in extent and quality of normative data necessitates careful analysis and consideration in making decisions about which multiscale inventory(s) to use and how to interpret the test results obtained. However, with adequate consideration of the potential influences and limitations of these multiscale inventories, the potential benefits can far outweigh the effort required.

In light of the strengths and limitations of multiscale inventories, we offer a number of recommendations and caveats:

- **Evaluate the need for cultural or linguistic accommodations**: Assess the extent to which accommodations for language or culture are necessary.
    - Determine the individual's level of English fluency and acculturation to the dominant culture, including but not limited to length of time spent in the host country and the examinee's exposure to cultural norms of the region.
- **Ensure the appropriateness of multiscale testing**: Determine whether a suitable version of a multiscale inventory is available and appropriate to the needs of the case.
    - If a translated version has been identified, assess the extent and quality of validation research to determine the appropriateness of the instrument for the examinee's cultural and linguistic background. While a well-validated translation might have a substantial research base to support it, the evaluator should determine which aspects of the test have (and have not) been adequately "validated."
- **Use skilled interpreters for test administration**: When administering psychological tests to an individual whose dominant language differs from the evaluator's, ensure that a skilled interpreter is available.
    - If the examinee requires clarification for an item, the evaluator should paraphrase or explain the item and have the interpreter translate the paraphrased explanation rather than have the interpreter provide their own explanation.
    - Under no circumstances should an evaluator rely on an interpreter to translate a multiscale inventory during an evaluation. Only use standardized and commercially available translations.
- **Consider alternative normative data**: Examine the normative data used for test interpretation to ensure it aligns with the cultural background of the examinee.
    - When possible, plot the test responses against both the US norms and culturally specific norms to assess how differing normative data may influence the interpretation of results.

  - If culturally specific norms are unavailable, acknowledge these limitations in the report and interpret findings cautiously.

- **Use collateral information to contextualize findings:** Incorporate data from clinical observations and collateral sources, such as medical records or family interviews, to support and contextualize test findings.

  - The balance of test interpretations against other sources of data is even more critical when cultural and linguistic influences may have impacted test results, and test results alone may not fully capture the individual's circumstances or context.

5
Cognitive and Neuropsychological Assessment

Summary

This chapter addresses cultural influences on cognitive, intellectual, and neuropsychological assessments. Neurocognitive evaluations play a role in multiple forensic settings, including personal injury and vocational disability evaluations, criminal law issues (e.g., competence to proceed, applicability of the death penalty), and access to specialized services such as educational opportunities and resources designated for individuals with developmental disabilities. This chapter will address a range of factors that impact neurocognitive test performance, along with the importance of appropriate normative data on test administration and interpretation. Specific attention is paid to the conceptualization and measurement of intellectual functioning and the role of cognitive screening tools, followed by a review of research examining the cross-cultural use and equivalence of cognitive and neuropsychological tests. We also highlight the impact of bilingualism on test performance and the benefits and challenges of using verbal and non-verbal tests with individuals from linguistically, ethnically, and culturally diverse backgrounds.

Case Vignette

Mr. Y, a 39-year-old Yemeni man, was referred by the US Attorney's Office for an evaluation of his competence to waive his Miranda rights following an arrest for selling narcotics. At the time of his arrest, Mr. Y had been living in the US for approximately 15 years, working full-time in a small grocery store, and living independently with his wife and child. Prior to questioning, Mr. Y was read a summary (in English) of his Miranda rights by the arresting police officer. After each element of the Miranda warning was read aloud, Mr. Y initialed a form (also written

Cultural and Linguistic Considerations in Forensic Mental Health Assessment. Barry Rosenfeld and Alicia Nijdam-Jones, Oxford University Press. © Oxford University Press (2026).
DOI: 10.1093/9780190900991.003.0005

in English). Although Mr. Y initially denied his guilt, he later provided a written statement in English, with the "assistance" of the arresting officer, admitting that he was aware that one of the products in his store was a narcotic packaged under a false label. While Mr. Y appeared capable of communicating in English, both the interrogation and subsequent psychological evaluation were conducted with the assistance of an Arabic-speaking interpreter.

Before trial, Mr. Y's attorney questioned the adequacy of his waiver of his Miranda rights and retained a psychologist to support her motion to suppress the statement. The defense's psychologist diagnosed Mr. Y with an intellectual disability, concluding that his limited intelligence rendered him unable to appreciate his Miranda rights at the time he spoke with the police and signed the written statement. Despite Mr. Y's seemingly adequate adaptive functioning (e.g., working full-time and supporting his family), the psychologist cited the results of several non-verbal subtests of an English-language IQ test as evidence of an intellectual disability. No measures of cognitive effort, adaptive functioning, or specific questions assessing Mr. Y's Miranda comprehension were described in the report. When questioned about these omissions, the psychologist asserted that while no measures of cognitive effort, Miranda comprehension, or adaptive functioning had been "validated" on Yemeni immigrants, the non-verbal cognitive testing was appropriate in any culture or language. This evaluation raises several important questions: Was the defense expert's assessment of the available options accurate? Are non-verbal subtests an adequate basis for estimating an individual's intelligence? Does the legal issue at hand (e.g., waiver of Miranda rights) require additional evaluation of verbal comprehension?

Cognitive and neuropsychological assessments can inform diagnostic and functional evaluations by quantifying an individual's functioning across a range of different domains that include memory, language, visual and spatial skills, processing speed, and executive functioning (e.g., cognitive flexibility, decision-making). Performance on the tests used to assess these skills is typically based on a comparison to normative samples in order to gauge the individual's overall level of functioning, as well as the relative strengths and weaknesses they exhibit. However, these comparisons are not as straightforward as many evaluators would like to believe, as a number of linguistic and cultural factors can impact both test performance and the appropriateness of comparisons based on normative data. This chapter reviews some of the available tests and techniques that might be used to assess neurocognitive functioning, along with a range of factors that can impact test performance.

We express our sincere appreciation to Dr. Tedd Judd for his thoughtful comments on an earlier draft of this chapter.

Before we delve into the specific issues involved in neurocognitive testing, a brief reminder regarding motivation and effort is warranted. Regardless of any issues related to language, culture, or any other potential influences on test results, considering cognitive effort and motivation is a critical component of any neurocognitive evaluation—particularly those occurring in a forensic context. It is indisputable that insufficient effort can impede or invalidate test results obtained from a neurocognitive assessment. Published guidelines for neuropsychological evaluations highlight the importance of including multiple cognitive effort tests in any cognitive or neuropsychological evaluation, regardless of an examinee's cultural background or linguistic skills (Sweet et al., 2021). As discussed in detail in Chapter 3, cognitive effort testing (also referred to as performance validity testing) is an objective approach to assessing whether an individual has put forth adequate effort in the evaluation session. Because cognitive effort tests are also influenced by cultural and linguistic factors, the evaluator should begin by reviewing the material and recommendations made in Chapter 3, which covers this issue in more detail. In addition to considering effort and motivation, there are multiple influences that can impact performance on neurocognitive testing that are described in this chapter, followed by a sequential review of the three primary types of neurocognitive assessments: cognitive screening, assessment of intelligence, and neuropsychological testing.

Factors that Influence Cognitive and Neuropsychological Test Results

A large and growing body of research, largely based on research conducted with Spanish-speakers living in the US, has demonstrated that performance on neurocognitive tests differs significantly across culturally and linguistically diverse samples, particularly when compared to dominant English-speaking, non-Latine White adults. These effects generally remain even after controlling for the age, education, or gender effects that are frequently observed with many neurocognitive tests (e.g., Jacobs et al., 1997; Weiss et al., 2010). Rivera Mindt et al. (2019) argued that psychologists must be aware of the impact sociocultural factors have on neuropsychological test performance to ensure accurate clinical and diagnostic judgments, as research has demonstrated that quality of education, level of acculturation, primary language or bilingualism, and racism and stereotype threat may impact testing. Fujii (2018) proposed a helpful framework that can inform neuropsychological evaluations with culturally and linguistically diverse adults in forensic contexts. Fujii's ECLECTIC framework recommends that evaluators consider several sociocultural factors, including

Education (E), *Culture* (C) and acculturation, *Language* (L) spoken and English proficiency, *Economic* (E) issues, *Communication* (C) style, the *Testing situation* (T), *Intelligence* (I), and *Context of immigration* (C).

Of course, test data comprise only one part of a comprehensive forensic evaluation, and given the important consequences of neurocognitive assessments, clinicians must consider multiple sources, including behavioral observations, self-report, and collateral information (including but not limited to available records), not just test data, to inform the overall assessment. Gathering a thorough clinical and psychosocial history while incorporating Fujii's (2018) ECLECTIC framework can help the evaluator clarify diagnoses, identify areas of individual strengths and weaknesses, and identify changes in functioning. The following sections outline several sociocultural factors that can and often do impact cognitive and neuropsychological assessments.

Education: Level, Quality, and Literacy

The correlation between education and neurocognitive functioning, particularly on tasks such as vocabulary and reading ability, is well-established, and many commonly used neuropsychological tests (not just those that target verbal skills or literacy) are adjusted on the basis of years of education (Lezak et al., 2012; Neisser et al., 1996). Indeed, a growing body of research indicates that literacy and education mediate performance on non-verbal cognitive tasks too, indicating that non-verbal assessments are not immune to the influence of education (e.g., Rosselli & Ardila, 2003). For example, formal education is positively associated with operational thinking skills, functional brain organization, and working memory and may also influence an individual's visual perception, logical reasoning, and phonological processing (Ardila et al., 2010; Kosmidis et al., 2011). Therefore, it is critical that evaluators consider how literacy and the amount or quality of education may impact test results.

In the US and Canada, individuals are often asked how many years of education they have completed as a proxy measurement of educational achievement. However, when working with individuals from diverse social and cultural groups, years of education can be a misleading indicator of educational experience. Instead, information about the nature and quality of education is often much more useful for interpreting neuropsychological test performance (Manly et al., 2002). Because the nature and quality of education can depend on many factors—both for individuals from disadvantaged regions or communities within economically developed countries (such as the US and Canada) and for those from economically disadvantaged countries—simply asking about years of formal schooling without considering the focus of that education (e.g., religious instruction, specific vocational training, traditional academic subjects) could overestimate expected performance (Rivera Mindt et al., 2019). For example, research with Tibetan refugees revealed that formal education was almost entirely focused on religious training, and hence emphasized reading and oral communication skills but not subjects like mathematics, geography, or world history. While this type of education will help develop verbal skills and literacy, knowledge in other domains is often far weaker.

Rivera Mindt and colleagues (2019) recommend using both objective measures and self-reports to assess the quality of education with individuals from culturally and linguistically diverse backgrounds. For example, the English-language Wide Range Achievement Test (Wilkinson & Robertson, 2017), the Reading Recognition subtest, or the Wechsler Test of Adult Reading (Wechsler, 2001) correlate strongly with quality of education while controlling for years of schooling, race and ethnicity, and socioeconomic status (Crowe et al., 2013; Sayegh et al., 2014). Although some of these tests (or analogous ones) are available in Spanish (e.g., the Word Accentuation Test; Del Pino et al., 2018), resources are far more limited for individuals whose dominant language is neither English nor Spanish. Nevertheless, evaluators are encouraged to seek details about the individual's educational experience, including subject matter, perceived quality, the ratio of students to teachers, the geographic region (e.g., rural, urban, suburban), length of classes and the school year, and perceived relationships with teachers. This information may help clarify the nature and quality of education received. Furthermore, discrepancies between years of education and quality of education should be noted in the evaluation and inform the selection of testing materials, especially in cases where reading level may impact test selection.

Culture and Acculturation

Cultural values and norms may also impact performance on standardized neurocognitive measures. For example, speed-based tests are not always reliable indicators of functioning when used cross-culturally, given that these tests require an examinee to prioritize rapid responding to novel stimuli. While many cultures emphasize the importance of timely task completion, particularly in educational and social contexts, and often reinforce trial-and-error strategies, some cultural groups do not share these norms. For example, some rural or agrarian cultural groups may be less likely to value rigid timetables or feel any need to finish a task quickly or within a prescribed time limit. Researchers who examined timed cognitive tests, such as Block Design, have found that members of the Arhuaco Indigenous community in Colombia could not finish the tasks within the allotted time, and many could not complete the tasks at all, even when given unlimited time (Ardila & Moreno, 2001). This may reflect differences in values relating to processing, with some cultures prioritizing depth of processing over speed (Sternberg & Grigorenko, 2008).

While examples drawn from highly distinctive cultures provide interesting examples of cultural influences on thought and behavior, cultural differences often exist even within cultural regions that we tend to think of as relatively similar, such as Western Europe and North America. In a comparison of Wechsler Adult Intelligence Scale-IV (WAIS-IV) normative data, Scandinavian participants demonstrated slower processing speed and poorer working memory compared to US, German, and French samples, while the European samples performed better than the US samples on reasoning tasks (Roivainen, 2019). These differences were hypothesized to reflect a greater prioritization of speed over accuracy by Americans but stronger educational systems in Europe, as well as differences in the articulation of digits (i.e., number of syllables) in the Nordic languages. In cases where an individual's cultural background may not prioritize rapid responding, Rivera Mindt et al. (2019) suggest examining qualitative information such as the errors an individual makes, along with "testing the limits" by determining if they can finish tasks when given more time. Additionally, inquiring (after completion of testing) about the motivations and approach the individual used to complete tasks may improve the clinician's understanding of the individual's performance.

Different cultural experiences may also afford differential exposure to and value placed on various types of tasks. For example, matrix-based testing is critical to many non-verbal reasoning tasks (e.g., non-verbal measures of intelligence discussed later in this chapter), but this type of test assumes familiarity with the organization of images into rows and columns, which is not a universal way of organizing knowledge and may be unfamiliar to some cultural groups. Similarly, different lived experiences may bolster or impede an individual's development of visuospatial skills, making these tasks easier for some groups than others. For example, Ostrosky-Solis et al. (2004) found that Indigenous adults in Mexico who were illiterate and worked as farmers or basket weavers performed better on tests measuring visuospatial skills than non-Indigenous adults (who were also illiterate) from urban areas. These and other studies have demonstrated that the strength of some neurocognitive skills may depend on their importance and frequency of use by the individual or in their culture. In short, cognitive and neuropsychological assessments that only incorporate the values and norms of the dominant culture may not accurately gauge an individual's true abilities and strengths.

Acculturation

As discussed in Chapter 1, clinicians working with individuals from diverse backgrounds should consider the nature of an individual's acculturation to the culture in which tests have been developed before deciding which neurocognitive tests and normative data are most appropriate for that person. Research has demonstrated that assimilation to the dominant culture is significantly associated with performance on many neurocognitive assessment tools.[1] Individuals whose cultural beliefs and experiences are dissimilar to the dominant culture, or who are less assimilated to that culture, frequently demonstrate poorer performance on tasks assessing abstraction/executive functioning, attention, working memory, language skills, visuo-construction abilities, and learning when compared to individuals who are similar to the normative sample (Cagigas & Manly, 2014; Rivera Mindt et al., 2019). However, a systematic review by Tan et al. (2021) examining the impact of acculturation on neuropsychological test performance among various ethnic groups found that tests of delayed memory (both verbal and visuospatial) appear to be less impacted by acculturation (based on a systematic measure) than other neurocognitive domains. In contrast, they identified a much stronger association between acculturation and performance on several verbal and non-verbal tests, with "less" acculturation corresponding to poorer performance (i.e., lower scores).[2]

One solution to the potential bias due to acculturation is to apply demographically and ethnically appropriate norms. However, such norms are not always available, particularly for infrequently studied cultural groups (i.e., most of the world). In practice, when there is no normative data that closely matches the individual's characteristics, clinicians are encouraged to think critically about the test results—and whether some tests are even appropriate to administer and interpret. The impact of acculturation may be less of a concern if the individual scores within the range of normal functioning, since deviations from the normative sample are much more likely to impede performance rather than mask genuine deficits. However, if an individual appears impaired or performs more poorly than expected, the evaluator should consider the potential impact of acculturation, especially if the individual appears to have a low level of acculturation with the dominant culture (Rivera Mindt et al., 2019).

[1] While most of this research has been conducted in the US, a growing literature has focused on immigrants living in Western Europe (e.g., Neilson et al., 2019).

[2] As noted in Chapter 1, while acculturation is best conceptualized as a multidimensional construct, much of the published research has treated this construct as a unidimensional variable with "higher" levels of acculturation reflecting greater assimilation to the dominant culture.

Language and Bilingualism

Before any cognitive or neuropsychological testing can be administered, clinicians must consider which language would be most appropriate for testing and whether or not they have sufficient competence to conduct the evaluation themselves. A clinician who speaks the same language as the examinee may still face challenges during a cognitive or neuropsychological evaluation, potentially impacting the accuracy of the assessment. Linguistic differences or errors may be missed by the clinician who does not recognize relevant cultural influences or fails to perceive subtle neuropsychiatric symptoms that would be recognized by someone more familiar with the examinee's cultural background.

Even when using tests developed in the examinee's dominant language, it is important for the clinician to consider where the test was created, as there may be significant linguistic and cultural differences across dialects even within the same language. For example, some terminology and questions in the WAIS developed for use with Mexican adults (Wechsler, 2013) may not be as meaningful or relevant to Spanish-speaking adults from Argentina or Puerto Rico. Similarly, among English-speaking North Americans, someone from Canada may not be familiar with the items that are culturally specific within the US, such as historical figures or geography that might be less widely known among Canadians.[3]

The language of test administration can also impact performance through the length of words, particularly on tests that measure verbal fluency or working memory. Kempler et al. (1998) found that even when controlling for the effects of age and education, Spanish-speaking participants named fewer animals than Chinese-, English-, and Vietnamese-speaking participants on a timed verbal fluency test. They explained that not only were animal names much longer in Spanish than in Vietnamese, but that the variety of animals differed across groups, suggesting that there may be less exposure to diverse types of animals through books, television, movies, and zoos in rural parts of the world (where the non-English-speaking participants originated). Similarly, Lau and Hoosain (1999) found that language and the sound duration of digits may also impact working memory tests, with Chinese speakers performing better on mental arithmetic tasks than Japanese speakers, both of whom performed better than English speakers.

Of course, as discussed in Chapter 4, inaccurate translations may also impact performance on neurocognitive tests, particularly if the evaluator (or test instructions) uses complex terminology, such as technical words or phrasing that

[3] English-language versions of the WAIS have been developed for Canada, Australia/New Zealand, and the United Kingdom, each with different normative data.

are unfamiliar to the individual. Therefore, it is critical that clinicians consider whether it is appropriate to use translated scales and/or instructions unless adequate normative data is available using the specific test and translation. Absent this assurance, the risk of errors in the estimation of neurocognitive functioning may outweigh the potential value of the information generated from testing.

Bilingualism

Bilingualism also impacts an individual's cognitive development and performance on neurocognitive tests, improving some domains but hindering others. For example, bilingualism, when compared to monolingualism, is usually associated with stronger performance on attention tasks, executive control, and episodic memory. However, bilingualism appears to disadvantage performance (regardless of the language tested) on tasks measuring verbal comprehension and production. Individuals who are fluent in two languages typically have lower scores on tasks relating to expressive and receptive vocabulary, including picture naming, word comprehension and production, and semantic fluency (Cagigas & Manly, 2014; Rivera Mindt et al., 2019).

Even for fully bilingual individuals, test administration and language can impact performance. For instance, in one study of self-reported Spanish-English bilingual adults (all of whom lived in Los Angeles at the time of testing but reported a wide range of countries of origin, including multiple Latin American and Caribbean countries, as well as the US), participants recalled more digits in English than in Spanish (López et al., 2016). However, when the authors analyzed the number of syllables participants recalled correctly per string, their performance was actually better in Spanish, consistent with Roivainen's (2019) suggestion that digit articulation may impact recall. Therefore, assessing fluency in both languages is essential to best determine how to proceed with a neuropsychological or cognitive evaluation of a bilingual individual (Rivera Mindt et al., 2008). This assessment can include both objective and subjective measures, as performance can vary depending on the specific skills that are being assessed (e.g., speaking, listening, writing, or reading). Subjective techniques include simply asking about the individual's linguistic preferences across situations and contexts (e.g., reading, watching television) and the extent and quality of their formal education in each language. On the other hand, objective measures can compare performance and proficiencies across languages, such as verbal fluency tests and picture naming.

In English-speaking countries, linguistic proficiency among bilingual individuals is usually divided into three categories: English-dominant, non-English language-dominant, or bilingual (i.e., roughly comparable abilities in English and a second language; Rivera Mindt et al., 2008). If the individual is English-dominant or truly bilingual, they can be evaluated in English without a bilingual examiner, though the caveats noted above must be considered when interpreting test performance. If the individual's primary (dominant) language is not English, the individual should be evaluated in their dominant language, ideally by a clinician who is fluent in the examinee's preferred language.[4] Regardless of the evaluator's linguistic skills, utilizing standardized tests developed and "normed" with individuals who are similar to the examinee's cultural and linguistic identities should always be prioritized.

Economic Issues

Although not typically conceptualized as a cultural issue, socioeconomic status and country-level (or regional) economic development may also impact an individual's neurocognitive test performance. Individuals who are raised in poverty typically have lower levels of cognitive functioning across several domains, including memory, language, executive functioning, and processing speed (e.g., Arentoft et al., 2015; Ursache & Noble, 2016), all of which typically result in lower scores on corresponding neurocognitive tests (Gottfried et al., 2003). Growing up in poverty is associated with multiple social factors that can contribute to poorer performance on neurocognitive testing. These influences include an increased risk of traumatic and/or chaotic home and neighborhood environments, a greater risk of direct exposure to traumatic experiences (e.g., victimization), and less opportunity for parents to read to their children, all of which can impact a child's vocabulary and comprehension skills (Fujii, 2018). Associations between socioeconomic factors and cognitive functioning have also been found at the national level. Lynn and Vanhanen (2006) found a strong correlation (r = .57) between a country's gross domestic product (GDP) and mean scores on a test of overall intellectual functioning. Considering the strength of the relationship between socioeconomic factors and neurocognitive functioning, considering the potential impact of economic factors on test performance is advisable.

Situational Influences

Familiarity with the testing situation involved in a cognitive or neuropsychological evaluation is not universal. Sitting in a room alone with an unknown evaluator who asks an individual to complete unfamiliar tasks (often while

[4] While this is often feasible for Spanish speakers, finding a locally licensed clinician trained in the administration of neuropsychological measures who is fluent in a language other than Spanish can be challenging, if not frankly impossible.

holding a stopwatch or timer) can be a strange and uncomfortable experience for individuals who have not been previously exposed to psychological testing. This lack of familiarity with the testing situation may demand more cognitive energy for an examinee to focus their attention on the neurocognitive tasks (Nell, 2000). This discomfort can be exacerbated when the evaluator is a member of the opposite sex or is simply unfamiliar to them, the latter of which is almost always the case in a forensic setting. For example, some individuals from Latine cultures question the utility of completing tasks that involve manipulating blocks when asked to by a stranger, as they may not perceive the relevance of this activity to the legal situation that gave rise to the evaluation (Ardila, 2007).

When discomfort or unfamiliarity with the testing situation is anticipated, the clinician should devote adequate time to establishing rapport with the examinee—not simply asking a handful of questions before they begin administering tests. Many neuropsychologists spend very little time conducting an interview, let alone establishing rapport with the examinee in advance of testing, and often rely on other individuals to conduct the testing (e.g., a psychometrist). Still, establishing rapport is even more critical when working with individuals who are unfamiliar with standardized testing. Explaining the purpose of testing and acknowledging the unusual nature of some of the tasks that will be administered can help decrease the examinee's discomfort and improve motivation to perform optimally. Nevertheless, discomfort with testing, both in terms of the novelty of the setting as well as the challenging nature of the tasks administered, can adversely impact performance.

Stereotype Threat and Racial Socialization

A related situational influence on neurocognitive testing is stereotype threat. Stereotype threat occurs when an individual becomes anxious in a situation where they will be evaluated, fearing that their performance will confirm a negative stereotype that is held about a component of their identities (Steele & Aronson, 1995). Even when an individual may have average or above-average cognitive abilities, anxiety can negatively impact executive functioning and working memory as the individual is distracted by the need to suppress negative thoughts and emotions (Johns et al., 2008). Stereotype threat has been shown to impact performance with multiple groups who have traditionally faced discrimination, including Black and Latine individuals, and women (Schmader et al., 2008).

Microaggressions, intentional and unintentional comments or behaviors that suggest negative attitudes toward stigmatized and marginalized groups, may also impact an examinee's comfort during the testing situation, impeding rapport

(Owen et al., 2014) and hindering performance on neurocognitive tests (Thames et al., 2013). This can be exacerbated when testing contains images that are seen as culturally insensitive or even overtly racist, triggering negative emotions in the examinee. Byrd et al. (2021) cite the image of a noose contained within a frequently used neuropsychological test (the Boston Naming Test) as an example of such stimuli. They suggested that images such as this can elicit stereotype threat, possibly leading to problems concentrating, reduced engagement, early termination of a testing session, or a desire to refuse future assessments. Byrd and colleagues argued that clinicians need to actively engage in antiracist assessment practices to ensure that we do not perpetuate racism and harm by using potentially harmful stimuli in our evaluations. Although the extent to which microaggressions and/or stereotype threat impact neurocognitive test performance has not been widely studied, consideration of, and taking steps to minimize this possible influence is nevertheless advisable.

Types of Neurocognitive Assessments

Once contextual factors have been considered, the evaluator must determine the type of neurocognitive assessment needed. Broadly speaking, neurocognitive assessments can be divided into three broad categories: cognitive screening tools, measures of intellectual functioning, and more narrowly focused neuropsychological assessment tools. The following pages discuss these three approaches to neurocognitive assessments, with an emphasis on available techniques for individuals who are culturally and/or linguistically diverse and the extent of research support for various tests and techniques.

Cognitive Screening Tools

Screening tools, while useful in many settings, are used infrequently in forensic assessments, where diagnostic clarity is often critical. Nevertheless, some clinicians employ cognitive screening tools to determine whether a more thorough neurocognitive assessment is warranted, particularly in long-term care settings such as forensic hospitals and correctional facilities. These instruments are typically comprised of a brief battery of questions and/or tasks to assess several neurocognitive domains, generating a summary score that can be used to quantify the likelihood of impairment. Although many such tools exist, only a handful of well-established screening tools have been translated into and evaluated across diverse languages and cultural groups.

Perhaps the most commonly used screening tool for identifying possible cognitive impairment is the Montreal Cognitive Assessment (MoCA; Nasreddine et al., 2005), a brief instrument that elicits attention, memory, and visual processing abilities in order to detect cognitive impairment. According to the official website (https://mocacognition.com), the MoCA is available in nearly a 100 languages and dialects, and a large body of research has supported its utility with many different cultural, diagnostic, and educational groups (Cova et al., 2022). Although optimal cut-scores for detecting mild cognitive impairment may vary by race, ethnicity, and education (Milani et al., 2018), dozens of translated versions are available from the MoCA website (unlike many of the tools described later in this chapter), along with versions intended for visually- and/or hearing-impaired individuals. In short, this instrument has considerable potential for cases in which a brief screening tool is warranted, but because it is intended as a screening tool, it prioritizes sensitivity over specificity, resulting in many individuals identified as needing a more thorough evaluation who are ultimately determined to have no clinically significant cognitive impairment. Moreover, while some of these translated versions have at least some published validation data to support their utility, many do not.

Another cognitive screening tool that has potential cross-cultural utility, albeit much less widely used, is the Rowland Universal Dementia Assessment Scale (RUDAS; Storey et al., 2004). The RUDAS was developed with the specific goal of cross-cultural utility, and particularly for those with limited literacy, which makes it a good alternative to tools that require literacy, such as the Mini-Mental State Exam (MMSE; Folstein et al., 1975). Research with the RUDAS has typically shown little to no association with gender, years of education, or language preference, but has been studied much less frequently outside of Australia, particularly in culturally and linguistically diverse samples. Nevertheless, a recent meta-analysis of ten RUDAS studies included data from twenty-three countries, including Australia, Germany, Spain, Denmark, Sweden, Norway, Greece, Belgium, and India (Chithiramohan et al., 2024). Although much of this research examined concordance with another screening tool (the MMSE), the RUDAS has also shown good sensitivity and specificity for identifying dementia.

Many clinicians also utilize individual neuropsychological instruments for screening purposes, despite having a more specific focus. For example, tools such as the Trail Making Test (which has a non-verbal version: the Color Trails Test) and the Stroop test are often used to screen for potential neurocognitive impairment. Because these instruments are better conceptualized as neuropsychological tests rather than true screening tools (since they do not cover a range of functions or abilities), they are not reviewed here but are discussed later in this chapter.

Assessing Intellectual Abilities

Measures of intellectual functioning have particular importance in forensic mental health assessments, as the identification of intellectual disability (characterized by deficits in intellectual functioning–typically an IQ score about 70 or below–and significant impairment in adaptive functioning across conceptual, social, or practical domains) can have important ramifications in many criminal and civil forensic settings. However, assessing intellectual functioning in individuals from culturally or linguistically diverse backgrounds presents unique challenges and requires careful consideration, particularly when the accuracy of a diagnosis of intellectual disability (ID) is critical. For example, in the US, a diagnosis of ID can render a criminal defendant ineligible for the death penalty, making the diagnosis a literal life or death determination.[5] Indeed, many contentious "*Atkins* hearings" hinge on whether an individual's performance on IQ testing warrants an ID diagnosis, particularly when such a diagnosis had not been assigned prior to being charged with a capital offense.

Many evaluators cope with the challenge of cultural and linguistic diversity by simply relying on non-verbal tests (as described in the vignette at the beginning of this chapter). This practice assumes, incorrectly, that simply avoiding verbal tasks will eliminate any possible sources of bias. This assumption ignores an extensive research literature demonstrating that verbal abilities, which comprise a range of functions, are a central aspect of intelligence. Indeed, many of the psycho-legal questions addressed by forensic psychologists rely heavily on verbal abilities, such as evaluations of competence to stand trial or waive one's *Miranda* rights.[6] Moreover, as will be discussed elsewhere in this chapter, research has increasingly demonstrated that non-verbal tasks are also vulnerable to cultural biases, though admittedly these biases are often less obvious than the problems that arise from translating verbal tasks (e.g., vocabulary items are likely to have different levels of difficulty when translated). Indeed, the search for "culture-fair" IQ tests (given the absence of truly "culture-free" cognitive tests) has been the impetus for many of the debates regarding the very nature of intelligence.

[5] In *Atkins* v. *Virginia*, 536 U.S. 304 (2002), the US Supreme Court ruled that executing an intellectually disabled adult violated the Constitutional prohibition against cruel and unusual punishment. Although subsequent decisions (e.g., *Hall v. Florida, 2017*) have placed greater emphasis on the adaptive functioning prong of the diagnosis, an IQ score within the range of ID is typically a prerequisite to any successful application.

[6] In the US, individuals suspected of a crime must be informed of their constitutional right to silence (i.e., not to speak with police), as well as the presence of an attorney during any questioning, even if they cannot provide one for themselves. These warnings, grounded in *Miranda v. US (1966)* is colloquially referred to as the *Miranda* warning.

Theories of Intelligence

Theories of intelligence typically distinguish explicit and implicit approaches, essentially mirroring the emic and etic methodologies used in cross-cultural research described in Chapter 1. Explicit theories of intelligence, which are the focus of most psychological research and assessment tools, are proposed as hypotheses and then evaluated through empirical investigation. Explicit theories assume that the nature of intelligence is largely similar across cultures and seek to "validate" data generated by their measures across diverse cultures. In contrast, implicit theories are formulated within a specific cultural context, reflecting how people in that context conceptualize and manifest intelligence, including both its extent and malleability. Hence, implicit theories influence how an individual perceives and evaluates their own or others' intelligence, whereas explicit theories are typically measured using a systematic assessment technique that can presumably be applied universally, across a range of cultures (e.g., a standardized test that has been translated into a different language than it was developed in, and then evaluated in a specific sample).

Mental health professionals rely primarily on explicit theories of intelligence, most of which are grounded in Charles Spearman's (1904) early research theorizing an overarching general intelligence (*g*) and/or Louis Thurstone's (1938) theory of multiple factors of intelligence. For example, the Cattell-Horn (Horn & Cattell, 1966) theory of intelligence posits that general intelligence is made up of different abilities that comprise two broad factors: fluid intelligence (quick thinking and reasoning) and crystallized intelligence (accumulated knowledge and vocabulary). By contrast, Howard Gardner's (1983) theory of multiple intelligences suggests there are at least eight different aspects of intelligence: linguistic, logical/mathematical, spatial, bodily-kinesthetic, musical, interpersonal, intrapersonal, and naturalist. Gardner described intelligence as the "biopsychological potential to process information that can be activated in a cultural setting to solve problems or create products that are of value in a culture" (Gardner, 2000, p. 28). However, only some of these types of intelligence are typically measured by the tools most often used in forensic and neuropsychological evaluations.

In the context of a cross-cultural cognitive assessment, Gardner's theory allows for considerable variance in what constitutes intelligence. For instance, Romani culture emphasizes musical and interpersonal skills demonstrated through oral storytelling (Sternberg, 2007). While an expert musician and gifted storyteller might be considered highly intelligent, traditional theories of intelligence, such as those of Spearman or Cattell-Horn, might classify an illiterate Romani storyteller as having low intelligence based on their limited knowledge of facts, vocabulary, or arithmetic ability. This distinction between generalized and specialized theories of intelligence has important implications for gauging intelligence in the context of cultural differences, where limited literacy or a lack of familiarity with the tasks included in a traditional measure of intellectual functioning (including non-verbal, problem-solving tasks) may limit the utility of these assessment tools. Despite the appeal of more inclusive conceptualizations of intelligence, it is unclear whether an evaluator could realistically utilize such an approach in a forensic evaluation, given the vulnerability of such an approach to a *Daubert* or *Frye* challenge.[7]

Differences in both cultural values and implicit theories of intelligence also impact the learning emphasized in schools, with educational systems in economically developed countries prioritizing memorization, speed, and efficiency (e.g., using the fewest steps possible to achieve a solution). In addition, silence is often viewed as indicating a lack of knowledge (Sternberg, 2007). Conversely, research conducted in Africa demonstrated that listening more and speaking less are valued and respected traits (Durojaiye, 1993; Irvine, 1978), despite the negative associations these behaviors might have in Western cultures. In one study contrasting academic functioning and practical intelligence in a rural village in Western Kenya, researchers found that culturally relevant skills such as knowledge of herbal medicines (used to combat local parasitic illnesses) were actually *negatively* correlated with Western-style assessments of intelligence and academic achievement, suggesting that standard methods of conceptualizing intelligence may be misleading when applied to someone from a culture with very different values and experiences (Sternberg et al., 2001).

The distinction between explicit and implicit theories of intelligence highlights the importance of contextualizing any assessment of cognitive abilities in the examinee's culture in order to adequately understand the relationship between cognitive and functional abilities. Not surprisingly, standard Western measures of intellectual functioning may underestimate the functional abilities of someone from a cultural background that does not emphasize the same elements of performance that Western educational systems and cognitive assessment tools emphasize.

Assessing intellectual functioning

As noted above, one common approach to evaluating intellectual functioning in individuals from culturally and linguistically diverse backgrounds is through the use of one of the many non-verbal measures. These range from the non-verbal subscales of a standard intelligence test, such as the WAIS,

[7] The requirements for admissibility of expert testimony under *Daubert* (*Daubert v. Merrill Dow Pharmaceuticals, 1993*) and *Frye* (*Frye v. US*, 1923) should be well-known to most readers, and are described in detail in Melton et al. (2018).

now in its fifth edition (WAIS-5; Wechsler, 2024), to a measure specifically developed to assess intelligence through non-verbal means, such as the Test of Nonverbal Intelligence (TONI), currently in its fourth edition (TONI-4; Brown et al., 2010). There are strengths and weaknesses to applying non-verbal subtests from a standardized intelligence test, depending on a range of considerations. For example, if appropriate normative data against which to compare observed scores are absent or if there is no established translation of the instructions, clinicians are forced to rely on assumptions of equivalency that are at best questionable. More importantly, there is little doubt that culture can impact performance on non-verbal measures, as is discussed elsewhere in this chapter.

According to the publisher's website, there are multiple translations of the WAIS available.[8] However, as is the case with many translations of established psychological tests (e.g., the MMPI, discussed in Chapter 4), the limited accessibility of these scales, not to mention the time and cost necessary to obtain a translated version of the WAIS, often impedes the feasibility of this option. For clinicians working in a setting where a particular translation is likely to be used with some regularity, investing in an established test is likely worthwhile. For example, a clinician living in the Southwestern US might find the purchase of the Mexican translation of the WAIS-IV to be a worthwhile investment.[9] However, investing in a Mandarin Chinese translation of the WAIS-IV (developed for use in Taiwan) is likely impractical for a clinician tasked with evaluating a single Mandarin speaker (barring highly unusual circumstances, such as a very high-profile situation where time constraints and financial resources are not a concern). Moreover, many of the available WAIS translations (or standardizations, such as the Australian or UK versions of the English-language WAIS) have been developed for countries that are rarely the subject of forensic evaluations for clinicians who do not practice in that country (e.g., Belgium, Austria, Greece, Sweden). Nevertheless, the publisher recommends using the test in the individual's dominant language for recent immigrants and provides contact information for the various adaptations, in cases where time and cost do not preclude purchasing a translated IQ test.

It should be noted that while multiple translated versions of the WAIS-IV are commercially available, decisions about which version to use may still be complicated. For example, in an evaluation of a Salvadoran woman, it was unclear whether the Mexican or European Spanish version of the test would be

[8] With the recent transition from the WAIS-IV to the WAIS-5 (in the Fall of 2024), the availability of updated foreign language translations of the WAIS will likely lag by several years. Hence, the WAIS translations currently listed are still based on the WAIS-IV.

[9] Purchasing the Mexican version of the WAIS-IV is not as simple as visiting a website and entering a credit card, as the test is distributed by a company located in Mexico City.

preferable, since no version developed and normed on a Salvadoran sample is available.[10] Moreover, normative data for these tests can vary considerably, highlighting the potential importance of this decision (Duggan et al., 2019). In the case of the Salvadoran woman evaluated by one of us, the Spanish normative data generated far lower scaled scores (based on the same raw scores) than the Mexican version—a discrepancy of more than twenty points in the Full Scale IQ (see Table 5.1 for a comparison of the normative data based on the same raw scores). Interestingly, this woman's performance fell between these two extremes when scored using US normative data—which might have been used by an evaluator who did not have ready access to a Spanish-language WAIS (perhaps justifiably, based on the fact that she had lived in the US for a number of years and spoke English with sufficient fluency as to require little assistance from an interpreter for most of the evaluation). Because of the magnitude of these discrepancies, with Mexican norms generating a Full Scale IQ in the Borderline range and all of the WAIS-IV index scores at or above 70, this decision could have meant the difference between life and death had it been an *Atkins* evaluation, as a diagnosis of intellectual disability would be easily supported by US and

Table 5.1 WAIS-IV scores for a 53-year-old Salvadoran woman based on differing normative datasets

Scale/Subscale	US	Mexico	Spain
Full Scale IQ	63	74	53
Verbal Comprehension	61	70	51
Perceptual Reasoning	75	78	66
Working Memory	69	73	69
Psychomotor Speed	71	81	67
Block Design	7	6	5
Similarities	3	4	2
Digit Span	4	5	4
Matrix Reasoning	5	6	4
Vocabulary	4	5	4
Arithmetic	5	5	5
Symbol Search	5	7	4
Visual Puzzles	6	6	5
Information	3	3	1
Digit Symbol	4	6	4

[10] Although Chilean and Colombian versions of the WAIS-IV have also been published, these are similar to the Mexican version in that cultural adaptations have resulted in only minor changes to item content and scoring, but normative data differ substantially (Duggan et al., 2019).

Spanish normative data, but the Mexican data are far more equivocal. These discrepancies highlight the importance of utilizing appropriate normative data and perhaps considering different sets of normative data when questions about the optimal benchmark are unclear.

The TONI-4 is another common approach to evaluating intelligence in individuals from diverse backgrounds, particularly for those who do not speak Spanish, French, or Mandarin (the languages most likely to justify obtaining a translated version of the WAIS). The TONI-4 was designed to evaluate general intelligence by assessing aptitude, abstract reasoning, and problem-solving in children and adults between 6 and 89 years of age. It is an untimed test that consists of 60 items that are arranged by level of difficulty and takes approximately 15 to 20 min to administer. Test instructions are available in non-verbal (pantomime) or oral format, with official translations in Spanish, French, German, Turkish, Chinese, Vietnamese, Korean, and Tagalog. Individuals can respond to items using gestures such as pointing, nodding, or blinking, further minimizing reliance on verbal interactions. The TONI-4 was normed using a sample of 2272 people stratified by age group and roughly matching the 2007 US population with regard to geographic region, gender, race, ethnicity (Latine vs. non-Latine), educational attainment, family income, and exceptionality status (e.g., learning disability, speech-language disorder). The TONI-4 has demonstrated good reliability (coefficient alpha > .90) in gender/racial/ethnic sub-groups from the normative sample, with minimal differences in mean index scores across groups (Brown et al., 2010).

However, limited research has examined the accuracy of IQ estimates based on the TONI-4, particularly when used with individuals from diverse cultures and languages. One study (Ghazali et al., 2018) of a culturally and linguistically diverse group of Malaysian youths (including Chinese, Malay, Iban, and Bidayuh speakers) found adequate test-retest reliability (r = .77) and concurrent validity with another non-verbal measure of general intellectual functioning (Raven's Progressive Matrices). However, much of the existing (and limited) research addressing cross-cultural validity (e.g., in India, Jamaica, Taiwan, and among Indigenous Peoples in Canada) used earlier versions of the TONI. Given the limited research gauging the accuracy of the TONI-4 against a more comprehensive measure of intellectual functioning (e.g., the WAIS), particularly in culturally and linguistically diverse groups, caution should be exercised when important clinical decisions rest on a precise IQ score (e.g., the presence or absence of intellectual disability).

Another non-verbal measure of general intellectual functioning that has been studied across a range of cultures and languages is Raven's Progressive Matrices (RPM). This test comprises three versions (Standard Progressive

Matrices, Colored Progressive Matrices, and Advanced Progressive Matrices), each of which has multiple forms. The RPM tests have been the subject of extensive research across numerous countries, languages, and cultures. A 2015 meta-analysis identified 305 research studies conducted in 48 countries over a 64-year period (1950–2014), including more than 200,000 total participants (Wongupparaj et al., 2015). Although most of the samples found were from economically developed countries (Western Europe, the US, Canada, and Australia), many were from countries with emerging or developing economies in Africa, Latin America, and Asia. Of note, the authors found a significant positive correlation between publication year and mean scores, indicating that performance improved over time. A similar phenomenon, known as the Flynn effect, has been consistently observed with multiscale intelligence tests such as the WAIS, whereby scores typically increase over time (Flynn, 1984). Interestingly, this effect was roughly twice as strong among more economically developed countries compared to countries with emerging or developing economies. Thus, while Raven's Progressive Matrices holds some appeal given the substantial research base supporting its utility, the lack of updated normative data complicates the interpretation of this test.

In sum, despite the importance of accurately assessing intellectual functioning in many forensic settings, the available tools are relatively limited, and the existing research on the tools that do exist is often modest. When feasible, the use of a comprehensive measure to assess intelligence, such as a translated official version of the WAIS is ideal, though the quality of the available normative data likely varies considerably across translations (we have not reviewed each translation). Moreover, we recognize that logistical constraints, such as the cost and time required to obtain a translated version of the WAIS, may limit the feasibility of some approaches. All of these caveats raise questions about whether the accuracy of existing tools is indeed superior to simply utilizing a non-verbal test such as the TONI or RPM, or even administering the non-verbal subtests of the WAIS (assuming adequate translation of subtest instructions). While the data presented in Table 6.1 demonstrate that non-verbal tests are also influenced by the choice of normative data, the discrepancies observed on non-verbal subtests are generally more modest than those observed for verbal subtests (as evidenced by the relatively larger discrepancy in Verbal Comprehension index scores compared to the other WAIS-IV index scores). However, absent any evidence to support the accuracy of interpretations based on US normative data, forensic evaluators faced with an individual from a unique cultural and/or linguistic background may consider a test such as the RPM, which is specifically designed for this purpose, to be preferable despite its limitations.

Neuropsychological Evaluations

Comprehensive neuropsychological evaluations are typically more important in forensic settings than are assessments of overall intellectual functioning. In civil settings, identifying neurocognitive damage or impairment can significantly impact compensation awarded in personal injury cases, or support vocational disability and workman's compensation claims (among many other potential issues). In criminal settings, neurocognitive impairment can help mitigate culpability for criminal behavior or impact a range of other legal issues (e.g., competence to stand trial, transfer of a juvenile to adult court). In immigration court, relief from deportation may also hinge on a finding of cognitive deficits, particularly if tied to past physical abuse (e.g., in support of an asylum claim, as discussed in Chapter 8). Given the importance of comprehensive neuropsychological assessments and the ever-growing range of neuropsychological assessment tools available, understanding the cross-cultural validity of these tools is critical.

Many commonly used neuropsychological tools are non-verbal, although verbal instructions are almost always required for test administration. As noted previously, the lack of verbal stimuli or responding does not negate cultural influences on test validity. There is, however, growing support for many neuropsychological tests. Multiple test batteries have been translated into (or developed in) Spanish, many of which have adequate normative and validity data to permit some degree of confidence in test interpretation. Rivera Mindt et al. (2019) identified several Spanish-language neuropsychological batteries, most of which were developed in either Spain or Mexico. These include La Batería Neuropsicológica en Español (Artiola i Fortuny et al., 1999), the NEUROPSI (Ostrosky-Solís et al., 1999) and the NEUROPSI: Attention and memory battery (Ostrosky-Solís et al., 2007), La Batería Neuropsicológica de Funciones Ejecutivas y Lóbulos Frontales-3 (Flores Lázaro et al., 2012), La Batería IV Woodcock-Muñoz (Alvarado et al., 2019), the Woodcock-Muñoz Language Survey III (Woodcock et al., 2010), the Evaluación Neuropsicológica Infantil-2 (Villaseñor et al., 2013), the Neuropsychological Screening Battery for Latinos (Pontón et al., 1996), the Spanish and English Neuropsychological Assessment Scales (Mungas et al., 2004, 2005), the Repeatable Battery for the Assessment of Neuropsychological Status Update-Spanish (Randolph, 2012), and the Spanish NIH Toolbox Cognition Battery (Casaletto et al., 2016). Of course, the extent of empirical support for these batteries varies widely and should be carefully investigated before being incorporated into a forensic neuropsychological evaluation.

In addition to established batteries, Arango-Lasprilla et al. (2015) published Spanish-language normative data for many commonly used neuropsychological tests based on data from 12 Latin American countries (and is currently developing and norming a comprehensive Latin American neuropsychological assessment battery). Although the sample sizes from most of these countries precluded a detailed analysis of age, education, and racial effects, these data provide a starting point for the neuropsychologist motivated to analyze test results in relation to a specific country or region. The need to examine culturally relevant norms carefully has become increasingly apparent, and contrasts sharply with past practices, which typically collapsed data from heterogeneous samples of Spanish-speakers drawn from a range of Latin American countries into a single "Spanish-language" normative sample.

Although most of the cross-cultural neuropsychological research has focused on Spanish speakers, a number of studies have examined neuropsychological tests used in other languages and cultures. One such example is the Canadian Study of Health and Aging, which focused on the detection of dementia in French- and English-speaking Canadians. They used confirmatory factor analysis to examine the equivalence of French and English versions of multiple neuropsychological tests (Tuokko et al., 2009). Although these findings have not been replicated, this study supports the comparability of French and English versions of an assessment battery, particularly for long-term memory and visuospatial abilities (only partial invariance was found for verbal abilities). However, given some of the cultural similarities between French- and English-speaking Canadians, the extent to which these results would replicate across other cultures is unknown (e.g., French-speaking West Africans). Another large-scale effort to examine the cross-cultural validity of neuropsychological tests is the European Consortium on Cross-Cultural Neuropsychology. This consortium has already published several studies using the European Cross-Cultural Neuropsychological Test Battery and the RUDAS (described earlier in this chapter), contrasting Western European participants with those from Eastern Europe, North Africa, India, and Pakistan (e.g., Nielsen et al., 2018, 2019).

A number of researchers have also examined the utility of individual neuropsychological tests in a wide range of diverse populations, often providing normative data to facilitate interpretation. For example, research teams in Asia have examined multiple neuropsychological measures in Mandarin- (Qi et al., 2022, 2023), Vietnamese- (McCauley et al., 2023), and Korean-speaking adults (Ryu & Yang, 2023; York et al., 2023). Korean translations exist for the California Verbal Learning Test (Kim & Kang, 1999), the Boston Naming Test (Kim & Na, 1999), and the Consortium to Establish a Registry for Alzheimer's Disease-Korean version (Lee et al., 2002, 2004). Similarly, several tests have been translated into Arabic, some of which have published normative data for different Arabic-speaking peoples (e.g., Egyptian, Lebanese, and Saudi; see Fasfous et al., 2017; Poreh et al., 2012; Zeinoun et al., 2022). However, despite the continued growth of language and culture-specific translations of neuropsychological tests and normative data, accessing these tests often depends on the ability to locate study authors and their willingness to share translated test stimuli and/or normative data. Very few of these instruments are commercially available, with the exception of some of the Spanish-language tools noted above.

Cross-Cultural Equivalence of Neuropsychological Measures

As noted above, while many instruments have established translations into languages other than English (i.e., linguistic equivalence), the availability of these tools does not necessarily mean that the validity or psychometric equivalence of the tests or instruments has been systematically evaluated. A key issue is the quality of the reference groups utilized to develop the measure's norms and the extent to which the comparison samples adequately reflect the characteristics of the individual being tested. For many of the measures that are commonly used in the US, adjusted norms take into account relevant demographic characteristics of the examinee, such as age, years of education, and racial/ethnic background. Cagigas and Manly (2014) suggest using demographically adjusted norms in several situations, specifically when (a) the selected tests have adequate construct validity, (b) there is a diagnostic question underlying the testing, (c) the examinee's characteristics are consistent with the reference population used to develop the norms, (d) selection bias and preclinical cognitive functioning or impairment do not invalidate the normative sample's representativeness, and (e) there is evidence indicating that demographic adjustments improve diagnostic accuracy.

Despite these cautions, some research has demonstrated strong support for the use of neuropsychological tests developed for and standardized in North America but subsequently applied in novel settings. For example, Adjorlolo (2016, 2018) found moderate to strong support for the diagnostic utility of executive functioning tests (the Stroop, Trail Making Test, and Controlled Oral Word Association Test) in a sample of Ghanaian adults with a history of Traumatic Brain Injury (TBI). However, the authors did not report descriptive data for their samples (those with TBI and a healthy comparison sample), so it is not possible to determine how their results might differ from North American normative datasets. Moreover, all participants were tested in English (which was a second language for most, if not all, participants), further limiting the ecological validity of this study.

Nuanced normative data is even less likely when using translated (or adapted) versions of tests that were developed for non-English speaking individuals. When normative data are available from specific countries or regions, these samples are typically derived from urban areas and may not adequately represent individuals from rural parts of the country. This selection bias can lead to an overdiagnosis of cognitive impairment in culturally and linguistically diverse groups when compared to members of the majority population. Issues with translation and normative data are particularly problematic when using verbally mediated tests. In our experience, it is not uncommon for clinicians to simply ask an interpreter, either during the evaluation or in advance, to translate testing materials into the individual's dominant language. While perhaps acceptable for simple instructions needed to administer non-verbal tests, it is hard to envision a scenario in which this would be advisable for most tests or testing situations. For example, an interpreter, or even a psychologist with some degree of fluency in the examinee's dominant language, may not be able to translate materials in a way that ensures cultural equivalence. Cultural equivalence requires adequate translatability across several domains of meaning: item content, semantic, technical, criterion, and conceptual (Canino & Bravo, 1994). Content equivalence requires that each test item is relevant and meaningful to the individual, while semantic equivalence requires that the language and terms used in the translation have the same meaning in both languages and cultures. Even resolving conflicts between precise translation (sometimes referred to as linguistic equivalence) and semantic equivalence can be challenging. Technical equivalence asks whether the assessment technique utilized (e.g., reading and writing) is effectively the same across cultures, while conceptual equivalence relates to whether the translated measure still assesses the same underlying construct. Criterion equivalence refers to whether the translated tool can predict the same outcomes as the original. Asking an interpreter to undertake this process without specialized training, whether before or during an evaluation, raises questions about each aspect of the translation process, potentially distorting the tool in ways that are not known.

Research on the Boston Naming Test (Kaplan et al., 1983) highlights the challenges of translating even a seemingly simple verbal test into another language for cross-cultural application. This neuropsychological tool assesses confrontation naming by presenting the individual with sixty pictures arranged in order of difficulty. However, research has demonstrated considerable variability in performance across cultures, which has necessitated adaptations to ensure cultural equivalence. In the Greek version, for example, four items (pretzel, doorknocker, stethoscope, and scroll) were changed to be more culturally relevant (Patricacou et al., 2007). The Argentinean version of the test was reordered because some items were more difficult for this cultural group than for the US samples on which the test was developed (Fernández & Fulbright, 2015). The need for cultural adaptations to psychological measures that depict visual stimuli demonstrates that even though a test may be classified as verbal, there may still be cultural biases in visual stimuli that impact performance. Interestingly, verbal language tests involving list-learning (e.g., the California Verbal Learning Test) appear to be less impacted by the language in which the test is administered, suggesting that this test may tap the same skill across different cultures and languages (Gasquoine et al., 2007). In short, clinicians must consider the research supporting the equivalence of verbal tests across cultural or linguistic differences before their administration.

Because they rely less on verbal stimuli, clinicians often prefer non-verbal tests for evaluating linguistically diverse individuals, especially when the evaluator does not speak the same primary language as the examinee. There are many strengths to non-verbal neurocognitive measures. They often require minimal verbal instruction, and some have established, readily available translations of the instructions. However, non-verbal cognitive tests also have critical shortfalls when applied cross-culturally. At the broadest level, it bears reiterating that non-verbal tests are not culture-free, nor do they eliminate the impact of culture or language on testing performance. Even when instructions are translated, test development may utilize norms, values, or culturally specific stimuli that belong to the majority culture, such as the value of responding quickly. Non-verbal measures may also rely on cognitive and neurocognitive skills that are not as well developed, or not as valued, in certain cultures. For example, numerous studies have shown that in comparison to English speakers, Spanish-speaking older adults demonstrate worse performance on category fluency, visuospatial, and visuo-constructional measures, such as recognition memory and multiple-choice matching (Jacobs et al., 1997). Similarly, a study of Taiwanese adults indicated that performance on the Wisconsin Card Sorting Test, a non-verbal measure of executive functioning, was substantially worse than expected based on normative data from the US, and showed little evidence of age, education, or gender effects (Shan et al., 2008). These differences reiterate the importance of adequate normative data to support interpretations based on both verbal and non-verbal neuropsychological tests. Of course, it is also critical to consider the link between the skills and abilities targeted by the neurocognitive assessment and the forensic questions at issue. Reliance on non-verbal assessment techniques is of limited utility when an evaluator is asked to assess a legal function that is predominantly "verbal," such as capacity to waive *Miranda* rights (as highlighted in the opening vignette) or testify in one's own defense, because non-verbal tests are unlikely to elucidate problems with verbal comprehension, learning disabilities, or aphasia.

Revisiting the Vignette

One central question posed by the opening vignette is whether reliance on non-verbal portions of an English-language IQ test is an appropriate method for assessing intellectual functioning, particularly in the context of a *Miranda* waiver. Based on the preceding discussion, the short answer is no. While non-verbal IQ tests can minimize certain linguistic demands, they are neither culture-free nor sufficient to assess verbal capacities such as understanding *Miranda* rights. Moreover, without culturally relevant normative data, the results of these tests may yield inaccurate conclusions about even non-verbal domains of intellectual functioning.

This vignette also highlights the importance of distinguishing between general functioning and specific legal capacities. While non-verbal IQ tests may provide an overall estimate of the individual's intellectual functioning, a waiver of *Miranda* rights hinges on verbal comprehension and practical understanding—skills that non-verbal measures cannot adequately capture. In this case, an assessment of adaptive functioning, including daily problem-solving and communication skills, would be critical in evaluating Mr. Y's ability to understand his rights and/or determine whether an intellectual disability diagnosis is warranted.[11] A more comprehensive assessment would evaluate Mr. Y's language proficiency, legal understanding, and adaptive functioning within his own cultural and linguistic context. Hence, non-verbal subtests of an English-language measure of intelligence alone are not sufficient for gauging someone's verbal and adaptive functioning abilities.

While worrisome from a procedural standpoint, the police officer's decision to read and present the *Miranda* warnings in English is not typically a matter for the forensic evaluator to weigh in on. Instead, the courts rely on forensic evaluators to assess Mr. Y's capacity to understand the warning as it was presented. While adequate cognitive testing may have indicated that Mr. Y was capable of understanding the *Miranda* warning, that does not mean that he actually did understand it. A test of English-language reading ability would likely help clarify this question. The defense expert's report also failed to address critical elements of forensic neuropsychological or cognitive evaluations, such as adaptive functioning or effort testing (Chapter 3). As discussed in Chapter 2, competence evaluations are not simply based on test scores, but must include an assessment of real-world functional abilities. The

[11] It should be noted that competence to waive a constitutional right is not contingent on a diagnosis of intellectual disability, as a range of other explanations can be offered (absent a formal diagnosis) to support an opinion that the waiver was not "knowing and voluntary."

absence of these measures in Mr. Y's evaluation raises significant concerns about the validity of the expert's conclusions.

In sum, this vignette underscores the need for forensic evaluators to use culturally and linguistically appropriate methods that align with the specific psycho-legal question at hand. When assessing verbal legal capacities, such as a *Miranda* waiver, reliance on non-verbal IQ measures alone is inadequate and risks generating misleading conclusions. Although the defense's expert may be correct that there are no measures of cognitive effort, *Miranda* comprehension, or adaptive functioning "validated" on Yemeni immigrants,[12] reviewing collateral information, observational data, and culturally and linguistically appropriate neurocognitive assessment tools would have strengthened the validity of the evaluation. Such an approach could have provided critical insights into Mr. Y's functional abilities, legal understanding, and capacity to appreciate the rights outlined in the *Miranda* warning.

Summary and Recommendations

Considering the current state of cross-cultural cognitive and neuropsychological assessment, some clinicians may feel discouraged and unsure about how best to proceed. Numerous sociocultural factors can impact testing, including level and quality of education, level of acculturation, primary language or bilingualism, economic issues, communication style, the unique testing situation, and cultural differences in the very meaning of "intelligence." With the presence of so many factors that can bias or impact testing and interpretation, and the potential for norms that are not appropriate to use with culturally and linguistically diverse examinees, how can one complete a culturally fair and accurate evaluation? Although imperfect, being mindful of the multiple factors that can impact neurocognitive testing is a crucial first step to improving a clinician's competence and the appropriateness of testing and test interpretation. We offer several recommendations based on the existing research and our clinical experience that can improve the quality and accuracy of neurocognitive testing with individuals from culturally and linguistically diverse backgrounds:

[12] It should be noted that tools developed and intended for non-English speaking examinees are increasingly common. For example, see https://riversideinsights.com/arabiya-intelligence-achievement for an example of Arab-language cognitive assessment tools. As noted throughout this volume, the availability of such tools does not necessarily correspond to adequate normative data, particularly for languages that encompass a wide range of cultures (e.g., Spanish, Arabic).

- **Prepare the individual for the evaluation**: To optimize the individual's comfort and understanding during the testing situation assessment process, it is important to inform them of the purpose and process of the current assessment.
    - Inform the examinee of the purpose and process of the evaluation in advance, and particularly the relevance of standardized testing.
    - Where appropriate and aligned with standardized testing procedures, explain the nature of the tests to reduce discomfort and unfamiliarity with the testing situation.
- **Gather sociocultural contextual information**: Sociocultural information should be elicited prior to the evaluation, as it will guide test selection and interpretation.
    - Information about education, acculturation, language proficiency, economic issues, and immigration context can—and should—inform the interpretation of test results.
    - Consider the individual's unique cultural context, background, and values, particularly as they relate to implicit theories of intelligence.
    - Keep in mind that individuals raised in poverty may have experienced factors that influence cognitive development, such as limited access to educational resources or, in some cases, traumatic experiences; if relevant, this information should be considered when interpreting test results.
- **Assess bilingualism and language proficiency**: Evaluate bilingualism and language fluency to guide decisions about the appropriate language(s) for testing.
    - Use both subjective methods (e.g., self-reports about language use and preferences) and objective measures (e.g., verbal fluency tests) to assess bilingualism and level of fluency across languages. This assessment should guide decisions about which language is most appropriate for testing based on the individual's dominant language or fluency level.
    - Consider testing in both languages if possible and appropriate.
- **Evaluate normative data and test limitations**: Determine whether the selected measures have adequate normative data for the individual's cultural and linguistic background.

- Investigate the strengths and weaknesses of each tool with members from the examinee's cultural group(s).
- Examine qualitative information, such as the errors an individual makes in testing, and consider testing the limits of performance on timed test items (i.e., to determine whether the examinee can finish timed tasks if given more time or under different conditions).
- Disclose the potential limitations of any measures used in the forensic report.
- Investigate whether specific measures have adequate normative data (or if new instruments or norms have become available) that may better suit the examinee's background.

- **Interpret sociocultural contextual factors**: Consider sociocultural contextual factors in the interpretation of neurocognitive test results.

  - Low scores may reflect genuine cognitive deficits or impairments, but the potential influence of cultural or linguistic factors should not be dismissed.
  - Be careful not to erroneously attribute actual deficits to cultural or linguistic issues, while remaining cautious about over-pathologizing.
  - Balance test results with observations and collateral information to provide a comprehensive evaluation.

- **Disclose decisions about translations and norms**: Document the use of translations, selection of normative data, and any deviation from standard procedures in the final report.

  - This ensures transparency and allows others to evaluate the appropriateness of the evaluator's methods.

6
Assessment of Risk for Violence and Reoffending

Summary

This chapter reviews the clinical and research literature on the assessment of risk for future violence and non-violent criminal behaviors in culturally diverse individuals. We summarize the existing research on the cross-cultural use of assessment instruments, highlighting potential sources of bias that might impact these tools. The extent of empirical support for both actuarial and structured professional judgment tools in cross-cultural settings is reviewed, along with the role of culturally specific risk factors. In addition, we review widely used tools for gauging risk of interpersonal violence, non-violent criminal behavior, and specific forms of offending (e.g., sexual reoffending, intimate partner violence) in both adults and adolescents. Finally, given its central role in assessing risk of both violent and non-violent recidivism, we discuss the cross-cultural applicability of the construct of psychopathy, along with recommendations for practice.

Case Vignette

Ali M, a twenty-six-year-old Jordanian immigrant, was arrested and charged with assaulting a police officer with a baseball bat during a confrontation outside of his home. Mr. M had been under surveillance by the police department due to a series of internet postings he made in support of Islamic fundamentalist groups. He was approached by two police officers for questioning one evening while walking in his neighborhood. After the interaction became heated, Mr. M walked back into his home and returned carrying a baseball bat. According to the arresting officer's statement, Mr. M assaulted one of the officers, hitting him several times in the arm and back, before being restrained by a second officer. He was referred by his

Cultural and Linguistic Considerations in Forensic Mental Health Assessment. Barry Rosenfeld and Alicia Nijdam-Jones, Oxford University Press. © Oxford University Press (2026).
DOI: 10.1093/9780190900991.003.0006

attorney for an evaluation of his risk of future violence in hopes of negotiating a plea bargain that would reduce his potential prison sentence.

Upon interview, Mr. M reported having been born and raised in Amman, Jordan, the oldest of six children born to a middle-class family with a father who owned a popular restaurant. He had attended a private secondary school where he learned English and completed his college degree in engineering at a Jordanian university. Mr. M immigrated to the US approximately three years before his arrest to pursue a master's degree in engineering, but intended to return to Jordan eventually, to work and raise his family. Although he spoke English fluently, the evaluator questioned the applicability of existing risk assessment instruments due to his cultural background. A search of the literature revealed no research studies examining risk factors for general violence or criminal reoffending (not terrorism) among Middle Eastern individuals. Can the evaluator simply apply his or her "standard" approach to risk assessment (i.e., a clinical interview, record review, and structured professional judgment tool)? Are there any unique considerations that the evaluator should be aware of or tools that can be used to guide this evaluation? What other steps would be appropriate to take before, during, or after beginning this assessment?

There is little dispute that the use of structured risk assessment tools improves the accuracy of evaluations that address an individual's risk for future violence or criminal behavior. In fact, there has been a steady improvement in the accuracy of violence risk assessment over the past few decades, corresponding to the emergence of structured risk assessment tools. These tools have been developed to guide clinicians as they identify and consider risk factors for violence and criminal recidivism and integrate these risk factors into clinical judgments about an individual's relative risk.

As is evident from the preceding chapters, the utility of forensic assessment measures with culturally and linguistically diverse populations is a growing concern internationally. The field of risk assessment is no different, as the potential consequences of errors can be significant, whether that means failing to detect someone who presents a high risk of future violence or wrongly identifying a low-risk individual as posing a high risk of violence. Because culture is integral to an individual's decision-making processes, it has the potential to influence when or why someone engages in violence or criminal behavior, as well as guide the selection of interventions that might reduce this risk. Culture also shapes personal values and perceptions, as well as the anticipated social response to one's actions (Krug et al., 2002). However, the most widely used (and frequently

We express our deepest appreciation to Dr. Stephen Hart for his feedback on an earlier draft of this chapter.

studied) risk assessment tools have been developed in the United States and Canada (Singh et al., 2011). Although some of these tools have integrated findings from research conducted around the world, this research base is primarily drawn from studies conducted in Western European and Australasian countries, raising questions about the validity of these tools when used with culturally diverse populations.

The Supreme Court of Canada highlighted the importance of considering culture in the 2018 case of *Ewert v. Canada*. The Court ruled that the Correctional Service Canada (CSC) had breached their legal obligation to ensure that the risk assessment tools used to evaluate an offender's risk of recidivism were appropriate for use with culturally or ethnically underrepresented populations, focusing specifically on their use with Indigenous adults. The Court ruled that before the CSC may resume using risk assessment tools, they must "conduct research into whether and to what extent [the tools] are subject to cross-cultural variance when applied to Indigenous offenders" (*Ewert v. Canada, 2018*, p. 199). Although specific to Indigenous adults in Canada, the *Ewert* case highlights a growing concern regarding cross-cultural validity in forensic evaluations, with some scholars stating the "issues of generalizability raised would logically apply to *any* psychometric tool used in a forensic/clinical context" (Haag et al., 2016, p. 66). Yet, despite increased attention focused on the cross-cultural validity of risk assessment measures, few studies specifically examine whether cultural bias exists in the construction of these tools, let alone whether predictive validity is moderated by racial, ethnic, or cultural status (Carter & Forsyth, 2007; Gonzalez et al., 2014).

In countries with large, culturally diverse populations, like the US, Canada, Australia, and the UK (among many others), it is particularly important that risk assessment tools be empirically evaluated in the populations they might be used with. Including risk assessment measures in forensic evaluations has become increasingly common, and many administrators and policymakers have actually mandated the use of specific tools through local policies and legislation (Monahan & Skeem, 2014). Over half of the fifty US states utilize risk assessment tools to inform parole decisions (Harcourt, 2008), and nearly as many states routinely use risk assessment measures in criminal sentencing decisions (Starr, 2014). Given the cultural diversity of individuals involved in the criminal legal system, it is critical that both the assessment tools and forensic evaluators themselves are responsive to cultural factors that might influence the accuracy of these tools.[1]

[1] Although risk assessments also occur in settings outside of the criminal legal system (e.g., employment, national security settings), we have framed this chapter around the criminal legal system given that this is the most common, and perhaps most challenging setting for such assessments—and because violence virtually always constitutes a form of criminal behavior, regardless of the setting in which it arises.

Unfortunately, despite high rates of diversity in the criminal legal systems of most economically developed countries, as well as a growing reliance on structured risk assessment tools around the world, relatively little research has actually evaluated the accuracy of risk assessment tools with members of diverse cultural groups. Fewer still have attempted to identify culturally relevant risk factors that might improve the accuracy of these tools in specific populations or cultures. Although several violence risk factors appear to be universal across cultures (e.g., a history of violent behavior, young age, presence of paranoid or violent ideation), there may be risk and protective factors that are unique to some populations.[2] Likewise, there are certainly cultural and political considerations that impact interventions and risk mitigation strategies, both within and across countries. Sociopolitical influences—such as systemic inequities, colonial histories, discrimination, and socioeconomic marginalization—shape both the emergence and interpretation of risk; considering these structural realities helps ensure that risk judgments are contextualized rather than pathologizing the effects of broader injustices. Furthermore, potentially important risk factors (e.g., psychopathy) may also manifest differently across cultures, raising questions about whether they can be accurately assessed in a specific individual from a divergent cultural background. In short, culturally appropriate risk assessment tools are critical to distinguishing genuinely high-risk individuals from those with a lower risk for violence or recidivism. This chapter reviews some of the most commonly used risk assessment tools, including violence risk assessment measures and instruments for evaluating general criminal recidivism and sexual violence, as well as the role of culture in the assessment of psychopathy.

Risk Assessment Approaches

Regardless of the context, evaluating an individual's risk for violence or general criminal recidivism requires a thorough and objective (i.e., as free from bias as possible) evaluation. Such an evaluation typically includes, at a minimum, reviewing relevant records and a clinical and diagnostic interview.[3] There is also a growing consensus that the evaluation process is improved by the use of a structured risk assessment tool. However, additional reliance on collateral sources of information can be particularly critical to the evaluation process when the examinee's cultural background differs from that of the evaluator or the dominant

[2] A growing research literature has focused on the identification and integration of protective factors into violence risk assessment, much of which has originated in Western Europe. However, we are aware of very little cross-cultural research that has examined the extent to which culture influences protective factors. Hence, this chapter does not address the research on protective factors.

[3] Considerations for clinical and diagnostic interviewing are described in detail in Chapter 2 and will not be repeated here.

cultural context. Interviews with family, friends, treatment providers, or members of the examinee's community can often provide critical information to help contextualize the data elicited. These sources may help evaluators differentiate culturally normative beliefs, attitudes, and behaviors from those unique to the individual, or identify culturally specific risk and protective factors that might not otherwise have been recognized. Combined with the use of a structured risk assessment instrument to guide the evaluation, this background information will help the examiner more accurately identify individual, situational, cultural or sociopolitical factors that may increase the risk of violence or non-violent criminal behavior. The goal of this process is not simply to estimate the nature and degree of any risk posed by an individual, but rather to evaluate the extent to which the person can modulate these risk factors, and to identify external controls and resources that might reduce the likelihood of negative outcomes.

Selection of a risk assessment tool, however, requires careful consideration given the strengths and limitations of the different assessment approaches. These approaches can be broadly distinguished by the two main methodologies used: actuarial decision-making tools and techniques that rely on professional judgment. Actuarial Risk Assessment Instruments (ARAIs) provide a set of fixed and explicit decision rules that are associated with specific outcomes (e.g., interpersonal violence, sexual offending, criminal behavior). These tools do not measure unique aspects of the individual, but rather rely on characteristics that have been demonstrated (in past research) to distinguish those who have and have not engaged in the type of problem behavior being assessed. Using an ARAI allows the evaluator to estimate the likelihood of negative outcomes (e.g., violence, recidivism) in a group of individuals with a similar degree of risk factors, either generating a probability of occurrence over a specified time period (e.g., 34% risk of violence over the next five years) or placing the individual into a categorical risk category (e.g., above average, average, or below average risk). An important benefit of ARAIs is transparency in the scoring and algorithm, as the risk considered and the weight applied to each are explicitly defined, limiting the opportunity for discretion or bias on the part of the evaluator.[4] However, ARAIs typically ignore many important risk factors or overweigh concerns that

[4] Minimizing the risk of evaluator bias does not necessarily eliminate the opportunity for systematic biases, given that some identified risk factors may be inherently biased in favor of, or against, specific subgroups. For example, ARAI's address risk of recidivism, which by definition only pertains to individuals that have already been convicted of a crime. Hence, these tools may be systematically biased against those who are from marginalized backgrounds that are more likely to be arrested, charged and convicted of a crime. Moreover, research has demonstrated an "allegiance effect" with ARAIs that, while weaker than with less structured approaches, is still notable (Murrie et al., 2009). This literature demonstrates that ratings with risk assessment tools tend to point toward greater risk when the assessment is paid for by the state (e.g., seeking to retain an individual or justify a longer sentence) and lower risk when paid for by attorneys seeking discharge from a secure facility or a shorter/non-carceral sentence.

have been successfully resolved, and leave no opportunity to account for unique considerations such as an examinee's cultural background or sociopolitical context. By focusing heavily on static risk factors, most ARAIs provide little to no guidance in developing risk management and intervention strategies.

Professional judgment approaches enable more discretion in determining what risk factors to consider, how to determine their presence or absence, and how much weight should be accorded to the risk factors identified. Although some clinicians continue to rely on their own experience and training, without the benefit of any structured approach (i.e., unstructured professional judgment), there is little evidence that decisions made with unstructured professional judgment are consistent across (or even within) professionals, and this approach has little evidence to support its predictive accuracy. The Structured Professional Judgment (SPJ) approach was developed in response to shortcomings in unstructured professional judgment by merging the benefits of actuarial methods (increased transparency and reliability) with the need to individualize the risk assessment process for the specific examinee. The SPJ approach guides clinicians to identify empirically supported risk factors that should be considered in a risk assessment but relies on the evaluator's clinical judgment in determining how to weigh and integrate these risk factors into risk judgments (e.g., low, moderate, and high).

An SPJ approach to violence risk assessment typically defines a series of risk factors that are associated with violence, increasing the consistency (reliability) across clinicians and the transparency of the decision process. Furthermore, by considering the relevance of these risk factors for the individual being evaluated, SPJ-based risk assessments can inform risk management strategies and help improve decision-making for individual cases. Importantly, the flexibility of the SPJ approach also allows for the possibility of adapting the tool to individuals whose backgrounds differ from the cultural and sociopolitical context(s) in which the tools were initially developed, in this way facilitating their use with people from diverse cultural backgrounds. That said, little research has assessed when and how, or even if these tools should be modified to account for unique cultural or sociopolitical influences that might impact the meaning and importance of the risk factors targeted (discussed in more detail later in this chapter).

Most of the cross-cultural research on risk assessment has used an etic perspective to assess the utility of existing tools when applied to a novel population or setting (see Chapter 1 for a more thorough explanation of this approach). While important, etic research does not necessarily facilitate the identification of culturally specific risk or protective factors, which are more readily identified using emic research strategies. The following section will review several commonly used instruments to assess violence risk, general recidivism, sexual recidivism, and intimate partner violence, as well as the existing evidence for their use with culturally and linguistically diverse adults.[5]

Violence Risk Assessment Research

Interpersonal violence has been defined as the "actual, attempted, or threatened infliction of bodily harm on another person" (Douglas et al., 2013, p. 36) that occurs when an individual has engaged in "an act (or omission), with some degree of willfulness, that caused or had the potential to cause physical or serious psychological harm to another person or persons" (Douglas et al., 2013, p. 37). Violence can be physical, verbal, or psychological and occurs in many contexts, including community and institutional settings (e.g., psychiatric and correctional facilities), the home, or at a school or workplace. Mental health clinicians worldwide are often responsible for assessing, managing, and monitoring the risk of violence, and there is growing evidence demonstrating the utility of risk assessment tools in these evaluations internationally (Singh et al., 2014). Several actuarial and SPJ tools have been developed to inform violence risk judgments, including the Violence Risk Appraisal Guide tools (VRAG; Harris et al., 1993) and its revised version (VRAG-R; Rice et al., 2013), as well as the Historical-Clinical-Risk Management-20 (HCR-20; Webster et al., 1995), now in its third iteration (HCR-20^{V3}; Douglas et al., 2013). A number of similar tools have also been developed for specific settings and populations, including the Structured Assessment of Violence Risk in Youth (SAVRY; Borum et al., 2006), an SPJ violence risk assessment tool developed for use with adolescents.[6]

Prior to describing these tools, it is important to review key methodological issues in risk assessment research, which often emphasize predictive accuracy as measured by the Area Under the Curve (AUC) statistic. Although the AUC statistic, which is based on the sensitivity and specificity of a tool across all possible cut-scores, allows for comparisons across studies, its meaning differs significantly in the context of risk assessment compared to other prediction contexts (e.g., identifying feigning, as discussed in Chapter 3). Most importantly, risk assessment tools aim to evaluate the likelihood of specific outcomes, such as violence or general recidivism. However, individuals classified as high risk may

[5] This chapter does not address the handful of tools that are designed to assess highly specific forms of violence, such as honor killings or terrorism. While these tools specifically target issues linked to cultural and sociopolitical contexts, research supporting these tools is largely based on anecdotal or retrospective analysis, and limited evidence exists to support their predictive validity.

[6] Many other tools exist for assessing violence risk, both in specific settings (e.g., school, the workplace) and populations (e.g., those accused or convicted of stalking, child abuse), but are not discussed in this chapter due to limited research support for their utility, both in general and with culturally diverse individuals in particular.

be restricted in their ability to demonstrate this risk, often remaining detained until their risk level decreases. Additionally, while ARAIs typically provide little assistance in reducing risk (other than through incapacitation), the primary goal of risk assessment is usually to identify interventions that can mitigate risk. Consequently, a high-risk individual who has been successfully supported in the community (which is obviously a positive outcome) would be classified as an "incorrect prediction" because they did not engage in violence. Conversely, someone identified as low risk who engages in violence does not necessarily indicate an incorrect classification, as some low-risk individuals are expected to act violently (i.e., low risk does not equate to no risk). Thus, while improvements over chance suggest enhanced predictive accuracy, achieving perfect accuracy is neither realistic nor desirable, as it implies inadequate risk mitigation or management.[7] Despite these limitations, the AUC remains the primary metric for gauging and comparing the effectiveness of risk assessment tools across different samples, settings, *and cultures*, and is relied upon to provide some evidence of adequacy.

VRAG

Among the many ARAIs developed to assess the risk of violence, the VRAG/VRAG-R is one of the most widely used. Developed in Canada with adults who had been hospitalized in a forensic psychiatric facility, the VRAG generates a probabilistic estimate based on a weighted algorithm of twelve risk factors identified in a large study. Like most ARAIs, the calculation of violence risk is based almost entirely on static (historical) risk factors that are not amenable to change. Nevertheless, numerous studies by independent research teams have found that the VRAG/VRAG-R has adequate predictive accuracy for predicting violence and criminal recidivism. However, of importance for this chapter, the vast majority of participants in the VRAG normative sample (Canadian adults with a history of charges or convictions for violent offenses, most of whom also had serious mental health problems) were White males who were released from long-term custodial settings in the 1980s and 1990s.

[7] There are multiple other limitations to risk assessment research that are too numerous to detail here, beginning with the equal weighting of sensitivity and specificity in calculating the AUC statistic. This equal weighting is rarely appropriate in real-world settings, as "errors" (false positives and false negatives) carry vastly different implications. For instance, in violence risk assessment, sensitivity is typically prioritized; failing to identify or intervene with someone who later commits a violent act poses significant societal risks. In contrast, although unjustified liberty restrictions are harmful, they are often perceived as less socially damaging than the consequences of a violent incident. Conversely, in the context of feigning detection (discussed in Chapter 3), specificity (avoiding false positives) typically takes precedence, as mistakenly identifying a genuine responder as feigning can lead to severe personal and professional repercussions for the examinee.

When used with adults from culturally or linguistically diverse backgrounds, the utility of the VRAG/VRAG-R has generated multiple concerns. For instance, the emphasis on criminal history variables (which constitute half of the VRAG items) may result in inflated risk estimates for members of marginalized racial or ethnic groups (e.g., Indigenous or Black individuals), whose criminal history may reflect systemic bias and racism in policing and the criminal legal system. The static nature of the items is another concern, as it precludes consideration of contextual, cultural, sociopolitical, or individual factors in estimating an individual's risk for violence. For example, while research has consistently demonstrated a link between substance abuse and violence, the inability to distinguish between those with an active or recent substance use disorder versus those who have abstained from substance abuse for many years (or decades) prevents the VRAG from considering individual variations in these risk factors. Of course, the reliance on a fixed, predetermined algorithm also prevents integration of any culturally specific risk factors—or any protective factors (since none are included in the VRAG).

Nevertheless, there is some empirical support for the use of the VRAG with culturally diverse adults in the United States and abroad. For example, our recent study examined the VRAG-R in a sample of men incarcerated in a Mexico City prison, finding relatively good predictive accuracy (AUC = .74) for institutional violence over a 3-month follow-up period (Cortvriendt et al., 2024). However, little research has examined the use of the VRAG/VRAG-R with other culturally or linguistically diverse groups, such as Latine individuals living in the US. Given the limited research support for the VRAG/VRAG-R in culturally diverse samples, clinicians should be cautious when applying this tool in the context of cultural or ethnic diversity and should avoid relying on probabilistic estimates based on the existing normative data, given the potential for inflated risk ratings and the questionable generalizability of the normative samples.

The HCR-20

One of the first and most frequently used SPJ risk assessment tools is the HCR-20 (Webster et al., 1995). The HCR-20 guides clinicians in considering twenty well-established risk factors that fall into three time periods: historical factors (Historical scale), the individual's recent clinical presentation (Clinical scale), and areas of potential future problems (Risk Management scale, see Table 6.1). Although initially developed in Canada, the HCR-20 has been widely used in Europe and the US, as well as in dozens of other countries around the world.

Table 6.1 HCR-20 risk factors

Historical Scale *(History of problems with...)*	**Clinical Scale** *(Recent problems with...)*	**Risk Management Scale** *(Future problems with...)*
H1. Violence H2. Other Antisocial Behavior H3. Relationships H4. Employment H5. Substance Use H6. Major Mental Disorder H7. Personality Disorder H8. Traumatic Experiences H9. Violent Attitudes H10. Treatment/Supervision Response OC-H. Other considerations	C1. Insight C2. Violent Ideation or Intent C3. Symptoms of Major Mental Disorder C4. Instability C5. Treatment/ Supervision Response OC-C. Other Considerations	R1. Professional Services and Plans R2. Living Situation R3. Personal Support R4. Treatment/Supervision Response R5. Stress or Coping OC-R. Other Considerations

Using the HCR-20, clinicians rate the degree to which each risk factor is present using a 3-level format (No = *the risk factor is absent*; P = *the risk factor is possibly or partially present*; Yes = *the risk factor is present*), as well as the relevance of each identified risk factor for the individual's future violence risk (*Low, Moderate*, or *High*). Although the presence of more risk factors and/or more high relevance ratings typically corresponds with a higher level of risk, clinicians use these ratings to develop a risk formulation and generate three Summary Risk Ratings (*Overall Risk for Future Violence/Case Prioritization, Risk for Serious Physical Harm, Risk for Imminent Violence*), each of which is rated as *Low, Moderate or High.*[8]

The utility of the HCR-20 has been examined in hundreds of research studies conducted in over 25 countries, typically generating moderate to large effect sizes for predicting violence (O'Shea et al., 2013; Singh et al., 2011). However, studies that apply the HCR-20 to culturally or linguistically diverse samples have typically used an etic approach, simply translating the instrument and applying it directly to a different culture or country.[9] Using this approach, studies have

[8] Much of the risk assessment literature described here has relied on file review without incorporating a clinical interview (this is typically less relevant for ARAIs but is a significant limitation with SPJ tools). In addition, many early studies simply summed the number of risk factors present rather than individualizing the weighting and interpretation of risk factors (which effectively converts an SPJ tool into a simple, unweighted ARAI).

[9] The revision process for the HCR-20 third edition did include feedback solicited from researchers in several Western European countries including Sweden, Norway, Germany, the UK, and the Netherlands.

demonstrated strong support for the HCR-20 using samples from the UK, Australia, and Western Europe, typically generating AUC estimates of about .70. A handful of studies have also examined the HCR-20 in non-Western samples, including studies conducted in locations in Asia, Latin America, and Africa. For example, two studies conducted in China have utilized the HCR-20 in psychiatric settings, both of which supported the tool's utility. Lv et al. (2013) used a Chinese translation of the HCR-20 in a sample of psychiatric patients diagnosed with schizophrenia, finding an AUC of .72 for the HCR-20 total score. More recently, Chen et al. (2023) found even stronger results using an authorized Chinese translation of the tool in individuals with a history of psychiatric treatment either in a psychiatric hospital (n = 93) or while in prison (n = 53). They found strong predictive accuracy for violent behavior at both the 6-week and 6-month follow-up assessments (AUC = .82 and .80, respectively), including violence that occurred either in the institution or in the community following discharge.

The handful of studies conducted in Latin America have varied in their support of the HCR-20. In a sample of Argentinian adults, Folino (2015) followed participants for an average of 3.5 years after their release from prison. The predictive accuracy of the HCR-20 for violent behavior was somewhat lower than what has typically been found in US and Western European samples (AUC = .62). On the other hand, Sada et al. (2016) found excellent short-term predictive accuracy (mean follow-up = 25 days) in a sample of adults in a Mexican psychiatric hospital (AUC = .86). We also utilized a Spanish translation of the HCR-20 to assess the risk of institutional violence in 114 inmates in a Mexico City prison. However, unlike previous studies, we used an emic approach to develop and identify culturally relevant risk factors that could be integrated into the HCR-20,[10] based on interviews with experienced forensic mental health professionals in Latin America (Nijdam-Jones, García-López, et al., 2020, 2021, 2023). We found strong predictive accuracy for the modified version of the HCR-20, with an AUC of .73 to .74. Although the culturally relevant risk factors did not significantly improve the predictive accuracy over the standard HCR-20 items,[11] individuals who engaged in institutional violence during the 3-month follow-up period had significantly higher risk ratings than those who did not on several

[10] Although this study characterized, measured and analyzed the identified culturally relevant risk factors as unique variables (i.e., risk factors), these variables are better conceptualized as culturally specific *manifestations* of existing risk factors (e.g., H8: Traumatic experiences, H9: Violent attitudes).

[11] Demonstrating statistically significantly differences in AUC estimates typically requires exceptionally large samples. Hence, many of the studies reported here indicate seemingly large differences that are, with very few exceptions, not *statistically* significant (despite what might appear to be *clinically* significant differences).

culturally relevant risk factors that had been identified (e.g., problems with *machismo*, *familismo*,[12] and indirect or direct violence exposure).

A handful of other studies have also applied the HCR-20 in other cultural contexts but have not directly addressed its utility in gauging violence risk. For example, Adjorlolo and Chan (2019) rated the HCR-20 in a sample of individuals imprisoned in Ghana, comparing those who had been previously incarcerated (i.e., recidivists) with those who had not (i.e., non-recidivists). They found strong interrater reliability and internal consistency for the HCR-20, as well as excellent accuracy in predicting recidivism based on the total number of items present (AUC = .87) and for the combined presence and relevance ratings (AUC = .89). However, the retrospective nature of this study, its focus on criminal recidivism rather than violence, and the reliance on "total scores" from the HCR-20 rather than summary risk ratings are notable limitations. Similarly, Sea and Bang (2021) examined the reliability and concurrent validity of the HCR-20 in a sample of 80 incarcerated Korean adults, most of whom had been convicted of serious violent offenses (e.g., homicide, rape, assault, robbery). Psychologists who were trained by the HCR-20 developers demonstrated excellent interrater reliability for both summary risk ratings and the sum of item presence ratings. However, because no follow-up data regarding violent behavior was obtained in this study, concurrent validity relied on correlations with other measures, such as the Psychopathy Checklist (r = .43) and a Korean violence risk tool (r = .33). Hence, while these studies provide some support that the HCR-20 can and is being used consistently in a wide range of cultures and countries, the existing empirical support (outside of Western Europe and Australia) is best characterized as modest.

Several studies have also examined racial or ethnic group differences when using the HCR-20 with different cultural groups in the US. For instance, Fujii et al. (2005), in their study of 108 adults hospitalized in a Hawaiian psychiatric facility found that HCR-20 total score had the lowest predictive accuracy for the Asian American (AUC = .58) and European American samples (AUC = .64), and the highest predictive accuracy for the Native Hawaiian group (AUC = .73). While these AUC estimates did not differ significantly, the authors did identify significant differences in the relevance of multiple individual risk factors across these ethnic groups, indicating that individual risk factors may be more salient in some ethnic groups than others. For example, they found that impulsivity was a more salient risk factor for Asian American participants, whereas young age at the first violent incident was more salient in the European American sample. Several risk factors were more salient for the Native Hawaiian participants,

[12] Familismo refers to a strong sense of loyalty, unity and reliance on family members that is common in many Latin American counties.

including relationship instability and low feasibility of risk-management plans. These findings demonstrate that identifying cultural differences that may impact the salience of risk factors across cultures could help the evaluator gauge and intervene to lower violence risk.

In sum, while research examining the utility of the HCR-20 in culturally and ethnically diverse samples is encouraging, the variability in predictive accuracy and the limited range of studies conducted in non-Western countries highlight the need for more systematic research with culturally diverse samples. A clear strength of the SPJ approach is that it permits the evaluator to incorporate relevant risk factors that are not explicitly addressed in the standard risk factors, yet little research has attempted to identify culturally specific risk factors (or manifestations of known risk factors) that can be integrated into the risk assessment process. Without such research, the degree to which such adaptations to the standard risk factors are necessary is not altogether clear, and likely depends on both culture and the context for the evaluation.

The SAVRY

The SAVRY (Borum et al., 2006) is another commonly used SPJ risk assessment tool, specifically intended for adolescents between the ages of 12 to 18. Developed in the US, the SAVRY includes twenty-four risk factors (rated as *Low, Moderate*, or *High)* across three categories: historical, individual, and social/contextual. In addition, the SAVRY includes six protective items (rated as *Present* or *Absent*) such as prosocial involvement, social support, and commitment to school. Like the HCR-20, the SAVRY also allows the evaluator to incorporate other relevant risk and protective factors that might inform their risk assessment, providing the flexibility to address unique cultural considerations.

The SAVRY and its manual have been translated into multiple languages (primarily Western European), but much of the research addressing cross-cultural utility has focused on comparisons between Indigenous and non-Indigenous youth in Canada and Australia. This literature has consistently found that Indigenous youth receive higher scores on the SAVRY (when items are summed) than non-Indigenous youth. However, total score and summary risk ratings have generated widely divergent estimates of predictive accuracy, with AUC estimates ranging from .64 to .84 for both violence and criminal behavior in samples of Indigenous youth (e.g., Lovatt et al., 2022; Muir & Viljoen, 2022; Shepherd et al., 2014).

Moreover, when predictive accuracy is considered through the lens of sensitivity and specificity (rather than AUC analyses, which weigh these equally), potentially important differences emerge. For example, Muir et al. (2020) found that the SAVRY correctly identified relatively few Indigenous Canadian youth as low risk, and they were more often rated as high risk for violent recidivism when compared to White adolescents, suggesting that the tool may have exaggerated violence risk in Indigenous youth. Based in part on their consultation with Indigenous "youth justice professionals," the authors suggested that these results may reflect the impact of colonialism and racial inequities in both the Canadian criminal legal system and health care systems more broadly, resulting in a greater degree of unmet needs and increasing perceived violence risk. In a subsequent paper, Muir et al. (2023) recommended that clinicians be more culturally responsive in their risk assessments by considering sources of risk (e.g., historical loss) or consulting with Indigenous professionals. Shepherd and Willis-Esqueda (2018) offered a similar conclusion based on their interviews with Indigenous professionals involved in the legal and health care systems. They suggested that the SAVRY may perpetuate negative labeling and does not facilitate the cultural and colonial contextualization of behaviors, norms, and practices that may be unique to Indigenous youth. Taken together, these studies suggest that while the SAVRY may have adequate predictive accuracy when used with Indigenous youth, there is a need for greater consideration of cultural factors and cultural sensitivity when evaluating and developing risk management strategies for Indigenous adolescents.

The need for evaluators to consider cultural and immigration factors was also highlighted by Munoz and Venta (2022) in their study of Latine youth who had recently immigrated to the US. They examined the concurrent validity of the SAVRY in predicting conduct problems in a sample with no known history of delinquent or criminal behavior. Although the SAVRY total score was significantly correlated with self-reported conduct problems (r = .38), it was not associated with caregiver reports of conduct problems (r = .17). Interestingly, the authors found that acculturation stress was also a significant predictor of conduct problems in their sample, emphasizing the need to consider other risk indicators when working with immigrant youth.

Research on the SAVRY with adolescents outside of North America has also demonstrated variable results, often finding lower levels of predictive accuracy for violent recidivism than those observed in Western countries. For example, studies examining the SAVRY in Chinese and Singaporean youth have generated relatively modest effect sizes (AUC = .66 to .68), but somewhat stronger accuracy in predicting general recidivism (AUC = .72; Chu et al., 2016; Zhou et al., 2017). However, a Canadian study found much stronger predictive accuracy for the SAVRY for both violent and nonviolent recidivism among Asian Canadians (AUC= .81 and .89) compared to White Canadians (AUCs = .71 and .77; Li et al., 2020).

Taken together, the existing research suggests that although the SAVRY may be an effective tool for some populations, individual, sociopolitical, and cultural factors should be considered. For example, acculturation and acculturative stress, the impact of colonization, and immigration status may adversely impact the predictive validity of the SAVRY. Culturally unique protective factors may also be important for understanding a youth's risk of violence, despite a lack of research addressing this topic. In short, while there is little research to guide the adaptation of the SAVRY, cultural and contextual considerations should nevertheless be incorporated into the risk assessment and formulation process.

General Recidivism

As evident from the previous section, much of the research on SPJ tools such as the HCR-20 and SAVRY has also addressed general criminal recidivism in addition to violent behavior. These studies have often observed somewhat higher levels of predictive accuracy for "any" recidivism, likely due to the greater frequency of criminal behavior compared to violence. However, the overlap in predictors for violence and general recidivism highlights the generalizability of that literature for more broadly focused risk assessments. There are also numerous instruments that have been developed and utilized in correctional settings, typically to guide decision-making around pre-trial release or post-conviction sentencing. Of these instruments, only one has been the subject of sufficient cross-cultural research to warrant review, though it primarily focuses on racial/ethnic differences in North American samples.

Level of Service Inventory (LSI)

The LSI and its revised version, the LSI-R (Andrews & Bonta, 1995), are frequently used for evaluating the risk of general recidivism in a wide range of settings and countries. Along with related instruments, such as the LSI Case Management Inventory (LS/CMI) and a youth version (YLS/CMI), these ARAIs were developed in Canada to identify criminogenic risk factors and intervention needs that impact recidivism. The LSI is based on the Risk-Needs-Responsivity model (RNR, Andrews et al., 1990), which emphasizes the importance of matching the level of services provided to an offender's risk for reoffending (the Risk principle) and tailor interventions to the individual's specific criminogenic needs (the Needs principle), while taking into account the individual differences in learning style, motivations, and abilities (the Responsivity principle). However, more recent scholarship has highlighted the need for culturally responsive adaptations even within the RNR model, to ensure these frameworks align with diverse sociocultural and systemic contexts (e.g., Burgess & Nijdam-Jones, 2024).

Although the LSI has been widely used in Western, English-speaking countries (US, UK, Canada, and Australia), there is little evidence that this tool has gained widespread acceptance in other regions of the world (Singh et al., 2014). Moreover, research that has examined this tool in North American samples has demonstrated differential utility when examined across different cultural and ethnic groups. Olver et al. (2014) conducted a meta-analysis of 128 studies ($k = 151$ independent samples, $N = 137{,}931$ participants), finding that although the LSI-R was a significant predictor of both violent and general recidivism across several ethnic groups (e.g., Indigenous, Asian, Black, and Latine), the effect sizes were much larger for the non-White samples. Furthermore, although ethnicity was a significant moderator of effect size, geographic region explained more variance in effect sizes than race/ethnicity, with the largest effect sizes being found in Canadian studies and studies from Western Europe and Australia, while the smallest effect sizes were found in US samples.

Another meta-analysis of the LSI with Indigenous Americans also found racial/ethnic disparities in its performance (Wilson & Gutierrez, 2014), as some subscales had lower predictive accuracy for Indigenous adults than non-Indigenous adults. The LSI also under-classified low-scoring Indigenous adults but accurately estimated recidivism rates for those who showed greater risk (i.e., obtained higher total scores). Nevertheless, they concluded that the LSI still retains some utility for predicting recidivism in Indigenous individuals, despite the weaker accuracy compared to non-Indigenous samples. From our community-based research, we have heard from Indigenous practitioners who question the conceptual validity of the LSI for Indigenous peoples, noting that several of its indicators (e.g., limited education, unstable employment, or family members with criminal involvement) reflect the effects of longstanding colonial legacies and sociopolitical inequities rather than individual criminogenic propensities. In sum, while research with the LSI/LSI-R has demonstrated adequate predictive validity across racial and ethnic subgroups of offenders in North America, greater caution should be exercised when gauging risk in minoritized groups and with Latine and Indigenous individuals in particular. Its utility in settings that differ more dramatically from North America and Western Europe (e.g., Asia, Latin America, and Africa) is essentially unknown.

Sexual Recidivism

Static-99/99R

Among the large number of ARAIs specifically designed to assess risk of sexual reoffending, one of the more widely used is the Static-99 and its subsequent revisions (Static-99R; Static-2002, Static-2002R; Hanson & Thornton, 2000; Helmus et al., 2012). Like other ARAIs, the Static-99/R uses an algorithm to calculate the probability of reoffending based on the weighted coding of ten risk factors. Risk can be described as the percentage of individuals in that score range who committed a sexual re-offense within five or ten years following their initial release, or can be characterized using qualitative descriptors (*Very Low Risk, Below Average Risk, Average Risk, Above Average Risk*, and *Well Above Average Risk*). The Static measures are widely used in several English-speaking countries, such as the US, Canada, the UK, and Australia, as well as many Western European nations, with materials and/or training available in French, Swedish, Finnish, Polish, German, and Dutch. Despite having been developed in Canada, research with European samples has actually demonstrated higher levels of predictive accuracy, with AUCs typically ranging from .75 to .79 (e.g., Gonçalves et al., 2020; Långström, 2004; Martens et al., 2017; Schmidt et al., 2017). The handful of studies examining the Static-99R in Asian countries (Japan, South Korea, Singapore) have also found strong predictive accuracy (AUCs = .70 to .76; Harada et al., 2023; Lee et al., 2023; Tsao & Chu, 2021) but accuracy has been considerably lower in North American samples, with AUCs typically ranging from .60 to .70 (Helmus et al., 2021, 2022). This may reflect the greater influence of systemic biases in policing and prosecution in North American samples, given the heavy reliance on previous criminal charges and convictions in the Static tools.

In light of the widespread use of these tools across diverse cultures, it is perhaps surprising that so little research has directly examined cross-cultural differences within and between subgroups. One exception, a study by Långström (2004), found lower predictive accuracy for recent immigrants or ethnic minorities living in Sweden compared to those of traditional Swedish descent. Similarly, a German study by Schmidt et al. (2017) found that although the Static-99R was effective at predicting sexual recidivism for individuals with a European background, it was not effective when predicting recidivism among immigrants from the Middle East and North Africa.

Studies based in North America have also questioned the utility of the Static-99/R when used with individuals who identify as Latine. For example, Varela et al. (2013) found that the Static-99 and Static-99R had relatively weak, though statistically significant (i.e., better than chance) predictive accuracy for identifying sexual reoffending among Black (AUCs = .62 to .69) and White, non-Latine adults (AUCs = .59 to .65) but not for Latine individuals (AUC = .56 to .58). While other studies have found stronger predictive accuracy with Latine samples (e.g., Hanson et al., 2014; Lee & Hanson, 2017), they continue to show poorer performance in Latine individuals relative to Black and White, non-Latine samples. Interestingly, Leguízamo et al. (2017) found that the Static measures had good predictive accuracy for Latine individuals born in the US and Puerto Rico (AUCs = .77 to .82) but poor predictive accuracy for individuals from other Latin American countries (AUCs = .47 to .52). Those authors speculated that predictive accuracy for the immigrant samples may have been impeded by limited access to historical information (e.g., criminal history).

Studies examining the predictive accuracy of the Static measures with Indigenous samples have also been mixed. For example, several Australian and Canadian studies have demonstrated weaker predictive accuracy for the Static-99 with Indigenous adults when compared to non-Indigenous adults (Lee et al., 2020; Smallbone & Rallings, 2013; Spiranovic, 2012). A meta-analysis of the Static-99R by Ahmed et al. (2023) synthesized eighteen studies examining the instrument with White, Black, Indigenous, Asian, and Latine adults from Canada, the US, Australia, and Singapore. They found the weakest predictive accuracy with Indigenous and Latine individuals (AUCs = .64 for both subgoups), whereas it performed somewhat better with Black (AUCs = .67 to .76), White (AUC = .68 to .71), and Asian adults (AUCs = .75). This pattern of results supports the possibility of cultural bias in the Static-99R and indicates the need for caution when administered with individuals from culturally and linguistically diverse backgrounds.

Violence Risk Scale—Sexual Offender version (VRS-SO)

The VRS-SO (Wong et al., 2003) is an increasingly popular ARAI for gauging risk of sexual reoffending, in part because it is the only ARAI intended to gauge changes in risk over time (e.g., in response to treatment). The VRS-SO uses seven static and seventeen dynamic items, with the dynamic items organized into three factors: Sexual Deviance, Criminality, and Treatment Responsivity. However, the VRS-SO has been primarily studied in English-speaking Canadian samples and has demonstrated variable predictive validity (AUC = .61 to .81). Similarly, studies in other economically developed countries, such as New Zealand (Beggs & Grace, 2010) and Germany (Gaunersdorfer & Eher, 2023), have generated similar levels of support. Notably, a study by Olver et al.

(2018) that compared Indigenous and non-Indigenous Canadians found slightly (though not significantly) higher predictive accuracy for the non-Indigenous sample (AUCs = .70 to .75) compared to Indigenous adults (AUCs = .62 to .70). While the VRS-SO has a number of appealing qualities, including its use of multiple dynamic items (unlike virtually all other ARAIs) and its focus on measuring treatment-related changes in risk, the limited research literature examining its utility in diverse samples raises questions about the extent to which it can be reliably used with individuals from diverse backgrounds.

Sexual Violence Risk-20 (SVR-20) and Risk of Sexual Violence Protocol (RSVP)

The most widely used SPJ tools for assessing risk of sexual violence in adults are the SVR-20 (Boer et al., 1997) and the RSVP (Hart et al., 2003), both of which are now in their second edition. These tools, which were developed by the same research team and have largely overlapping item content, differ in the extent to which they focus on estimating risk of re-offense (the SVR-20) versus developing risk management and intervention strategies (the RSVP). Like other SPJ instruments, these tools guide the clinician to consider empirically supported risk factors that are associated with sexual recidivism and are used to render risk judgments using an ordinal qualitative scale (*Low, Moderate, High*).

The SVR-20 has predominantly been studied in English-speaking (including the UK and Australia) and Western European countries (e.g., Spain, Sweden, Austria, the Netherlands, and Germany; Rettenberger et al., 2009) and has demonstrated moderate to good predictive validity. However, a handful of studies have examined the SVR-20 in non-EuroAmerican contexts. For example, a study conducted in Singapore found strong predictive accuracy for sexual recidivism (AUC = .78) among men sentenced to a term of probation following a conviction for a sexual offense (Tsao & Chu, 2021), exceeding the predictive validity of the Static-99 (AUC = .70). However, another qualitative study examining the perspectives of Latin American forensic mental health professionals involved in sex offense risk assessments raised concerns about the SVR-20. Aparcero et al. (2020) found that while the instrument was often used in several Latin American countries, the professionals interviewed expressed concern about the lack of research supporting its validity in this context. Additionally, some professionals identified potentially important socio-cultural risk factors that are not included in the tool (e.g., involvement in subcultures where incest may be more acceptable) or reflect culturally specific risk factors (e.g., *machismo*) that appear relevant to evaluating an individual's risk for sexual recidivism. Given that SPJ tools facilitate the integration of unique and/or culturally relevant risk factors, this possibility should be explored whenever conducting a risk assessment with an individual from a less familiar cultural background.

Juvenile Sex Offender Assessment Protocol-II (J-SOAP-II)

Although little research has examined the differential utility of SPJ instruments with ethnically diverse adults, two studies have examined differences in the predictive accuracy of the J-SOAP-II (Prentky & Righthand, 2003), an SPJ instrument designed for evaluating risk in juveniles convicted of a sex offense. Martinez and colleagues (Martinez et al., 2007) retrospectively coded the J-SOAP-II in a sample of 60 Black and Latine youths evaluated in an urban outpatient treatment setting in the US. They found strong predictive accuracy for sexual recidivism (AUC = .78) but noted that predictive accuracy was much stronger for the Dynamic subscale (comprised of the Treatment Response and Community Supports scales) compared to the Static subscale (comprised of the Sexual Deviance and Antisocial Behaviors scales). A subsequent study by this research group, with juveniles who had been incarcerated following a sexual offense, examined differences in predictive accuracy between Black, Latine, and White, non-Latine youths (Martinez et al., 2015). They found no predictive accuracy for the J-SOAP-II with Latine youths on the J-SOAP-II total or subscale scores, whereas AUC estimates were above .70 for non-Latine White youths on all subscales. Predictive accuracy with Black youths was more variable, with adequate predictive validity for the Dynamic subscale and total score, but not for the Static subscale. However, the modest sample size in this study, particularly for the Latine and White, non-Latine samples, limited the conclusiveness of these findings (many of which were not significant, either in isolation or when compared to one another). Nevertheless, these findings are consistent with growing evidence to suggest that sex offender risk assessment tools may require adaptation when applied to Latine individuals, regardless of age. Furthermore, the weak support for static risk factors (which include a history of antisocial behaviors) supports the growing concern that traditionally marginalized individuals may generate inflated risk estimates based on systemic biases in the criminal legal system(s), particularly in North America.

Intimate Partner Violence

Intimate partner violence (IPV) is prevalent in many parts of the world, where some forms of physical violence against women are often regarded as acceptable or even justified (e.g., Nigeria: Adegoke & Oladeji, 2008; Ghana: Amoakohene,

2004; China: Liu & Chan, 1999), sometimes as a means of restricting women's autonomy or resolving conflict (e.g., Pakistan: Ali & Khan, 2007; South Africa: Jewkes et al., 2002). Despite the prevalence of IPV worldwide, relatively little research has addressed the cross-cultural utility of risk assessment tools used to gauge the likelihood of reoffending among individuals who have engaged in this behavior.

Spousal Assault Risk Assessment (SARA)

Like other SPJ tools created by Canadian researchers at Simon Fraser University, the SARA guide (now in its third edition; Kropp & Hart, 2015) has been widely used and translated into numerous languages. However, while a recent review identified 28 published studies of the SARA, most of these were conducted in Canada (k = 14) or the US (k = 7), with the remainder in Sweden, Portugal, Argentina, and New Zealand (Allard et al., 2024). In one of the few published studies conducted outside of North America and Western Europe, Arbach and Folino (2021) monitored twelve Argentinian men for an average of eight months, identifying recidivism using court records. They found adequate predictive validity for the summary risk ratings (low, moderate, or high), with an AUC of .64, providing preliminary support for this tool when used by Latin American professionals. More recently, Hogan and Corăbian (2024) examined the utility of the SARA-3 in Indigenous and non-Indigenous Canadian adults charged with an intimate partner violence offense. They observed higher risk ratings among the Indigenous sample, who were nearly four times more likely to be rated as high risk than non-Indigenous individuals, and also found that those identified as Indigenous were more frequently rearrested even after controlling for risk level and history of prior IPV convictions. While their analyses did not address whether predictive accuracy levels differed, they noted that this effect may not solely reflect differential processing by the criminal legal system, as Indigenous adults also had a higher likelihood of uncharged allegations. Given the importance of accurately identifying risk of IPV, particularly given the potential for severe outcomes such as intimate partner homicide, the need for additional research to guide these evaluations is clear.

Assessment of Psychopathic Personality

The construct of psychopathy has unique relevance for risk assessment, regardless of whether the assessment concerns violence, non-violent criminal reoffending, sexual offenses, or other forms of problematic behavior.

Research has consistently demonstrated the importance of considering psychopathic personality traits, highlighting the substantial association with a wide range of problematic behaviors.[13] Measures used to gauge psychopathic personality traits have also been translated into countless languages, and a substantial body of research has supported their utility across diverse cultures.

Much of the early cross-cultural research on psychopathy focused on differences between racial-ethnic groups in the US, in part because the most widely used tool, the Psychopathy Checklist-Revised (PCL-R; Hare, 2003), was developed with predominantly White Canadians of European descent. The PCL-R consists of twenty items based on an individual's behavior and functioning over their lifetime (see Table 6.2). The initial version of the PCL-R described a 2-factor model for psychopathy (interpersonal and affective, and social deviance), but Hare subsequently expanded this model to include four facets, two within each factor (interpersonal, affective, lifestyle, and antisocial).

Early research on the PCL-R focused on comparisons between incarcerated samples of Black and White males, demonstrating considerable overlap in the correlates of PCL-R scores, but some differences in the factor structure of the scale and the salience of individual items. In fact, Fanti et al. (2018) concluded

Table 6.2 PCL-R items, facets, and factors

Factor 1 (Interpersonal/Affective)		Factor 2 (Social Deviance)	
Facet 1 (Interpersonal)	**Facet 2 (Affective)**	**Facet 3 (Lifestyle)**	**Facet 4 (Antisocial)**
• Superficial charm • Grandiose sense of self-worth • Pathological lying • Manipulative	• Lack of remorse • Shallow affect • Callous/lack of empathy • Failure to accept responsibility	• Need for stimulation • Parasitic lifestyle • Lack of realistic, long-term goals • Impulsivity • Irresponsibility	• Poor behavioral controls • Early behavioral problems • Juvenile delinquency • Revocation of conditional release • Criminal versatility

Items not included in factors
• Promiscuous sexual behavior
• Many short-term marital relationships

[13] In the case of sexual offending, this association appears to be indirect, mediated by the presence of deviant sexual arousal (Hawes et al., 2013).

that "the commonly recognized dimensions of psychopathy may not manifest similarly in African American and European American samples" (p. 537). For example, Thornquist and Zuckerman (1995) found a significant association between psychopathy ratings and impulsivity in non-Latine White adults in the US, but no such associations for Black or Latine individuals. Similarly, Walsh (2013) found expected levels of predictive validity for the PCL-R among Black and non-Latine White adults with a history of criminal offending, but no significant association in Latine adults. Some research has attributed these differences to a moderating influence of socioeconomic status (e.g., Walsh & Kosson, 2007), but research has provided inconsistent support for this explanation. Nevertheless, despite some potential differences, associations between psychopathy and renewed violent and/or criminal behavior have been largely similar across racial-ethnic groups, supporting the relevance of this instrument for risk assessment in North America and Western Europe.

What is less clear is the extent to which psychopathy manifests differently in cultures beyond North America and Western Europe. To be sure, anecdotal accounts have described psychopathic individuals in a wide range of settings, including African and Indigenous North American tribes (Murphy, 1976). However, systematic research on psychopathy in non-Western samples has been much less common. Data from non-Western countries (e.g., Brazil, Bulgaria, Burundi, Ecuador, Iran) have provided support for some elements of the psychopathy construct but offer little evidence of its predictive utility. Neumann et al. (2012) analyzed self-report psychopathy ratings in a sample of more than 30,000 individuals from 58 countries. They concluded that the factor structure of psychopathy ratings was generally consistent across the world, but their methodology precluded the identification of specific cultural or linguistic differences, as they collapsed highly diverse countries into broad regional categories (North America, Central/South America, Northern Europe, Eastern Europe, Southern Europe, Middle East, Africa, Oceania, South/Southeast Asia, and East Asia). Moreover, despite some promising findings, very little research has addressed the utility of psychopathy ratings in the primary domain where it is believed to be relevant: risk assessment. In their sample of 113 Korean offenders who had completed a prison sentence and/or term of probation, Lee and Kim (2010) found that PCL-R scores were modestly but significantly correlated with recidivism ($r = .22$; AUC = .67). Not surprisingly, this association was largely driven by the Lifestyle and Antisocial facets (i.e., Factor 2 of the PCL-R; $r = .25$) rather than Interpersonal and Affective facets (Factor 1; $r = .09$), a finding that has consistently emerged in research with North American and European samples. Folino (2015) assessed the predictive utility of the PCL-R in an Argentinian sample of 153 males who had been released from prison following criminal convictions. These authors also observed better predictive validity for the Lifestyle and

Antisocial facets for both general and violent recidivism (AUCs between .60 and AUC = .64) compared to the Interpersonal and Affective facets (AUCs between .51 and .53). A prospective study by Schmid et al. (2025) evaluated the predictive validity of the PCL-R in predicting institutional violence among incarcerated adults in Mexico. The PCL-R total score and Factor 2 demonstrated strong predictive accuracy for institutional violence during the first three months after the assessment (AUC = .74), whereas Factor 1 showed much weaker predictive utility (AUC = .58). In short, while the construct of psychopathy appears to be relatively consistent across cultures, existing research suggests that the predictive utility of this construct is largely due to items reflecting behavioral problems rather than the Interpersonal and Affective aspects. Moreover, the extent to which measures of psychopathy need to be adapted to better account for cultural differences in the expression of this construct is still largely unknown, as is the extent to which it adds to the identification of individuals at high risk for future criminal or violent behavior, particularly in the context of a more thorough risk assessment (e.g., the HCR-20).

Revisiting the Vignette

The vignette raised the question of whether a violence risk assessment should, or must, be tailored to an individual's cultural background and context. While the absence of robust cross-cultural research in this area poses challenges, evaluators cannot overlook the potential influence of culture and context on risk factors and interpretations. There is certainly a benefit to considering culturally specific risk factors, but evaluators must remain cautious about overgeneralizing findings from populations for whom these tools were not developed, and where their use has not been adequately studied. The absence of research should not preclude consideration of well-established risk factors; however, this consideration should include questioning whether the available information is sufficient to inform important clinical-legal decisions. For example, does the apparent absence of any known history of violence or criminal behavior convey a lower risk of future violence? Or could such a history exist that is not known to the evaluator?

Consultation with mental health professionals familiar with Jordanian culture, or the Middle East more generally, might also help the evaluator to identify and consider risk factors that are potentially relevant. For example, the internet postings that gave risk to police surveillance may be benign in light of the individual's religion or cultural background—or could reflect an advanced degree of "radicalization" and the potential of a serious threat. Alternatively, despite the defendant's middle-class upbringing, the strict and often abusive practices reportedly employed by Jordanian police may have instilled such fear of the police that his behavior seems understandable. While a tool such as the HCR-20 (or another tool more specifically geared toward terroristic threat assessment, if warranted by the referral question) might be a useful starting point, these tools must be used with an understanding of the cultural and systemic influences that may shape the examinee's behavior to better inform risk management and intervention. Additional considerations are no doubt worth exploring to identify factors that might increase or decrease an individual's level of risk.

Moreover, even when rigorous cross-cultural measures are available, the evaluator should consider whether context might impact the importance of these risk factors. For instance, while research conducted in the Middle East may highlight region-specific risk factors, these findings may not always apply to individuals who have migrated and now live in a different cultural and legal system. Would research conducted in the Middle East accurately reflect the importance of these same risk factors for individuals living in the US (where the risk would presumably take place)? It is easy to envision risk factors that might have relevance in one part of the world, under particular circumstances, that are less salient when that individual is located in a completely different context. Hence, cross-cultural adaptations and contextual considerations are crucial, particularly when applying tools developed for use in Western populations to individuals from other regions. For example, while research on adults in a Mexican prison is a useful starting point for identifying culturally specific risk factors, this research may not accurately reflect the utility of those risk factors for Mexican adults living in the US or Canada. Evaluators must carefully assess the validity of risk factors and tools within the specific cultural and environmental context of the examinee.

Summary and Recommendations

As is evident from the preceding pages, the potential for biased or incomplete assessment of risk is substantial when evaluating individuals from culturally diverse backgrounds, even when they are born and raised in the same country as the evaluator. Although risk assessment tools are increasingly used around the world, very little research has sought to identify culturally specific risk or protective factors that might impact (or improve) the accuracy and utility of existing tools. Likewise, there are potential sources of bias that should be considered even when evaluating individuals from culturally and linguistically diverse backgrounds within the countries where risk assessment research has typically been conducted, such as the US, Canada, Australia, and Europe. For example, sociopolitical factors, such as systemic discrimination in policing practices and criminal sanctions, economic disadvantages, and the enduring effects of colonization and trauma, may inflate perceptions of risk in minoritized individuals. There are no simple solutions to this challenge, but evaluators are encouraged to research possible sources of bias, identify any culturally relevant risk and protective factors (or manifestations of known risk factors), and consider the extent to which available risk assessment tools are adequate for guiding risk judgments in the individual they are tasked with evaluating. Although the flexibility of SPJ assessment tools provides evaluators with the opportunity to incorporate idiosyncratic risk or protective factors into their analyses, identifying these factors can be a challenging task.

- **Consider the examinee's cultural and social background**: Gather information about the examinee's social and cultural context related to the problematic behavior.
    - Consider whether collateral sources of information can help contextualize the examinee's behavior; interviews with family members, community leaders, or culturally knowledgeable professionals can provide invaluable information.
    - Assess systemic and contextual influences such as discrimination, socioeconomic challenges, and historical trauma that may affect the examinee's actions, both historically and in the future.
    - Verify the consistency of information elicited by considering multiple sources of collateral information to reduce the risk of misinterpretation or bias.
    - Reflect on how sociopolitical factors (e.g., criminalization of poverty, racialized surveillance, colonization) may influence both the behaviors being assessed and the systems responding to them.
- **Select the appropriate approach for structuring the risk assessment**: Determine the most appropriate approach and/or instrument for the specific risk assessment context.
    - Evaluate the empirical support for the available tools relative to the specific cultural context, setting, and referral question.
    - Consider whether tools may be biased in light of the examinee's personal or cultural background, while recognizing that not all cultural differences necessarily indicate bias.
    - Adapt tools when appropriate by incorporating cultural and contextual considerations into their application or risk formulation to improve relevance and cultural responsiveness.

  - Where applicable document how cultural and contextual adaptations were made, and note any limitations related to generalizability or validation in the specific population.

- **Identify and incorporate culturally specific risk or protective factors**: Identify culturally specific factors to increases the evaluator's ability to consider the full range of influences on the examinee's background and behavior.

  - When feasible, cultural experts or mental health professionals with expertise or who share the examinee's background can provide insights into unique risk or protective factors.
  - Incorporate culturally relevant protective factors, such as family ties, community support, or spiritual beliefs, into the risk formulation to provide a balanced assessment.
  - Consider the interaction between cultural factors and systemic influences, such as the impact of colonization or acculturative stress.

- **Develop risk management strategies tailored to cultural context**: Are there culturally relevant risk-reduction strategies that may be particularly useful—or unhelpful, given the examinee's unique socio-cultural background?

  - Identify culturally appropriate risk-reduction strategies and feasibility of intervention approaches to ensure they are culturally responsive.
  - Incorporate cultural strengths and resources into risk management plans to enhance their effectiveness.
  - If applicable, monitor and adjust interventions over time to ensure they remain responsive to the examinee's evolving needs and circumstances.

- **Acknowledge and mitigate bias in risk assessments**: Be mindful of the potential for bias in risk assessments and take proactive steps to mitigate it.

  - Consider the impact of systemic discrimination on perceptions of risk and evaluate how historical or ongoing inequities may influence the assessment.
  - Avoid over-reliance on static factors that may disproportionately impact marginalized groups, and balance these with dynamic and protective factors.

  - Use of structured professional judgment tools can facilitate the incorporation of unique cultural considerations that are not considered in actuarial instruments.
  - Reflect on and challenge personal biases to ensure they do not inadvertently influence risk evaluations or recommendations.

- **Reflect on ethical challenges in culturally responsive risk assessments**: Ensure that evaluations balance cultural responsivity with objective forensic standards.

  - Engage in training or consultation to address evaluator biases.
  - Consult with experts or colleagues if/when ethical dilemmas arise.
  - Document the rationale for decisions involving cultural considerations to maintain transparency and accountability.
  - When systemic inequities limit available options or services, explicitly note these barriers in the report to support advocacy for appropriate resources.

7
Assessment of Children and Families

Summary

This chapter reviews cultural issues that relate to three main areas of family law: child custody, evaluations of potential child abuse, and termination of parental rights. We emphasize the importance of understanding family structure, cultural norms, and sociopolitical factors in conducting culturally sensitive evaluations as they pertain to each of these evaluation contexts. Specifically, the chapter highlights research that impacts the evaluation and decision-making processes, and underscores the importance of considering culturally appropriate interventions when working with children, adolescents, and families. Psychological test use in the context of family-based evaluations, along with ethical considerations in conducting culturally sensitive evaluations and research in this area are also discussed.

Case Vignette

Tina J was referred for an evaluation of her risk of committing future child abuse in conjunction with a petition to terminate her parental rights. Ms. J is a 28-year-old, unmarried, cisgendered Jamaican–American female who has lived in the US since age 10. She has two sons, who were 7 and 9 years old at the time of the evaluation. She had been living in subsidized public housing with her sons and her mother with a physical disability, working sporadically as a home health aide. Approximately 11 months before the evaluation, Ms. J's younger son reported to his first-grade teacher that his mother had beaten him after he spilled food at the dinner table. The teacher subsequently reported possible child maltreatment, including both child abuse and medical neglect. Following an investigation, this allegation was "substantiated" by the child welfare agency, and the two children were placed in foster care. Roughly 6 months after their placement, the agency began proceedings to terminate Ms. J's parental rights and allow the foster family to adopt the children.

Cultural and Linguistic Considerations in Forensic Mental Health Assessment. Barry Rosenfeld and Alicia Nijdam-Jones, Oxford University Press. © Oxford University Press (2026).
DOI: 10.1093/9780190900991.003.0007

The agency cited Ms. J's resistance to interventions, including mandatory parenting classes, and "difficult" behavior during supervised visits (e.g., arguments with the supervising case worker).

During the evaluation, Ms. J expressed considerable mistrust of the child welfare system, referencing her own experiences as both a parent and as a child herself. She repeatedly characterized the system as racist and specifically identified the caseworker assigned to supervise her family visits as being hostile and judgmental. She added that when she was a child, her mother had also been accused of maltreatment and neglect, asserting that her mother's poverty and disability had been misinterpreted as neglect. She recalled having been placed in foster care for roughly 3 years. She cited her suspicion of both the child welfare agency and the health care system more generally in justifying her failure to seek medical treatment for her children when they were ill. Available records confirmed her report that neither of her sons had experienced any serious medical problems beyond minor illnesses or injuries, but that both were somewhat undernourished and periodically described by their teachers as disheveled and wearing dirty, tattered clothing. In addition, Ms. J acknowledged (and available records substantiated) a history of crack cocaine use before the birth of her oldest son, along with several prior arrests for prostitution and possession of narcotics; she had no record of arrests since the birth of her oldest son.

The evaluator, while recognizing the potential influence of poverty and past experiences with systemic discrimination and racism on both Ms. J's behavior, expressed concern about possibly normalizing problematic and potentially harmful behaviors that could reflect genuine risk factors for future abuse and maltreatment. What steps can the evaluator take to balance the competing goals of protecting the long-term welfare of the two children without ignoring the possible role of systemic influences on these putative risk factors? What would an antiracist approach to this evaluation look like?

Cultural influences, whether pertaining to minoritized individuals within their country of origin or those who identify with culturally or linguistically diverse groups from another part of the world, can inject a unique set of challenges into the assessment of children and families. This chapter focuses on settings in which the forensic evaluation of children and families arises with some regularity, including child custody evaluations, assessment of risk for abuse and maltreatment, and the termination of parental rights. Because each of these evaluation settings focuses, at least in part, on issues related to parenting, understanding cultural practices, values, and norms can play a critical role in

We express our sincere appreciation to Jonathan Gould for his invaluable feedback on an earlier version of this chapter.

evaluating the family structure and parenting styles that can influence these assessments.

As with any assessment that invokes cultural considerations, the forensic evaluator must approach family-based assessments with respect for the cultural background of all participants (i.e., with cultural humility) while simultaneously distinguishing culturally normative family dynamics from those that are not. There are multiple reasons why working with families can be complicated, including the sensitive and potentially stigmatizing nature of the legal cases and the frequent cultural belief that family matters should stay within the family or community. Therefore, evaluators are encouraged to be particularly sensitive to and respectful of the individual's (and family's) values and preferences while still gathering the information needed to complete a thorough evaluation.

This chapter reviews several essential considerations in the assessment of children and families, including cultural differences in family structure and parenting styles, the impact of acculturation on child-caregiver dynamics, and the role of family and culture in child development. Whereas all forensic evaluations require a consideration of the individual being evaluated, this chapter expands that focus to include the *family's* cultural background and origins (both immediate and extended), the context(s) in which family members were born and raised, and the nature of acculturation for all relevant parties. Understanding cultural models of parenting used by grandparents can also clarify how parenting practices have shaped those being evaluated, including their perception of parent roles and what is viewed as normative within their cultural groups across generations. Specific considerations in child sexual abuse, child custody, and termination of parental rights are also discussed. Although we use the term *parents* throughout this chapter, we acknowledge the broad diversity of family structures and caregivers in households and that not all evaluated families will align with the stereotypical two-parent household.

Family Structure and Parenting Styles

Historically, parenting styles and practices refer to observable behavior that parents and caregivers use in interactions with their children. Research has typically used two dimensions to describe parenting practices: parental control and parental support. Parental control is characterized as the behavioral (e.g., demands, supervision, rewards/punishments) or psychological (e.g., manipulation of thoughts and feelings) methods a caregiver implements to manage and regulate a child's behavior (Barber, 1996). On the other hand, parental support is the extent to which parents are involved, accepting, emotionally available, warm, and responsive to their children (Cummings et al., 2000). It may already be evident from these descriptions that cultures vary tremendously in the nature of parental control and the extent to which "support" is defined by the qualities listed.

Parenting styles have been further delineated into four main approaches to parenting: authoritative, authoritarian (or disciplinarian), permissive (or indulgent), and neglectful (or uninvolved) (see Figure 7.1; Baumrind, 1971; Macoby & Martin, 1983). These approaches differ in the extent to which they place demands or expectations on the child and in their responsiveness to the child's needs or problems (Macoby & Martin, 1983). Demandingness refers to the extent to which parents exert control over, or have expectations of their children's behavior, whether in academic, social, or athletic settings. In contrast, responsiveness relates to the degree to which parents are sensitive (or attuned to), warm, and accepting of their children's psychological and developmental needs, such as recognizing when a child is overwhelmed, and modulating their expectations in response to that recognition (versus forcing the child to "tough it out"). Authoritative parenting is characterized by high levels of demandingness and high levels of warmth and responsiveness, and is the most common parenting preference in North America. In contrast, authoritarian parenting is characterized by high levels of demandingness, typically expressed through power, but low levels of responsiveness to the child's emotional needs. This often presents as parents who have high expectations of their children, expect strict obedience,

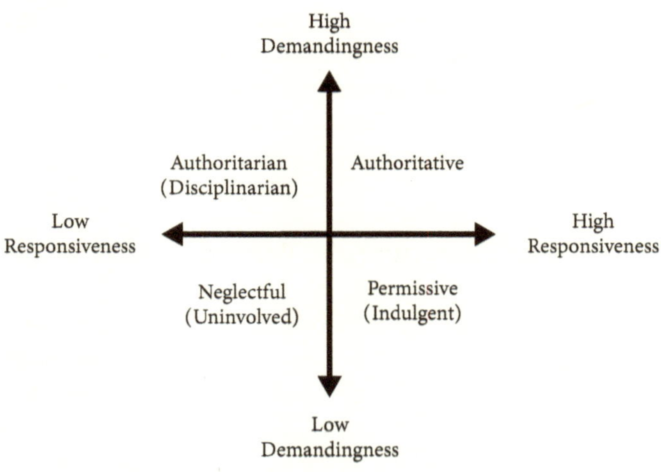

Figure 7.1 Parenting styles

Note. Adapted from Baumrind (1971) and Maccoby & Martin (1983). Expressions and impacts of parenting styles may vary across cultural contexts

and use coercive power tactics. Permissive parenting falls at the other extreme, with emotionally responsive but undemanding parents who typically impose few rules or boundaries on their children. Neglectful parenting is characterized by low demandingness and low responsiveness, resulting in parents with limited involvement in their children's development. Although this model is often conceptualized as categorical, both dimensions (demandingness and responsiveness) are clearly continuous variables, with individual parents falling along these two continuums. Moreover, parents may also exhibit differential levels of demandingness and responsiveness toward different children, whether because of gender norms (e.g., higher expectations of boys than girls) or differential abilities (e.g., nurturing and accepting of a disabled child's limitations while placing demands on a more able child).

Perhaps not surprisingly, these parenting models vary substantially across cultural groups, not only in terms of how they are expressed by parents, but the extent to which parents fit these models of parenting "types" and the association between the impact of parenting styles and child behaviors. For example, some cultural norms emphasize independence and value personal desires over those of the group, whereas others prioritize cohesion and the family's needs over individual interests. This distinction mirrors the individualist-collectivist distinction or continuum that is sometimes applied to cultures. Parents from a culture that values the community over the individual will more frequently emphasize a person's responsibility to their family, as opposed to the idiocentric norm more highly valued by parents from cultures that emphasize individualism and focus on the child's movement toward autonomy throughout development.

A substantial research literature has focused on differences in parenting styles based on cultural or contextual factors. However, it should be obvious that this simple typology does not fully capture many of the complex and potentially relevant behaviors that characterize cross-cultural differences in parenting practices (Choi et al., 2013; Domènech Rodriguez et al., 2009). For instance, research from North America has typically demonstrated better outcomes for children raised by authoritative parents compared to authoritarian or overly permissive parents (e.g., less externalizing behaviors, better mental health, and academic outcomes; Park et al., 2010). However, Middle Eastern and Asian families are often described as more authoritarian and cite the need to ensure that children grow up to display the discipline and toughness necessary to thrive in a challenging or highly competitive environment (Chao & Tseng, 2002). One study of Canadian families found that higher levels of "parental harshness" were associated with more child behavioral problems for Canadian families of European descent, but lower levels of child behavioral problems for families who had emigrated from South Asia (Ho et al., 2008). Similarly, an authoritarian parenting style might be more beneficial for young children of inner city families when concerns exist regarding a need for toughness in a challenging environment (Ali & Frederickson, 2011).

Despite these broad generalizations, parenting practices and expectations vary, particularly as children age, and often require parents to accommodate their parenting styles to changes in the needs of the child. For example, in many Asian cultures, children under six are typically given considerable latitude, with little expectation that they will obey rules or adhere to expected norms, but these expectations are strictly enforced with older children. In their study of the role of culture in Indonesian parenting practices, Riany et al. (2017) described the phenomena of *during ngerti*, which reflects the belief that children under six cannot understand behavioral expectations and therefore should not be punished for misbehavior. They note that similar beliefs are common in many Asian countries, including Japan, China, and India. Hence, parenting styles may not be as fixed as researchers often assume, necessitating an awareness of the relationship between one's immediate and cultural context to understand the unique family dynamics and parenting styles in culturally diverse families.

Cultural norms also impact parents' involvement with their children. Capps et al. (2010) studied Chinese and Mexican immigrant fathers, finding different engagement patterns between those whose cultural background emphasized the father's role as primarily providing discipline (more common in Chinese immigrant fathers) versus those who perceived their role as teachers and caregivers (more common among Mexican immigrant fathers). This may reflect norms that emphasize the disciplinary role to garner obedience and maintain harmony with their children (Hulei et al., 2006), as some Asian family structures are described as "strict father, kind mother" (Molenda-Kostanski, 2016). Thus, fathers who adhere to a strict cultural role of authoritarian fatherhood may spend limited time with their children unless they need to discipline or control their child's behavior (Julian et al., 1994; Lin & Fu, 1990).

The concept of "childhood" and how children are expected to interact with the world around them also differs across families and cultures, which may in turn impact parenting practices (Cacuci et al., 2021). In cultures that value collectivism, families typically emphasize group interactions and well-being, and therefore may strictly enforce the expectation that their children respect group rules and authority. Even as adults, grown children in many such cultures are expected to be deferential to their parents as repayment for having raised them (Riany et al., 2017). In short, these cultural norms can influence perceptions and values regarding a child's role in the family and can impact how they discuss or even disclose family matters, such as abuse or maltreatment.

Family Acculturation

As with culturally responsive evaluations of an individual, assessment of a family unit requires considering the entire family's pattern of acculturation. However, in addition to acculturation, many immigrant families also engage in *enculturation*, the process by which they learn and maintain their own cultural ways (Gonzales et al., 2008). Enculturation and acculturation are orthogonal processes in that more acculturation to the adopted country does not require less enculturation–or the reverse. Distinguishing acculturation and enculturation is crucial to the assessment of children and families because differences in acculturation may provide insight into the extent to which the specific family values reflect their cultural heritage versus those of the dominant local culture or idiosyncratic beliefs and values that are unique to the family. For example, in some Asian American families, fathers are often expected to provide economic support for their family and frequently maintain traditional patriarchal roles, holding values that may differ from what is (or has become) culturally normative in communities that value individualism. However, acculturation may also change the way fathers interact with their children. One study of Asian American fathers found that more acceptance of the adopted culture was associated with higher levels of other forms of parental involvement, such as teaching responsibility, school encouragement, support of the child's mother, spending time and talking together, praise and affection, developing talents and future concerns, reading and homework support, and attentiveness (Molenda-Kostanski, 2016). Several studies examining the impact of acculturation on parenting values and practices have highlighted the utility of language proficiency as a metric for acculturation, in contrast to the length of residence in the US (e.g., Cabrera et al., 2006). For example, Capps et al. (2010) found that English language use and proficiency among Chinese and Mexican immigrant fathers were positively associated with involvement in cognitively stimulating activities with their children, whereas the length of time living in the US was not.

The Role of Family, Culture, and Systems in Child Development

Bronfenbrenner's bioecological model (Bronfenbrenner & Morris, 2006), an evolution of his earlier ecological systems theory (1979), provides a framework for understanding the role of family and culture in child development. Within the forensic context, it can help evaluators situate the child within a broader web of relationships and social influences, organized across five interrelated systems (see Figure 7.2). At the center of the model is the child, whose behavior and outcomes are shaped by their genetic makeup, developmental factors, psychosocial history, and cultural and intersectional identities, such as their ethnicity, gender, socioeconomic status, disability, sexual orientation, religion, or immigration status. Surrounding the child in the first level is the microsystem, the set of environments and relationships that influence their daily life. These include the child's parents, siblings, teachers, peers, extended family, and health workers. The mesosystem is next, and it reflects the interactions among the different

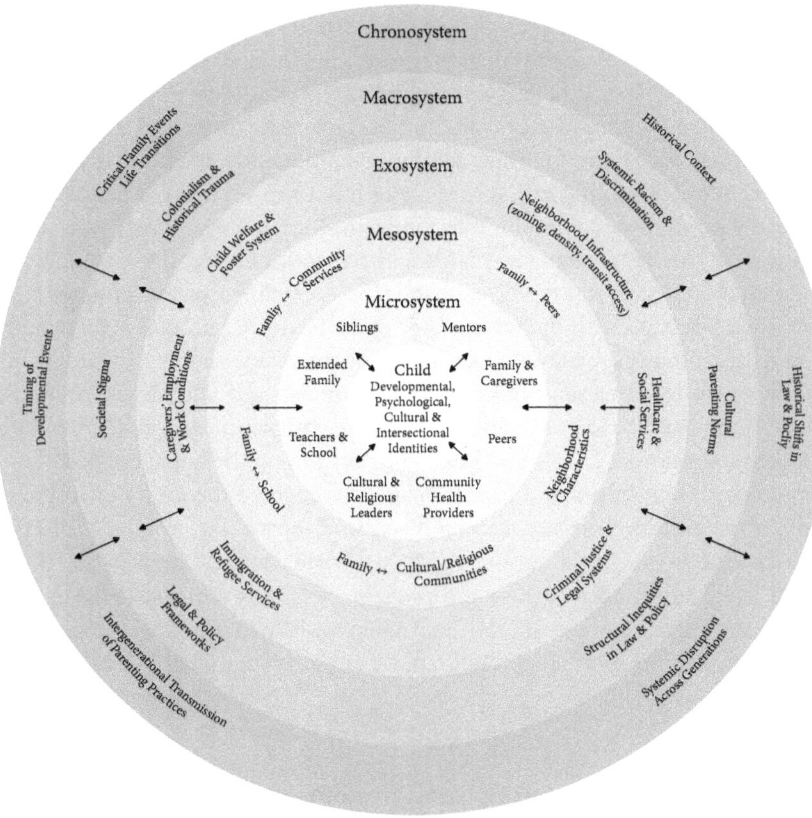

Figure 7.2 Biocological systems model for forensic assessment

Note. Adapted from Bronfenbrenner's bioecological model (Bronfenbrenner & Morris, 2006). This version centers on structural, cultural, and systemic factors relevant to culturally responsive forensic evaluations of children and families. The chronosystem reflects temporal influences across the lifespan and generations. Intersectionality is integrated across all layers, highlighting how systems of power and identity shape experiences at each ecological level (see also Vélez-Agosto et al., 2017).

microsystems, such as how the child's family, school, peers, religious or cultural leaders, and community-based health and service providers interact with each other. The third level is the exosystem, and it includes the broader structures that can impact the child's life more indirectly, such as their caregiver's work conditions, child welfare services, immigration or refugee supports, community-level healthcare and legal services, and neighborhood characteristics (e.g., physical and social infrastructure). Next, the macrosystem includes the overarching cultural attitudes, ideologies, and structural conditions that shape the other systems. These may consist of both explicit ideas about race, ethnicity, gender, and class as well as implicit beliefs about everyday life (e.g., norms around family roles, employment, consumption, or behavior). The macrosystem also encompasses both legal and policy frameworks, and the structural inequities embedded in how these systems are developed and applied. These inequities, which are reinforced through systemic racism, colonialism, discrimination, and intergenerational trauma, influence institutional practices and parenting norms across cultural contexts. Finally, the chronosystem represents time and cuts across all other systems. It includes historical events, social or environmental change, and life transitions, including the timing of developmental milestones and the cumulative effects of structural inequities unfolding across the lifespan and between generations.

Bronfenbrenner's framework can help evaluators conceptualize the range of factors, including cultural and ever-broader social contexts, that influence children and families, whether the focus of the evaluation is on custody determinations, assessment of child maltreatment, or any other relevant topic (see Vélez-Agosto et al., 2017 for a discussion on the integration of culture in this model). Fontes (2005, 2022) drew upon Bronfenbrenner's ecological systems theory to consider the role of culture in perpetuating child maltreatment, emphasizing the fact that the child's home and family are impacted by their cultural background (including, ethnicity, religion, ideologies), which in turn affects and is affected by proximal social systems including their neighborhood, employment or school, health providers and peers. These systems can help the evaluator understand the family dynamics that can influence an individual child and their family, including but not limited to the perpetration of child maltreatment. Clinicians are advised to both widen and narrow their focus to better understand how child abuse occurs within the context of multiple systems and consider the range of factors that can perpetuate or reduce the risk for child maltreatment (Fontes, 2022). The following pages review some of the more common forensic assessment settings involving children and families, highlighting cultural influences that can complicate these assessments.

Child Custody Evaluations

With the ever-growing diversification of most developed countries, the number of bicultural and multicultural families in the US, Canada, and Western European countries is steadily increasing. Of course, as the number of multicultural families grows, the number of separations or divorces among these families also increases. The number of children under 18 with immigrant parents has been increasing as well. In 1990, 13.4% of children in the US were from immigrant families, whereas by 2019, this number had risen to 25.8% (Migration Policy Institute, n.d.). Of course, even when families or individuals are born and raised in the country where the evaluation takes place, cultural factors may impact the extent to which the evaluator genuinely understands the range of influences that might be relevant to determining a child's "best interest."[1]

When conducting child custody evaluations with families or individuals from culturally and linguistically diverse backgrounds, it is critical to consider the families' social and cultural context and the legal and geographic context (Shear & Drozd, 2013). However, only a handful of US states have statutory provisions requiring evaluators and courts to consider culture in determining the child's best interest (Mabry, 2013). For example, the 2023 Minnesota statute on Custody and Support of Children on Judgment (Minn. Stat. § 518.17, 2023) identified a set of specific factors that the court should consider in custody decisions, two of which relate specifically to culture. These provisions reference "a child's physical, emotional, cultural, spiritual, and other needs, and the effect of the proposed arrangements on the child's needs and development" (Minn. Stat. § 518.17 Subd. 1(a)(1)). In addition, courts must consider "the willingness and ability of each parent to provide ongoing care for the child; to meet the child's ongoing developmental, emotional, spiritual, and cultural needs; and to maintain consistency and follow through with parenting time" (Minn. Stat. § 518.17 Subd. 1(a)(7)). This provision further notes that "there are many ways that parents can respond to a child's needs with sensitivity and provide the child love and guidance, and these may differ between parents and among cultures" (Minn. Stat. § 518.17 Subd. 1(b)(3)). Perhaps not surprisingly, these provisions were added after a custody dispute involving a multiracial family where both parents wanted their children to be exposed to and practice elements of their own cultural backgrounds (Mabry, 2013).

When disputes arise regarding child custody arrangements, mental health evaluations are often relied on to gauge each parent's ability to meet the unique

[1] A thorough discussion of the "best interest" standard is beyond the scope of this chapter. The interested reader is directed to other authoritative sources (e.g., Emery et al., 2005; Gould & Martindale, 2007).

needs of the child. There are several resources available to inform clinicians of the best practices for child custody evaluations, including the American Academy of Child and Adolescent Psychiatry (AACAP) Practice Parameters for Child Custody Evaluation (Herman, 1997), the American Psychological Association (APA) Guidelines for Child Custody Evaluations in Family Law Proceedings (APA, 2022), and the Association of Family Conciliation Courts (AFCC) Guidelines for Parenting Plan Evaluations in Family Law Cases (AFCC, 2022). Although not always necessary, psychological testing is also a common element of these evaluations (Chiu, 2014), highlighting the need to select measures with sufficient validity for the individual's cultural background. Although a wide range of instruments exist that are potentially informative, multiscale instruments such as the MMPI are commonly used (see Chapter 4 for a more thorough discussion of these instruments, and in particular, issues related to the available normative data). Several specialized instruments have also been developed or adapted for use in custody evaluations, such as the Child Behavior Checklist (CBCL) (Achenbach & Rescorla, 2001). While few of these measures have been adapted for cross-cultural use, the CBCL has been translated into multiple languages and adapted for numerous cultural contexts (e.g., Spanish, Arabic, Korean, Turkish; Dumenci et al., 2004; Wild et al., 2012; Yunis et al., 2007). However, the relevance of tools like the CBCL for custody determinations is far from clear, as identification of behavioral problems in a child says little about a parent's ability to provide an adequate environment for that child.

The APA's Guidelines for Child Custody Evaluations highlight the importance of a multimodal assessment approach to inform the analysis and synthesize data collected. In cases where the psychologist may be insufficiently familiar with the family's cultural or ethnic background, they are encouraged to engage in culturally informed, non-discriminatory evaluation practices, seek peer consultation, and review relevant research (Guideline 6; APA, 2022). As described in previous chapters, this research should begin in advance of the evaluation. Identifying topics that warrant discussion can be critical to conducting an adequate interview, and many potentially important issues may be identified during pre-evaluation research and consultation. For example, child custody evaluators must be aware of and consider the significance that culture and religion play in the family's life (AFCC, 2022; Herman, 1997). Similarly, evaluators should consider the availability of resources in the family's community (both current and proposed, if applicable) and the importance of these factors (religious, cultural, and community) to the child's developmental growth. Not surprisingly, these issues are significant and often far more complex when parents have different cultural backgrounds (Herman, 1997). Furthermore, evaluators should recognize that ongoing research or consultation may be needed as the evaluation progresses, particularly if unexpected considerations emerge during initial interviews.

Given the importance of understanding the parents' cultural heritage and beliefs, an evaluation should also include an analysis of how the parents have previously navigated any differences in cultural parenting practices (e.g., parental roles and responsibilities, intergenerational processes)—and the degree to which these arrangements were satisfactory or successful. Not surprisingly, disputes over cultural and parenting practices may be the source of many of the conflicts leading to divorce (and custody disputes), so gauging the strength of not only the parents' preferences but the extent to which other members of their respective culture share those preferences may help differentiate reasonable versus unreasonable expectations. Likewise, the evaluator should also examine how parents have engaged in parenting post-separation and whether those practices are consistent with or different from the parenting model used when the parents were together.

Understanding the child's (or children's) needs is another critically important aspect of a culturally informed evaluation, whether those needs are unique to the specific child (e.g., special needs) or are common to most children of their age and culture. Depending on age and developmental stage, children may feel a strong connection to their family's culture but are nevertheless affected by external factors such as their peer group. The child's acculturation, as well as that of the parents, also requires consideration, as it is not uncommon for children to be far more assimilated into the dominant cultural context than their parents. Moreover, differing acculturation patterns may impact both child and parent preferences, perhaps leading to diverging goals and interests.

Mabry (2013) developed a checklist for judges and lawyers to consider when reviewing custody cases, highlighting a range of cultural factors that should be considered in decision-making. Adapted for forensic mental health evaluators, the following factors highlight cultural and religious issues relevant to assessing each parent's capacity to meet the child's developmental and cultural needs, the availability of community supports, and the potential impact of systemic influences on parenting and decision-making (see Table 7.1):

When relocation may be an outcome for the child, the emotional and psychological impact of an international or domestic move must also be assessed (see Austin, 2016, for a thorough discussion of these issues). These cases arise when an expatriate spouse finds themselves alone in their ex-partner's culture or country after separation, perhaps impacting their professional opportunities and economic independence.[2] Evaluators should consider how changes in place (the

[2] This situation is most readily apparent when a partner immigrates to the US for the relationship, or the reverse, when a partner emigrates or moves abroad to their partner's home country.

Table 7.1 Culturally and religiously relevant factors in child custody evaluation

- Opportunities for cultural and religious experiences in the parent's community
- Opportunities to interact with extended family members and community members
- Exposure to heritage, language, and traditions within the home
- Each parent's ability to meet the child's cultural, spiritual, and linguistic needs
- Each parent's willingness to support and educate the child in the other parent's culture or religion
- Each parent's practices and whether they are consistent with those typical of their cultural group
- The child's cultural, spiritual, and religious preferences (as developmentally appropriate)
- The parent's preferences and how they have negotiated cultural differences historically
- A parent's cultural or familial ties to another country or region
- The likelihood of international relocation or abduction related to cultural identity fulfilment
- The impact of cultural beliefs and values on parenting styles and discipline practices
- The child's ability to adapt to or cope in a different cultural environment
- The influence of systemic or external factors (e.g., discrimination, immigration status, economic barriers)
- The degree of acculturation and enculturation differences between parents and their impact on family functioning
- Availability of culturally congruent community, spiritual, or language supports in each parent's environment
- The presence of protective cultural or community mechanisms that promote stability and resilience
- The potential impact of prioritizing one parent's cultural identity on a bicultural or multicultural child

Note: Adapted from Mabry (2013), expanded to reflect systemic, acculturation, and resilience factors described in this chapter.

destination country, neighborhood, and social-cultural milieu) may impact the child's relationships and experiences (Shear & Drozd, 2013), perhaps limiting opportunities for the child to maintain a connection to the cultural roots of one or both parents. The extent to which cultural resources are equally available may be an important consideration, and jurisdictional differences may impact everything from the evaluation process to the factors that must be considered. Shear and Drozd (2013) encourage evaluators to assess the risks, benefits, specific

However, similar considerations can arise when partners are from markedly different regions of the same country, such as a parent from a small, rural town in the Midwestern US and another from an urban, coastal city.

provisions, and safeguards associated with each of three possible outcomes in a relocation case: cases in which the child either moves to a new community with the relocating parent, cases where the child stays with the parent remaining in the current community, or cases where the parents decide to stay in the same community and not relocate the child.

These considerations provide a broad overview of a highly complex and nuanced evaluation process. The range of possible influences of culture and religion on custody evaluations is extraordinarily wide, partly because these considerations apply to all involved parties (and may include grandparents or multiple siblings with different needs and preferences). Moreover, the stakes of these evaluations are high, sometimes leading to highly contentious outcomes. Hence, consultation with someone well-versed in the relevant cultures is often a critical step in conducting a thorough custody evaluation.

Child Abuse and Maltreatment

A second type of forensic mental health evaluation involving children and families involves allegations of child abuse and maltreatment. Although mental health professionals should not be asked to confirm the presence or absence of maltreatment,[3] several questions arise concerning the risk of continued abuse by individuals who have already been determined to have engaged in abuse or maltreatment. Allegations of abuse can also arise in the context of child custody evaluations, but are more common in the context of sexual abuse or foster care placements. An extension of this type of evaluation, addressed separately later in this chapter, involves the termination of parental rights.

Like child custody, evaluations conducted in the context of child protection also benefit from guidelines established by professional organizations such as the APA (2013) and the AACAP (Kraus et al., 2011). While the guidelines promulgated by the APA are surprisingly silent on issues of cultural diversity (other than noting the potential for biases on the part of both evaluator and society more generally), the AACAP emphasizes the need for cultural competence on the part of the evaluator. Even so, the AACAP guidelines do not address issues such as cultural traditions that may condone, or at least complicate, the assessment of child maltreatment, focusing instead on issues such as the need to consider whether parents will support the child's involvement in cultural traditions.

[3] While we recognize that forensic mental health professionals may be asked to render opinions on whether abuse or maltreatment has occurred, we consider these decisions to be legal determinations that should be made by the trier of fact (e.g., a court or administrative body).

Of course, some forms of child maltreatment are unequivocal regardless of the cultural background of the child or parent. For example, female genital mutilation continues to have some support among some communities in parts of Africa, the Middle East, and Southeast Asia (Ayenew et al., 2024; United Nations International Children's Emergency Fund, 2024), even when it is illegal. The extent to which this practice is accepted varies dramatically, both within and across countries. Nevertheless, because female genital mutilation is illegal in virtually all countries, and unambiguously so in Western countries where most forensic evaluations take place, it would clearly constitute a form of child abuse. Moreover, research has suggested that support for this practice is more common among women who acknowledge having physically assaulted their children, highlighting the link between genital mutilation and child maltreatment (Afifi & Von Bothmer, 2007).

Other than extreme examples, such as female genital mutilation, other forms of maltreatment, such as corporal punishment, present more complex challenges due to cultural variations in what forms of punishment are considered acceptable. Corporal punishment can take a range of forms, from striking or hitting a child with the hand to flogging, caning, or striking with belts or other objects. Several courts have noted variations in cultural values and beliefs regarding whether corporal punishment is an acceptable form of physical discipline for children. Nevertheless, some forms of corporal punishment have been banned in over sixty countries (Freeman, 2010). However, for families whose cultural heritage approves the use of corporal punishment, even some seemingly severe forms of punishment may still be viewed as acceptable and appropriate ways to discipline children. On the other hand, parenting behaviors that are relatively common in many North American cultures, such as isolating infants in their room to sleep, feeding a child on a strict schedule, or letting a child "cry it out," may be viewed as neglectful or harmful in many cultures, further demonstrating the importance of culture in understanding parenting behaviors (Korbin, 1981). Because definitions of child abuse and neglect differ across cultures, evaluators must understand the cultural context in which allegations of abuse have arisen, including what disciplinary techniques are considered appropriate and whether these techniques are genuinely harmful (Renteln, 2010).

Jill Korbin, a cultural and medical anthropologist, noted that what may be perceived as maltreatment in many Western cultures may not actually cause harm to the child and may be culturally normative (Korbin, 1980, 1981). Korbin proposed three levels of analysis to assess child abuse or neglect cross-culturally. First, evaluators should determine whether the behaviors are perceived as acceptable in the family's heritage or culture, even if they are viewed as inappropriate or harmful in the dominant culture. Second, the evaluator should identify what constitutes child maltreatment in the family's own culture, to better contextualize the behavior in question and determine whether it deviates from culturally acceptable behavior in that community. Lastly, evaluators should understand the structural and societal factors that perpetuate child abuse and maltreatment, such as poverty or inadequate health care, nutrition, and housing. She concluded that understanding the parent's and family's beliefs and intentions around their behavior, as well as how the child perceives the actions, is critical to evaluating allegations of child maltreatment. These considerations do not mean that all culturally accepted methods of discipline or socialization are exempt from being labeled as child abuse or maltreatment, but investigating the cultural roots of the behaviors can better inform the legal system's response and identify appropriate interventions.

One example of questionable parenting behavior common to some Southeast Asian cultures is "coining" (*cao gio* or *cheut sah*), a folk medicine approach used to treat illnesses such as the common cold or influenza. This treatment involves putting oil on the body and using a coin to rub all over the body, often causing temporary bruising from burst blood vessels. Without an understanding of this cultural practice, the actions and resulting bruising could be perceived as child maltreatment (Davis, 2000), but given the intent and cultural context, this judgment would often be premature. On the other hand, reliance on coining for cases of severe medical illness (in lieu of available medical treatments) may constitute a form of medical neglect. Another example, common to some Latin American families, is the use of *hincar* as a form of discipline. This technique involves having the child kneel (bare-kneed) on uncooked rice for several minutes, typically causing significant pain. Although the indentations left by the rice are temporary, this form of discipline has typically been characterized as a form of physical abuse, even when utilized for short periods of time (Fontes & O'Neill-Arana, 2008). In short, rather than making blanket assumptions about behaviors, evaluators should consider several factors to inform decisions around whether unfamiliar culturally specific methods of discipline constitute child maltreatment, including the child's age, the severity and duration of the actions, and the overall frequency of punishment (see Table 7.2).

As evident from the opening vignette, cultural influences on child maltreatment cases are not limited to non-Western cultures. However, one must be aware that disproportionate involvement in child maltreatment proceedings often reflects systemic factors rather than behavioral or cultural characteristics. Minoritized groups in the US, Canada, and other Western countries are disproportionately involved in child maltreatment proceedings, despite research indicating that rates of abuse and maltreatment are roughly comparable across

Table 7.2 Factors to inform decisions about whether a culturally specific form of discipline constitutes child maltreatment

Factor	Considerations for Evaluators
1. Age of the child	Younger children have limited understanding of intent and consequences; developmental stage affects potential psychological and physical harm.
2. Frequency of the punishment	Occasional use may differ from a pattern of recurrent or escalating punishment.
3. Apparent physical and emotional effects of the punishment	Assess for injury, lingering pain, fear, or humiliation; note whether the child appears distressed or frightened.
4. Duration of the punishment	The length of time or repetition can transform a culturally normative act into abuse (e.g., being made to stand with arms outstretched for 5 minutes versus an hour).
5. Severity of the punishment	Consider degree of physical risk (e.g., burning, hitting with objects, forced ingestion of substances). Any act causing injury or serious pain constitutes maltreatment regardless of cultural origin.
6. Invasiveness of the punishment	Actions that interfere with essential bodily functions (e.g., eating, drinking, sleeping, toileting, or movement) are inherently abusive.
7. Intent and context	Evaluate the parent's intent (discipline vs. harm), awareness of potential impact, and availability of culturally endorsed alternatives.
8. Cultural meaning and community norms	Determine whether the practice reflects a broader cultural tradition or idiosyncratic belief, and whether community standards view it as acceptable or harmful.
9. Systemic and situational influence	Consider contextual stressors (e.g., poverty, migration, discrimination) that may contribute to parenting behaviors while maintaining focus on child safety.

Note: Adapted from Fontes and O'Neill-Arana (2008), expanded to incorporate developmental, contextual, and systemic factors consistent with the framework presented in this chapter.

racial and ethnic groups (e.g., Fluke et al., 2003; Putnam-Hornstein et al., 2013). Although some of the evidence for racial bias in child maltreatment evaluations and decision-making may be attributable to the confounding role of poverty, increasing research highlights racial and ethnic biases at various stages of the referral, evaluation, and decision-making process (e.g., Palusci & Botash, 2021).

Indeed, systemic racism and biases are so widely recognized in child welfare settings that any evaluation of parents or children must consider the extent to which historical abuses may impact the willingness of parents to both seek assistance when it might be available and to cooperate with proposed interventions when required (e.g., Miller et al., 2013). Evaluators must not only be aware of the potential role of ethnic or racial factors that influence systemic factors (e.g., the likelihood of an investigation being initiated or deemed "founded" against people of color), but also their own assumptions and biases. For example, a parent's rejection of proposed (or mandated) interventions may reflect cultural mistrust that is grounded in historical abuses rather than a lack of concern for or appreciation of potential negative consequences of not participating. Understanding these influences requires evaluators to critically examine how systemic biases shape racial and ethnic disparities in child welfare involvement. This includes recognizing how historical and structural inequalities impact attitudes and behaviors, while integrating knowledge of cultural norms, traditions, and values that may be relevant to the specific evaluation.

Child Sexual Abuse

A particularly challenging form of child maltreatment is child sexual abuse, which is defined as the intentional touching of a child for one's own sexual gratification. When incidents of child sexual abuse are identified, several questions may be asked of a mental health evaluator, including assessing the understanding and motivation of the perpetrator (who is often, but not always a family member), gauging the appropriateness of the family's response (e.g., in the context of child neglect or maltreatment evaluations), and helping determine what if any interventions are necessary for the child. Each of these questions requires consideration of cultural factors that may influence the perceptions and behaviors of the involved parties.

Although criminal prosecution for child sexual abuse is the typical response, interventions for individuals convicted of child sex abuse can vary dramatically based on the assessment of the perpetrator's understanding of their actions. Moreover, the influence of cultural factors on the risk for child sexual abuse has been increasingly recognized (Guerra et al., 2021). For example, culture may impede the reporting of child sexual abuse, as some cultures are reluctant to disclose the occurrence of child sexual abuse, particularly to the authorities (e.g., Baker & Dairy, 2003). It is important to note that while all forms of sexual abuse are prohibited, cultural factors may nonetheless influence the intent of sexual contact between family members and, by extension, the legal system's response.

In one notable case, the Supreme Court of Maine upheld an acquittal in a case where an Afghani refugee father was charged with sexual assault for kissing his infant son's penis (*State v. Kargar*, 1996). After an extensive investigation and trial, the Court determined that although the father violated the law, his actions were deemed a *de minimis* violation because there was no sexual gratification involved and because, culturally, "kissing a young child on every part of his body is considered a sign only of love and affection for the child" until the child becomes a toddler.

Some cultural traditions and norms may seem inappropriate to evaluators unfamiliar with them. For example, in some Persian-influenced cultures, it is common for women (e.g., grandmothers) to shower with the young boys in their families. This practice is thought to be grounded in the country's history. Indoor plumbing was uncommon even in the early 20th century, so bathing was communal and *hammams* (communal baths) were used in shifts based on gender. Because many children were raised by their grandmothers, young boys would be taken to bathe with older women until they were 6 to 9 years of age. Even after indoor plumbing became relatively common, the tradition of children bathing with grandmothers continued, although this practice may be less frequent now. In short, differentiating sexual versus non-sexual motives underlying ostensible sexual contact between adults and children can help determine the risk of further sexual contact and thereby play a critical role in decision-making.

Cultural factors can also protect children from sexual abuse, even when a family member is identified as being at risk for sexually offending or reoffending. Membership in cultural groups that are intolerant of adults who engage in sexual activity with children, those that highly value women and children, or have extended family and males directly involved in child-rearing can all serve as protective factors that reduce the risk of child sexual abuse (Fontes & Plummer, 2010). Additionally, close maternal relationships, social and cultural sanctions against sexual abuse, normative perceptions of children as non-sexual, encouragement of children's independence and ability to voice their needs, and socialization that discusses sexuality and consent are factors that can further decrease the risk of sexual victimization. The availability of other formal and informal resources for child protection also plays a crucial role in mitigating risk.

Barriers to Reporting Sexual Abuse

While reports of sexual victimization are not rare, numerous barriers may impact the willingness of children and family members to disclose child sexual abuse, some of which are based in culture. Fontes and Plummer (2010) cited shame, social taboos and modesty, sexual scripts, honor, respect, and patriarchy as factors that might inhibit disclosure of child sexual abuse. For example, while feelings of shame may be present across a wide range of cultures, it is especially salient in cultures where discussing sexuality is actively discouraged. Unfortunately, when a child from a culture that emphasizes shame does get the courage to disclose sexual abuse to an adult, they may not be believed or even accused of lying, further reinforcing feelings of shame and self-blame, which in turn may hinders efforts by an evaluator to understand the incident that gave rise to the evaluation (Gilligan & Akhtar, 2006; Gupta & Ailawaldi, 2005).

Religious beliefs may also prohibit discussions of sexual activity because of cultural norms that portray discussions of sexuality or an individual's body as taboo. Katzenstein and Fontes (2017) identified several religious and cultural groups that prohibit discussing transgressions outside of their community. Examples include the Mesira law in the Hassidic culture and the Jewish Orthodox value of Chillul Hashem, or Lashon Hara, which prohibit speech that could defame someone's image or esteem. Similarly, some Chinese cultures view family issues as private matters and believe that outsiders, including legal authorities, should not be involved (Xie et al., 2017). Additionally, the disclosure of sexual abuse may bring shame to the individual and family, and family members may be worried about how neighbors, friends, and community members will perceive the abused child. Part of what may drive feelings of shame are cultural taboos, combined with an emphasis on modesty, which Fontes and Plummer (2010) cite as a reason why sexual education in Puerto Rican families is largely nonexistent. Even if a child tries to avoid the perpetrator, being unable to discuss the actions and knowing that the topic is taboo often prevents disclosure. Moreover, the inability to receive needed help following abuse has been associated with a range of adverse outcomes, such as an inability to build trusting relationships and a higher likelihood of engaging in risky sexual behaviors, substance abuse, and even self-harm or suicide (Gupta & Ailawaldi, 2005).

Cultural beliefs around the importance of maintaining a girl's virginity may also impact whether a child will disclose sexual abuse, for fear of hindering their desirability as future brides. Among some communities where family honor and shame are associated with female sexual purity, family members may even engage in what are sometimes called "honor killings" of female family members who are perceived as being "damaged" or bringing disgrace upon their families, including women or girls who are victims of sexual assault (Gengler et al., 2021). Additionally, some cultural groups may accord greater status—and reliability—to males than females, which can lead to family members disbelieving girls who report that a male family member has sexually assaulted them.

Although these barriers may impede efforts to understand the nature and intent of reported sexual abuse, the forensic mental health evaluator should maintain an open, supportive, and objective stance toward the evaluation. Providing the victim or the abuser with an opportunity to engage in a candid and non-judgmental discussion can facilitate a more thorough and accurate evaluation. This information can also be critical to accurate assessments of the need for treatment (of both the perpetrator and the child), as well as gauging the risk of continued sexual offending.

Termination of Parental Rights

The termination of parental rights (TPR) is typically the last resort in cases of child maltreatment, as it has lasting impacts on all parties involved. Termination of parental rights is more common with younger children and may occur even before the child has developed a meaningful attachment to the biological parent(s). These cases arise when governmental child welfare agencies identify neglect or abuse that is sufficiently severe, or the risk of continued maltreatment is so high, that the child may need to be permanently removed from their biological parent's care. Termination severs any opportunity for reunification and places the child in foster care or an adoptive home. Grounds for terminating parental rights may involve a history of severe or chronic abuse or neglect of one or more children in the household, but can also be based on sexual abuse, child abandonment, parental incapacity (e.g., due to long-term, serious mental illness or substance use), or failure of the parent to provide support or maintain contact with the child. In 2016, it was estimated that parents of one in a hundred children in the US have had parental rights terminated before their child turned eighteen, a number that has doubled since 2000 (Wildeman et al., 2020).

In the US, TPR cases disproportionately affect traditionally marginalized and economically disadvantaged groups. In 2016, an estimated 3% of Indigenous American children, 1.5% of Black children, and 1% of White children were the subject of TPR findings that permanently removed them from further contact with their biological parent(s). These disparities are even more alarming when noting that Indigenous American families are less likely to undergo child welfare investigations than White families, but are nearly three times more likely to have their children placed into foster care and have parental rights terminated. Furthermore, despite the fact that rates of child maltreatment do not appear to differ across race in the US, Black and Indigenous children are significantly more likely to be placed in foster care. A study of children born in California in 2002 found that Black children were more than twice as likely as White children to be referred for maltreatment, have their cases substantiated, and enter foster care before age five (Putnam-Hornstein et al., 2013). These disparities persisted even after accounting for socioeconomic and health factors associated with child maltreatment and child protective services (CPS) involvement. Although considerable debate exists regarding the extent to which racial biases drive these disparities in rates of referral to CPS, placement in foster care, and TPR proceedings, it is clear that many of the risk factors for child maltreatment, such as poverty and incarceration, also differ by race.

Like custody evaluations, decisions around the termination of parental rights are grounded in the best interest of the child standard. In addition to considering the perceived threat of serious harm due to a caregiver's actions (e.g., physical or sexual abuse) or lack of actions (physical or emotional neglect), some jurisdictions also consider the length of time a child has been in foster care as one criterion for decision-making. Mental health professionals are periodically asked to evaluate children and/or parents to address referral questions related to TPR. These questions include assessing the caregiver's risk of continued abuse or neglect, their engagement and progress in interventions (and amenability to treatment more generally), and the child's current functioning. All of these questions can inform treatment or intervention needs and inform decisions about the risks and benefits of TPR.

Many of the cultural considerations already articulated in this chapter also apply to TPR evaluations. These include contextualizing the underlying behaviors in the family's cultural background to determine whether behaviors deemed abusive may be culturally accepted. In cases where problematic behaviors are culturally normative, the evaluator should consider the extent of harm caused, whether the parent(s) recognize that harm, and whether they indicate a willingness to modify their behaviors in accordance with prevailing legal standards. However, due to the overrepresentation of children from Indigenous and Black families, it is also critical to consider the impact of colonization and systemic racism and its effect on the families involved. Understanding the impact of historical trauma, colonization, and institutional practices that have impacted Indigenous and Black communities and destabilized families (Evans-Campbell, 2008) is critical in evaluating families in this context and informing culturally appropriate intervention recommendations.

Another important consideration in evaluating child maltreatment is the extent to which psychological testing can aid in these evaluations. Although several approaches have been developed and promoted, the accuracy of risk assessments intended to assist in gauging the level of risk has generated considerable controversy. Of note, many of the structured clinical judgment measures developed for child abuse risk assessments are best characterized as simple checklists of risk factors, lacking the comprehensive methodology of the well-established structured professional judgment (SPJ) tools described in the preceding chapter. Nevertheless, a meta-analysis by Van der Put and colleagues (2017) demonstrated significantly stronger predictive accuracy for actuarial measures compared to structured clinical judgment tools in gauging risk of renewed child maltreatment. It should be noted, however, that unlike the actuarial tools used in most violence risk assessments, child abuse risk assessment tools do not typically generate a probability of reoffending, but rather simply identify the number of risk factors. Of note, this review also concluded that tools intended to gauge the risk of recurrence were significantly weaker than those intended to screen the general population for risk of abuse (which is of little relevance in TPR evaluations). However, very few of these studies utilized samples from outside the US (e.g., the Netherlands and Japan), and only one, from Texas, focused squarely on Latine adults.

One instrument that is frequently used in child maltreatment assessments is the Child Abuse Potential Inventory (CAPI) (Milner & Wimberley, 1979). Like many child maltreatment risk assessment tools, the CAPI was developed to differentiate those at greater or lesser risk for child abuse. Multiple translations of the CAPI have been developed and published, including in Mandarin, Arabic, Spanish, Dutch, Thai, Japanese, Portuguese, Greek, Finnish, Turkish, and German (e.g., Al Abduwani et al., 2017; Milner & Crouch, 2012). However, while many of these studies have shown adequate ability to discriminate between abusive and non-abusive parents, little evidence exists for the predictive validity of the CAPI, or any other child maltreatment risk assessment tool, in forensic evaluations, in part because it has limited capacity to identify distorted or socially desirable responding.

Revisiting the Vignette

As evident from the chapter, many evaluations of child abuse and/or termination of parental rights must disentangle situational factors that might explain problematic parenting behaviors. In this vignette, little evidence is presented to suggest that the children have suffered significant physical harm, but the evaluator would certainly need to focus on assessing this risk. The evaluator must contextualize Ms. J's behavior to differentiate culturally normative behaviors, those influenced by poverty or systemic barriers, and actions that genuinely place the children at risk of harm. While establishing rapport in this evaluation may be challenging, a good clinical interview can also help the evaluator to better understand the mother's perspective.

To approach this evaluation using an antiracist lens, the evaluator should consider the role of systemic biases in shaping the current family's situation and the child welfare agency's actions. It would be beneficial to consult the literature or cultural experts to better understand how systemic factors, such as structural racism, economic inequality, and intergenerational trauma from the mother's own involvement in the child welfare system, might have influenced Ms. J and her actions, mistrust, and alleged hostility. It is critical to distinguish between these systemic influences and any personal characteristics (beyond socioeconomic factors) that may contribute to neglect and/or abuse. For example, the evaluator should inquire into her resistance to interventions (e.g., parenting classes), exploring whether cultural inappropriateness, accessibility issues, or systemic mistrust accounts for her lack of engagement. Identifying culturally safe intervention options might reduce her apparent resistance. Collateral contact with other family and friends of the mother (perhaps including previous employers) might also help elucidate whether personality or behavioral problems are potential contributing factors.

Assessing Ms. J's parenting strengths and protective factors is also necessary to ensure a balanced evaluation of her parenting capabilities. For instance, the evaluator might consider Ms. J's apparent resilience, her sobriety (if accurate), her lack of criminal involvement since the birth of her children, and any evidence that the children's basic medical needs have been met. Further, understanding the children's experiences and perspectives of Ms. J's parenting is crucial. Therefore, it would be important to assess their attachment to their mother, their developmental and cultural needs, and how placement may or may not align with these needs. Ultimately, this evaluation requires balancing the protection of the children's welfare with a culturally informed understanding of Ms. J's experiences. Incorporating cultural humility, focusing on strengths, and applying an antiracist lens will help ensure that recommendations are both equitable and effective.

Summary and Recommendations

Forensic evaluations of children and families are inherently complex because of the importance of the legal issues at hand and the multiple relationships that impact parent-child interactions. When cultural influences come into play, the evaluation becomes even more challenging. The examples in this chapter highlight many of the ways in which culture and systems can impact family structures and parenting styles, as well as the willingness to disclose child maltreatment or child sexual abuse. Working with culturally diverse families requires sensitivity, thoughtfulness, and centering the family using an ecological systems framework, which nests the individual child in the center of a complicated system of relationships and influences. We offer several recommendations based on the existing research and our clinical experience that can improve the quality and accuracy of forensic evaluations with families from culturally and linguistically diverse backgrounds:

- **Collect contextual cultural information**: Evaluate the family's cultural background, origins, social structures, and acculturation patterns to contextualize behaviors.

    - Where family members were born and raised, as well as their cultural background and acculturation, may impact family dynamics and parenting practices.
    - Examine intergenerational influences on parenting styles, including traditions, norms, and values passed down within the family.
    - Evaluate how parenting practices align with cultural norms, including differences in demandingness and responsiveness.
    - Assess the broader cultural models of parenting and the diverse values they encompass, including whether they emphasize communal responsibilities or prioritize individual autonomy.

- **Evaluate social and culturally specific risk and protective factors**: Integrate into the evaluation specific social and cultural factors that influence risk and protective mechanisms to ensure a balanced and accurate understanding.

    - Identify protective mechanisms such as extended family networks, community support, and cultural rituals that promote resilience and well-being.
    - Assess the role of systemic influences, including poverty and systemic racism, in shaping parenting behaviors and family dynamics.

- **Contextualize child maltreatment allegations**: Determine whether the behaviors deemed problematic deviate from cultural norms and assess potential harm within the family's sociocultural and systemic context:

    - Evaluate whether the behaviors in question are considered acceptable or harmful in the family's cultural context, while maintaining legal standards for child safety. Although these considerations do not mean that all culturally sanctioned methods for discipline or socialization should be immune from being defined as child abuse or maltreatment, investigating the cultural roots of the behaviors can better inform recommendations.
    - Consider societal factors, such as access to resources or historical trauma, that may contribute to or mitigate the behaviors in question.

- **Use multimodal, culturally informed practices**: To the extent possible, engage in non-discriminatory, evidence-based evaluation methods tailored to the family's cultural context.
    - Incorporate multimodal assessment approaches, including interviews, collateral information, and structured professional judgment tools.
    - When relevant, seek cultural consultants or those who share the examinee's culture to enhance understanding of culturally specific practices and dynamics.
- **Reflect on bias and systemic influences**: Evaluate the impact of systemic biases and personal assumptions on the evaluation process and outcomes.
    - Assess the role of systemic discrimination and historical injustices in shaping family dynamics and access to resources.
    - Reflect on personal biases to ensure they do not inadvertently influence findings or recommendations.
- **Center the child's developmental needs**: Focus on the child's developmental stage, unique needs, and perspective to guide culturally responsive recommendations.
    - Evaluate the child's acculturation level and how it relates to parental practices and systemic influences.
    - Assess and report the child's perspective on family dynamics.

8
Evaluations for Asylum and International Human Rights Violations

Summary

No area of forensic psychology is more consistently challenged by issues of language and culture than cases involving immigration and international human rights. Almost by definition, cases that arise in these legal settings involve immigrants from or citizens of other countries, many of whom speak little or no English. Forensic mental health professionals who work in these settings are routinely confronted with a range of challenges that stretch the boundaries of their expertise, both in terms of the psycho-legal questions that arise as well as the accommodations that may be necessary to provide culturally fair and accurate assessments. This chapter summarizes the contours of immigration court and provides an overview of the types of questions that usually give rise to forensic mental health evaluations. This review is followed by an overview of issues that arise in international human rights cases. In addition, we discuss elements of the assessment process (e.g., diagnostic instruments, assessment of feigning) that, while covered in depth in other chapters, raise unique questions in immigration and human rights cases.

Case Vignette

Tenzin X is a 42-year-old Tibetan man who entered the US without legal authorization. After living in the US for roughly three years, he was arrested during a "sweep" of the factory where he worked and was placed in removal proceedings. Mr. X described a history of torture and abuse inflicted by the Chinese authorities prior to leaving his country of origin and had been receiving healthcare services (including mental health treatment) through a non-profit program for survivors of torture. That program had arranged for a pro bono attorney, who subsequently retained an expert to provide input into the extent of any psychological symptoms

Cultural and Linguistic Considerations in Forensic Mental Health Assessment. Barry Rosenfeld and Alicia Nijdam-Jones, Oxford University Press. © Oxford University Press (2026).
DOI: 10.1093/9780190900991.003.0008

or mental disorder(s) that might support his claim of past torture. In addition, his attorneys requested an evaluation of whether symptoms of a mental disorder might have impacted Mr. X's ability to seek asylum within the one-year window specified by US law. The evaluation was conducted through a Tibetan-speaking interpreter, but psychological testing was limited by the relative dearth of standardized instruments developed for or adapted for use with Tibetans. Because of this limitation, the evaluator relied primarily on the clinical interview, supplemented with medical records (documenting injuries that he attributed to the Chinese authorities) and Tibetan translations of self-report inventories that target symptoms of depression, anxiety, and posttraumatic stress disorder (PTSD) to gauge the nature and severity of his reported symptoms. The evaluator subsequently opined that Mr. X's symptoms were "consistent with" his report of past traumatic experiences. Is this an appropriate approach for an asylum evaluation? Does the failure to utilize structured diagnostic instruments (e.g., the CAPS-5) or feigning tools (e.g., the TOMM) render this opinion invalid? Does the nature of immigration proceedings alter perceptions of what procedures are acceptable?

No area of forensic psychology is more consistently challenged by issues of language and culture than those involving immigration and international human rights. Regardless of the country where these cases arise, immigration and human rights cases almost invariably involve individuals who do not speak the primary language of the host country where their case is being heard. Thus, forensic mental health professionals who work in these settings are routinely confronted with challenges that stretch the boundaries of their expertise, both in terms of the psycho-legal questions that arise and the accommodations that may be necessary to provide culturally fair and accurate assessments. However, despite the unique and challenging nature of evaluations conducted for immigration purposes or in international courts, little scholarship has been generated to inform these evaluations, and the guidance available for clinicians who choose to work in immigration and international settings is extremely limited (Mercado et al., 2022; Tazi et al., 2023). This chapter provides a brief overview of the typical psycho-legal issues, as well as suggestions for navigating these challenging evaluations. It should be noted that while many of the clinical issues that arise in immigration and international legal settings are common across all jurisdictions, legal standards and practices differ markedly across geographic and political regions. Because coverage of even a subset of the countries and jurisdictions is beyond the scope of this chapter, we focus on US immigration law, with occasional reference to other settings that may generate similar issues.

The authors express their appreciation to Dr. Cassandra Bailey for her helpful comments on an earlier draft of this chapter.

Immigration Court Proceedings

In the US, the laws and procedures that govern immigration court differ markedly from those encountered by mental health clinicians working in the more common legal settings of criminal, civil, or family courts. These differences include the procedures that apply to the court, the rights of those who appear in immigration court (typically termed the "respondent"), and the role of mental health professionals. Few of these unique characteristics benefit the respondent, and mental health professionals routinely find themselves searching for guidance that does not seem to exist. Hence, it seems appropriate to begin this chapter with a brief overview of some relevant aspects of Immigration Law that give rise to forensic mental health evaluations. It should also be noted that while the fundamental laws that govern US immigration court proceedings change infrequently, administrative decisions about how these laws should be applied are often more malleable (e.g., whether or where to detain individuals awaiting the resolution of an asylum application). As a result, there is considerable variability in the conditions that immigrants and asylum seekers experience (e.g., migration, detention), the likelihood of successful applications (whether for asylum or other forms of relief), and the availability of legal counsel over time and across geographic regions.

Definitions and Distinctions

Important distinctions exist among individuals evaluated in relation to immigration court proceedings, depending on their legal status. One such distinction hinges on whether the individual entered the US with legal authorization. For example, many individuals enter the US as refugees, having been granted refugee status abroad due to credible threats in their country of origin that endanger the safety of themselves or a family member. Others migrate to escape similarly dangerous conditions but cannot secure authorization to enter the US, so they request asylum at a US port of entry (e.g., an international airport or land border with Mexico or Canada). Many others enter the US with a time-limited authorization (e.g., a tourist visa) and do not leave when their visa has expired. Finally, some individuals enter the US without authorization, often aided by smugglers or human traffickers, often at significant personal risk and expense. Legal status at the time of US entry is essential because many cases heard in immigration court may also involve criminal charges. Of course, those living in the US with valid legal authorization may still face "removal" if their actions are deemed problematic (e.g., following a conviction for a criminal offense). In the following pages, these distinctions will be addressed in more detail, where relevant.

Applications for Asylum

A large proportion of immigration court evaluations involve individuals who have requested asylum. Asylum applications typically arise from one of two possible routes; most often, they are the result of direct or "affirmative" requests for asylum from individuals who arrive at a US land border (arriving from, or via, Mexico or Canada) or other ports of entry (i.e., international airports, by boat). Upon presentation to a US Customs and Border Protection (CBP) agent, every individual is (or should be, according to US law) given the opportunity to assert a fear for their safety if returned to their country of origin. Despite growing resistance to asylum more generally, US law requires that the CBP officer ask the individual whether they have any such fear before deportation proceedings can be initiated.[1]

A somewhat less common route to asylum hearings is for individuals who have already entered the US and are subject to possible removal (often referred to as a "defensive" request). The law provides for a one-year period in which that person can file a formal request for asylum that would, if granted, provide a more permanent status.[2] Although asylum applicants may be permitted entry into the US if they are deemed not to present a risk of harm or flight, an increasingly large proportion of these individuals are held in detention facilities (often regional jails) for extended periods of time. Because a critical element of asylum applications is the demonstration of a credible fear for one's safety, and this fear is typically premised on some actual harm that has already occurred, mental health professionals may be asked to evaluate the legitimacy of an individual's reported traumatic experiences. There are, of course, many other pathways into immigration court (Barber-Rioja et al., 2023), some of which are discussed separately, but the central role of trauma in asylum hearings has led to increasing reliance on mental health expertise.

Removal Proceedings for Those Already in the US

Many immigration court respondents have never submitted an asylum application but are living in the US when they are identified as having broken the law

[1] Disturbingly, the requirement that CBP officers specifically ask about a fear of return is often ignored, as evidenced by a study by the U.S. Commission on International Religious Freedom (Keller et al., 2005). This multi-faceted study found, among other things, that CBP officers often failed to ask about a fear of return. When CBP officers did ask, and the individual expressed a fear of return, they often actively discouraged the person by warning them that they would likely be detained and separated from their family members if they did not retract that expression of fear.

[2] The one-year limit can be waived when compelling circumstances (possibly including mental health symptoms) are deemed to justify an exception (Barber-Rioja et al., 2023).

and therefore face removal. Historically, deportation was primarily reserved for those convicted of a serious criminal offense, particularly those convicted of a violent crime. A primary justification for deporting those convicted of a serious crime was a fear that these individuals, whether they entered the country with legal authorization (e.g., refugee status) or without (e.g., crossing the border without being detected), would present a danger to others and should therefore not be allowed to remain in the country. However, in recent years, there has been a growing emphasis on identifying individuals whose only "crime" is having entered the US without authorization or overstayed an otherwise legal entry (e.g., having entered on a tourist or student visa and then remaining in the US beyond the expiration date of the visa), eliminating any pretext of dangerousness as the basis for removal. Like individuals who affirmatively seek asylum, these individuals may also be subject to detention while awaiting the resolution of their cases.

Individuals who entered the US legally but were subsequently deemed "removable" by Immigration and Customs Enforcement (ICE) are required to demonstrate that they qualify for some form of relief and should therefore be allowed to remain in the US legally (Barber-Rioja et al., 2023). There are several legal arguments that can satisfy the requirement of relief (see Table 8.1), including asylum if the individual demonstrates a credible threat to their safety if returned to their country of origin. However, removal proceedings can also be canceled for many other reasons, including a finding that removal would cause extreme hardship to other US citizens or legal permanent residents (e.g., family members, such as children born in the US) or the presence of mitigating factors that outweigh the illegal convictions. For example, an individual who has no history of serious felony convictions (as defined by immigration law) or has been the victim of a crime or domestic violence within the US might also be eligible for relief under a U visa or the Violence Against Women Act (34 USC § 12291). These various routes of entry into the immigration court system give rise to a range of different psycho-legal issues, some of which are described in more detail below.

Common Types of Forensic Evaluations in Immigration Court

Over the past two decades, the use of mental health evaluations in immigration court has become increasingly common. Despite the limited resources available to most individuals involved in immigration court proceedings (even when represented by an attorney), immigration attorneys have increasingly sought

Table 8.1 Common types of immigration evaluations

Asylum	Individuals are eligible for asylum when they can demonstrate a "well-founded fear of persecution" related to one or more of the five protected characteristics: race, religion, nationality, membership in a particular social group, or political orientation. The fear of persecution can be based on past experiences of trauma or abuse, or on anticipated future persecution and must be deemed "objectively reasonable."
Competence to Proceed	Case law establishes the right to assistance upon demonstration that a respondent's mental disease or disability substantially impairs his or her capacity to understand the proceedings and provide relevant information, whether through an attorney or direct testimony.
Extreme Hardship Waivers	Individuals who can demonstrate that removal would result in "exceptional and extremely unique" hardship to another US citizen or legal permanent residents (typically children, a spouse, or parents). These waivers only require the presence of a legal qualifying relative who would suffer the hardship and does not apply to the respondent him or herself, however the hardship cannot simply be due to family separation, economic disadvantage, or inferior medical care unless these losses would result in significant emotional or psychological harm.
Violence Against Women Act	Victims of intimate partner violence inflicted by a US citizen or legal resident may be eligible for permanent legal status and/or cancelation of removal proceedings. Those over 14 years old are also required to demonstrate that they are "of good moral character," with the proviso that illegal or immoral acts (e.g., drug use, prostitution) may not disqualify applicants if they can demonstrate that their actions were also the result of abuse.
U Visa	Immigrants who have been the victim of, or witness to, a serious crime and have suffered mental or physical consequences as a result of that experience may be eligible to remain in the US and apply for a "green card." Successful applications typically require demonstration of "permanent or serious harm to the appearance, health, or physical or mental soundness of the victim."
T Visa	Individuals who enter the US as victims of human trafficking are eligible for this form of relief, if they have been forced to engage in labor and would experience "extreme hardship" if forced to leave the US.
Suspension of Deportation for Crimes of Moral Turpitude	Deportation proceedings may be suspended or terminated upon demonstration that the immigrant has been rehabilitated and does not pose a risk to others if allowed to remain in the US.

forensic mental health evaluations to support their clients. The most common foci of these evaluations include, but are not limited to, the following:

1. "Validating" the respondent's account of trauma and credible fear.
2. Evaluating competence to proceed in immigration court.
3. Assessment of extreme hardship or other mitigating factors (e.g., mental illness or substance abuse that might mitigate a history of criminal offending).
4. Applications for bail relief or mitigation (e.g., based on a low risk of future violent or criminal behavior).
5. Justification for a delay in filing for asylum (i.e., after the one-year period has expired).
6. Need for treatment or services not available in the respondent's country of origin.

Although there are elements of the forensic evaluation that are unique to some of these psycho-legal issues, many elements apply equally to some or all of them—including issues of language and culture that invariably complicate these evaluations.

Allegations of Trauma and Maltreatment

A cornerstone of asylum applications, as well as a possible justification for having delayed filing for asylum, is the belief that one would be in jeopardy if returned to their country of origin.[3] Therefore, the assessment of past traumatic experiences is often a critical piece of evidence in many asylum hearings and can be particularly compelling for many immigration court judges. Affidavits attesting to the nature and frequency of persecution within a particular country or region, or even the political or social conditions more generally, are commonly offered in immigration court. However, presenting evidence that the respondent has actually experienced this abuse is far more compelling than simply identifying the country or region as one in which a high risk of victimization exists. Hence, forensic evaluators will often obtain a detailed history of past traumatic experiences suffered by a respondent and are encouraged to conduct a thorough assessment of PTSD symptoms in order to provide a link between the individual being evaluated and their report of past experiences.

[3] In order to qualify for asylum, the basis for this perceived fear must fit into one of the established categories: persecution based on race, religion, nationality, political beliefs, or membership in a specific social group.

Although PTSD symptoms do not verify the respondent's description of past abuse or maltreatment, the importance of a systematic assessment of past trauma and PTSD symptoms is strongly encouraged by international guidelines. One example is the *Manual on Effective Investigation and Documentation of Torture and Other Cruel, Inhumane or Degrading Treatment or Punishment* (also known as the *Istanbul Protocol*; Iacopino et al., 1999; United Nations Office of the High Commissioner for Human Rights, 2022). This set of recommended procedures has been adopted by organizations around the world to facilitate the comprehensive assessment and documentation of torture and other forms of abuse. Among the many relevant aspects of the *Istanbul Protocol* is the emphasis on mental health evaluations and diagnoses, with particular attention to the presence (or history) of PTSD. Although the *Istanbul Protocol* does not offer specific recommendations for assessing trauma and abuse, thorough documentation (including photographic evidence of injuries) is strongly encouraged. Likewise, systematic interview approaches (described in more detail later in this chapter) can improve the reliability of PTSD diagnostic assessments. However, the assessment of PTSD is often limited by the reliance on diagnostic criteria that may not adequately capture culturally unique symptom manifestations.

Perhaps not surprisingly, there are many challenging aspects to assessing trauma and its sequelae, one of the most obvious being that PTSD is just one of many possible responses to trauma and maltreatment. Research with refugees and asylum seekers has consistently found high rates of anxiety and depression (usually far exceeding rates of PTSD), ranging from 25% to 50% of refugees and those arriving at the US border seeking entry (Keller et al., 2017). The rates are even higher in US detention centers and jails, with more than 75% of individuals in these settings reporting clinically significant symptoms of anxiety and depression (Keller et al., 2003). Rates of PTSD, on the other hand, are usually in the range of 25% to 40%, and rarely exceed 50%, even among individuals who have experienced severe forms of trauma. Of course, anxiety, depression, and PTSD, while perhaps the most common, represent only a subset of the diagnoses that may be relevant in immigration court proceedings; substance use (which is highly comorbid with PTSD), developmental disabilities, and even psychosis are not rare. Hence, while PTSD warrants and typically receives particular attention in immigration court proceedings, clinicians must be prepared to evaluate the full range of serious mental disorders.

Of course, the journey to the US can also be fraught with dangers, compounding any sequelae of pre-migration trauma and loss. The impact of pre-migration trauma can also be exacerbated even after entering the US, where immigrants are often subject to discrimination and harassment, unfair working conditions, and harsh living circumstances. In extreme cases, physical violence and human trafficking can greatly exacerbate any pre- and peri-migration symptoms. Hence, a key element to many evaluations for immigration court is disentangling, to the extent possible, symptoms and functional impairments that appear attributable to pre-migration experiences, even if those difficulties were subsequently exacerbated by peri- and post-migration trauma (Bailey & Widner, 2022; Tazi et al., 2023).

In many cases, a comprehensive medical evaluation can help identify evidence of scarring or physical impairments that are consistent with the individual's reported traumatic experiences. However, not only will the ability to link medical findings with specific trauma vary based on the nature of the findings and reported trauma, but this assessment typically requires expertise in the medical evaluation or treatment of trauma survivors. Torture treatment centers exist in many metropolitan centers around the US and internationally, and can often be a valuable resource for identifying a medical professional who possesses the expertise to examine and document physical evidence of trauma.

Another important complication when evaluating the sequelae of trauma and abuse is the growing evidence of cross-cultural differences in the manifestation of mental disorders in general, and in how trauma-based symptoms are expressed more specifically. Rasmussen and colleagues (2014) reviewed research on posttraumatic stress symptoms in non-Western countries, drawing heavily on studies conducted in refugee settlements. They found that syndromes reflective of PTSD as conceptualized by the *DSM* and *ICD* were relatively uncommon—at least as far as the specific diagnostic criteria are concerned. However, symptoms reflective of distress and dysphoria were frequent and highly diverse, not only in the nature of the symptoms but their perceived etiology (within the specific culture) and recommended interventions. In fact, some research has suggested that culture may impede the expression of some elements of diagnostic criteria, precluding diagnosis with the formal criteria. Sachs and colleagues (2008), in their study of Tibetan refugees living in India, found that individuals who reported experiencing torture prior to migration rarely exhibited the "avoidance" symptoms required for a diagnosis of PTSD. They cited religious beliefs, including the perception that one's experiences are a function of Karma, to explain the tendency to accept and embrace traumatic experiences rather than avoid reminders or discussions of past events.

Unfortunately, very little guidance exists on identifying these phenomena across diverse cultures, as the literature on cultural variations in distress and mental disorders is still relatively limited. Moreover, courts in the US may limit testimony to diagnoses established in the DSM, regardless of whether existing criteria optimally characterize the manifestations of trauma-based symptoms that arise in a particular asylum applicant. A diagnosis of PTSD, on the other hand, is often considered the "gold standard" (whether justifiable or not) for demonstrating that an individual has suffered from past trauma. Hence, while awareness of culturally specific symptoms of distress can (and should) certainly inform the assessment process, diagnostic conclusions may be more useful (i.e., acceptable to judges or immigration officials) if framed in the context of established diagnostic criteria. For example, a clinician might opine that an individual satisfies many, but not all, of the criteria for PTSD but cite cultural factors in explaining deviations from the diagnostic criteria. Testimony regarding the symptoms that reflect past abuse need not satisfy all criteria for a formal diagnosis to provide compelling evidence of past trauma and abuse, provided a plausible justification for the opinion can be offered.

Challenges to Assessing the Validity of PTSD Symptoms

A common concern raised in immigration court proceedings is the potential for deliberate distortion in the report of both past traumatic experiences and PTSD symptoms. Several self-report and clinician-rated instruments have been developed and evaluated in assessing PTSD symptom severity, but relatively little research has examined the potential for deliberate distortion (i.e., malingering). For example, the Clinician-Administered PTSD Scale (CAPS, most recently revised to conform to DSM-5 criteria [CAPS-5]; Weathers et al., 2018) is often considered the gold standard instrument for establishing the presence of a PTSD diagnosis. This structured interview, which has been translated into Spanish, provides specific questions and follow-up prompts to guide the clinician in rating the presence and severity of PTSD symptoms. The CAPS also includes items to gauge the duration, functional interference, and "validity" of the person's report. However, like the many self-rated instruments (e.g., the PTSD Checklist for DSM-5 or PCL-5, Harvard Trauma Questionnaire, Trauma Symptom Inventory) that have been translated and evaluated in diverse languages and cultures, these tools rely almost entirely on the individual's self-report. Hence, they are easily manipulated by individuals seeking to present themselves as more distressed than they really are. Although implausibly high scores on a self-report questionnaire (i.e., markedly exceeding those found in individuals known to have severe PTSD) might raise concerns about deliberate symptom exaggeration (e.g., Schroeder & Bieu, 2024), the lack of well-established validity indices and the limited availability of translated versions of these questionnaires can limit their utility in many forensic settings.

There are self-report questionnaires that systematically address the possibility of deliberate symptom exaggeration. For example, the Trauma Symptom Inventory, currently in its second edition (TSI-2; Briere, 2011), includes two validity scales, including the Atypical Response (ATR) scale. Although the TSI-2 has been translated into several languages that have potential utility in both forensic evaluations in general and asylum evaluations in particular (e.g., Spanish, French), a review of existing research found limited ability to discriminate between individuals feigning PTSD and honest responders (Roberts et al., 2022). Weiss and Rosenfeld (2017), in their study of French- and English-speaking West African immigrants who had been granted asylum, found that the TSI-2 ATR scale had little ability to detect feigned PTSD (and accuracy did not differ depending on whether the TSI-2 was administered in French or English). Moreover, individuals identified as having significant PTSD symptoms obtained only modest elevations on the "Trauma" factor of the TSI-2, raising questions about the tool's sensitivity for identifying individuals with genuine PTSD in this population. Given the modest effectiveness of the TSI-2 in past research, Roberts and colleagues (2022) recommended that the TSI-2 only be used in conjunction with another instrument with more substantial discriminatory power in identifying feigned PTSD symptoms, such as the Personality Assessment Inventory (PAI) or Minnesota Multiphasic Personality Inventory (MMPI) (see Chapter 4).

However, differentiating feigned from genuine PTSD symptoms on the MMPI-2 and PAI is also challenging, even among English-speaking individuals. Nijdam-Jones and colleagues (2020) conducted a meta-analysis of research examining the utility of the MMPI-2 in detecting feigned PTSD symptoms and found large effect sizes for most scales. However, genuine patients with PTSD typically generated elevated scores on many of the scales designed to detect feigned responding, often due to the diverse range of symptoms associated with PTSD. Thus, evaluators must exercise caution when interpreting test data related to PTSD, particularly given the risk of inaccurately labeling genuinely impaired individuals as feigning (i.e., "false positive" findings).

It should be noted that while concerns about feigning are often raised in immigration court, there is little evidence to suggest that immigration court respondents are prone to fabricate or exaggerate PTSD symptoms. Although feigning is certainly possible, and no doubt occurs occasionally, systematic assessment of feigning is often used to provide support for the validity of the individual's reported symptoms (i.e., by demonstrating the absence of feigned symptoms as indirect support of the individual's report). As such, evaluators may administer scales specifically designed to identify feigned symptoms potentially relevant to PTSD. For example, because memory or concentration problems are plausible symptoms of PTSD and may be fabricated or exaggerated by an individual attempting to feign PTSD symptoms, evaluators may administer cognitive effort measures such as the Test of Memory Malingering or the Dot Counting Test (see Chapter 3). Another test specifically designed to identify feigned PTSD symptoms, but which has limited research in refugee or immigrant samples, is the Morel Emotional Numbing Test (Morel, 1998). Of course, the risk of false positives exists with any of these instruments and appears to be greater among those with low levels of education and limited literacy (Nijdam-Jones & Rosenfeld, 2017; Nijdam-Jones et al., 2019b). Nevertheless, each has potential utility, provided the evaluator interprets test data with appropriate caution, such as requiring considerable evidence (beyond test findings alone) before concluding that an individual's symptom report is not genuine.

Competence to Proceed in Immigration Court

Another increasingly common basis for mental health evaluations in immigration court pertains to competence to proceed. Although many forensic mental health professionals are familiar with the standards and procedures for evaluating competence to stand trial (also known as adjudicative competence), important differences exist between competence evaluations in criminal and immigration proceedings. For example, unlike individuals facing criminal charges in the US, immigration court respondents are entitled to rely on legal representation but are not provided with an attorney if they cannot arrange for one themselves. Not surprisingly, roughly half of all immigration court respondents represent themselves in court (i.e., appear *pro se*), and many others are assisted by non-attorneys, including paralegals, friends, or family members. Thus, for many respondents, there are few people, if any, in a position to identify and react to impairments that might adversely impact the legal process. Therefore, this responsibility typically falls on the immigration court judge, who holds the primary responsibility for addressing concerns about the fairness of the legal proceedings. The judge is charged with providing procedural safeguards whenever concerns arise about an individual's ability to receive a fair hearing (US Department of Justice, 2007). For example, immigration court respondents with mental illness or intellectual disabilities are at greater risk of an unfair outcome such as unjustified removal. This risk is largely due to a limited ability to exercise their rights, such as providing evidence to the court, questioning witnesses, or challenging witnesses who provide inaccurate or disparaging testimony (Human Rights Watch, 2010). In fact, US law asserts that the judge "shall not accept an admission of removability from an unrepresented respondent who is incompetent" (8 CFR § 1240.10(c)).

Unfortunately, the processes for identifying and responding to questions about competence when applied to immigration court proceedings are far less developed than those applied to the criminal courts, where tens of thousands of trial competence evaluations occur annually. Even the establishment of a legal standard for competence in immigration court is a relatively recent development, particularly compared to the *Dusky* standard for competence to stand trial, which was established more than half a century earlier (*Dusky v. US*, 1960).[4] The primary case outlining criteria for competence to proceed in immigration court is *Matter of M-A-M* (2011), in which a Jamaican respondent with permanent resident status in the US faced removal due to past criminal convictions. The respondent, who had been diagnosed with schizophrenia, appeared in immigration court without representation and had difficulty answering simple questions posed by the judge. Despite having informed the judge about his mental illness (and presenting medical records that corroborated his diagnosis), the judge failed to inquire into or make a finding regarding his competence to participate in the proceedings. After the respondent was deemed removable due to his criminal convictions, he obtained legal representation and appealed the removal decision based on the argument that the immigration judge did not address the issue of competence or provide any safeguards to ensure a fair hearing. The Board of Immigration Appeals (BIA), in response to this appeal, held:

> The test for determining whether an alien is competent to participate in immigration proceedings is whether he or she has a rational and factual understanding of the nature and object of the proceedings, can consult with the attorney or representative if there is one, and has a reasonable opportunity to examine and present evidence and cross-examine witnesses.
>
> (BIA, 2011, p. 479)

Although this standard largely mirrors the *Dusky* standard for competence in criminal court proceedings, there are also significant differences between these two standards. For example, because many immigration court respondents do not have an attorney, competence to proceed in immigration court requires consideration of the individual's ability to perform some of the tasks that would typically be delegated to an attorney, such as presenting evidence and cross-examining witnesses. Moreover, when questions arise regarding a respondent's competence, the immigration court judge is expected to take steps to assess the degree of any impairment, typically by asking questions to assess the person's mental state and understanding of the proceedings. This often involves the judge asking the respondent questions to gauge their understanding of specific aspects of the immigration court proceedings or even simply assessing their ability to respond appropriately to any questions. Soliciting relevant medical records is another judicial response to concerns about a respondent's competence. Although referral to a mental health professional for a competence evaluation is only required when the judge does not feel qualified to make a

[4] In *Dusky v. US*, the Supreme Court ruled that competence to stand trial required "sufficient present ability to consult with his lawyer with a reasonable degree of rational understanding -and whether he has a rational as well as factual understanding of the proceedings against him" (p. 402).

determination about the respondent's competence (based on the available evidence), attorneys or other involved parties may seek a mental health evaluation to assist in this process. Perhaps not surprisingly, given the challenging nature of competence evaluations, immigration court judges are increasingly inclined to request a formal evaluation by a psychiatrist or psychologist.

Another critical distinction between criminal and immigration court proceedings is the standard of proof, which was the focus of another important US case: *Matter of J-S-S* (2015). Because immigration court proceedings are not intended to be adversarial, both sides are expected to collaborate with the judge to assist in the competence determination. Hence, "neither party bears a formal burden of proof in immigration proceedings to establish whether or not the respondent is mentally competent, but where indicia of incompetence are identified, the immigration judge should determine if a preponderance of the evidence establishes that the respondent is competent" (p. 683). In criminal court cases, on the other hand, clear and convincing evidence is typically required before a defendant is found incompetent to stand trial. Perhaps most importantly, once an immigration court respondent is deemed incompetent, the judge is expected to determine appropriate safeguards to protect that individual's rights, such as providing the respondent with some type of legal representation (although not necessarily an attorney).

Evaluating Competence to Proceed in Immigration Court

Given the limited legal and clinical attention paid to competence in immigration court, it is not surprising that little guidance exists regarding how an evaluator should evaluate a respondent whose competence has been questioned. A review by Tazi et al. (2023) identified only six published articles focusing on competence to proceed in immigration court, which is a stark contrast to the voluminous research literature focused on adjudicative competence in criminal court. However, Aparcero (2023) recently adapted an instrument initially developed to guide adjudicative competence evaluations, the Fitness Interview Test-Revised (FIT-R, Roesch et al., 2006), for use in immigration court proceedings. This tool, termed the Fitness Interview Test–Immigration Court version (FIT-IC), guides the evaluator to consider four domains of competence: (a) factual knowledge of the nature and object of the proceedings (e.g., the type of proceedings, charges against them, why they are facing removal); (b) appreciation of the individual's rights and the potential outcome of the proceedings (e.g., right to representation, present favorable information, examine and object to evidence); (c) ability to make decisions related to the proceedings and communicate information effectively (e.g., to explain their reasons for migration and describe potentially relevant experiences); and (d) ability to consult with an attorney or representative (e.g., trust in the representative, ability to convey relevant information). To date, only preliminary data has supported the utility of this instrument, based primarily on expert review of the tool and the perceived relevance of its elements. Furthermore, like most instruments developed to assess competence to stand trial, there are no scores generated to differentiate competent from incompetent respondents. Rather, the FIT-IC is intended to provide structure and guidance to the evaluation process and is likely to greatly improve the thoroughness and accuracy of clinical opinions.

Another critical difference between competence to stand trial in criminal court and competence to proceed in immigration court is that the latter frequently involves individuals with little or no understanding of the US legal proceedings. Thus, the evaluator must distinguish between those individuals who are simply unfamiliar with the process but are capable of understanding information when it is explained to them versus those who are unable to comprehend the information even when it is presented in a manner that should be understandable. Unfortunately, many attorneys, judges, and even some forensic evaluators provide information using terminology that would challenge even well-educated US citizens (few of whom are familiar with immigration law). Any attempt to explain the legal proceedings needs to be sufficiently straightforward, conveying relevant information in a manner that individuals with no legal background and limited fluency should be able to comprehend. Likewise, the presence of some intellectual limitations or psychological symptoms does not necessarily preclude an adequate understanding of the relevant information, provided it has been conveyed in clear, simple language. This approach should not be interpreted to mean that an accurate understanding of and ability to meaningfully participate in the proceedings is not important. However, an immigration court respondent need not have the legal expertise of an attorney or judge (or even an educated layperson), merely a level of understanding and ability commensurate with the demands of the case.

In identifying the specific domains that comprise competence to proceed in immigration court, the US Executive Office for Immigration Review (EOIR) identified the following specific abilities:

1. Rational and factual understanding of:
   a. the nature and object of the proceeding;
   b. the privilege of representation, including but not limited to the ability to consult with a representative if one is present;
   c. the right to present, examine, and object to evidence;
   d. the right to cross-examine witnesses; and

    e. the right to appeal.
2. Reasonable ability to:
    a. make decisions about asserting and waiving rights;
    b. respond to the allegations and charges in the proceeding; and
    c. present information and respond to questions relevant to eligibility for relief

(EOIR, 2013, p. 2)

In breaking down these domains of knowledge and ability, Filone and King (2015) identified several critical elements contained within the EOIR guidelines. However, they also caution that an adequate assessment of competence to proceed in immigration court requires the evaluating clinician to understand the proceedings themselves. Specifically, the evaluator must understand the core elements of the legal process, including the different types of hearings, relief options, and potential outcomes. In terms of the rational and factual understanding of information, the respondent should have a general understanding of the specific type of proceeding they are facing, including the adversarial nature of the proceedings and the role of immigration court personnel (e.g., judge, ICE attorney petitioning for removal). Notably, the adversarial system may be confusing for respondents who are from countries that rely on non-adversarial approaches to legal decision-making. Hence, it is often helpful for the evaluator to have some understanding of how legal proceedings work in the respondent's country of origin, as a reference point for identifying (and possibly explaining) differences. Respondents should also know what allegations or charges have been raised (which should be documented in the Notice to Appear that all respondents receive) and the potential outcome of their case, including granting relief from removal or removal, which is typically accompanied by at least a ten-year ban on readmission to the US.

In assessing the individual's knowledge of their rights and ability to make decisions related to these rights, Filone and King (2015) recommended assessing whether the respondent is aware that *pro bono* legal representation may be available through various service agencies. Even when an attorney cannot be secured, legal assistance and advocacy resources are often available to assist the *pro se* respondent. However, respondents should also know that the likelihood of obtaining relief is greater when they have formal legal representation. Respondents should also understand their right to appeal an adverse decision, and evaluators are advised to inquire why and how the respondent would file an appeal. Although these suggestions are not intended to provide a comprehensive overview of the process of evaluating competence to proceed in immigration court, they do highlight critical differences between the evaluation process in criminal and immigration court evaluations. Evaluators who undertake these evaluations should begin by reviewing the relevant legal guidance and some of the research literature and legal scholarship available.

Assessment of Potential Mitigating Factors in Respondents Facing Removal

Another growing area in which mental health professionals can impact immigration court proceedings is the assessment of mitigating factors. These can be factors relevant to the respondents themselves (e.g., history of gainful employment, experience with intimate partner violence, mental health or substance abuse problems that do not rise to the level of incompetence) or factors relevant to other involved parties (e.g., if removal will cause extreme hardship for one or more US citizens, such as a child or other family member). Many of these evaluations will overlap substantially with evaluations for sentencing or mitigation conducted for criminal court, but a focus on other involved parties can present several unique challenges. To begin with, issues of informed consent are more complex when other parties are involved in the evaluation, since personal information conveyed during the interview may be repeated in court. This issue requires careful consideration of the nature and content of any informed consent disclosure.

Potentially mitigating information can also have unintended consequences. A history of substance use or severe mental illness, for example, can result in discriminatory assumptions about the person's potential for renewed substance use or potential for criminal behavior more generally (particularly when substance abuse involves illegal substances). The evaluating clinician should consider this potential when communicating information in either written reports or courtroom testimony, as negative repercussions may be minimized by presenting adequate context. For example, while some immigration court judges may perceive a history of mental illness as a reason for removal, the greater availability of and willingness to engage in necessary mental health treatment may help offset this perception. On the other hand, a history of gainful employment, a limited (or distant past) criminal history, or recovery from substance use may support an argument that the respondent does not pose a threat to society that would warrant removal.

The strongest arguments for avoiding removal are typically those based on hardships that would be faced by young children, who may be US citizens if they were born in the US, even if neither parent had legal authorization to enter or remain in the country. Even without clear financial or emotional dependence, interviews with friends and family may provide strong evidence to justify termination of removal proceedings if other forms of support for dependents are more readily available in the US (e.g., educational or medical needs). However, an argument that necessary medical treatment is less adequate or less readily available in the respondent's country is not necessarily a sufficient basis for remaining in the US.

Finally, perhaps the most compelling argument for terminating removal proceedings is a history of victimization or exposure to criminal activity. Existing US law provides a mechanism for individuals to qualify for a U visa if they have been the victim of a crime or have been helpful in detecting or investigating a crime committed against others. Intended to encourage immigrants to report crimes they know about or to assist in the prevention or prosecution of criminal activity, this mechanism can provide temporary legal status for the victim and family members and may also include work authorization and a possible path to citizenship. However, the process of seeking U visa eligibility requires documentation provided by a law enforcement agency or judge attesting to a person's role in the criminal activity (e.g., crime victim, witness). Hence, clinicians should be aware of the requirements for the U visa, particularly when evaluating someone who is not represented by an attorney, and therefore may not be aware of this pathway to delaying or terminating removal proceedings.

As noted above, several of these pathways to termination of removal proceedings hinge on a demonstration (or argument) that the individual does not pose a significant risk of harm to the community. Hence, many evaluations conducted for immigration court proceedings are bolstered when they are accompanied by an assessment that the respondent is at low risk for violence or criminal behavior. A thorough review of risk assessment, both generally and in the context of cultural and linguistic diversity, is beyond the scope of this chapter but is addressed in Chapter 6.

International Human Rights Violations

A less common but certainly no less important aspect of "international" forensic practice pertains to international human rights violations. Human rights violations are addressed through a wide range of legal proceedings, depending on the country and the context for the alleged violations. In general, these proceedings are often grounded in the United Nations Universal Declaration of Human Rights, which was first promulgated in the wake of the atrocities committed by Nazi Germany. The declaration outlines a series of fundamental human rights and provides a basis for identifying violations (and justifying sanctions for these violations). When blatant violations of these fundamental rights have occurred, such as genocide, torture, or maltreatment of minority groups, standing or time-limited courts may be developed to address the perpetrators of this maltreatment. For example, the United Nations International Criminal Court has provided such a forum for, or assistance in, redressing violations that have occurred during periods of political unrest. Examples of these *ad hoc* courts include the International Criminal Tribunals for Rwanda and the Former Yugoslavia and the Special Court for Sierra Leone. Many countries have also established legal forums for addressing mistreatment that has occurred within a country, such as the Canadian Human Rights Tribunal and the National Human Rights Commission in India. Although opportunities to provide forensic mental health testimony occasionally arise during these legal proceedings, relatively few mental health professionals have the opportunity to work in these settings. On the other hand, civil litigation is a far more common setting for addressing international human rights violations, as the involvement of the military or multinational corporations in cases of alleged abuse occurs with some frequency.

Cases that arise in international courts carry a range of complications, not least of which is the need to understand the relevant legal issues that pertain to these courts. Admissibility of different types of testimony and the rules that govern who may be deemed an expert witness and what topics may be testified to can all vary depending on the nature of the court and the specific issues involved in the case. When evaluations are conducted outside the US, issues of licensure may also be relevant, as some countries and legal proceedings will prohibit testimony from an expert who is not licensed to practice in that country, whereas others are less restrictive and will accept expert testimony from anyone who meets a requisite level of qualification, regardless of where they typically practice. Clinical psychologists must also be aware of their own licensing board's rules for cross-jurisdictional clinical practice, to ensure that they are not in violation of their own state's licensure requirements.

Perhaps not surprisingly, many international human rights cases hinge on the same set of issues that arise in immigration court proceedings, with particular emphasis on PTSD that results from traumatic experiences. However, many of these cases involve widespread trauma and abuse, including both traumas that were directly observed as well as others suffered by friends, family members, or even strangers. As a result, understanding the social, economic, and political conditions in the country where a human rights case arose can be essential to evaluating the nature and impact of the events that gave rise to the legal case. Not only is this information crucial to understanding the context for the case at hand, but an awareness of the social and political climate in the respondent's country of origin can be critical to establishing rapport. A useful starting point in such cases is a literature review to determine whether any ethnographic or mental health research has been conducted with survivors (e.g., studies of refugee mental health, or descriptive reports of atrocities).

One challenging issue in cases that involve allegations of government abuse is the potential for the person being evaluated to harbor concerns about disclosing information to an interpreter. Although not ideal in many circumstances, it may be necessary to utilize an interpreter who has no connection to the country in which the case arose, to minimize concerns about the individual or their family's safety due to the information disclosed. Given that many international human rights cases involve multiple plaintiffs, it may be feasible to invest time and resources into vetting and training interpreters, given that an interpreter (or set of interpreters) may be used for multiple evaluations. This scenario is a stark contrast to the typical immigration court evaluation, where resources to provide for even a court-sanctioned interpreter are often limited or non-existent.

Likewise, in our experience, international human rights cases that involve multiple plaintiffs often occur over extended periods of time. Hence, the opportunity often exists to consult with researchers or clinicians who have experience with the language or culture of the individual(s) being evaluated, perhaps identifying information in advance that can be integrated into the evaluation (e.g., culturally unique clinical symptoms). Moreover, while translation and back-translation of instruments are rarely advisable in routine practice, resources might be available to develop or obtain translated versions of structured diagnostic tools such as the CAPS-5 (to assess PTSD symptoms, albeit as operationalized by the DSM-5) or the self-report symptom rating scales previously described. In some cases, purchasing an international translation of the MMPI may even be feasible, particularly when time and resources are not in short supply. Identifying researchers who have developed and published validity data supporting neurocognitive or symptom validity tools can also generate resources that are rarely available in routine clinical practice, where time and funding constraints may not permit such access.

Many of these same concerns arise when human rights violations are the subject of civil litigation. For example, litigation that arose from the infamous Abu Ghraib prison abuse was initially raised in US Federal courts in the form of a lawsuit against the subcontractor who operated the prison. Similarly, former Guantanamo Bay defendants have occasionally attempted to sue US government officials for the damages inflicted by military personnel. Although many of these cases are ultimately unsuccessful, international human rights violations that survive "summary judgment" (i.e., a motion to resolve a civil complaint due to a lack of any material facts in dispute) may require formal evaluations and testimony in some forum (e.g., deposition or trial). While the legal proceedings may not differ from "routine" civil litigation, the importance of understanding the cultural issues, both within the country at large and within the specific region or subculture where the case arose, can be critical to both the evaluation process and to providing adequate support for any conclusions generated.

Revisiting the Vignette

Evaluations conducted for the purpose of asylum applications and related matters (as described in the vignette) are often limited by the inability to access potentially relevant collateral information—and, hence, rely substantially on self-report data. This vignette describes a common situation in these evaluations, as only self-report questionnaires were identified as potentially useful. While such instruments are rarely used (or recommended) for typical forensic evaluations, they can be a useful supplement to what might otherwise be sole reliance on the clinical interview. However, we would disagree with the conclusion that measures of symptom (or performance) validity cannot be addressed, given the relatively strong support for non-verbal instruments such as the TOMM. That said, care must be taken to avoid false positives, particularly given Mr. X's limited educational background and likely lack of familiarity with psychological testing. Thus, while the interpretation of the TOMM should be necessarily cautious (i.e., not considering the established cut-off score as a firm threshold), there have been a number of studies supporting its utility across diverse cultures and languages (e.g., Chinese and West African immigrants living in the US).

On the other hand, the expectation that an evaluator utilizes a structured diagnostic interview, like the CAPS-5, is often unrealistic. First, we are unaware of a Tibetan translation of the CAPS-5 and would discourage evaluators from asking an interpreter to translate the tool during the evaluation. While the evaluator can certainly utilize a CAPS-5 to guide their own interview (e.g., to ensure adequate coverage of PTSD criteria), the failure to map an asylum interview onto the specific elements of the DSM is not crucial, particularly given the evidence that cultures manifest trauma responses differently. The evaluator may also benefit from consulting with professionals affiliated with a refugee or torture treatment center, or those with expertise in Tibetan culture, to better contextualize Mr. X's experiences and better understand Tibetan manifestations of trauma. Of course, the evaluator should document culturally specific expressions of distress including somatic complaints or spiritual interpretations of suffering, despite a lack of alignment with DSM-based PTSD criteria. Therefore, using language such as "consistent with PTSD" would be appropriate for this context, where the goal is to identify symptoms that might support an asylum claim, not to definitively ascertain the accuracy of the diagnosis.

Summary and Recommendations

Cases that arise in immigration court and international human rights settings are almost inherently "cross-cultural" but have many unique elements that challenge even the most culturally responsive forensic mental health professional. In addition to the clinical issues that are addressed throughout this book, the legal contours of these evaluations are unfamiliar to many mental health professionals. Moreover, far less guidance exists for these evaluations, either in the published research literature or in textbooks, as these topics are studied, discussed, and taught far less often than many of the more "traditional" criminal or civil legal issues. Thus, clinicians are left with limited guidance as to what to expect and how to navigate the unique challenges that arise. However, because many of these challenges center around issues of trauma and PTSD, and a growing body of research has emerged to assist clinicians exploring these topics, practitioners have ever-increasing resources upon which to draw. This may include seeking consultation with experts familiar with the country or region that the examinee(s) originated from, as well as optimal (and suboptimal) techniques to elicit the relevant clinical data. In this chapter, we highlighted some of the central topics that arise in immigration court and international human rights cases, as well as outlined some of the resources and approaches that might improve practice in these important areas. Nevertheless, there is a critical need for further research and scholarship surrounding these topics, which is the focus of the final chapter in this volume. These limitations notwithstanding, we offer the following recommendations:

- **Clarify the legal standards and context**: Understand the legal framework and cultural context of the evaluation to ensure a relevant and accurate assessment.
    - Align assessment methods with the psycho-legal questions and legal standard being addressed.
    - Consult knowledgeable authorities or resources to understand the political, social, and cultural background of the examinee's country of origin (assuming the evaluator lacks sufficient knowledge).
- **Ensure interpreter impartiality and competence**: Choose interpreters carefully to support accurate and confidential evaluations.

  - To the extent possible, the evaluator should select interpreters who are neutral and not directly connected to the examinee's community or government to avoid concerns about safety or bias.
  - Train interpreters, when feasible, on the sensitive nature of forensic evaluations to enhance the quality of interpretation and maintain confidentiality.

- **Recognize cultural variability in trauma symptoms**: Account for cultural differences in the manifestation of trauma symptoms to avoid misdiagnosis or oversight.

  - Acknowledge that trauma-based symptoms may not align with DSM criteria for PTSD and consider culturally informed diagnostic frameworks.
  - Recognize the limitations of standardized PTSD structured interview approaches (e.g., the CAPS-5) when used in cross-cultural contexts. Adapt or supplement with culturally responsive alternatives to capture diverse trauma symptoms accurately.

- **When used, adapt structured interviews to the cultural context**: Use structured tools flexibly to accommodate cultural differences and linguistic limitations.

  - Employ tools like the CAPS-5 as a guide for covering diagnostic criteria without rigid adherence when cultural factors influence symptom expression.
  - Supplement structured interviews with open-ended questions to capture culturally specific nuances of trauma and distress.
  - Disclose any deviations from standardized administration in the forensic report.

- **Address feigning with cultural sensitivity**: Evaluate for possible malingering with appropriate caution, recognizing the inflated risk of false positive in many cross-cultural contexts.

  - Use validated tools like the TOMM, MMPI, or PAI cautiously, interpreting results in conjunction with other data.
  - Consider the examinee's educational background, literacy, and familiarity with testing when interpreting validity indices.

- **Disentangle systemic and individual factors**: Evaluate how systemic, peri-migration, and post-migration factors interact with individual behaviors and symptoms.

    - Assess the impact of discrimination, poverty, and systemic barriers on mental health and functioning.
    - Distinguish between trauma-related symptoms and those arising from ongoing stressors or cultural adaptation challenges.

9
Developing a Culturally Informed Research Agenda

Summary

The preceding chapters have identified numerous topics that have received limited research attention or empirically supported guidance. This chapter summarizes some of the immediate, most significant, and potentially remediable gaps in our existing knowledge. We focus on how culture shapes the phenomenology of mental disorders, the structure and accuracy of psychological testing, acculturation processes, the sociopolitical context of evaluations and forensic case formulation. A second major area of discussion is the need to establish helpful and feasible guidelines, with the ultimate goal of a consensus on "best practices" for forensic mental health professionals working with individuals from culturally and linguistically diverse backgrounds. While best practices necessarily evolve over time, establishing a process for gauging the utility of existing and proposed practices–and to determine when adaptations are needed–is a critical component of any set of recommendations. Finally, we address training models for enhancing cultural competence and the need to facilitate the dissemination of relevant information to professionals who confront challenging clinical situations.

This book began with a what we thought would be a simple task: Providing concrete and empirically informed guidance for forensic evaluators who work with individuals from culturally and linguistically diverse backgrounds. Our experience conducting these evaluations and navigating the myriad challenges that have arisen served as the foundation for this book. However, reviewing and summarizing the existing literature has highlighted how little we, as a profession, know about many important topics. Indeed, the process of writing this book has often felt like swimming in quicksand. While the research base continues to grow (relatively quickly in some subject areas but less so in others), our awareness of the gaps in our knowledge has become even more glaring.

Cultural and Linguistic Considerations in Forensic Mental Health Assessment. Barry Rosenfeld and Alicia Nijdam-Jones, Oxford University Press. © Oxford University Press (2026).
DOI: 10.1093/9780190900991.003.0009

Because of the steadily evolving literature, we have tried to highlight general principles that will hopefully remain relevant for the foreseeable future—and not be outdated before the book is published! To facilitate this, we have continued to amend and update content as we become aware of new and relevant findings. However, there will undoubtedly be important publications that we were unaware of or that were published between submitting a completed manuscript and the book's eventual publication. This is particularly true in domains that are the focus of more frequent research attention in forensic mental health, such as the assessment of malingering and violence risk. Other areas, such as the assessment of children and families and international human rights, grow far more slowly and have an even more pressing need for research attention. The present chapter aims to summarize some of those gaps, review strategies for addressing these issues in a way that may inform forensic mental health practice, and hopefully identify reachable goals for the next generation of researchers and clinicians.

What Do We Need to Know?

The gaps in our knowledge of cultural influences can seem insurmountable at times. For example, it is unrealistic to think that every psychological or neurocognitive test can be adequately cross-validated and "normed" in every language and population. In fact, it's not altogether clear what adequately normed even means. How large must a sample be to represent a population accurately? We know bigger samples are better than smaller samples, but how small is too small? Do we need separate studies, or should more than one research group examine an issue or population? These methodological questions have no correct answer but highlight the complexity of establishing normative data for any specific population. But what even *is* the population of interest? For example, do we need a series of studies with individuals living in Pakistan to understand the relevant cultural influences on specific forensic questions (which differ depending on the questions)? Can we extrapolate from research conducted *in* Pakistan to Pakistani immigrants who have been living in the US for months or years? If not, do we also need research examining differences between Pakistani immigrants living in the US, Canada, and England to understand how the immigration process or local culture might impact study findings? There are no simple answers to these questions, but there is little doubt that expanding our research base can help address some of the more pressing issues.

Although cross-cultural research has expanded rapidly in recent years, a disturbing proportion of this research continues to classify large and diverse populations under a single label, like pan-Asian, pan-Latine or pan-Indigenous groups. Moreover, even attempts to narrow these broad labels can be challenging. For example, one might choose to focus on a specific part of Asia, such as India—a country that is home to 22 different official languages (not including English), numerous major religions, and an incredibly wide range of cultures. Is it preferable to collect a representative sample that is proportional to the languages, beliefs, or cultures that characterize India, or does that approach (which is commonly used in the US to account for race/ethnicity in normative data) mask potentially important differences found in specific communities? The challenges to recognizing and analyzing diversity in research with heterogeneous samples cannot be overstated, which is a setup for frustration.

One way to inform these questions and circumvent the endless search for culturally and linguistically appropriate normative data is to identify general principles that can be applied across a range of ethnocultural settings and populations. The clearest example of this approach is the large body of research contrasting individualist and collectivist cultures (e.g., Darwish & Huber, 2003; Greif, 1994; Triandis, 2001). This literature grew in popularity during the last quarter of the twentieth century, with hundreds of publications using the individualist/collectivist framework to examine cultural differences in attitudes, behaviors, values, and customs. At the broadest level, individualist cultures are generally associated with North America, Western Europe, and Australia/New Zealand, whereas collectivist cultures are more common in Asia, Africa, and Latin America. While this distinction generated many interesting findings regarding how people in different societies tend to view themselves in relation to others, understanding the extent to which any individual person or subgroup adheres to these values requires a separate level of analysis. Moreover, research has suggested that even the wording of scales to measure individualism and collectivism is influenced by the cultural variables being measured, indicating that the interpretation of questions about the individualism–collectivism continuum are impacted by the cultural background of the respondent, regardless of content (Shulruf et al., 2011). In short, the circularity that has been observed when measuring the constructs of individualism and collectivism has provided limited help to our understanding of cultural and historical influences that might impact specific forensic psychological questions. Nevertheless, armed with the starting point of examining broad cultural trends, forensic psychologists can begin to investigate a set of possible influences that might affect the accuracy of the tools, techniques, and inferences that guide our work.

An example of what this might look like in practice begins with examining a broad set of cultural groups in a region (e.g., Latine individuals from Latin America), with attention to patterns both within and across these groups. Our study of the false positive rate with the Test of Memory Malingering (TOMM) across eight Latin American countries (described in Chapter 3) is a relatively simple example of this approach applied to a specific forensic question (Nijdam-Jones et al., 2017). The need for reliable methods for gauging cognitive effort is uncontested, and of particular concern is the potential for false positives—identifying someone as failing to put forth adequate effort (or deliberately trying to perform poorly) when their performance is actually impaired by factors specific to their cultural, personal, or sociopolitical background. Our study found heightened concern about false positives in some Latin American countries, yet there was little evidence that individuals in neighboring countries were similarly disadvantaged. Of particular interest, this study found a significant association between TOMM accuracy rates and education, age, and level of a country's economic development. These data help clarify the factors that might influence test results, and one could plausibly justify extending the findings from that study to make inferences about other, similar cultural groups. For example, the TOMM is unlikely to generate high rates of false positives in someone from Uruguay, given the similarities to Argentina and Mexico (both of which demonstrated low false positive rates) in terms of educational systems and economic development. However, the TOMM would likely be more problematic for individuals from El Salvador or Haiti, where economic development and the average level of education are much lower (i.e., roughly similar to Bolivia, which showed a much higher rate of false positives). Unfortunately, few studies have examined tools or techniques within such a broad range of individuals and cultures (and admittedly, our access to these data was fortuitous, thanks to a large, multinational study conducted by our co-authors). Nevertheless, the principles remain important: Examining differences within subgroups that share cultural similarities and languages can be essential for developing generalizable data. Even if it is impractical to collect samples that permit a nuanced analysis of individual subgroups or subcultures, simply collecting accurate and detailed background data can facilitate a greater understanding of cultural and contextual influences.

Another setting where focused research can help our field begin to identify patterns that have potential importance for forensic mental health evaluations is the assessment of cognitive functioning. Like the surge of interest in the collectivism/individualism spectrum, the last century saw considerable attention focused on understanding cultural differences in the construct of intelligence. Debates about the very nature of this construct were often heated and led to the innovative research efforts that demonstrated the importance of culture in how we understand and evaluate cognitive functioning. Much of this attention was focused on developing "culture-free" measures of intelligence (e.g., Cattell, 1940; Sternberg, 2004), though these efforts were met with limited success. Yet while there is general agreement that culture plays an unusually large role in how we conceptualize and measure intelligence, the forensic evaluator confronted with a monolingual Vietnamese-speaking criminal defendant charged with capital murder has no clear pathway for evaluating this defendant's intelligence if asked to assist in determining whether the *Atkins* decision (prohibiting the execution of intellectually disabled individuals) applies to this individual. Are language-free cognitive tests such as the Raven's Progressive Matrices or the Test of Non-verbal Intelligence (TONI) sufficiently accurate for this purpose? As discussed in Chapter 5, the somewhat dated research base supporting these approaches to measuring intelligence has languished despite the ever-growing importance of questions that hinge on their results.

What if, instead of evaluating this monolingual Vietnamese immigrant for pending criminal charges, the evaluation required identifying neurocognitive damages from toxic chemical exposure? Do we have *any* neurocognitive assessment tools or appropriate normative data to guide us? Whether researchers should continue to invest time and resources into evaluating existing language-free tests or put greater emphasis on exploring the generalizability of translated adaptations of more comprehensive batteries (e.g., the Wechsler scales or Repeatable Battery for Assessment of Neuropsychological Status) is not a decision we (the authors) are equipped to make. Still, there is clearly a need for greater attention to assessing neurocognitive functioning in non-English speaking individuals.

Another area in which research is sorely lacking, particularly regarding forensic applications, is the conceptualization and measurement of processes of acculturation. As researchers, we have tried to examine the influence of acculturation in many of our studies, including those focusing on test accuracy and legal decision-making. Although several measures exist that purport to measure acculturation, we have been struck by how simplistic both the understanding and measurement of this construct are—and how limited the options for quantifying acculturation are. A surprising number of studies (including some of our own) have relied on simple indices like the number of years living in an English-speaking country (e.g., US, Canada or Australia), or the proportion of time spent speaking English (for those whose dominant language is not English).

We claim no particular expertise in understanding this challenging construct, but it is clear that we need a more sophisticated understanding of what acculturation means and how to reliably and accurately operationalize this construct. For example, while theories of acculturation identify two or more "dimensions" that comprise acculturation, few measurement tools incorporate this approach (one exception is the Bidirectional Acculturation Scale for Hispanics; Marin & Gamba, 1996). Instead, researchers often apply a Eurocentric lens, focusing on the extent to which immigrants conform to the norms and values of the dominant cultural context. Without a more sophisticated method of assessing and analyzing acculturation, understanding the impact of different acculturation patterns or approaches on critical variables will continue to languish. Not only are improved tools for gauging acculturation necessary, but a more rigorous approach is clearly needed when considering this potentially important influence on important psycho-legal issues.

Expanding Research Methodologies

While large-scale research approaches may be needed for many of the norm-referenced questions that arise in forensic assessment, these are not the only methodological approaches that can help us understand cultural influences. Qualitative data collection and analysis are equally important, but an under-utilized technique for understanding cultural diversity. A common tool for understanding unusual medical cases, case studies and qualitative methods are still relatively infrequent in psychological research publications. One example of a qualitative approach might involve surveying experts, mental health professionals, or routine citizens to elicit their opinions and perspectives on potentially relevant issues. Another example might involve case studies of atypical presentations or unusual test results. Qualitative methods have been an invaluable approach to identifying culturally unique symptom manifestations or rare explanations for problematic behaviors (e.g., Fabian et al., 2018; Hinton et al., 2010; Krause, 1989).

The accumulated knowledge from qualitative research or descriptive studies can also form the basis for more sophisticated data analysis, which may yield more generalizable information. One such example was the previously described study by Rasmussen and colleagues (2014), who examined culturally specific idioms of distress from around the world. They combined data from case studies, focus groups, ethnographic interviews, formal surveys, and research with individuals living in their country of origin or as refugees living in a range of Western countries. Using cluster analysis, they integrated these diverse research findings into a series of symptom patterns that they interpreted as reflecting more somatic-based symptoms, anxiety-based symptoms, dysphoric symptoms, and behavioral disturbances. Although cluster analysis may be of more academic interest than a technique that provides concrete guidance in any specific forensic evaluation (and the underlying research base has likely expanded considerably in the decade since this paper was published), their findings can help contextualize culturally unique symptoms into categories that map onto existing models of psychopathology. Moreover, the very existence of such an extensive research base describing culturally unique symptoms is a valuable resource to anyone tasked with evaluating an individual from one of the many countries and cultures targeted by these studies. Of course, this type of synthesis is only possible if individual researchers publish findings from small samples, case studies, and broad-based surveys of potentially relevant populations.

The very existence of culturally specific symptoms of distress raises another critical set of questions regarding the application of Western diagnostic models. There is little consensus as to whether culturally specific symptoms should be formally integrated into an existing diagnostic scheme. Should we modify our diagnostic criteria to improve recognition of clinically significant impairment or distress in cultures/subgroups where we have evidence to support such deviations? If so, what would that process look like? Would we permit the substitution of culturally unique symptoms for other established symptoms of a known disorder, or can/should we simply keep applying the DSM as is, regardless of whether it optimally captures the disorder as it manifests in another culture? Does the rigid application of DSM criteria *ever* make sense when individual differences are so crucial? Although we are not prepared to answer these questions, we would argue that the appropriate response is to spur further research, whether in the form of systematic epidemiological data, surveys of expert clinicians, or any other approach that might provide guidance and support for the evaluator confronted with a challenging case. While we don't anticipate answering many of the complex questions raised in these pages, we hope that the next generation of researchers begins to chip away at some of them.

Another crucial aspect to expanding our methodological approaches is the inclusion of community-based participatory research (CBPR) (e.g., Wallerstein & Duran, 2006). This approach partners researchers with stakeholders and individuals with lived experience in forensic mental health services in order to ground research in a more ecologically valid and socially informed framework. A growing trend in psychology is to actively involve those directly impacted by services in developing research aimed at improving these services, including research design, implementation, and analysis. Engaging with community partners ensures we address the right questions, using language that is understandable and accessible to stakeholders, when developing culturally responsive forensic mental health services.

Importantly, CBPR situates forensic research within its broader sociopolitical context, recognizing that inequities in mental health and involvement with the legal system are often shaped by historical and structural forces such as colonization, systemic racism, and socioeconomic marginalization. By naming these influences explicitly, CBPR moves beyond simply "including diverse voices" to transforming how research questions are framed and whose knowledge is valued. This approach is particularly relevant for research with culturally and linguistically diverse communities and can aid clinicians and researchers in better identifying biases in existing tools. For instance, CBPR can illuminate cultural, linguistic, and sociopolitical factors that shape assessment processes and outcomes. This participatory approach enhances the quality of the research by incorporating diverse perspectives and lived experiences, and helps build trust and collaboration between researchers and the communities we serve.

Community-based research often yields relevant and actionable findings that can be directly applied to improve forensic assessment services for equity-seeking groups. By valuing the voices and needs of those most affected by our assessments, we can adapt forensic assessment practices to be more effective and culturally safe. This strategy helps bridge the gap between research and practice, ensuring that forensic mental health services are responsive to the needs of culturally and linguistically diverse communities, rather than imposing existing structures and frameworks that may not be optimal. Additionally, the CBPR approach contributes to the decolonization of research methodologies by challenging traditional power dynamics and valuing culturally diverse knowledge systems and perspectives.

Improving Multicultural Practice

Perhaps one of the most important research goals for advancing forensic practice with culturally diverse individuals is identifying and articulating what constitutes "best practices." Achieving this goal requires moving beyond the traditional experimental designs that most mental health professionals are accustomed to. Instead, it involves gauging the perceived adequacy of various practices, techniques, opinions, or diagnoses. This process typically relies on the views of potentially relevant stakeholders such as judges, other mental health professionals, and members of relevant cultural communities to which an examinee belongs. Although these data may help shape questions about best practices, they can also be helpful in identifying culturally insensitive behaviors, thereby decreasing the risk that problematic behaviors will continue. For example, judges have periodically cited what they perceive as inadequate attention to the role of culture in forensic psychological evaluations, as evidenced by cases arising in Washington state. In *State of Washington v. Sisouvanh* (2012), the Washington Supreme Court deemed a forensic psychologist's assessment inadequate because the evaluating clinician "refused to acknowledge the importance of cultural competence and failed to reasonably account for the need for cultural competence in his or her evaluation" (pp. 624–625). More recently, the Washington Supreme Court reiterated the importance of cultural competence by affirming a lower court's decision to discount the opinion of evaluators who "made no attempt to evaluate [the defendant] in a culturally appropriate fashion" (*State of Washington v. Ortiz-Abrego*, 2017; p. 413).

However, while egregious examples of culturally insensitive practices may be readily apparent (and some have served as the basis for the case vignettes that opened preceding chapters), little research has attempted to refine what approaches might be optimal. This might be surprising given that several guidelines and recommendations have been propagated over the years. For example, the *DSM-IV* first introduced the concept of cultural formulation in 1994, and a revised and expanded version of the Cultural Formulation Interview (CFI) was included in the *DSM-5*—which means that virtually every forensic mental health professional already has a copy! Yet, despite the widespread availability of this tool, research has only recently begun to examine whether the CFI is perceived as helpful in achieving its goals (Lewis-Fernandez et al., 2020). Of course, many of the goals of the CFI may appear tangentially relevant to forensic mental health assessments, such as expressing empathy and enhancing rapport with examinees or identifying potential treatment goals that fall outside the primary diagnosis (or legal issue). While rapport is undoubtedly a valuable component of any mental health assessment, whether forensic or otherwise, the CFI does not directly address many assessment goals that challenge the forensic mental health professional. For example, understanding how the US legal system might differ from the examinee's understanding of legal practices (e.g., in their culture or country of origin), or the examinee's expectations from the assessment process, and the extent to which they can develop a trusting relationship with an attorney (if one is available) can be essential components of forensic evaluations, yet are not addressed by the CFI.[1]

Similarly, understanding an examinee's expectations regarding the nature and outcome of any necessary interventions, whether they are interventions traditionally utilized by mental health professionals or reflect Indigenous or culturally based practices, can be critical to many forensic questions, including gauging damages in personal injury evaluations, assessing parenting behaviors (e.g., including treatment decisions for children), determining competence to accept or reject treatment, and a range of other questions that arise in forensic mental health evaluations. In short, while the availability of the CFI—or other proposed techniques to enhance the cultural relevance of forensic mental health assessments represents an important step forward, further research is clearly needed to enhance these tools. Perhaps more importantly, the extent to which the CFI and other proposed techniques actually accomplish their stated goal of improving mental health assessments of culturally diverse individuals requires external validation.

To date, the most thorough analysis of what might constitute best practices in culturally informed forensic mental health assessment is a qualitative study by Fanniff and colleagues (2023). These authors used a Delphi-type survey to elicit

[1] This should not be taken as a criticism of the CFI, as it was not developed as a tool for improving *forensic* assessments.

information from experienced forensic psychologists with expertise in cross-cultural issues. Among the primary practices identified as critical to developing cultural competence were the following:

1. The need to attend training on how cultural identities impact the assessment process;
2. Reading newly published materials relevant to culturally informed practices (i.e., to stay abreast of recent developments);
3. Self-monitoring one's case selection and patterns of opinions as they relate to cultural identities;
4. Reflecting on one's own identity, beliefs, and privilege; and
5. Consulting with peers and supervisors regarding cultural considerations.

In addition, these authors outlined numerous tasks and steps that should occur before (i.e., preparatory to), during, and after (e.g., during case formulation and report writing) the evaluation process, many of which have been discussed in the preceding chapters. Although this approach to identifying best practices is an important starting point, the frequency with which these practices are actually undertaken by the typical clinician (or even by the experts who were surveyed) remains an unanswered question. Hence, the results of Fanniff et al.'s survey should be seen as an important starting point, but questions about what approach will best achieve these goals (e.g., self-exploration, consideration of how one's own intersecting identities might impact decision-making) are often less apparent. Likewise, research evaluating the extent to which recommended steps impact case outcomes is sorely needed and will no doubt prove challenging. Of course, the extent to which recommended practices apply to a particular case at hand will undoubtedly vary and therefore requires at least some level of cultural sophistication to determine whether a recommendation or technique is actually relevant.

Ironically, perhaps the most crucial set of issues identified by Fanniff et al. are also the least understood: The extent to which cultural differences impact clinician behaviors and opinions. While the impact of biases on human behavior is undisputed, we are not aware of any systematic research examining how cultural differences might impact the "bottom line" opinions that forensic mental health professionals offer. No doubt many would like to believe that they are "color-blind" when it comes to the influence of race, gender, and ethnicity, but this belief remains largely untested in the work of forensic mental health professionals (though researchers frequently examine the extent to which these factors impact jury decisions, employment decisions, and a host of other important outcomes). Admittedly, this is a challenging undertaking and one that is fraught with potential embarrassment. What would it mean if an evaluator determined that they consistently assigned higher psychopathy ratings to Black examinees compared to White examinees? The most obvious explanation would be racial bias, but have alternative explanations been adequately explored and ruled out? Early research on violence risk suggested that Black adults with a mental disorder were more likely to engage in violence than White adults with a mental disorder. However, subsequent research that controlled for socioeconomic disadvantage found no significant association between race and violent recidivism (Silver, 2000). Without large-scale studies that rigorously account for such covariates, our ability to understand how sociocultural variables shape clinical decision-making remains severely limited.

Moreover, eliciting the data necessary for such an analysis may be politically untenable. Would a state office of mental health or correctional system agree to provide the requisite data to analyze questions that pertain to biased practices? We have had little success obtaining data that would permit an examination of biases in forensic mental health decision-making. And the list of potentially confounding variables in any such analysis is often overwhelming—and frequently equally unavailable. Do we simply assume that a White psychologist of European descent will demonstrate more bias when evaluating a Spanish-speaking immigrant than a Latine psychologist of Mexican descent? Or is the level of bias more likely influenced by the evaluator's unique personal and family background, linguistic skills, experience with individuals from a region similar to the examinee, and perhaps even the nature of the evaluation being conducted? Are we even capable of consistently identifying bias within ourselves? These are just a handful of the questions that challenge our abilities to develop a culturally informed practice, virtually all of which have been ignored in the existing research literature.

One potential solution, admittedly long-term, is increasing the diversity among forensic mental health professionals. While greater diversity among mental health professionals, and researchers in particular, may improve the cultural sensitivity of both evaluations and the research that underlies them, empirical evidence is limited. However, a recent study indicated that racially and ethnically marginalized researchers possess a deeper awareness and understanding of culturally responsive research practices (Gilbert & Pasque, 2023). This suggests that their perspectives can be especially valuable for identifying cultural nuances and reducing biases in both assessment and research contexts. Furthermore, drawing from CBPR literature, it becomes clear that psychologists from diverse backgrounds can enrich evaluation methods. Of course, increasing the profession's diversity is probably not within the power of most readers of this book. Nonetheless, the responsibility for fostering a diverse workforce rests with all of us, whether we work in clinical, academic, or research settings.

Building Cultural Competence

As the preceding pages indicate, the need to identify knowledge and skill gaps does not necessarily lend itself to finding solutions that will increase knowledge and enhance skills. Hence, another important need for researchers is improving actual clinical practice (beyond simply reading this book). In the US, the American Psychological Association's Commission on Accreditation has long required formal training in multicultural psychology. These guidelines have consistently emphasized the importance of diversity, defined broadly by the ADDRESSING model: Age and generational differences, Developmental disability, Disability acquired later, Religion, Ethnicity, Socio-economic status, Sexual orientation, Indigenous heritage, National origin, and Gender (Hays, 2008). Psychology graduate programs either fulfill this requirement through a free-standing course (often titled Multicultural Psychology) or through relevant content embedded into multiple different courses (and sometimes both). Yet there is considerable variability in the content of these courses, with many focusing heavily on race and ethnicity within the US and rarely considering the broader range of issues that apply to culturally and linguistically diverse individuals. Moreover, within the subfield of forensic psychology, the extent to which students or established professionals attend to these issues varies dramatically. In this context, cultural competence involves more than the acquisition of discrete skills and reflects an ongoing, reflective process that incorporates cultural humility, responsiveness, and attention to power, context, and systemic inequities in forensic practice.

One option for developing and sustaining cultural competence in a specific domain (such as forensic mental health assessment) is through continuing education workshops. One of us has offered these workshops for more than 15 years, originally in person but increasingly through online and on-demand formats. Workshops are a logical approach for professionals interested in the subject matter, particularly when attendance is voluntary and the subject matter is selected by the attendees (from a range of available options). However, many workshops are institution-driven rather than learner-driven, with content selected by an administrator or clinical director and attendance either expected or required. Our experience from conducting institution-level workshops is that interest level and attention vary dramatically among the attendees, with some who are visibly uninterested and distracted by other activities.

The growth of online and on-demand workshops[2] has significantly increased the availability of continued education opportunities. Particularly with

[2] Online workshops are typically scheduled, synchronous experiences that largely mimic the traditional in-person workshop model. On-demand workshops are usually pre-recorded and can be completed in multiple sessions, with the timing determined by the participant.

on-demand workshops, interested professionals no longer need to wait for an opportunity to attend an in-person training or worry about scheduling conflicts. However, on-demand workshops do not provide the same level of engagement or interaction as in-person workshops, and attendees do not have the benefit of learning from questions and answers generated by other attendees, which is typical of both in-person and (to a lesser extent) virtual workshops. Virtual (online) workshops provide some of the advantages of in-person workshops, as the experience is typically synchronous, held at a pre-determined time (or times), so attendees can ask questions and learn from questions asked by others. Another clear advantage of online workshops is that attendees often have access to internationally recognized experts, which would not otherwise be feasible (whether due to cost or scheduling logistics). On the other hand, maintaining the interest of attendees through a video screen is far more challenging (in our experience) than during an in-person workshop, and is even more challenging with pre-recorded, on-demand workshops than with online workshops. In short, there are advantages and disadvantages to each of these approaches to continuing education in support of culturally safe practice. Unfortunately, research on the effectiveness of alternative training models has been virtually absent, so how can we determine whether one approach is superior to others—or whether one workshop is better than another when both focus on the same topic?

The need for research examining modes of training is not unique to forensic mental health assessment, particularly given that cultural competence requires ongoing development rather than mastery. A recent review of cultural competence training programs for general mental health providers found that rigorous research designs were virtually absent (Chu et al., 2022). Of the 40 identified studies, only three (7.1%) utilized a randomized controlled trial (RCT), and the vast majority simply analyzed changes in attendee knowledge and attitudes based on pre- and post-workshop questionnaires. Indeed, most workshops rely solely on attendee self-assessment to measure outcomes. This is a common and accessible approach, regardless of whether self-assessment corresponds to behavioral changes (versus, for example, social desirability; Constantine & Ladany, 2000). Moreover, because of the timing of Chu et al.'s review, virtually all the workshops they analyzed were conducted in person. On-demand workshops predated the COVID-19 pandemic, but the movement from in-person to virtual workshops and training programs has exploded in recent years. As both attendees and presenters, we are acutely aware of the differences in these formats, particularly when workshop attendance is mandated by an employer rather than sought by a clinician who has identified the need for improved skills.

Independent study is another option for continuously expanding one's cultural competence, particularly given the steadily growing research and scholarship supporting culturally safe and antiracist practice in many relevant domains (assessment tools, culturally unique symptom manifestations, and different forms of bias that might impact our objectivity). We all have the opportunity (though not necessarily enough time) to keep abreast of recent developments in research and scholarship; however, the effectiveness of a self-directed approach to expanding cultural competence is also unknown. The circularity inherent in the self-directed approach is also probably apparent, since clinicians who seek out and attend to the growing research literature are likely to be those who already have substantial cultural competence.

Established professionals may also find it helpful to seek consultation from a colleague when confronted with a referral that challenges their current level of cultural competence, though some professionals decline those referrals altogether. We would discourage the latter approach for two reasons. First, it may risk depriving an examinee of a true subject matter expert simply because cultural issues complicate the evaluation. Second, it deprives the evaluator of the opportunity to expand their expertise and knowledge base, albeit by forcing them to consider issues they may have previously not engaged with. In our experience, the greatest learning opportunities have come from precisely those cases where we had to stretch the boundaries of our expertise, doing research outside of the case materials, and occasionally seeking outside consultation to learn more about the relevant issues. However, the extent to which "boundary stretching" is actually viewed as helpful to the professional, versus possibly giving rise to challenges in court, is yet another question that would benefit from systematic research.

Given the undisputed importance of motivation, perhaps a more important question is how to incentivize the desire for cultural competence. Readers of this book are clearly not the target audience for this question, but many of us have encountered clinicians who seem surprisingly unaware of their limited cultural competence, even when they are well-respected for their work in other aspects of forensic mental health assessment. How do we transform cultural competence from a box to be checked off to an ongoing movement toward cultural humility, cultural safety, and improved skills, knowledge, and understanding? Given the wealth of unique clinical (and personal) experiences that can come from expanded cultural competence, this should seem like a relatively easy question to answer. However, this probably reflects our own biases and interests rather than a more general truism that applies to all. Unfortunately, without an intrinsic motivation to consistently improve one's cultural competence as a lifelong practice, there is little doubt that we risk stagnation.

Concluding Thoughts

The importance of understanding and appreciating cultural and linguistic diversity in forensic mental health assessments is ever-growing, and opportunities to enhance these skills are available all around us. As researchers and clinicians, we can make valuable contributions to this growing field while simultaneously strengthening our own clinical skills. Moreover, by making cultural and linguistic diversity central to our work as forensic mental health professionals, we can expand our understanding of our own strengths, weaknesses, privileges, and biases. This process, coupled with embracing cultural humility and the ongoing need for enhanced cultural competence, has the potential to improve the accuracy of forensic mental health evaluations and, by extension, benefit the individuals and systems that we serve. We hope this book serves as a helpful starting point—and certainly not the end!

References

Achenbach, T. M., & Rescorla, L. A. (2001). *Manual for the ASEBA school-age forms & profiles*. Burlington: University of Vermont, Research Center for Children, Youth, & Families.

Adegoke, T. G., & Oladeji, D. (2008). Community norms and cultural attitudes and beliefs factors influencing violence against women of reproductive age in Nigeria. *European Journal of Scientific Research*, *20*(2), 265–273.

Adjorlolo, S. (2016). Ecological validity of executive function tests in moderate traumatic brain injury in Ghana. *The Clinical Neuropsychologist*, *30*(sup1), 1517–1537. https://doi.org/10.1080/13854046.2016.1172667

Adjorlolo, S. (2018). Diagnostic accuracy, sensitivity, and specificity of executive function tests in moderate traumatic brain injury in Ghana. *Assessment*, *25*(4), 498–512. https://doi.org/10.1177/1073191116646445

Adjorlolo, S., & Chan, H. C. O. (2019). Risk assessment of criminal offenders in Ghana: An investigation of the discriminant validity of the HCR-20V3. *International Journal of Law and Psychiatry*, *66*, 101458. https://doi.org/10.1016/j.ijlp.2019.101458

Afifi, M., & Von Bothmer, M. (2007). Egyptian women's attitudes and beliefs about female genital cutting and its association with childhood maltreatment. *Nursing and Health Sciences*, *9*(4), 270–276. https://doi.org/10.1111/j.1442-2018.2007.00366.x

Aguilar, C., Bailey, C., Karyadi, K. A., Kinney, D. I., & Nitch, S. R. (2021). The use of performance validity tests among inpatient forensic monolingual Spanish-speakers. *Applied Neuropsychology: Adult*, 1–9. https://www.tandfonline.com/doi/full/10.1080/23279095.2021.1970555

Ahmed, S., Lee, S. C., & Helmus, L. M. (2023). Predictive accuracy of Static-99R across different racial/ethnic groups: A meta-analysis. *Law and Human Behavior*, *47*(1), 275–291. https://doi.org/10.1037/lhb0000517

Al Abduwani, J., Sidebotham, P., Al Saadoon, M., Al Lawati, M., & Barlow, J. (2017). The child abuse potential inventory: Development of an Arabic version. *Child Abuse and Neglect*, *72*, 283–290. https://doi.org/10.1016/j.chiabu.2017.08.012

Ali, S., & Frederickson, N. (2011). The parenting dimensions of British Pakistani and White mothers of primary school children. *Infant and Child Development*, *20*, 313–329. https://doi.org/10.1002/icd.696

Ali, T. S., & Khan, N. (2007). Strategies and recommendations for prevention and control of domestic violence against women in Pakistan. *Journal of Pakistan Medical Association*, *57*(1), 27–32. https://ecommons.aku.edu/pakistan_fhs_son/171

Allard, V., Higgs, T., & Slight, M. (2024). Psychometric properties of the Spousal Assault Risk Assessment from samples of people having perpetrated intimate partner violence. *Trauma, Violence, & Abuse*, *25*(5), 3777–3795. https://doi.org/10.1177/15248380241262275

Altarriba, J., & Santiago-Rivera, A. L. (1994). Current perspectives on using linguistic and cultural factors in counselling the Hispanic client. *Professional Psychology, Research and Practice*, *25*(4), 388–397. https://doi.org/10.1037/0735-7028.25.4.388

Alvarado, C. G., Shrank, F. A., McGrew, K. S., Mather, N., & Woodcock, R. W. (2019). *Batería IV Woodcock-Muñoz*. Riverside Insights.

American Academy of Psychiatry and the Law. (2005). *Ethics guidelines for the practice of forensic psychiatry*. https://aapl.org/docs/pdf/ETHICSGDLNS.pdf

American Psychiatric Association. (2022). *Diagnostic and statistical manual of mental disorders, fifth edition, text revision* (DSM-5-TR). Washington DC: American Psychiatric Association Press.
American Psychological Association. (2022). *Guidelines for child custody evaluations in family law proceedings*. Retrieved from https://www.apa.org/practice/guidelines/child-custody-evaluations.pdf
American Psychological Association. (2013). Specialty guidelines for forensic psychology. *American Psychologist, 68*, 7–19. https://doi.org/10.1037/a0029889
American Psychological Association. (2017a). *Ethical principles of psychologists and code of conduct*. Washington, DC: Author. Retrieved from https://www.apa.org/ethics/code
American Psychological Association. (2017b). *Multicultural guidelines: An ecological approach to context, identity, and intersectionality*. Washington, DC: Author. Retrieved from http://www.apa.org/about/policy/multicultural-guidelines.pdf
American Psychological Association. (2019a). *APA guidelines for psychological practice for people with low-income and economic marginalization*. Washington, DC: Author. Retrieved from https://www.apa.org/about/policy/guidelines-low-income.pdf
American Psychological Association. (2019b). *APA race and ethnicity guidelines in psychology*. Washington, DC: Author. Retrieved from http://www.apa.org/about/policy/race-and-ethnicity-in-psychology.pdf
American Psychological Association. (2023). *Inclusive language guide* (2nd ed.). https://www.apa.org/about/apa/equity-diversity-inclusion/language-guidelines.pdf
Amoakohene, M. I. (2004). Violence against women in Ghana: A look at women's perceptions and review of policy and social responses. *Social Science & Medicine, 59*(11), 2373–2385. https://doi.org/10.1016/j.socscimed.2004.04.001
Anderson, J. L., Plantz, J., Glocker, S., & Zapf, P. A. (2022). The MacCAT-CA and the ECST-R in competence to stand trial evaluations: A critical review and practical implications. *Journal of Personality Assessment, 104*(2), 281–288, https://doi.org/10.1080/00223891.2021.2006671
Andrews, D. A., & Bonta, J. (1995). *The LSI–R: The level of service inventory–revised*. Multi-Health Systems.
Andrews, D. A., Bonta, J., & Hoge, R. D. (1990). Classification for effective rehabilitation: Rediscovering psychology. *Criminal Justice and Behavior, 17*, 19–52. https://doi.org/10.1177/0093854890017001004
Aparcero, M. (2023). *Development and validation of a standardized instrument to assess competence in immigration court*. Fordham University.
Aparcero, M., Nijdam-Jones, A., Rosenfeld, B., & García-López, E. (2020). Sex offender risk assessment in Latin America: An exploratory study. *Professional Psychology: Research and Practice, 51*(5), 467–476. https://doi.org/10.1037/pro0000271
Aparcero, M., Picard, E. H., Nijdam-Jones, A., & Rosenfeld, B. (2023). Comparing the ability of MMPI-2 and MMPI-2-RF validity scales to detect feigning: A meta-analysis. *Assessment, 30*(3), 744–760. https://doi.org/10.1177/10731911211067535
Appazov, A. (2016). *Expert evidence and international criminal justice*. New York: Springer.
Arango-Lasprilla, J. C., Rivera, D., Longoni, M., Saracho, C. P., Garza, M. T., Aliaga, A., Rodríguez, W., Rodríguez-Agudelo, Y., Rábago, B., Sutter, M., Schebela, S., Luna, M., Ocampo-Barba, N., Galarza-del-angel, J., Bringas, M. L., Esenarro, L., Martínez, C., García-Egan, P., & Perrin, P. B. (2015). Modified Wisconsin Card Sorting Test (M-WCST): Normative data for the Latin American Spanish speaking adult population. *NeuroRehabilitation, 37*(4), 563–590. https://doi.org/10.3233/nre-151280
Arango-Lasprilla, J. C., Ayearst, L. E., Rivera, D., Dini, M. E., Olabarrieta-Landa, L., Ramos-Usuga, D., Perrin, P. B., & McCaffrey, R. (2024). Test of Memory Malingering 2nd Edition: Normative data from cognitively intact adults living in

Spain. *Applied Neuropsychology: Adult*, 1–7. https://doi.org/10.1080/23279095.2024.2421450

Arbach, K., & Folino, J. (2021). La valoracion del riesgo de reincidencia en imputados por violencia contra la pareja: Un estudio longitudinal con la guia SARA [Risk assessment of intimate partner violent reoffending: A longitudinal study with the Spousal Assault Risk Assessment guide]. *Anuario de Psicología Jurídica, 31*(1), 35–44. https://doi.org/10.5093/apj2021a4

Archer, R. P., Buffington-Vollum, J. K., Stredny, R. V., & Handel, R. W. (2006). A survey of psychological test use patterns among forensic psychologists. *Journal of Personality Assessment, 87*(1), 84–94. https://doi.org/10.1207/s15327752jpa8701_07

Archer, R. P., Handel, R. W., Ben-Porath, Y. S., & Tellegen, A. (2016). *Minnesota Multiphasic Personality Inventory-Adolescent-Restructured Form (MMPI-A-RF): Administration, scoring, interpretation, and technical manual.* Minneapolis: University of Minnesota Press.

Ardic, F. C., Kose, S., Solmaz, M., Kulacaoglu, F., & Balcioglu, Y. H. (2019). Reliability, validity, and factorial structure of the Turkish version of the Structured Inventory of Malingered Symptomatology (Turkish SIMS). *Psychiatry and Clinical Psychopharmacology, 29*(2), 182–188. https://doi.org/10.1080/24750573.2019.1599237

Ardila, A. (2007). The impact of culture on neuropsychological test performance. In B. Uzzell, M. Ponton, & A. Ardila (Eds.), *International handbook of cross-cultural neuropsychology* (pp. 23–44). Lawrence Erlbaum Associates.

Ardila, A., & Moreno, S. (2001). Neuropsychological test performance in Aruaco Indians: An exploratory study. *Journal of the International Neuropsychological Society, 7*(4), 510–515. https://doi.org/10.1017/S1355617701004076

Ardila, A., Bertolucci, P. H., Braga, L. W., Castro-Caldas, A., Judd, T., Kosmidis, M. H., Matute, E., Nitrini, R., Ostrosky-Solis, F., & Rosselli, M. (2010). Illiteracy: The neuropsychology of cognition without reading. *Archives of Clinical Neuropsychology, 25*(8), 689–712. https://doi.org/10.1093/arclin/acq079

Arentoft, A., Byrd, D., Monzones, J., Coulehan, K., Fuentes, A., Rosario, A., Miranda, C., Morgello, S., & Rivera Mindt, M. (2015). Socioeconomic status and neuropsychological functioning: Associations in an ethnically diverse HIV+ cohort. *Clinical Neuropsychologist, 29*(2), 232–254. https://doi.org/10.1080/13854046.2015.1029974

Artiola I Fortuny, L., Hermosillo, R. D., Heaton, R. K., & Pardee, R. E. I. (1999). *Manual de normas y procedimien- tos para la Batería Neuropsicológica en Español.* Brookfield: Swets & Zeitlinger.

Association of Family and Conciliation Courts. (2022). *Guidelines for parenting plan evaluations in family law cases.* Retrieved from: https://www.afccnet.org/Portals/0/Committees/2022%20Parenting%20Plan%20Guidelines.pdf?ver=pL0FdZapJmsbfUvQ6zzN-A%3D%3D

Atkins v. *Virginia*, 536 U.S. 304 (2002).

Austin, W. G. (2016). Comment on Parkinson and Cashmore's (2015) research and proposal for reforming child custody relocation law: child custody evaluator and psychological perspecitve. *Family Court Review, 54*(4), 620–631. https://doi.org/10.1111/fcre.12247

Australian Bureau of Statistics. (2024). *Prisoners in Australia.* Retrieved from https://www.abs.gov.au/statistics/people/crime-and-justice/prisoners-australia/latest-release

Ayenew, A. A., Mol, B. W., Bradford, B., & Abeje, G. (2024). Prevalence of female genital mutilation and associated factors among women and girls in Africa: A systematic review and meta-analysis. *Systematic Reviews, 13*(1), 26. https://doi.org/10.1186/s13643-023-02428-6

Bachman, J. G., & O'Malley, P. M. (1984). Yea-saying, nay-saying, and going to extremes: Black-White differences in response styles. *Public Opinion Quarterly, 48*(2), 491–509. https://doi.org/10.1086/268845

Bailey, C. A., & Widner, K. (2022). The nexus between immigration status, policy, and proceedings, and mental health. *Current Opinion in Psychology, 47*, 1–9. https://doi.org/10.1016/j.copsyc.2022.101411

Baird, A., Mejia, C., Booth, J., Collins, R., & Wisdom, N. (2023). Cross-cultural utility of performance validity indicators in a community sample from Kampala, Uganda. *Journal of the International Neuropsychological Society, 29*(S1), 750–751. https://doi.org/10.1017/S1355617723009347

Bajjaleh, C., Braw, Y. C., & Elkana, O. (2021). Adaptation and initial validation of the Arabic version of the Word Memory Test (WMTARB). *Applied Neuropsychology: Adult*, 1–10. https://doi.org/10.1080/23279095.2021.1923495

Baker, K. A., & Dairy, M. (2003). Cultural norms versus state law in treating incest: A suggested model for Arab families. *Child Abuse and Neglect, 27*, 109–123. https://doi.org/10.1016/S0145-2134(02)00505-7

Bamford, K. W. (1991). Bilingual issues in mental health assessment and treatment. *Hispanic Journal of Behavioral Sciences, 13*, 377–390. https://doi.org/10.1177/07399863910134002

Barber-Rioja, B., Akinsulure-Smith, A. M., & Vendzules, S. (2023). *Mental health evaluations in immigration court: A guide for mental health and legal professionals.* New York: New York University Press.

Barber-Rioja, V., & Rosenfeld, B. (2018). Addressing linguistic and cultural differences in the forensic interview. *International Journal of Forensic Mental Health, 17*(4), 377–386, https://doi.org/10.1080/14999013.2018.1495280.

Barber, B. K. (1996). Parental psychological control: Revisiting a neglected construct. *Child Development, 67*(6), 3296–3319. https://doi.org/10.2307/1131780

Barnett, J. E., Wise, E. H., Johnson-Greene, D., & Buckey, S. (2007). Informed consent: Too much of a good thing or not enough? *Professional Psychology: Research and Practice, 38*(2), 179–186. https://doi.org/10.1037/0735-7028.38.2.179

Baumrind, D. (1971). Current patterns of parental authority. *Developmental Psychology Monograph, 4*, 1–103. http://dx.doi.org/10.1037/h0030372

Bayles, B. P., & Katerndahl, D. A. (2009). Culture-bound syndromes in Hispanic primary care patients. *The International Journal of Psychiatry in Medicine, 39*(1), 15–31. https://doi.org/10.2190/PM.39.1.b

Beggs, S. M., & Grace, R. C. (2010). Assessment of dynamic risk factors: An independent validation study of the Violence Risk Scale: Sexual offender version. *Sexual Abuse, 22*(2), 234–251. https://doi.org/10.1177/1079063210369014

Ben-Porath, Y. S., & Tellegen, A. (2008). *MMPI-2-RF manual for administration, scoring, and interpretation.* University of Minnesota Press.

Ben-Porath, Y. S., & Tellegen, A. (2020). *MMPI-3 technical manual.* University of Minnesota Press.

Berry, J. W. (2005). Acculturation: Living successfully in two cultures. *International Journal of Intercultural Relations, 29*(6), 697–712. https://doi.org/10.1016/j.ijintrel.2005.07.013

Berry, J. W. (1997). Immigration, acculturation, and adaptation. *Applied Psychology, 46*(1), 5–34. https://doi.org/10.1111/j.1464-0597.1997.tb01087.x

Berry, J. W., Kim, U., Power, S., Young, M., & Bujaki, M. (1989). Acculturation attitudes in plural societies. *Applied Psychology, 38*(2), 185–206. https://doi.org/10.1111/j.1464-0597.1989.tb01208.x

Betancourt, H., & López, S. R. (1993). The study of culture, ethnicity, and race in American psychology. *American Psychologist, 48*, 629–637. https://doi.org/10.1037/0003-066X.48.6.629

Betancourt, J. R., Green, A. R., Carrillo, J. E., & Aneneh-Firempong, O. II. (2003). Defining cultural competence: A practical framework for addressing racial/ethnic disparities in health and health care. *Public Health Reports, 118*, 293–302.

Boer, D. P., Hart, S. D., Kropp, P. R., & Webster, C. D. (1997). *Manual for the Sexual Violence Risk-20: Professional guidelines for assessing risk of sexual violence*. Vancouver, British Columbia, Canada: Mental Health, Law, and Policy Institute.

Boone, K. B., Lu, P., & Herzberg, D. (2002). *The dot counting test manual*. Western Psychological Services.

Bopp, L., Aparcero, M., & Rosenfeld, B. (2022). Detecting symptom exaggeration and minimization using translated versions of the MMPI-2 and MMPI-2-RF: A systematic review and preliminary meta-analysis. *Law and Human Behavior, 46*(1), 81–97. https://doi.org/10.1037/lhb0000469

Borum, R., Bartel, P., & Forth, A. (2006). *Manual for the structured assessment for violence risk in youth (SAVRY)*. Odessa, FL: Psychological Assessment Resources.

Briere, J. (2011). *Trauma Symptom Inventory-2nd edition (TSI-2) professional manual*. Psychological Assessment Resources.

Bronfenbrenner, U. (1979). *The ecology of human development*. Cambridge, MA: Harvard University Press. https://doi.org/10.4159/9780674028845

Bronfenbrenner, U., & Morris, P. A. (2006). The bioecological model of human development. In R. M. Lerner & W. Damon (Eds.), *Handbook of child psychology: Theoretical models of human development* (6th ed., pp. 793–828). John Wiley & Sons, Inc. https://psycnet.apa.org/record/2006-08774-014

Brown, L., Sherbenou, R. J., & Johnsen, S. K. (2010). *Test of nonverbal intelligence* (Vol. 4th ed.). TX: PRO-ED.

Bureau of Prisons Statistics. (2022). *Inmate citizenship*. Federal Bureau of Prisons. Retrieved from https://www.bop.gov/about/statistics/statistics_inmate_citizenship.jsp

Burgess, B., & Nijdam-Jones, A. (2024). Culturally responsive offender rehabilitation: future directions. In M. Daffern & C. M. Chu (Eds.), *Approaches to offender rehabilitation in Asian jurisdictions: Integration of western models and cultural adaptations* (pp. 245–261). Routledge. https://doi.org/10.4324/9781003360919

Burke, P. (2017). *Popular culture in early modern Europe*. New York, NY: Routledge.

Burneo-Garcés, C., Fernández-Alcántara, M., Aguayo-Estremera, R., & Pérez-García, M. (2020). Psychometric properties of the spanish adaptation of the personality assessment inventory in correctional settings: An ESEM Study. *Journal of Personality Assessment, 102*(1), 75–87. http://doi.org/10.1080/00223891.2018.1481858

Butcher, J. N. (Ed.). (1996). *International adaptations of the MMPI-2: Research and clinical applications*. University of Minnesota Press.

Butcher, J. N., Dahlstrom, W. G., Graham, J. R., Tellegen, A. M., & Kaemmer, B. (1989). *Minnesota Multiphasic Personality Inventory-2 (MMPI-2): Manual for administration and scoring*. University of Minnesota Press. https://doi.org/10.1037/t15120-000

Butcher, J. N., Williams, C. L., Graham, J. R., Archer, R. P., Tellegen, A., Ben-Porath, Y. S., & Kaemmer, B. (1992). *MMPI–A (Minnesota Multiphasic Personality Inventory–Adolescent): Manual for administration, scoring, and interpretation*. University of Minnesota Press.

Byrd, D. A., Rivera Mindt, M. M., Clark, U. S., Clarke, Y., Thames, A. D., Gammada, E. Z., & Manly, J. J. (2021). Creating an antiracist psychology by addressing professional complicity in psychological assessment. *Psychological Assessment, 33*(3), 279–285. https://doi.org/10.1037/pas0000993.

Cabrera, N., Shannon, J., West, J., & Brooks-Gunn, J. (2006). Parental interactions with Latino infants: Variation by country of origin and English proficiency. *Child Development, 77*(5), 1190–1207. https://doi.org/10.1111/j.1467-8624.2006.00928.x

Cacuci, S. A., Bull, R., Huang, C. Y., & Visu-Petra, L. (2021). Criteria-based content analysis in child sexual abuse cases: A cross-cultural perspective. *Child Abuse Review, 30*(6), 520–535. https://doi.org/10.1002/car.2733

Cagigas, X. E., & Manly, J. J. (2014). *Cultural neuropsychology: The new norm* (M. W. Parsons & T. A. Hammeke, Eds. 3rd ed.). https://doi.org/10.1037/14339-008
Came, H., & Griffith, D. (2018). Tackling racism as a "wicked" public health problem: Enabling allies in anti-racism praxis. *Social Science & Medicine, 199*, 181–188. https://doi.org/10.1016/j.socscimed.2017.03.028
Canino, G., & Bravo, M. (1994). The adaptation and testing of diagnostic and outcome measures for cross-cultural research. *International Review of Psychiatry, 6*(4), 281–286. https://doi.org/10.3109/09540269409023267
Capps, R. C., Bronte-Tinkew, J., & Horowitz, A. (2010). Acculturation and father engagement with infants among Chinese- and Mexican-origin immigrant fathers. *Fathering, 8*, 61–92. https://doi.org/10.3149/fth.0801.61
Carter, R. T., & Forsyth, J. M. (2007). Examining race and culture in psychology journals: The case of forensic psychology. *Professional Psychology: Research and Practice, 38*(2), 133–142. https://doi.org/10.1037/0735-7028.38.2.133
Casaletto, K. B., Umlauf, A., Marquine, M., Beaumont, J. L., Mungas, D., Gershon, R., Slotkin, J., Akshoomoff, N., & Heaton, R. K. (2016). Demographically corrected normative standards for the Spanish language version of the NIH toolbox cognition battery. *Journal of the International Neuropsychological Society, 22*(3), 364–374. https://doi.org/10.1017/S135561771500137X
Cattell, R. B. (1940). A culture-free intelligence test. I. *Journal of Educational Psychology, 31*(3), 161–179. https://doi.org/10.1037/h0059043
Chang, Y.-T., Rosenfeld, B., Tam, W.-C. C., Teng, C-Y. & Han, Y. (2023). A study of the TOMM and DCT in Chinese-speaking Immigrants with Limited English proficiency in the United States. *International Journal of Forensic Mental Health, 22*(1), 1–13. https://doi.org/10.1080/14999013.2022.2027048
Chao, R. K., & Tseng, V. (2002). Parenting of Asians. In M. H. Bornstein (Ed.), *Handbook of parenting* (2nd ed.) 59–93. Mahwah, NJ: Lawrence Erlbaum Associates.
Chen, C., Lee, S.-Y., & Stevenson, H. W. (1995). Response style and cross-cultural comparisons of rating scales among East Asian and North American students. *Psychological Science, 6*(3), 170–175. https://doi.org/10.1111/j.1467-9280.1995.tb00327.x
Chen, Y., Douglas, K. S., Zhang, Z., Xiao, C., Wang, H., Wang, Y., & Ma, A. (2023). Evaluating the HCR-20V3 violence risk assessment measure with mentally disordered offenders and civil psychiatric patients in China. *Behavioral Sciences & the Law, 41*(4), 186–206. https://doi.org/10.1002/bsl.2614
Chithiramohan, T., Santhosh, S., Threlfall, G., Hull, L., Mukaetova-Ladinska, E. B., Subramaniam, H., & Beishon, L. (2024). Culture-fair cognitive screening tools for assessment of cognitive impairment: A systematic review. *Journal of Alzheimer's Disease Reports, 8*(1), 289–306. https://doi.org/10.3233/ADR-230194
Chiu, E. Y. (2014). Psychological testing in child custody evaluations with ethnically diverse families: Ethical concerns and practice recommendations. *Journal of Child Custody, 11*(2), 107–127. https://doi.org/10.1080/15379418.2014.919245
Choi, Y., Kim, Y. S., Kim, S. Y., & Park, I. J. K. (2013). Is Asian American parenting controlling and harsh? Empirical testing of relationships between Korean American and Western parenting measures. *Asian American Journal of Psychology, 4*(1), 19–29. https://doi.org/10.1037/a0031220
Chu, C. M., Goh, M. L., & Chong, D. (2016). The predictive validity of SAVRY ratings for assessing youth offenders in Singapore: A comparison with YLS/CMI ratings. *Criminal Justice and Behavior, 43*(6), 793–810. https://doi.org/10.1177/0093854815616842
Chu, W., Wippold, G., & Becker, K. D. (2022). A systematic review of cultural competence trainings for mental health providers. *Professional Psychology: Research and Practice, 53*(4), 362–371. https://dx.doi.org/10.1037/pro0000469
Clarke, I. III. (2000). Extreme response style in cross-cultural research: An empirical investigation. *Journal of Social Behaviour and Personality, 15*(1), 137–152.

Clegg, C., Fremouw, W., & Mogge, N. (2009). Utility of the structured inventory of malingered symptomatology (SIMS) and the assessment of depression inventory (ADI) in screening for malingering among outpatients seeking to claim disability. *Journal of Forensic Psychiatry & Psychology, 20*, 239–254. https://doi.org/10.1080/14789940802267760

Cofresí, N. I., & Gorman, A. A. (2004). Testing and assessment issues with Spanish-English bilingual Latinos. *Journal of Counseling and Development, 82*(1), 99–106. https://doi.org/10.1002/j.1556-6678.2004.tb00290.x

Constantine, M., & Ladany, N. (2000). Self-report multicultural counseling competence scales: Their relation to social desirability attitudes and multicultural case conceptualization ability. *Journal of Counseling Psychology, 47*(2), 155–164. https://doi.org/cxf8bk

Cook, A. N., & Hart, S. D. (2017). Violence risk assessment across nations and across cultures: Legal, clinical, and scientific considerations. In R. Roesch & A. Cook (Eds.) *Handbook of forensic mental health services* (pp. 131–152). New York: Routledge.

Correa, A. A. (2018). Beyond borders: Cultural and transnational perspectives of feigning and other response styles. In R. Rogers & S. Bender (Eds.), *Clinical assessment of malingering and deception* (4th ed., pp. 61–80). Guilford Press.

Correa, A. A., & Rogers, R. (2010). Cross-cultural applications of the PAI. In M. Blais, M. Baity, & C. Hopwood (Eds.), *Clinical applications of the personality assessment inventory* (pp. 135–148). Routledge.

Correa, A. A., Rogers, R., & Hoersting, R. (2010). Validation of the Spanish SIRS with monolingual Hispanic outpatients. *Journal of Personality Assessment, 92*(5), 458–464. https://doi.org/10.1080/00223891.2010.497430

Cortvriendt, J., García-López, E., Rosenfeld, B., & Nijdam-Jones, A. (2024). Predictive validity of the violence risk appraisal guide-revised in Mexico. *Journal of Threat Assessment and Management*. https://doi.org/10.1037/tam0000227

Council of Chairs of Training Councils. (2021). *CCTC 2020: Social responsiveness in health service psychology education and training toolkit*. Retrieved from https://www.cctcpsychology.org/wp-content/uploads/2023/04/CCTC_Socially-Responsive-HSP-Ed-Training_4-17-23.pdf

Cova, I., Nicotra, A., Maestri, G., Canevelli, M., Pantoni, L., & Pomati, S. (2022). Translations and cultural adaptations of the Montreal Cognitive Assessment: A systematic and qualitative review. *Neurological Sciences, 43*, 113–124. https://doi.org/10.1007/s10072-021-05716-y

Crişan, I., & Erdodi, L. (2022). Examining the cross-cultural validity of the test of memory malingering and the Rey 15-item test. *Applied Neuropsychology: Adult, 31*(5), 721–731. https://doi.org/10.1080/23279095.2022.2064753

Crişan, I., Matei, A., Avram, D.-L., Bunghez, C., & Erdodi, L. A. (2023). Full of SURPRISES: Performance validity testing in examinees with limited English proficiency. *Psychological Injury and Law, 16*(2), 177–198. https://doi.org/10.1007/s12207-023-09474-4

Crowe, M., Clay, O. J., Martin, R. C., Howard, V. J., Wadley, V. G., Sawyer, P., & Allman, R. M. (2013). Indicators of childhood quality of education in relation to cognitive function in older adulthood. *Journals of Gerontology Series A: Biomedical Sciences and Medical Sciences, 68*(2), 198–204. https://doi.org/10.1093/gerona/gls122

Cummings, E. M., Davies, P. T., & Campbell, S. B. (2000). *Developmental psychopathology and family process*. The Guilford Press

Darwish, A. F. E., & Huber, G. L. (2003). Individualism vs collectivism in different cultures: A cross-cultural study. *Intercultural Education, 14*(1), 47–56. https://doi.org/10.1080/1467598032000044647

Daubert v. Merrell Dow Pharmaceuticals, 113 S.Ct. 2786 (1993).

Davis, R. E. (2000). Cultural health care or child abuse? The Southeast Asian practice of cao gio. *Journal of the American Academy of Nurse Practitioners*, 12(3), 89–95. https://doi.org/10.1111/j.1745-7599.2000.tb00173.x

Del Pino, R., Peña, J., Ibarretxe-Bilbao, N., Schretlen, D. J., & Ojeda, N. (2018). Demographically calibrated norms for two premorbid intelligence measures: The word accentuation test and pseudo-words reading subtest. *Frontiers in Psychology*, *9*, 1950. https://doi.org/10.3389/fpsyg.2018.01950

Del Ser, T., Gonzalez-Montalvo, J. I., Martinez-Espinosa, S., Delgado-Villapalos, C., & Bermejo, F. (1997). Estimation of premorbid intelligence in Spanish people with the Word Accentuation Test and its application to the diagnosis of dementia. *Brain Cognition*. *33*(3), 343–356. https://doi.org/10.1006/brcg.1997.0877

Detullio, D., Messer, S. C., Kennedy, T. D., & Millen, D. H. (2019). A meta-analysis of the Miller Forensic Assessment of Symptoms Test (M-FAST). *Psychological Assessment*, *31*(11), 1319–1328. https://doi.org/10.1037/pas0000753

Dolovich, S., & Natapoff, A. (2017). *The new criminal justice thinking*. New York: NYU Press.

Domènech Rodriguez, M. M., Donovick, M. R., & Crowley, S. L. (2009). Parenting styles in a cultural context: Observations of "protective parenting" in first-generation Latinos. *Family Process*, *48*(2), 195–210. https://doi.org/10.1111/j.1545-5300.2009.01277.x

Douglas, K. S., Hart, S. D., Webster, C., & Belfrage, H. (2013). *HCR-20 (Version 3): Assessing risk for violence*. Burnaby BC, Canada; Mental Health, Law and Policy Institute, Simon Fraser University.

Duggan, E. C., Awakon, L. M., Loaiza, C. C., & Garcia-Barrera, M. A. (2019). Contributing towards a cultural neuropsychology assessment decision-making framework: Comparison of WAIS-IV norms from Colombia, Chile, Mexico, Spain, United States, and Canada. *Archives of Clinical Neuropsychology*, *34*(5), 657–681. https://doi.org/10.1093/arclin/acy074

Dumenci, L., Erol, N., Achenbach, T. M., & Simsek, Z. (2004). Measurement structure of the Turkish translation of the child behavior checklist using confirmatory factor analytic approaches to validation of syndromal constructs. *Journal of Abnormal Child Psychology*, *32*, 335–340. https://doi.org/10.1023/B:JACP.0000026146.67290.07

Durojaiye, M. O. A. (1993). Indigenous psychology in Africa. In U. K. J. W. Berry (Ed.), *Indigenous psychologies: Research and experience in cultural context* (pp. 211–220). Sage.

Dusky v.United States, 362 U.S. 402 (1960).

Edyburn, K. L., Dowdy, E., DiStefano, C., Bertone, A., & Greer, F. (2020). Measurement invariance of the English and Spanish BASC-3 behavioral and emotional screening system parent preschool forms. *Early Childhood Research Quarterly*, *51*, 307–316. https://doi.org/https://doi.org/10.1016/j.ecresq.2019.12.002

Emery, R. E., Otto, R. K., & O'Donahue, W. T. (2005). A critical assessment of child custody evaluations: Limited science and a flawed system. *Psychological Science in the Public Interest*, *6*(1), 1–29. https://doi.org/10.1111/j.1529-1006.2005.00020.x

Einesman, F. (1999). Confessions and culture: The interaction of *Miranda* and diversity. *Journal of Criminal Law and Criminology*, *90*, 1. https://scholarlycommons.law.northwestern.edu/jclc/vol90/iss1/1

Erdodi, L. A., Nussbaum, S., Sagar, S., Abeare, C. A., & Schwartz, E. S. (2017). Limited English proficiency increases failure rates on performance validity tests with high verbal mediation. *Psychological Injury and the Law*, *10*, 96–108. https://doi.org/10.1007/s12207-017-9282-x

Evans-Campbell, T. (2008). Historical trauma in American Indian/ Native Alaska communities: A multilevel framework for exploring impacts on individuals, families, and

communities. *Journal of Interpersonal Violence, 23*(3), 316–338. https://doi.org/10.1177/0886260507312290
Ewert v.Canada. 2018 SCC 30.
Executive Office for Immigration Review [EOIR]. (2013). *Phase I of plan to provide enhanced procedural protections to unrepresented detained respondents with mental disorders.* Retrieved from https://immigrationreports.files.wordpress.com/2014/01/eoir-phase-i-guidance.pdf.
Fabian, K., Fannoh, J., Washington, G. G., Geninyan, W. B., Nyachienga, B., Cyrus, G., Hallowanger, J. N., Beste, J., Rao, D., & Wagenaar, B. H. (2018). "My Heart Die in Me": Idioms of distress and the development of a screening tool for mental suffering in Southeast Liberia. *Culture, Medicine, and Psychiatry, 42*(3), 684–703. https://doi.org/10.1007/s11013-018-9581-z
Fanniff, A. M., York, T. M., Montena, A. L., & Bohnsack, K. (2022). Current practices in incorporating culture into forensic mental health assessment: A survey of practitioners. *International Journal of Forensic Mental Health, 21*(2), 146–163. https://doi.org/10.1080/14999013.2021.1952355
Fanniff, A. M., York, T., & Gutierrez, R. (2023). Developing consensus for culturally informed forensic mental health assessment: Experts' opinions on best practices. *Law and Human Behavior, 47*(3), 385–402. https://doi.org/10.1037/lhb0000531
Fanti, K. A., Lordos, A., Sullivan, E. A., & Kosson, D. S. (2018). Cultural and ethnic variations in psychopathy. In C. J. Patrick (Ed.) *Handbook of psychopathy* (pp. 529–569). Guilford Press.
Fasfous, A. F., Al-Joudi, H. F., Puente, A. E., & Pérez-García, M. (2017). Neuropsychological measures in the Arab world: A systematic review. *Neuropsychology Review, 27*(2), 158–173. https://doi.org/10.1007/s11065-017-9347-3
Fernández, A. L., & Fulbright, R. L. (2015). Construct and concurrent validity of the Spanish adaptation of the Boston Naming Test. *Applied Neuropsychology: Adult, 22*(5), 355–362. https://doi.org/10.1080/23279095.2014.939178
Filone, S., & King, C. M. (2015). The emerging standard of competence in immigration removal proceedings: A review for forensic mental health professionals. *Psychology, Public Policy, and Law, 21*(1), 60–71. https://doi.org/10.1037/law0000032.
Flores Lázaro, J. C., Ostrosky-Solís, F., & Lozano Gutiérrez, A. (2012). BANFE: Batería neuropsicológica de funciones ejecutivas y lóbulos frontales. In *México, DF* (Vol. Manual Moderno).
Fluke, J. D., Yuan, Y.-Y. T., Hedderson, J., & Curtis, P. A. (2003). Disproportionate representation of race and ethnicity in child maltreatment: Investigation and victimization. *Children and Youth Services Review, 25*(5–6), 359–373. https://doi.org/10.1016/S0190-7409(03)00026-4
Flynn, J. R. (1984). The mean IQ of Americans: Massive gains 1932 to 1978. *Psychological Bulletin, 95*(1), 29–51. https://doi.org/10.1037/0033-2909.95.1.29
Folino, J. O. (2015). Predictive efficacy of violence risk assessment instruments in Latin-America. *The European Journal of Psychology Applied to Legal Context, 7*(2), 51–58. https://doi.org/10.1016/j.ejpal.2014.11.006
Folstein, M. F., Folstein, S. E., & McHugh, P. R. (1975). "Mini-mental state": A practical method for grading the cognitive state of patients for the clinician. *Journal of Psychiatric Research, 12*(3), 189–198. https://doi.org/10.1016/0022-3956(75)90026-6
Fontes, L. A. (2005). *Child abuse and culture: Working with diverse families.* Guilford.
Fontes, L. A. (2022). Cultural competence in the field of child maltreatment. In R. Geffner, J. W. White, L. K. Hamberger, A. Rosenbaum, V. Vaughan-Eden, & V. I. Vieth (Eds.), *Handbook of interpersonal violence and abuse across the lifespan* (pp. 1403–1424). Springer.
Fontes, L. A., & O'Neill-Arana, M. R. (2008). Assessing for child maltreatment in culturally diverse families. In L. A. Suzuki, J. G. Ponterotto, & P. J. Meller (Eds.), *Handbook of*

multicultural assessment: Clinical, psychological, and educational applications (3rd ed., pp. 647–648). Jossey-Bass.
Fontes, L. A., & Plummer, C. (2010). Cultural issues in disclosures of child sexual abuse. *Journal of Child Sexual Abuse, 19*(5), 491–518. https://doi.org/10.1080/10538712.2010.512520
Frederick, R. I. (2003). *Validity indicator profile manual, revised.* Minnetonka, MN: Pearson Assessments.
Freeman, M. D. (2010). Upholding the dignity and best interests of children: International law and the corporal punishment of children. *Law and Contemporary Problems, 73*(2), 211–251. https://doi.org/10.1163/9789004219106_004
Freckelton, I., & Karagiannakis, M. (2014). Unfitness to stand trial under international criminal law: The influential decision of the International Criminal Tribunal of the former Yugoslavia in relation to Pavle Strugar and its ramifications. *Psychiatry, Psychology, and Law, 21*(4), 611–621. https://doi.org/10.1080/13218719.2014.934764
Frye v.U.S., 295 F. 1013 (D.C. Cir, 1923)
Fujii, D. E. (2018). Developing a cultural context for conducting a neuropsychological evaluation with a culturally diverse client: The ECLECTIC framework. *Clinical Neuropsychologist, 32*(8), 1356–1392. https://doi.org/10.1080/13854046.2018.1435826
Fujii, D. E., Tokioka, A. B., Lichton, A. I., & Hishinuma, E. (2005). Ethnic differences in prediction of violence risk with the HCR-20 among psychiatric inpatients. *Psychiatric Services, 56*(6), 711–716. https://doi.org/10.1176/appi.ps.56.6.711
Gany, F., Kapelusznik, L., Prakash, K., Gonzalez, J., Orta, L. Y., Tseng, C., & Changrani, J. (2007). The impact of medical interpretation method on time and errors. *Journal of General Internal Medicine, 22*, 319–323. https;//doi.org/10.1007/s11606-007-0361-7
Gardner, G. E. (1983). *Frames of mind: The theory of multiple intelligences.* Basic Books.
Gardner, H. E. (2000). *Intelligence reframed: Multiple intelligences for the 21st century.* Hachette UK.
Gasquoine, P. G., Croyle, K. L., Cavazos-Gonzalez, C., & Sandoval, O. (2007). Language of administration and neuropsychological test performance in neurologically intact Hispanic American bilingual adults. *Archives of Clinical Neuropsychology, 22*(8), 991–1001. https://doi.org/10.1016/j.acn.2007.08.003
Gaunersdorfer, K., & Eher, R. (2023). Die deutschsprachige Version der Violence Risk Scale – Sexual Offense Version (VRS-SO): Prädiktive und konvergente Validität und Kalibrierung des Fünf-Kategorien-Modells: The German-language Version of the VRS-SO: Predictive validity and calibration analyses of the five level risk and needs system. *Monatsschrift für Kriminologie und Strafrechtsreform, 106*(4), 301–313. https://doi.org/10.1515/mks-2023-0012
Gengler, J. J., Alkazemi, M. F., & Alsharekh, A. (2021). Who supports honor-based violence in the Middle East? Findings from a national survey of Kuwait. *Journal of Interpersonal Violence, 36*(11–12), NP6013-NP6039. https://doi.org/10.1177/0886260518812067
Ghamkhar Fard, Z., Pourshahbaz, A., Anderson, J., Shakiba, S., & Mirabzadeh, A. (2022). Assessing DSM-5 Section II Personality disorders using the MMPI-2-RF in an Iranian community sample. *Assessment, 29*, 782–805. https://doi.org/10.1177/1073191121991225
Ghazali, S. R., Chen, Y. Y., Kader, M. A., & Kadir, N. B. A. (2018). Validity and reliability of the Raven Coloured Progressive Matrices and the Test of Non-Verbal iIntelligence among Malaysian children. *ASEAN Journal of Psychiatry, 19*(2), 2231–7805.
Gilbert, C., & Pasque, P. A. (2025). Defining culturally responsive research: Learnings and tensions in minoritized researcher perspectives. *Journal of Diversity in Higher Education, 18*(4), 453–467. https://doi.org/10.1037/dhe0000522

Gilligan, P., & Akhtar, S. (2006). Cultural barriers to the disclosure of child sexual abuse in Asian communities: Listening to what women say. *British Journal of Social Work, 36*(8), 1361–1377. https://doi.org/10.1093/bjsw/bch309

Giromini, L., & Viglione, D. J. (2022). Assessing negative response bias with the Inventory of Problems-29 (IOP-29): A quantitative literature review. *Psychological Injury and Law, 15*(1), 79–93. https://doi.org/10.1007/s12207-021-09437-7

Giromini, L., Barbosa, F., Coga, G., Azeredo, A., Viglione, D. J., & Zennaro, A. (2020). Using the inventory of problems – 29 (IOP-29) with the Test of Memory Malingering (TOMM) in symptom validity assessment: A study with a Portuguese sample of experimental feigners. *Applied Neuropsychology: Adult, 27*(6), 504–516. https://doi.org/10.1080/23279095.2019.1570929

Giromini, L., Viglione, D. J., Pignolo, C., & Zennaro, A. (2018). A clinical comparison, simulation study testing the validity of SIMS and IOP-29 with an Italian sample. *Psychological Injury and Law, 11*, 340–350. https://doi.org/10.1007/s12207-018-9314-1

Golden, C. J., & Hutchings, P. S. (1998). The mental status examination. In M. Hersen & V. B. Van Hasselt (Eds.), *Basic interviewing* (pp. 107–128). Mahwah, NJ: Lawrence Erlbaum Associates

Gonçalves, L. C., Gerth, J., Rossegger, A., Noll, T., & Endrass, J. (2020). Predictive validity of the Static-99 and Static-99R in Switzerland. *Sexual Abuse, 32*(2), 203–219. https://doi.org/10.1177/1079063218821117

Gonzales, N., Germán, M., Kim, S., George, P., Fabrett, F., Millsap, R., & Dumka, L. (2008). Mexican American adolescents' cultural orientation, externalizing behavior and academic engagement: The role of traditional cultural values. *American Journal of Community Psychology, 41*(1–2), 151–164. https://doi.org/10.1007/s10464-007-9152-x

Gonzalez, E., Varela, J., Boccaccini, M., Damnjavonic, T., & Lawrence, J. (2014). *Risk assessment and cultural diversity: A study space analysis.* American Psychology-Law Society, New Orleans, LA.

Gostin, L. O. (1995). Informed consent, cultural sensitivity and respect for persons. *Journal of the American Medical Association, 274*, 844–845. https://doi.org/10.1001/jama.1995.03530100084039

Gottfried, A., Bathurst, K., Guerin, D., & Parramore, M. (2003). Socioeconomic status in children's development and family environment: Infancy throughout adolescence. In M. Bornstein & R. Bradley (Eds.), *Socioeconomic status, parenting and child development* (pp. 189–207). Lawrence Erlbaum.

Gould, J. W., & Martindale, D. A. (2007). *The art and science of child custody evaluations.* New York, NY: Guilford Press.

Green, D., & Rosenfeld, B. (2011). Evaluating the gold standard: A review and meta-analysis of the Structured Interview of Reported Symptoms. *Psychological Assessment, 23*(1), 95–107. https://doi.org/10.1037/a0021149.

Green, D., Rosenfeld, B., Belfi, B., Rohler, L. & Pierson, A. (2012). Use of measures of cognitive effort in detection of feigned psychiatric symptoms with pretrial criminal defendants. *International Journal of Forensic Mental Health, 11*(3), 181–190, http://doi.org/10.1080/14999013.2012.723665.

Greene, R. L. (2000). *The MMPI-2: An interpretive manual.* Allyn & Bacon.

Greif, A. (1994). Cultural beliefs and the organization of society: A historical and theoretical reflection on collectivist and individualist societies. *Journal of Political Economy, 102*(5), 912–950.

Greiffenstein, M. F., Baker, W. J., & Gola, T. (1994). Validation of malingered amnesic measures with a large clinical sample. *Psychological Assessment, 6*, 218–224. https://doi.org/10.1037/1040-3590.6.3.218

Guerra, C., Arredondo, V., Saavedra, C., Pinto-Cortez, C., Benguria, A., & Orrego, A. (2021). Gender differences in the disclosure of sexual abuse in Chilean adolescents. *Child Abuse Review*, *30*(3), 210–225. https://doi.org/10.1002/car.2672

Gupta, A., & Ailawaldi, A. (2005). Childhood and adolescent sexual abuse and incest: Experiences of women survivors in India. In S. J. Jejeebhoy, I. Shah, & S. Thapa (Eds.), *Sex without consent: Young people in developing countries* (pp. 171–186). Zed Books. https://doi.org/10.5040/9781350222519.ch-011

Guttfreund, D. G. (1990). Effects of language usage on the emotional experience of Spanish-English and English-Spanish bilinguals. *Journal of Consulting and Clinical Psychology, 58(*5), 604–607. https://doi.org/10.1037/0022-006X.58.5.604

Haag, A. M., Boyes, A., Cheng, J., MacNeil, A., & Wirove, R. (2016). An introduction to the issues of cross-cultural assessment inspired by Ewert v. Canada. *Journal of Threat Assessment and Management*, *3*(2), 65–75. https://doi.org/10.1037/tam0000067

Hall v. Florida. (2017), 572 U.S. 701

Hall, G. C. N., Bansal, A., & Lopez, I. R. (1999). Ethnicity and psychopathology: A meta-analytic review of 31 years of comparative MMPI/MMPI-2 research. *Psychological Assessment*, *11*(2), 186–197. https://psycnet.apa.org/doi/10.1037/a0039734

Hall, G. C., Yip, T., & Zarate, M. A. (2016). On becoming multicultural in a monocultural research world: A conceptual approach to studying ethnocultural diversity. *American Psychologist*, *71*, 40–51. https://doi.org/10/1037/a0039734

Hanson, R. K., & Thornton, D. (2000). Improving risk assessments for sex offenders: A comparison of three actuarial scales. *Law and Human Behavior*, *24*(1), 119–136. https://doi.org/10.1023/a:1005482921333

Hanson, R. K., Lunetta, A., Phenix, A., Neeley, J., & Epperson, D. (2014). The field validity of Static-99/R sex offender risk assessment tool in California. *Journal of Threat Assessment and Management*, *1*(2), 102–117. https://doi.org/10.1037/tam0000014

Harada, T., Nomura, K., Shimada, H., & Kawakami, N. (2023). Development of a risk assessment tool for Japanese sex offenders: The Japanese Static-99. *Neuropsychopharmacology Reports*, *43*(4), 496–504. https://doi.org/10.1002/npr2.12330

Harcourt, B. E. (2008). *Against prediction: Profiling, policing, and punishing in an actuarial age.* University of Chicago Press.

Hare, R. D. (2003). *The Hare psychopathy checklist-revised* (2nd ed.). Toronto, Canada: Multi-Health Systems.

Harris, G. T., Rice, M. E., & Quinsey, V. L. (1993). Violent recidivism of mentally disordered offenders: The development of a statistical prediction instrument. *Criminal Justice and Behavior*, *20*(4), 315–335. https://doi.org/10.1177/0093854893020004001

Hart, S. D., Kropp, P. R., Laws, D. R., Klaver, J., Logan, C., & Watt, K. A. (2003). *The risk for sexual violence protocol (RSVP): Structured professional guidelines for assessing risk of sexual violence.* Burnaby, BC: Mental Health, Law, and Policy Institute, Simon Fraser University.

Harzing, A.-W. (2006). Response styles in cross-national survey research: A 26-country study. *International Journal of Cross Cultural Management*, *6*(2), 243–266. https://doi.org/10.1177/1470595806066332

Hathaway, S. R., & McKinley, J. C. (1943). *The Minnesota multiphasic personality inventory.* University of Minnesota Press.

Hawes, S. W., Boccaccini, M. T., & Murrie, D. C. (2013). Psychopathy and the combination of psychopathy and sexual deviance as predictors of sexual recidivism: Meta-analytic findings using the Psychopathy Checklist—Revised. *Psychological Assessment*, *25*(1), 233–243. https://doi.org/10.1037/a0030391

Hays, P. A. (2008). *Addressing cultural complexities in practice: Assessment, diagnosis and therapy.* American Psychological Association Press.

Heilbrun, K. (2009). *Evaluation for risk of violence in adults.* Oxford University Press.

Heilbrun, K., Grisso, T., & Goldstein, A. (2008). *Foundations of forensic mental health assessment*. Oxford University Press

Helfrich, H. (1999). Beyond the dilemma of cross-cultural psychology: Resolving the tension between etic and emic approaches. *Culture & Psychology*, *5*, 131–153. https://doi.org/10.1177/1354067X9952002

Helmus, L. M., Hanson, R. K., Murrie, D. C., & Zabarauckas, C. L. (2021). Field validity of Static-99R and STABLE-2007 with 4,433 men serving sentences for sexual offences in British Columbia: New findings and meta-analysis. *Psychological Assessment*, *33*(7), 581–595. https://doi.org/10.1037/pas0001010

Helmus, L. M., Kelley, S. M., Frazier, A., Fernandez, Y. M., Lee, S. C., Rettenberger, M., & Boccaccini, M. T. (2022). Static-99R: Strengths, limitations, predictive accuracy meta-analysis, and legal admissibility review. *Psychology, Public Policy, and Law*, *28*(3), 307–331. https://doi.org/10.1037/law0000351

Helmus, L., Hanson, R. K., Thornton, D., Babchishin, K., & Harris, A. (2012). Absolute recidivism rates predicted by Static-99R and Static-2002R sex offender risk assessment tools vary across samples: A meta-analysis. *Criminal Justice and Behavior*, *39*(9), 1148–1171. https://doi.org/10.1177/0093854812443648

Herman, S. P. (1997). Practice parameters for child custody evaluation. *Journal of the American Academy of Child & Adolescent Psychiatry*, *36*(10), 57S–68S. https://doi.org/10.1097/00004583-199710001-00005

Hinton, D. E., Kredlow, M. A., Pich, V., Bui, E., & Hofmann, S. G. (2013). The relationship of PTSD to key somatic complaints and cultural syndromes among Cambodian refugees attending a psychiatric clinic: The Cambodian Somatic Symptom and Syndrome Inventory (CSSI). *Transcultural Psychiatry*, *50*, 347–370. https://doi.org/10.1177/1363461513481187

Hinton, D. E., Pich, V., Marques, L., Nickerson, A., & Pollack, M. H. (2010). Khyâl attacks: A key idiom of distress among traumatized Cambodia refugees. *Culture, Medicine, and Psychiatry*, *34*, 244–278. https://doi.org/10.1007/s11013-010-9174-y

Ho, C., Bluestein, D., & Jenkins, J. M. (2008). Cultural differences in the relationship between parenting and children's behaviour. *Developmental Psychology*, *44*(2), 507–522. https://doi.org/10.1037/0012-1649.44.2.507

Hofstede, G., & McCrae, R. R. (2004). Personality and culture revisited: Linking traits and dimensions of culture. *Cross-Cultural Research*, *38*, 52–88. https://doi.org/10.1177/1069397103259443

Hofstede, G., Hofstede, G. J., & Minkov, M. (2010). *Cultures and organizations: Software of the mind* (3 ed.). McGraw-Hill.

Hogan, N. R., & Corăbian, G. (2024). Investigating racial disparities in violence risk assessment using the Spousal Assault Risk Assessment Guide–Version 3 (SARA-V3): Structured professional judgment ratings and recidivism among indigenous and non-indigenous individuals. *Psychological Assessment*, *36*(5), 339–350. https://doi.org/10.1037/pas0001307.

Horn, J. L., & Cattell, R. B. (1966). Refinement and test of the theory of fluid and crystallized general intelligences. *Journal of Educational Psychology*, *57*(5), 253–270. https://doi.org/10.1037/h0023816

Hui, C. H., & Triandis, H. C. (1989). Effects of culture and response format on extreme response style. *Journal of Cross-Cultural Psychology*, *20*(3), 296–309. https://doi.org/10.1177/0022022189203004

Hulei, E., Zevenbergen, A. A., & Jacobs, U. C. (2006). Discipline behaviors of Chinese American and European American mothers. *Journal of Psychology*, *140*(5), 459–475. https://doi.org/10.3200/JRLP.140.5.459-475

Human Rights Watch. (2010). *Deportation by default: Mental disability, unfair hearings, and indefinite detention in the U.S. immigration system*. https://www.aclu.org/files/assets/usdeportation0710_0.pdf

Iacopino, V., Ozkalipci, O., & Schlar, C. (1999). The Istanbul Protocol: International standards for the effective investigation and documentation of torture and ill treatment. *Lancet, 354*(9184), 1117. https://doi.org/10.1016/S0140-6736(99)08381-6.

Institute for Crime and Justice Policy Research. (2021). *World prison brief.* University of London, U.K. Retrieved from https://www.prisonstudies.org/

Irvine, J. T. (1978). Wolof "magical thinking": Culture and conservation revisited. *Journal of Cross-Cultural Psychology, 9*(3), 300–310. https://doi.org/10.1177/002202217893003

Jacobs, D. M., Sano, M., Albert, S., Schofield, P., Dooneief, G., & Stern, Y. (1997). Cross-cultural neuropsychological assessment: A comparison of randomly selected, demographically matched cohorts of English-and Spanish-speaking older adults. *Journal of Clinical and Experimental Neuropsychology, 19*(3), 331–339. https://doi.org/10.1080/01688639708403862

Jewkes, R., Levin, J., & Penn-Kekana, L. (2002). Risk factors for domestic violence: Findings from a South African cross-sectional study. *Social Science & Medicine, 55*(9), 1603–1617. https://doi.org/10.1016/S0277-9536(01)00294-5

Johns, M., Inzlicht, M., & Schmader, T. (2008). Stereotype threat and executive resource depletion: Examining the influence of emotion regulation. *Journal of Experimental Psychology: General, 137*(4), 691–705. https://doi.org/10.1037/a0013834

Julian, T. W., McKenry, P. C., & McKelvey, M. W. (1994). Cultural variations in parenting: Perceptions of Caucasian, African-American, Hispanic, and Asian-American parents. *Family Relations, 43*(1), 30–37. https://doi.org/10.2307/585139

Kaplan, E., Goodglass, H., & Weintraub, S. (1983). *Boston Naming Test-2nd edition.* Lea & Febiger.

Katzenstein, D., & Fontes, L. A. (2017). Twice silenced: The underreporting of child sexual abuse in Orthodox Jewish communities. *Journal of Child Sexual Abuse: Research, Treatment, & Program Innovations for Victims, Survivors, & Offenders, 26*(6), 752–767. https://doi.org/10.1080/10538712.2017.1336505

Keller, A., Ford, D., Trinh-Shevrin, C., Meserve, C., Sachs, E., Leviss, J. A., Singer, E., Smith, H., Wilkinson, J., Kim, G., Allden, K., & Rosenfeld, B. (2003). Mental health of detained asylum seekers. *Lancet, 362,* 1271–1273. https://doi.org/10.1016/S0140-6736(03)14846-5

Keller, A., Joscelyne, A., Granski, M., & Rosenfeld, B. (2017). Pre-migration trauma exposure and mental health functioning among Central American migrants arriving at the US border. *PLOS ONE, 12*(1), e0168692. http://doi.org/10.1371/journal.pone.0168692.

Keller, A., Rasmussen, A., Reeves, K., & Rosenfeld, B. (2005). An evaluation of Credible Fear referrals in Expedited Removal at ports of entry in the United States. In M. Hatfield (Ed.) *Report on asylum seekers in expedited removal* (pp. 1–43). United States Commission on International Religious Freedom.

Kempler, D., Teng, E. L., Dick, M., Taussig, I. M., & Davis, D. S. (1998). The effects of age, education, and ethnicity on verbal fluency. *Journal of the International Neuropsychological Society, 4*(6), 531–538. https://doi.org/10.1017/S1355617798466013

Kim, H., & Na, D. L. (1999). Normative data on the Korean version of the Boston Naming Test. *Journal of Clinical Experimental Neuropsychology, 21,* 127–133. https://doi.org/10.1076/jcen.21.1.127.942

Kim, J. K., & Kang, Y. (1999). Brief report: Normative study of the Korean-California Verbal Learning Test (K-CVLT). *Clinical Neuropsychologist, 13*(3), 365–369. https://doi.org/10.1076/clin.13.3.365.1740

Korbin, J. (Ed.). (1981). *Child abuse and neglect: Cross-cultural perspectives.* University of California Press.

Korbin, J. E. (1980). The cultural context of child abuse and neglect. In H. Kempe & R. E. Helfer (Eds.), *The battered child* (3rd ed., pp. 21–35). University of Chicago Press.

Kosmidis, M. H., Zafiri, M., & Politimou, N. (2011). Literacy versus formal schooling: Influence on working memory. *Archives of Clinical Neuropsychology*, *26*(7), 575–582. https://doi.org/10.1093/arclin/acr063

Kraus, L. J., Thomas, C. R., & The Committee on Quality Issues. (2011). Practice parameter for child and adolescent forensic evaluations. *Journal of the American Academy of Child and Adolescent Psychiatry*, *50*(12), 1299–1312. https://doi.org/10.1016/j.jaac.2011.09.020

Krause, I. B. (1989). Sinking heart: A Punjabi communication of distress. *Social Science & Medicine*, *29*, 563–575. https://doi.org/10.1016/0277-9536(89)90202-5

Kropp P. R., Hart S. D. (2015). *SARA-V3. User guide for the third edition of the spousal assault risk assessment*. ProActive Resolutions.

Krug, E., Dahlberg, L., Mercy, J., Zwi, A., & Lozano, R. (Ed.). (2002). *World report on violence and health*. World Health Organization.

Kuper, A. (1999). *Culture: The anthropologists' account*. Cambridge, MA: Harvard University Press.

Långström, N. (2004). Accuracy of actuarial procedures for assessment of sexual offender recidivism risk may vary across ethnicity. *Sexual Abuse*, *16*(2), 107–120. https://doi.org/10.1177/107906320401600202

Lau, C. W., & Hoosain, R. (1999). Working memory and language difference in sound duration: A comparison of mental arithmetic in Chinese, Japanese, and English. *Psychologia*, *42*(3), 139–144.

Laurinaitytė, I., Laurinavičius, A., Ustinavičiūtė, L., Wygant, D. B., & Sellbom, M. (2017). Utility of the MMPI-2 Restructured Form (MMPI-2-RF) in a sample of Lithuanian male offenders. *Law and Human Behavior*, *41*(5), 494–505. https://doi.org/10.1037/lhb0000254

Lee, D. Y., Lee, K. U., Lee, J. H., Kim, K. W., Jhoo, J. H., Kim, S. Y., Yoon, J. C., Woo, S. I., Ha, J., & Woo, J. I. (2004). A normative study of the CERAD neuropsychological assessment battery in the Korean elderly. *Journal of the International Neuropsychological Society*, *10*(1), 72–81. https://doi.org/10.1017/S1355617704101094

Lee, J. H., Lee, K. U., Lee, D. Y., Kim, K. W., Jhoo, J. H., Kim, J. H., Lee, K. H., Kim, S. Y., Han, S. H., & Woo, J. I. (2002). Development of the Korean version of the consortium to establish a registry for Alzheimer's Disease Assessment Packet (CERAD-K): Clinical and neuropsychological assessment batteries. *Journals of Gerontology* - Series B *Psychological Sciences and Social Sciences*, *57*(1), 47–53. https://doi.org/10.1093/geronb/57.1.P47

Lee, S. C., & Hanson, R. K. (2017). Similar predictive accuracy of the Static-99R risk tool for White, Black, and Hispanic sex offenders in California. *Criminal Justice and Behavior*, *44*(9), 1125–1140. https://doi.org/10.1177/0093854817711477

Lee, S. C., Hanson, R. K., & Blais, J. (2020). Predictive accuracy of the Static-99R and Static-2002R risk tools for identifying indigenous and White individuals at high risk for sexual recidivism in Canada. *Canadian Psychology/Psychologie Canadienne*, *61*(1), 42–57. https://doi.org/10.1037/cap0000182

Lee, S. C., Hanson, R. K., & Yoon, J. S. (2023). Predictive validity of Static-99R among 8,207 men convicted of sexual crimes in South Korea: A prospective field study. *Sexual Abuse*, *35*(6), 687–715. https://doi.org/10.1177/10790632221139173

Lee, S. J., & Kim, M. (2010). Study on recidivism prediction capability of PCL-R for criminals in South Korea. *Korean Journal of Forensic Psychology*, *1*(1), 43–55.

Leguízamo, A., Lee, S. C., Jeglic, E. L., & Calkins, C. (2017). Utility of the Static-99 and Static-99R with Latino sex offenders. *Sexual Abuse*, *29*(8), 765–785. https://doi.org/10.1177/1079063215618377

Lewis-Fernández, R., Aggarwal, N. K., & Kirmayer, L. J. (2020). The cultural formulation interview: Progress to date and future directions. *Transcultural Psychiatry*, *57*(4), 487–496. https://doi.org/10.1177/1363461520938273

Lewis-Fernandez, R., Aggarwal, N. K., Hinton, L., Hinton, D. E., & Kirmayer, L. J. (2016). *DSM–5 handbook on the cultural formulation interview*. American Psychiatric Publishing.

Lezak, M., Howieson, D., Bigler, E., & Tranel, D. (2012). *Neuropsychological assessment* (5th ed.). NY: Oxford University Press.

Li, S. M. Y., Viljoen, J. L., Christiansen, A. K., & Muir, N. M. (2020). Predictive validity of the Structured Assessment of Violence Risk in Youth (SAVRY) among a sample of Asian Canadian youth on probation. *Law and Human Behavior, 44*(6), 485–501. https://doi.org/10.1037/lhb0000431

Lilienfeld, S. O., Wood, J. M., & Garb, H. N. (2000). The scientific status of projective techniques. *Psychological Science in the Public Interest, 1*(2), 27–66. https://doi.org/10.1111/1529-1006.002

Lin, C. C., & Fu, V. R. (1990). A comparison of child rearing practices among Chinese, immigrant Chinese, and Caucasian-American parents. *Child Development, 61*(2), 429–433. https://doi.org/10.1111/j.1467-8624.1990.tb02789.x

Liu, C., Liu, Z., Chiu, H. F., Carl, T. W.-C., Zhang, H., Wang, P., Wu, G., Mwansisya, T. E., Cao, L., Hu, A., Wang, Y., & Xue, Z. (2013). Detection of malingering: Psychometric evaluation of the Chinese version of the Structured Interview of Reported Symtpoms-2. *BMC Psychiatry, 13*(1). https://doi.org/10.1186/1471-244x-13-254

Liu, M., & Chan, C. (1999). Enduring violence and staying in marriage: Stories of battered women in rural China. *Violence Against Women, 5*(12), 1469–1492. https://doi.org/10.1177/10778019922183471

López, E., Steiner, A. J., Hardy, D. J., IsHak, W. W., & Anderson, W. B. (2016). Discrepancies between bilinguals' performance on the Spanish and English versions of the WAIS Digit Span task: Cross-cultural implications. *Applied Neuropsychology: Adult, 23*(5), 343–352. https://doi.org/10.1080/23279095.2015.1074577

Lovatt, K. M., Stockdale, K. C., & Olver, M. E. (2022). Dynamic violence risk, protective factors, and therapeutic change in a gender and ethnoculturally diverse sample of court-adjudicated youth. *Psychological Assessment, 34*(2), 105–124. https://doi.org/10.1037/pas0001071

Lustig, M. W., & Koester, J. (1999). *Intercultural competence: Interpersonal communication across cultures* (3rd ed.). Longman.

Lv, Y., Han, C.-B., & Wang, X.-P. (2013). The reliability and validity of the historical, clinical, risk management-Chinese version. *Chinese Journal of Clinical Psychology, 21*(6), 984–987.

Lynn, R., & Vanhanen, T. (2006). *IQ and global inequality*. Washington Summit Publishers.

Mabry, C. R. (2013). Blending cultures and religions: Effects that the changing makeup of families in our nation have on child custody determinations. *Journal of the American Academy of Matrimonial Lawyers, 26*(1), 31–50. https://www.aaml.org/wp-content/uploads/MAT102_6.pdf

Maccoby, E. E., & Martin, J. A. (1983). Socialization in the context of the family: Parent-child interaction. In P. H. Mussen (Series Ed.) & E. M. Hetherington (Vol. Ed.), *Handbook of child psychology: Vol. IV. Socialization, personality and social development* (4th ed., pp. 1–101). New York: Wiley.

Manly, J. J., Jacobs, D. M., Touradji, P., Small, S. A., & Stern, Y. (2002). Reading level attenuates differences in neuropsychological test performance between African American and white elders. *Journal of the International Neuropsychological Society, 8*(3), 341–348. https://doi.org/10.1017/S1355617702813157

Marin, G., & Gamba, R. J. (1996). A new measurement of acculturation for Hispanics: The Bidimensional Acculturation Scale for Hispanics (BAS). *Hispanic Journal of Behavioral Sciences, 18*, 297–316. https://doi.org/10.1177/07399863960183002

Marin, G., Gamba, R. J., & Marin, B. V. (1992). Extreme response style and acquiescence among Hispanics: The role of acculturation and education. *Journal of Cross-Cultural Psychology*, *23*(4), 498–509. https://doi.org/10.1177/0022022192234006

Martens, R., Rettenberger, M., & Eher, R. (2017). The predictive and incremental validity of the German adaptation of the Static-2002 in a sexual offender sample released from the prison system. *Legal and Criminological Psychology*, *22*(1), 164–179. https://doi.org/10.1111/lcrp.12080

Martin, P. K., Schroeder, R. W., Olsen, D. H., Maloy, H., Boettcher, A., Ernst, N., & Okut, H. (2020). A systematic review and meta-analysis of the Test of Memory Malingering in adults: Two decades of deception detection. *The Clinical Neuropsychologist*, *34*(1), 88–119. https://doi.org/10.1080/13854046.2019.1637027

Martinez, R., Flores, J., & Rosenfeld, B. (2007). Validity of the Juvenile Sex Offender Assessment Protocol-II (J-SOAP-II) in a sample of urban minority youth. *Criminal Justice and Behavior*, *34*(10), 1284–1295. https://doi.org/10.1177/0093854807301791

Martinez, R., Rosenfeld, B., Cruise, K., & Martin, J. (2015). Predictive validity of the J-SOAP-II: Does accuracy differ across settings? *International Journal of Forensic Mental Health*, *14*, 56–65. http://doi.org/10.1080/14999013.2015.1019683

Matsumoto, D. (1996). *Culture and psychology*. Pacific Grove, CA: Brooks/Cole.

Matter of J-S-S, 26 I&N Dec. 679 (BIA 2015).

Matter of M-A-M, 25 I&N Dec. 474 (BIA 2011).

McCallum, R. S. (2017). Context for nonverbal assessment of intelligence and related abilities. In R. S. McCallum (Ed.), *Handbook of nonverbal assessment* (pp. 3–19). Springer International Publishing.

McCauley, S. R., Nguyen, T., Nguyen, C., Strutt, A. M., Stinson, J. M., Windham, V. A., & York, M. K. (2023). Developing a culturally competent neuropsychological assessment battery for Vietnamese-speaking patients with suspected dementia. *Archives of Clinical Neuropsychology*, *38*(3), 485–500. https://doi.org/10.1093/arclin/acac035

Melton, G., Petrilla, J., Poythress, N., & Slobogin, C. (2018). *Psychological evaluations for the courts*, 4th ed. Guilford

Mercado, A., Antuña, C. S., Bailey, C., Garcini, L., Hass, G. A., Henderson, C., Koslofsky, S., Morales, F., & Venta, A. (2022). Professional guidelines for psychological evaluations in immigration proceedings. *Journal of Latinx Psychology*, *10*(4), 253–276. https://doi.org/10.1037/lat0000209

Merckelbach, H., & Smith, G. P. (2003). Diagnostic accuracy of the Structured Inventory of Malingered Symptomatology (SIMS) in detecting instructed malingering. *Archives of Clinical Neuropsychology*, *18*(2), 145–152. https://doi.org/10.1016/S0887-6177(01)00191-3

Meyer, G. J., Erdberg, P., & Shaffer, T. W. (2007). Toward international normative reference data for the comprehensive system. *Journal of Personality Assessment*, *89* (Suppl 1), S201–S216. https://doi.org/10.1080/00223890701629342

Mezzich, J. E., Caracci, G., Fabrega, H., & Kirmayer, L. J. (2009). Cultural formulation guidelines. *Transcultural Psychiatry*, *46*, 383–405. https://doi.org/10.1177/1363461509342942

Migration Policy Institute. (2015). *The limited English proficient population in the United States* in 2013. Retrieved from https://www.migrationpolicy.org/article/limited-english-proficient-population-united-states-2013

Migration Policy Institute. (n.d.). *U.S. immigration trends*. Retrieved from: https://www.migrationpolicy.org/programs/data-hub/us-immigration-trends#children

Mihretu, A., Teferra, S., & Fekadu, A. (2017). What constitutes problematic khat use? An exploratory mixed methods study in Ethiopia. *Substance Abuse Treatment, Prevention, and Policy*, *12*, 17. https://doi.org/10.1186/s13011-017-0100-y

Milani, S. A., Marsiske, M., Cottler, L. B., Chen, X., & Striley, C. W. (2018). Optimal cutoffs for the Montreal Cognitive Assessment vary by race and ethnicity. *Alzheimer's &*

Dementia: Diagnosis, Assessment & Disease Monitoring, 10(1), 773–781. https://doi.org/https://doi.org/10.1016/j.dadm.2018.09.003
Miller, H. A. (2001). *M-FAST: Miller Forensic Assessment of Symptoms Test professional manual.* Psychological Assessment Resources.
Miller, K. E., Omidian, P., Quraishy, A. S., Nasiry, S., Karyar, N. M., & Yaqubi, A. A. (2006). The Afghan symptom checklist: A culturally grounded approach to mental health assessment in a conflict zone. *American Journal of Orthopsychiatry, 76*(4), 423–433.
Miller, K. M., Cahn, K., Anderson-Nathe, B., Cause, A. G., & Bender, R. (2013). Individual and systemic/structural bias in child welfare decision making: Implications for children and families of color. *Children and Youth Services Review, 35*(9), 1634–1642. https://doi.org/10.1016/j.childyouth.2013.07.002
Millon, T., Grossman, S., & Millon, C. (2015). *Millon Clinical Multiaxial Inventory-IV (MCMI-IV).* Pearson Assessments.
Millon, T., Tringone, R., Grossman, S., & Millon, C. (2020). *Millon adolescent clinical inventory-II (MACI-II).* Pearson Assessments.
Milner, J. S., & Crouch, J. L. (2012). Psychometric characteristics of translated versions of the Child Abuse Potential Inventory. *Psychology of Violence, 2*(3), 239–259. https://doi.org/10.1037/a0026957
Milner, J. S., & Wimberley, R. C. (1979). Child Abuse Potential Inventory (CAPI) [Database record]. APA PsycTests. https://doi.org/10.1037/t65940-000
Ministry of Justice. (2022). *Prison population figures: 2022.* United Kingdom Ministry of Justice. Retrieved from https://www.gov.uk/government/publications/prison-population-figures-2022
Minnesota Statutes § 518.17. (2023). *Custody and support of children on judgment.* In 2023 Minnesota Statutes. Retrieved from https://www.revisor.mn.gov/statutes/cite/518.17
Miranda v. Arizona, (1966). 384 U.S. 436
Molenda-Kostanski, Z. (2016). *Asian American men and fatherhood: Relationship between acculturation, gender-role conflict, parenting self-efficacy, and father involvement.* Seton Hall University Dissertations and Theses (ETDs). 2204. https://scholarship.shu.edu/dissertations/2204
Monahan, J., & Skeem, J. L. (2014). Risk redux: The resurgence of risk assessment in criminal sanctioning. *Federal Sentencing Reporter, 26*(3), 158–166. https://doi.org/10.1525/fsr.2014.26.3.158
Morel, K. R. (1998). Development and preliminary validation of a forced-choice test of response bias for posttraumatic stress disorder. *Journal of Personality Assessment, 70*(2), 299–314. https://doi.org/10.1207/s15327752jpa7002_8.
Morey, L. C. (1991). *Personality assessment inventory.* Psychological Assessment Resources.
Morey, L. C. (2007). *Personality Assessment Inventory–Adolescent (PAI-A) professional manual.* Psychological Assessment Resources.
Muir, N. M., & Viljoen, J. L. (2022). Adverse childhood experiences and recidivism in indigenous and white female and male adolescents on probation. *Child Abuse & Neglect, 126,* 105512. https://doi.org/10.1016/j.chiabu.2022.105512
Muir, N. M., Viljoen, J. L., & Shepherd, S. M. (2023). Violence risk assessment tools and indigenous peoples: Colonialism as an underlying cause of risk ratings on the SAVRY. *International Journal of Forensic Mental Health, 22*(4), 289–301. https://doi.org/10.1080/14999013.2023.2178554
Muir, N. M., Viljoen, J. L., Jonnson, M. R., Cochrane, D. M., & Rogers, B. J. (2020). Predictive validity of the Structured Assessment of Violence Risk in Youth (SAVRY) with indigenous and caucasian female and male adolescents on probation. *Psychological Assessment, 32*(6), 594–607. http://doi.org/10.1037/pas0000816
Mungas, D., Reed, B. R., Crane, P. K., Haan, M. N., & González, H. (2004). Spanish and English Neuropsychological Assessment Scales (SENAS): Further development

and psychometric characteristics. *Psychological Assessment, 16*(4), 347–359. https://doi.org/10.1037/1040-3590.16.4.347

Mungas, D., Reed, B. R., Haan, M. N., & González, H. (2005). Spanish and English Neuropsychological Assessment Scales: Relationship to demographics, language, cognition, and independent function. *Neuropsychology, 19*(4), 466–475. https://doi.org/10.1037/0894-4105.19.4.466

Munoz, C. G., & Venta, A. C. (2022). Considerations when conducting violence risk assessments in immigrant youth: The roles of acculturation stress and criminal attitudes. *Journal of International Migration and Integration, 23*, 989–1009. https://doi.org/10.1007/s12134-021-00868-4

Murphy, J. (1976). Psychiatric labeling in cross-cultural perspective. *Science, 191*, 1019–1027.

Murrie, D. C., Boccaccini, M. T., Turner, D. B., Meeks, M., Woods, C., & Tussey, C. (2009). Rater (dis) agreement on risk assessment measures in sexually violent predator proceedings: Evidence of adversarial allegiance in forensic evaluation? *Psychology, Public Policy, and Law, 15*(1), 19–53. https://doi.org/10.1037/a0014897

Nasreddine, Z. S., Phillips, N. A., Bédirian, V., Charbonneau, S., Whitehead, V., Collin, I., Cummings, J. L., & Chertkow, H. (2005). The Montreal Cognitive Assessment, MoCA: A brief screening tool for mild cognitive impairment. *Journal of the American Geriatrics Society, 53*(4), 695–699. https://doi.org/10.1111/j.1532-5415.2005.53221.x

National Academies of Sciences, Engineering, and Medicine. 2025. *Rethinking race and ethnicity in biomedical research.* Washington, DC: National Academies Press. https://doi.org/10.17226/27913.

National Association of Social Workers. (2008). *NASW code of ethics (guide to the everyday professional conduct of social workers).* Washington, DC: NASW.

Neisser, U., Boodoo, G., Bouchard, T. J., Boykin, A. W., Brody, N., Ceci, S. J., Halpern, D. F., Loehlin, J. C., Perloff, R., Sternberg, R. J., & Urbina, S. (1996). Intelligence: Knowns and unknowns. *American Psychologist, 51*(2), 77–101. https://doi.org/10.1037/0003-066X.51.2.77

Nell, V. (2000). *Cross-cultural neuropsychological assessment: Theory and practice.* Lawrence-Erlbaum Associates.

Neumann, C. S., Schmitt, D. S., Carter, R., Embley, I., & Hare, R. D. (2012). Psychopathic traits in females and males across the globe. *Behavioral Sciences & the Law, 30*(5), 557–574. https://doi.org/10.1002/bsl.2038

Nguyen, D. L., & Kehmeier, D. F. (1980). The people of Indochina: The Vietnamese. In J. F. McDermott, W. S. Tseng, & T. W. Maretzki (Eds.), *Peoples and cultures of Hawai'i* (pp. 200–217). Hawai'i Press.

Nielsen, T. R., Segers, K., Vanderaspoilden, V., Beinhoff, U., Minthon, L., Pissiota, A., Bekkhus-Wetterberg, P., Bjørkløf, G. H., Tsolaki, M., Gkioka, M., & Waldemar, G. (2019). Validation of a European Cross-Cultural Neuropsychological Test Battery (CNTB) for evaluation of dementia. *International Journal of Geriatric Psychiatry, 34*(1), 144–152. https://doi.org/10.1002/gps.5002

Nielsen, T. R., Segers, K., Vanderaspoilden, V., Bekkhus-Wetterberg, P., Minthon, L., Pissiota, A., … Waldemar, G. (2018). Performance of middle-aged and elderly European minority and majority populations on a Cross-Cultural Neuropsychological Test Battery (CNTB). *The Clinical Neuropsychologist, 32*(8), 1411–1430. https://doi.org/10.1080/13854046.2018.1430256

Nijdam-Jones, A., & Rosenfeld, B. (2017). Cross-cultural feigning assessment: A systematic review of feigning instruments used with linguistically, ethnically, and culturally diverse samples. *Psychological Assessment, 29*(11), 1321–1336. https://doi.org/10.1037/pas0000438

Nijdam-Jones, A., Chen, Y., & Rosenfeld, B. (2020). Detection of feigned posttraumatic stress disorder: A meta-analysis of the Minnesota Multiphasic Personality Inventory-2

(MMPI-2). *Psychological Trauma: Theory, Research, Practice, and Policy, 12*(7), 790–798. https://dx.doi.org/10.1037/tra0000593.

Nijdam-Jones, A., García-López, E., Aparcero, M., & Rosenfeld, B. (2020). How do Latin American professionals approach violence risk assessment? A qualitative exploratory study. *International Journal of Forensic Mental Health, 19*(3), 227–240. https://doi.org/10.1080/14999013.2019.1707330

Nijdam-Jones, A., García-López, E., Merchan, L., Ruiz Guarneros, A., & Rosenfeld, B. (2021). Predictive validity of the HCR-20V3 with incarcerated males in Mexico City. *Criminal Justice and Behavior, 48*(10), 1450–1467. https://doi.org/10.1177/0093854821997520

Nijdam-Jones, A., García-López, E., Merchan, L., Ruiz Guarneros, A., & Rosenfeld, B. (2023). Cross-cultural violence risk assessment: Adapting the HCR-20V3 for incarcerated offenders in Mexico. *International Journal of Forensic Mental Health, 22*(1), 39–55. https://doi.org/10.1080/14999013.2022.2053000

Nijdam-Jones, A., Rivera, D., Rosenfeld, B., & Arango-Lasprilla, J. C. (2017). A cross-cultural analysis of the Test of Memory Malingering among Latin American Spanish-speaking adults. *Law and Human Behavior, 41*(5), 422–428. https://doi.org/10.1037/lhb0000250

Nijdam-Jones, A., Rivera, D., Rosenfeld, B., & Arango-Lasprilla, J. C. (2019a). *The effect of education, literacy, and culture on cognitive effort test performance: An examination of the TOMM in Colombia* [Paper presentation]. Annual Conference of the International Association of Forensic Mental Health Services, Montreal, Canada.

Nijdam-Jones, A., Rivera, D., Rosenfeld, B., & Arango-Lasprilla, J. C. (2019b). The effect of literacy and culture on cognitive effort test performance: An examination of the Test of Memory Malingering in Colombia. *Journal of Clinical and Experimental Neuropsychology, 41*(10), 1015–1023. https://doi.org/10.1080/13803395.2019.1644294

O'Shea, L. E., Mitchell, A. E., Picchioni, M. M., & Dickens, G. L. (2013). Moderators of the predictive efficacy of the Historical, Clinical and Risk Management-20 for aggression in psychiatric facilities: Systematic review and meta-analysis. *Aggression and Violent Behavior, 18*(2), 255–270. https://doi.org/10.1016/j.avb.2012.11.016

Olver, M. E., Sowden, J. N., Kingston, D. A., Nicholaichuk, T. P., Gordon, A., Beggs Christofferson, S. M., & Wong, S. C. P. (2018). Predictive accuracy of Violence Risk Scale–Sexual Offender version: Risk and change scores in treated Canadian Aboriginal and non-Aboriginal sexual offenders. *Sexual Abuse, 30*(3), 254–275. https://doi.org/10.1177/1079063216649594

Olver, M. E., Stockdale, K. C., & Wormith, J. S. (2014). Thirty years of research on the level of service scales: A meta-analytic examination of predictive accuracy and sources of variability. *Psychological Assessment, 26*(1), 156–176. https://doi.org/10.1037/a0035080

Ostrosky-Solís, F., Ardila, A., & Rosselli, M. (1999). NEUROPSI: A brief neuropsychological test battery in Spanish with norms by age and educational level. *Journal of the International Neuropsychological Society, 5*(5), 413–433. https://doi.org/10.1017/S1355617799555045

Ostrosky-Solís, F., Gómez-Pérez, M. E., Matute, E., Rosselli, M., Ardila, A., & Pineda, D. (2007). NEUROPSI attention and memory: Neuropsychological test battery in Spanish with norms by age and education level. *Applied Neuropsychology, 14*(3), 156–170. https://doi.org/10.1080/09084280701508655

Ostrosky-Solis, F., Ramirez, M., & Ardila, A. (2004). Effects of culture and education on neuropsychological testing: A preliminary study with indigenous and nonindigenous population. *Applied Neuropsychology, 11*(4), 186–193. https://doi.org/10.1207/s15324826an1104_3

Owen, J., Tao, K. W., Imel, Z. E., Wampold, B. E., & Rodolfa, E. (2014). Addressing racial and ethnic microaggressions in therapy. *Professional Psychology: Research and Practice, 45*(4), 283–290. https://doi.org/10.1037/a0037420

Pace, T. M., Robbins, R. R., Choney, S. K., Hill, J. S., Lacey, K., & Blair, G. (2006). A cultural-contextual perspective on the validity of the MMPI-2 with American Indians. *Cultural Diversity and Ethnic Minority Psychology, 12*(2), 320–333. https://doi.org/10.1037/1099-9809.12.2.320

Palusci, V. J., & Botash, A. S. (2021). Race and bias in child maltreatment diagnosis and reporting. *Pediatrics, 148*(1), e2020049625. https://doi.org/10.1542/peds.2020-049625

Park, Y. S., Kim, B. S. K., Chiang, J., & Ju, C. M. (2010). Acculturation, enculturation, parental adherence to Asian cultural values, parenting styles, and family conflict among Asian American college students. *Asian American Journal of Psychology, 1*(1), 67–79. https://doi.org/10.1037/a0018961

Patricacou, A., Psallida, E., Pring, T., & Dipper, L. (2007). The Boston Naming Test in Greek: Normative data and the effects of age and education on naming. *Aphasiology, 21*(12), 1157–1170. https://doi.org/10.1080/02687030600670643

Pavlenko, A., Hepford, E., & Jarvis, S. (2019). An illusion of understanding: How native and non-native speakers of English understand (and misunderstand) their *Miranda* rights. *The International Journal of Speech, Language and the Law, 26*, 2. https://doi.org/10.1558/ijsll.39163

Picard, E., Aparcero, M., Nijdam-Jones, A., & Rosenfeld, B. (2023). Identifying positive impression management using the MMPI-2 and the MMPI-2-RF: A meta-analysis. *The Clinical Neuropsychologist, 37*, 545–561. https://doi.org/10.1080/13854046.2022.2077237

Ponterotto, J. G., (1998). Charting a course for research in multicultural counseling and training. *The Counseling Psychologist, 26*(1), 43–68. https://doi.org/10.1177/0011000098261004

Pontón, M. O., Satz, P., Herrera, L., Ortiz, F., Urrutia, C. P., Young, R., D'Elia, L. F., Furst, C. J., & Namerow, N. (1996). Normative data stratified by age and education for the Neuropsychological Screening Battery for Hispanics (NeSBHIS): Initial report. *Journal of the International Neuropsychological Society, 2*(2), 96–104. https://doi.org/10.1017/S1355617700000941

Poreh, A., Sultan, A., & Levin, J. (2012). The Rey Auditory Verbal Learning Test: Normative data for the Arabic-speaking population and analysis of the differential influence of demographic variables. *Psychology & Neuroscience, 5*(1), 57–61. https://doi.org/10.3922/j.psns.2012.1.08

Poythress, N., Nicholson, R., Otto, R. K., Edens, J. F., Bonnie, R. J., Monahan, J., & Hoge, S. K. (1999). *The MacArthur competence assessment tool—criminal adjudication: Professional manual.* Psychological Assessment Resources.

Prentky, R., & Righthand, S. (2003). *Juvenile Sex Offender Assessment Protocol-II (J-SOAP-II) manual.* U.S. Department of Justice, Office of Justice Programs, Office of Juvenile Justice and Delinquency Prevention.

Putnam-Hornstein, E., Needell, B., King, B., & Johnson-Motoyama, M. (2013). Racial and ethnic disparities: A population-based examination of risk factors for involvement with child protective services. *Child Abuse & Neglect, 37*(1), 33–46. https://doi.org/10.1016/j.chiabu.2012.08.005

Qi, W. G., Hong, Y., Sun, X., Stinson, J. M., York, M. K., McCauley, S., & Strutt, A. M. (2023). A neuropsychological battery for the evaluation of dementia among mandarin-speaking older adults in the United States. *Archives of Clinical Neuropsychology, 38*(3), 446–458. https://doi.org/10.1093/arclin/acac085

Qi, W. G., Sun, X., & Hong, Y. (2022). Normative data for adult mandarin-speaking populations: A systematic review of performance-based neuropsychological instruments.

Journal of the International Neuropsychological Society, 28(5), 520–540. https://doi.org/10.1017/S1355617721000667

Ramet, S. P. (2011). Croatia and Serbia since 1991: An assessment of their similarities and differences. *Journal of Communist Studies and Transition Politics, 27*(2), 263–290. https://doi.org/10.1080/13523279.2011.564098

Ramos Usuga, D., Ayearst, L. E., Rivera, D., Krch, D., Perrin, P. B., Carrión, C. I., Morel Valdés, G. M., Loro, D., Rodriguez, M. J., Munoz, G., Drago, C. I., García, P., Rivera, P. M., & Arango-Lasprilla, J. C. (2024). A preliminary examination of the TOMM2 in a sample of Spanish speakers in the United States. *NeuroRehabilitation, 55*(2), 235–242. https://doi.org/10.3233/nre-240085

Randolph, C. (2012). *Repeatable Battery for the Assessment of Neuropsychological Status Update-Spanish (RBANS Update).*

Rasmussen, A., Eustache, E., Raviola, G., Kaiser, B., Grelotti, D. J., & Belkin, G. S. (2015). Development and validation of a Haitian Creole screening instrument for depression. *Transcultural Psychiatry, 52*(1), 33–57. https://doi.org/10.1177/1363461514543546

Rasmussen, A., Keatley, E., & Joscelyne, A. (2014). Posttraumatic stress in emergency settings outside North America and Europe: A review of the emic literature. *Social Science & Medicine, 109*, 44–54. https://doi.org/10.1016/j.socscimed.2014.03.015.

Rees, L. M., Tombaugh, T. N., Gansler, D. A., & Moczynski, N. P. (1998). Five validation experiments of the Test of Memory Malingering (TOMM). *Psychological Assessment, 10*, 10–20. https://doi.org/10.1037/1040-3590.10.1.10

Renteln, A. D. (2010). Corporal punishment and the cultural defense. *Law and Contemporary Problems, 73*(2), 253–279. https://www.jstor.org/stable/25766393

Rettenberger, M., Hucker, S. J., Boer, D. P., & Eher, R. (2009). The reliability and validity of the Sexual Violence Risk-20 (SVR-20): An international review. *Sexual Offender Treatment, 4*(2).

Rey, A. (1964). *The clinical examination in psychology.* University Press of France.

Reynolds, C. R., & Kamphaus, R. W. (2015). *Behavior assessment system for children manual-third edition.* Pearson.

Reznek, L. (2005). The Rey 15-item memory test for malingering: A meta-analysis. *Brain Injury, 19*(7), 539–543. https://doi.org/10.1080/02699050400005242

Rhoads, T., Leib, S. I., Resch, Z. J., Basurto, K. S., Castillo, L. R., Jennette, K. L., Soble, J. R. (2021). Relative rates of invalidity for the Test of Memory Malingering and the Dot Counting Test among Spanish-speaking patients residing in the USA. *Psychological Injury and Law, 14*, 269–280. https://doi.org/10.1007/s12207-021-09423-z

Riany, Y. E., Meredith, P., & Cuskelly, M. (2017). Understanding the influence of traditional cultural values on Indonesian parenting, *Marriage and Family Review, 53*(3), 207–226. https://doi.org/10.1080/01494929.2016.1157561

Rice, M. E., Harris, G. T., & Lang, C. (2013). Validation of and revision to the VRAG and SORAG: The Violence Risk Appraisal Guide — Revised (VRAG-R). *Psychological Assessment, 25*(3), 951–965. https://doi.org/10.1037/a0032878

Rivera Mindt, M., Arentoft, A., Coulehan, K., Summers, A. C., Tureson, K., Aghvinian, M., & Byrd, D. A. (2019). Neuropsychological evaluation of culturally/linguistically diverse older adults. In L. D. Ravdin, & H. L. Katzen (eds) *Handbook on the neuropsychology of aging and dementia* (pp. 25–48). Springer. https://doi.org/10.1007/978-3-319-93497-6_3

Rivera Mindt, M., Arentoft, A., Germano, K. K., D'Aquila, E., Scheiner, D., Pizzirusso, M., Sandoval, T. C., & Gollan, T. H. (2008). Neuropsychological, cognitive, and theoretical considerations for evaluation of bilingual individuals. *Neuropsychology Review, 18*(3), 255–268. https://doi.org/10.1007/s11065-008-9069-7

Roberts, J. M., Arbisi, P. A., John, M. A., & Seamans, R. N. (2022). The utility of the Trauma Symptom Inventory as a primary and secondary assessment instrument for forensic practice in legal settings. *Journal of Personality Assessment, 104*(2), 221–233. https://doi.org/10.1080/00223891.2022.2029461.

Roesch, R., Zapf, P. A., & Eaves, D. (2006). *Fitness interview test-revised: A structured interview for assessing competence to stand trial.* Professional Resource Press.

Rogers, R. (2018). Detection strategies for malingering and defensiveness. In R. Rogers & S. D. Bender (Eds.), *Clinical assessment of malingering and deception* (4th ed., pp. 18–41). Guilford Press.

Rogers, R., Correa, A., Hazelwood, L., Shuman, D., Hoersting, R. and Blackwood, H. (2009). Spanish translations of Miranda warnings and the totality of the circumstances. *Law and Human Behavior, 33*, 61–69. https://doi.org/10.1007/s10979-008-9129-9

Rogers, R., Sewell, K. W., & Gillard, N. D. (2010). *Structured interview of reported symptoms professional manual* (2nd ed.). Psychological Assessment Resources.

Rogers, R., Tillbrook, C. E., & Sewell, K. W. (2004). *Evaluation of competence to stand trial-revised (ECST-R).* Psychological Assessment Resources.

Roivainen, E. (2019). European and American WAIS IV norms: Cross-national differences in perceptual reasoning, processing speed and working member subtest scores. *Scandinavian Journal of Psychology, 60*(6) 513–519. https://doi.org/10.1111/sjop.12581

Rosenfeld, B., Green, D., Pivovarova, E., Dole, T., & Zapf, P. (2010). What to do with contradictory data: Approaches to the integrating of multiple malingering measures. *International Journal of Forensic Mental Health, 9*(2), 63–73. https://doi.org/10.1080/14999013.2010.499559

Rosenfeld, B., Sands, S., & Van Gorp, W. (2000). Have we forgotten the base rate problem? Methodological issues in the detection of distortion. *Archives of Clinical Neuropsychology, 15*(4), 349–359. https://doi.org/10.1093/arclin/15.4.349.

Rosselli, M., & Ardila, A. (2003). The impact of culture and education on non-verbal neuropsychological measurements: A critical review. *Brain and Cognition, 52*(3), 326–333. https://doi.org/10.1016/S0278-2626(03)00170-2

Ryan, J. J., Yamaguchi, T., & Kreiner, D. S. (2019). Preliminary validation of the Rey 15-item test and reliable digit span in native Japanese samples. *Psychological Reports, 122*(5), 1925–1945. https://doi.org/10.1177/0033294118792697

Ryu, H. J., & Yang, D. W. (2023). The Seoul Neuropsychological Screening Battery (SNSB) for comprehensive neuropsychological assessment. *Dementia and Neurocognitive Disorders, 22*(1), 1–15. https://doi.org/10.12779/dnd.2023.22.1.1

Sachs, E., Rosenfeld, B., Lhewa, D., Rasmussen, A., & Keller, A. (2008). Entering exile: Trauma, mental health and coping among Tibetan refugees arriving in Dharamsala, India. *Journal of Traumatic Stress, 21*, 199–208. https://doi.org/10.1002/jts.20324.

Sada, A., Robles-García, R., Martínez-López, N., Hernández-Ramírez, R., Tovilla-Zarate, C.-A., López-Munguía, F., Suárez-Alvarez, E., Ayala, X., & Fresán, A. (2016). Assessing the reliability, predictive and construct validity of historical, clinical and risk management-20 (HCR-20) in Mexican psychiatric inpatients. *Nordic Journal of Psychiatry, 70*(6), 456–461. https://doi.org/10.3109/08039488.2016.1159330

Sayegh, P., Arentoft, A., Thaler, N. S., Dean, A. C., & Thames, A. D. (2014). Quality of education predicts performance on the Wide Range Achievement Test-4th edition Word Reading subtest. *Archives of Clinical Neuropsychology, 29*(8), 731–736. https://doi.org/10.1093/arclin/acu059

Schmader, T., Johns, M., & Forbes, C. (2008). An integrated process model of stereotype threat effects on performance. *Psychological Review, 115*(2), 336–356. https://doi.org/10.1037/0033-295X.115.2.336

Schmid, A., García-López, E., Rosenfeld, B., & Nijdam-Jones, A. (2025). Predicting institutional violence: Utility of the psychopathy checklist-revised in a Mexican prison context. *Assessment.* Advance Online, 1–16. https://doi.org/10.1177/10731911251368062

Schmidt, S., Pettke, O., Lehmann, R. J. B., & Dahle, K.-P. (2017). Sexual offenders with and without a migration background from the Middle East and North Africa Crime scene behavior and risk assessment. *Forensische Psychiatrie, Psychologie, Kriminologie, 11*(4), 322–334. https://doi.org/10.1007/s11757-017-0441-4

Schroeder, R. W., & Bieu, R. K. (2024). Exploration of PCL-5 symptom validity indices for detection of exaggerated and feigned PTSD. *Journal of Clinical and Experimental Neuropsychology, 46*(2), 152–161. https://doi.org/10.1080/13803395.2024.2314728

Sea, J., & Bang, S. (2021). The interrater reliability and concurrent validity of the HCR-20 version 3 in South Korea. *Journal of Forensic Psychiatry and Psychology, 32*(6), 879–901. https://doi.org/10.1080/14789949.2021.1937279

Seaborn, B., Andrews, J. F., & Martin, G. (2010). Deaf adults and the comprehension of Miranda. *Journal of Forensic Psychology Practice, 10*(2), 107–132. https://doi.org/10.1080/15228930903446732

Sellbom, M., Flens, J., Gould, J., Ramnath, R., Tringone, R., & Grossman, S. (2022). The Millon Clinical Multiaxial Inventory-IV (MCMI-IV) and Millon Adolescent Clinical Inventory-II (MACI-II) in legal settings. *Journal of Personality Assessment, 104*(2), 203–220. https://doi.org/10.1080/00223891.2021.2013248

Sellbom, M., Laurinavičius, A., Ustinavičiūtė, L., & Laurinaitytė, I. (2018). The Triarchic Psychopathy measure: An examination in a Lithuanian inmate sample. *Psychological Assessment, 30*(7), e10–e20. https://doi.org/10.1037/pas0000603

Shan, I.-K., Chen, Y.-S., Lee, Y.-C., & Su, T.-P. (2008). Adult normative data of the Wisconsin Card Sorting Test in Taiwan. *Journal of the Chinese Medical Association, 71*(10), 517–522. https://doi.org/10.1016/S1726-4901(08)70160-6

Shear, L. E., & Drozd, L. M. (2013). To speak of all kinds of things: Child custody evaluations and the unique characteristics of relocations to foreign countries. *Journal of Child Custody, 10*(3–4), 325–358. https://doi.org/10.1080/15379418.2013.864937

Shein, E. (1990). Organizational culture. *American Psychologist, 45*, 109–119. https://doi.org/10.1037/0003-066X.45.2.109

Shepherd, S. M., & Willis-Esqueda, C. (2018). Indigenous perspectives on violence risk assessment: A thematic analysis. *Punishment & Society, 20*, 599–627. http://doi.org/10.1177/1462474517721485

Shepherd, S. M., Adams, Y., McEntyre, E., & Walker, R. (2014). Violence risk assessment in Australian Aboriginal offender populations: A review of the literature. *Psychology, Public Policy, and Law, 20*(3), 281–293. https://doi.org/10.1037/law0000017

Shepherd, S., & Lewis-Fernandez, R. (2016). Forensic risk assessment and cultural diversity: Contemporary challenges and future directions. *Psychology, Public Policy, and Law, 22*, 427–438. https://doi.org/10.1037/law0000102.

Sherman, E. M. S., Slick, D. J., & Iverson, G. L. (2020). Multidimensional malingering criteria for neuropsychological assessment: A 20-year update of the malingered neuropsychological dysfunction criteria. *Archives of Clinical Neuropsychology, 35*(6), 735–764. https://doi.org/10.1093/arclin/acaa019

Shiomi, K., & Loo, R. (1999). Cross-cultural response styles on the Kirton adaption-innovation inventory. *Social Behavior and Personality: An International Journal, 27*, 413–419. https://doi.org/10.2224/sbp.1999.27.4.413

Shulruf, B., Alesi, M., Ciochină, L., Faria, L., Hattie, J., Hong, F., Pepi, A.-M., & Watkins, D. (2011). Measuring collectivism and individualism in the third millennium. *Social Behavior and Personality: An International Journal, 39*(2), 173–187. https://doi.org/10.2224/sbp.2011.39.2.173

Shumaker, N., Long, T., Torres, A., Mercado, A., Marek, R. J., & Anderson, J. L. (2024). Exploring potential ethnic bias among MMPI-3 scales in assessing personality psychopathology. *Assessment (Advance Online)*. https://doi.org/10.1177/10731911241254341

Shura, R. D., Ord, A. S., & Worthen, M. D. (2022). Structured inventory of malingered symptomatology: A psychometric review. *Psychological Injury and Law, 15*(1), 64–78. https://doi.org/10.1007/s12207-021-09432-y

Silver, E. (2000). Race, neighborhood disadvantage, and violence among persons with mental disorders: The importance of contextual measurement. *Law and Human Behavior, 24*(4), 449–456. https://doi.org/10.1023/A:1005544330132

Singh, J. P., Desmarais, S. L., Hurducas, C., Arbach-Lucioni, K., Condemarin, C., Dean, K., Doyle, M., Folino, J. O., Godoy-Cervera, V., Grann, M., Ho, R. M. Y., Large, M. M., Nielsen, L. H., Pham, T. H., Rebocho, M. F., Reeves, K. A., Rettenberger, M., de Ruiter, C., Seewald, K., & Otto, R. K. (2014). International perspectives on the practical application of violence risk assessment: A global survey of 44 countries. *International Journal of Forensic Mental Health, 13*(3), 193–206. https://doi.org/10.1080/14999013.2014.922141

Singh, J. P., Grann, M., & Fazel, S. (2011). A comparative study of violence risk assessment tools: A systematic review and metaregression analysis of 68 studies involving 25,980 participants. *Clinical Psychology Review, 31*(3), 499–513. https://doi.org/10.1016/j.cpr.2010.11.009

Slick, D. J., Sherman, E. M. S., & Iverson, G. L. (1999). Diagnostic criteria for malingered neurocognitive dysfunction: Proposed standards for clinical practice and research. *Clinical Neuropsychologist, 13*(4), 545–561. https://doi.org/10.1076/1385-4046(199911)13:04;1-Y;FT545

Smallbone, S., & Rallings, M. (2013). Short-term predictive validity of the Static-99 and Static-99-R for indigenous and nonindigenous Australian sexual offenders. *Sexual Abuse, 25*(3), 302–316. https://doi.org/10.1177/1079063212472937

Smith, G. P., & Burger, G. K. (1997). Detection of malingering: Validation of the Structured Inventory of Malingered Symptomatology (SIMS). *Journal of the American Academy of Psychiatry and the Law, 25*, 183–189.

Spearman, C. (1904). "General intelligence," objectively determined and measured. *The American Journal of Psychology, 15*(2), 201–292. https://doi.org/10.2307/1412107

Spencer-Oatey, H. (2012). What is culture? A compilation of quotations. *Globalpad Core Concepts.* Retrieved from https://warwick.ac.uk/fac/soc/al/globalpad-rip/openhouse/interculturalskills_old/core_concept_compilations/global_pad_-_what_is_culture.pdf

Spiranovic, C. (2012). *The Static-99 and Static-99-R norms project: Developing norms based on Western Australian sex offenders.* University of Western Australia.

Starr, S. B. (2014). Evidence-based sentencing and the scientific rationalization of discrimination. *Stanford Law Review, 66*, 803–872.

State v.Kargar, 679 A.2d 81 (Me. 1996).

State v. Ortiz-Abrego, 187 Wash. 2d 394, 387 P.3d 638 (Wash. 2017).

State v. Sisouvanh, 175 Wash. 2d 607, 290 P.3d 942 (Wash. 2012)

Steele, C. M., & Aronson, J. (1995). Stereotype threat and the intellectual test performance of African Americans. *Journal of Personality and Social Psychology, 69*(5), 797–811. https://doi.org/10.1037/0022-3514.69.5.797

Sternberg, R. J. (2004). Culture and intelligence. *American Psychologist, 59*(5), 325–338. https://doi.org/10.1037/0003-066X.59.5.325

Sternberg, R. J. (2007). Intelligence and culture. In S. Kitayama & D. Cohen (Eds.), *Handbook of cultural psychology* (pp. 547–568). Guilford Press.

Sternberg, R. J., & Grigorenko, E. L. (2008). Ability testing across cultures. In L. A. Suzuki & J. G. Ponterottto (Eds.), *Handbook of multi-cultural assessment: Clinical, psychological, and education application* (3rd ed., pp. 449–470). Wiley.

Sternberg, R. J., Nokes, C., Geissler, P. W., Prince, R., Okatcha, F., Bundy, D. A., & Grigorenko, E. L. (2001). The relationship between academic and practical intelligence:

A case study in Kenya. *Intelligence, 29*(5), 401–418. https://doi.org/10.1016/S0160-2896(01)00065-4

Storey, J. E., Rowland, J. T. J., Conforti, D. A., & Dickson, H. G. (2004). The Rowland Universal Dementia Assessment Scale (RUDAS): A multicultural cognitive assessment scale. *International Psychogeriatrics, 16*(1), 13–31. https://doi.org/10.1017/S1041610204000043

Sue, D. W. (2001). Multidimensional facets of cultural competence. *The Counseling Psychologist, 29(*6), 790–821. https://doi.org/10.1177/0011000001296002

Sue, D. W. (2004). Whiteness and ethnocentric monoculturalism: Making the "invisible" visible. *American Psychologist, 59*(8), 761–769. https://doi.org/10.1037/0003-066X.59.8.761

Sue, D. W., & Sue, D. (2016). *Counseling the culturally diverse: Theory and practice.* 7th ed. John Wiley & Sons, Inc.

Sweet, J. J., Heilbronner, R. L., Morgan, J. E., Larrabee, G. J., Rohling, M. L., Boone, K. B., Kirkwood, M. W., Schroeder, R. W., Suhr, J. A., & Conference Participants. (2021). American Academy of Clinical Neuropsychology (AACN) 2021 consensus statement on validity assessment: Update of the 2009 AACN consensus conference statement on neuropsychological assessment of effort, response bias, and malingering. *The Clinical Neuropsychologist, 35*(6), 1053–1106. https://doi.org/10.1080/13854046.2021.1896036

Tam, W.-C. C., Chang, Y.-T., & Rosenfeld, B. (2023). A simulation study on the utility of the structured interview of Reported Symptoms-Second Edition (SIRS-2) in Taiwan Region adults. *Psychology, Crime & Law*, 1–12. https://doi.org/10.1080/1068316X.2023.2222214

Tan, Y. W., Burgess, G. H., & Green, R. J. (2021). The effects of acculturation on neuropsychological test performance: A systematic literature review. *The Clinical Neuropsychologist, 35*(3), 541–571. https://doi.org/10.1080/13854046.2020.1714740

Tazi, K. Y., Rogers, R., & Chang, Y.-T. (2023). Forensic evaluations for immigration courts: A critical commentary on legal and ethical considerations. *Psychological Injury and Law, 16*, 303–319. https://doi.org/10.1007/s12207-023-09489-x.

Thames, A. D., Hinkin, C. H., Byrd, D. A., Bilder, R. M., Duff, K. J., Mindt, M. R., Arentoft, A., & Streiff, V. (2013). Effects of stereotype threat, perceived discrimination, and examiner race on neuropsychological performance: Simple as black and white? *Journal of the International Neuropsychological Society, 19*(5), 583–593. https://doi.org/10.1017/S1355617713000076

Thornquist, M. H., & Zuckerman, M. (1995). Psychopathy, passive-avoidance learning and basic dimensions of personality. *Personality and Individual Differences, 19*(4), 525–534. https://doi.org/10.1016/0191-8869(95)00051-7

Thurstone, L. L. (1938). *Primary mental abilities.* University of Chicago Press.

Tombaugh, T. N. (1996). *Test of memory malingering (TOMM).* Multi-Health Systems, Inc.

Tombaugh, T. N. (1997). The Test of Memory Malingering (TOMM): Normative data from cognitively intact and cognitively impaired individuals. *Psychological Assessment,* 9(3), 260–268. https://doi.org/10.1037/1040-3590.9.3.260

Tombaugh, T. N., & McCaffrey, R. J. (unpublished test manual). *Test of Memory Malingering (TOMM 2) – 2nd edition.* Multi-Health Systems Inc.

Triandis, H. C. (2001). Individualism-collectivism and personality. *Journal of Personality,* 69(6), 907–924.

Trujillo, S. M., Green, J. A., & Carrillo, A. (2019). *Introduction to the language acculturation meter for Spanish-speaking English language learners (white paper).* PAR, Inc.

Tsao, I. T., & Chu, C. M. (2021). An exploratory study of recidivism risk assessment instruments for individuals convicted of sexual offenses in Singapore. *Sexual Abuse, 33*(2), 157–175. https://doi.org/10.1177/1079063219884575

Tuokko, H. A., Chou, P. H. B., Bowden, S. C., Simard, M., Ska, B., & Crossley, M. (2009). Partial measurement equivalence of French and English versions of the Canadian study of health and aging neuropsychological battery. *Journal of the International Neuropsychological Society, 15*(3), 416–425. https://doi.org/10.1017/S1355617709090602

U.S. Department of Justice, Executive Office for Immigration Review. (2007). *Immigration judge benchbook.* Retrieved from https://www.justice.gov/eoir/page/file/988046/download

United Nations International Children's Emergency Rund. (2024). *Female genital mutilation/cutting: A global concern – 2024 update.* Retrieved from https://data.unicef.org/resources/female-genital-mutilation-a-global-concern-2024/

United Nations Office of the High Commissioner for Human Rights. (2022). *Istanbul Protocol: Manual on the effective investigation and documentation of torture and other cruel, inhuman or degrading treatment or punishment.* Professional Training Series No. 8/Rev. 2. United Nations

U.S. Government Accountability Office. (2018). *Criminal alien statistics: Information on incarcerations, arrests, convictions, costs, and removals.* Publication GAO-18-433, Washington, DC.

Ursache, A., & Noble, K. G. (2016). Neurocognitive development in socioeconomic context: Multiple mechanisms and implications for measuring socioeconomic status. *Psychophysiology, 53*(1), 71–82. https://doi.org/10.1111/psyp.12547

Van der Put, C. E., Assink, M., & van Solinge, N. F. B. (2017). Predicting child maltreatment: A meta-analysis of the predictive validity of risk assessment instruments. *Child Abuse & Neglect, 73*, 71–88. https://doi.org/10.1016/j.chiabu.2017.09.016

Van Impelen, A., Merckelbach, H., Jelicic, M., & Merten, T. (2014). The Structured Inventory of Malingered Symptomatology (SIMS): A systematic review and meta-analysis. *The Clinical Neuropsychologist, 28*(8), 1336–1365. https://doi.org/10.1080/13854046.2014.984763

Varela, J. G., Boccaccini, M. T., Gonzalez, E., Jr., Gharagozloo, L., & Johnson, S. M. (2011). Do defense attorney referrals for competence to stand trial evaluations depend on whether the client speaks English or Spanish? *Law and Human Behavior, 35*(6), 501–511. https://doi.org/10.1007/s10979-010-9253-1

Varela, J. G., Boccaccini, M. T., Murrie, D. C., Caperton, J. D., & Gonzalez, E. (2013). Do the Static-99 and Static-99R perform similarly for White, Black, and Latino sexual offenders? *International Journal of Forensic Mental Health, 12*(4), 231–243. https://doi.org/10.1080/14999013.2013.846950

Vélez-Agosto, N. M., Soto-Crespo, J. G., Vizcarrondo-Oppenheimer, M., Vega-Molina, S., & García Coll, C. (2017). Bronfenbrenner's bioecological theory revision: Moving culture from the macro into the micro. *Perspectives on Psychological Science, 12*(5), 900–910. https://doi.org/10.1177/1745691617704397

Vernon, M., & Miller, K. (2001). Linguistic incompetence to stand trial: A unique condition in some deaf defendants. *Journal of Interpretation, 9*, 99–120.

Viglione, D. J., de Ruiter, C., King, C. M., Meyer, G. J., Kivisto, A. J., Rubin, B. A., & Hunsley, J. (2022). Legal admissibility of the Rorschach and R-PAS: A review of research, practice, and case law. *Journal of Personality Assessment, 104*(2), 137–161. https://doi.org/10.1080/00223891.2022.2028795

Viglione, D. J., Giromini, L., & Landis, P. (2017). The development of the Inventory of Problems–29: A brief self-administered measure for discriminating bona fide from feigned psychiatric and cognitive complaints. *Journal of Personality Assessment, 99*, 534–544. https://doi.org/10.1080/00223891.2016.1233882

Viljoen, J. L., Odgers, C., Grisso, T., & Tillbrook, C. (2007). Teaching adolescents and adults about adjudicative proceedings: A comparison of pre- and post-teaching scores on the MacCAT-CR. *Law and Human Behavior, 31*, 419–432. https://doi.org/10.1007/s10979-006-9069-1

Villaseñor, E. M., Rosselli, M., Ardila, A., & Solís, F. O. (2013). *Evaluación neuropsicológica infantil (ENI-2).* Manual Moderno.

Wallerstein, N. B., & Duran, B. (2006). Using community-based participatory research to address health disparities. *Health Promotion Practice, 7*(3), 312–323. https://doi.org/10.1177/1524839906289376

Walsh, Z. (2013). Psychopathy and criminal violence: The moderating effect of ethnicity. *Law and Human Behavior, 37*(5), 303–311. https://doi.org/10.1037/lhb0000017

Walsh, Z., & Kosson, D. S. (2007). Psychopathy and violent crime: A prospective study of the influence of socioeconomic status and ethnicity. *Law and Human Behavior, 31*, 209–229. https://doi.org/10.1007/s10979-006-9057-5

Weathers, F. W., Bovin, M. J., Lee, D. J., Sloan, D. M., Schnurr, P. P., Kaloupek, D. G., Keane, T. M., & Marx, B. P. (2018). The Clinician-Administered PTSD Scale for DSM-5 (CAPS-5): Development and initial psychometric evaluation in military veterans. *Psychological Assessment, 30*(3), 383–395. https://doi.org/10.1037/pas0000486

Webster, C. D., Eaves, D., Douglas, K. S., & Wintrup, A. (1995). *The HCR–20 scheme: The assessment of dangerousness and risk.* Simon Fraser University and Forensic Psychiatric Services Commission of British Columbia.

Wechsler, D. (2001). *Wechsler test of adult reading.* Psychological Corporation.

Wechsler, D. (2013). *Escala wechsler de inteligencia para adultos WAIS-IV.* Manual Moderno Mexico, Mexico City.

Wechsler, D. (2024). *Wechsler Adult Intelligence Scale (WAIS-5)* (5th ed.). Pearson U.S.

Weiss, L. G., Chen, H., Harris, J. G., Holdnack, J. A., & Saklofske, D. H. (2010). WAIS-IV use in societal context. In *WAIS-IV clinical use and interpretation* (pp. 97–139). Elsevier. https://doi.org/10.1016/b978-0-12-375035-8.10004-7

Weiss, R., & Rosenfeld, B. (2010). Cross-cultural validity in malingering assessment: The dot counting test in a rural Indian sample. *International Journal of Forensic Mental Health, 9*(4), 300–307. https://doi.org/10.1080/14999013.2010.526680

Weiss, R., & Rosenfeld, B. (2012). Navigating cross-cultural issues in forensic assessment: Recommendations for practice. *Professional Psychology: Research and Practice, 43*, 234–240. https://doi.org/10.1037/a0025850

Weiss, R., & Rosenfeld, B. (2017). Identifying feigning in trauma-exposed African immigrants. *Psychological Assessment, 29*(7), 881–889. https://doi.org/10.1037/pas0000381

Whaley, A. L. (1997). Ethnicity/race, paranoia, and psychiatric diagnoses: Clinician bias versus sociocultural differences. *Journal of Psychopathology and Behavioral Assessment, 19*(1), 1–20. http://dx.doi.org/10.1007/BF02263226

Whitman, M. R., Hansen, A. N., Ortega Medina, L., & Ben-Porath, Y. S. (2022). Psychometric properties of Spanish-language MMPI-3 scores in a Puerto Rican parental fitness evaluation setting. *Psychological Assessment, 34*(8), 803–809. https://doi.org/10.1037/pas0001140

Whitman, M. R., Holmes, K., Elias, L. S., Cappo, B. M., & Ben-porath, Y. S. (2024). Incremental validity of MMPI-3 and NEO PI-3 scores in public safety candidate pre-employment psychological evaluations. *Criminal Justice and Behavior, 51*(3), 331–352. https://doi.org/10.1177/00938548231219809

Widows, M. R., & Smith, G. P. (2005). *Structured inventory of malingered symptomatology professional manual.* Psychological Assessment Resources.

Wild, D., Furtado, T., & Angalakuditi, M. (2012). The translation and cultural adaptation of the Child Behavior Checklist for use in Israel (Hebrew), Korea, the US

(Spanish), India (Malayalam and Kannada), and Spain. *Psychology Research and Behavior Management, 2012*(5), 51–56. https://doi.org/10.2147/PRBM.S28009

Wildeman, C., Edwards, F. R., & Wakefield, S. (2020). The cumulative prevalence of termination of parental rights for U.S. children, 2000–2016. *Child Maltreatment, 25*(1), 32–42. https://doi.org/10.1177/1077559519848499

Wilkinson, G. S., & Robertson, G. J. (2017). *Wide range achievement test (WRAT-5)* (5th ed.). NCS Pearson.

WilsCon, H. A., & Gutierrez, L. (2014). Does one size fit all? A meta-analysis examining the predictive ability of the Level of Service Inventory (LSI) with Aboriginal offenders. *Criminal Justice and Behavior, 41*(2), 196–219. https://doi.org/10.1177/0093854813500958

Wisdom, N. M., Callahan, J. L., & Shaw, T. G. (2010). Diagnostic utility of the Structured Inventory of Malingered Symptomatology to detect malingering in a forensic sample. *Archives of Clinical Neuropsychology, 25*(2), 118–125. https://doi.org/10.1093/arclin/acp110

Wong, S. C. P., Olver, M. E., Nicholaichuk, T. P., & Gordon, A. (2003). *The Violence Risk Scale: Sexual Offender version (VRS-SO).*

Wong, T. M., & Fujii, D. E. (2004). Neuropsychological assessment of Asian Americans: Demographic factors, cultural diversity, and practical guidelines. *Applied Neuropsychology, 11*(1), 23–36. https://doi.org/10.1207/s15324826an1101_4

Wongupparaj, P., Kumari, V., & Morris, R. (2015). A cross-temporal meta-analysis of Raven's Progressive Matrices: Age groups and developing versus developed countries. *Intelligence, 49*, 1–9. https://doi.org/10.1016/j.intell.2014.11.008

World Health Organization. (2022). *ICD-11: International classification of diseases* (11th revision). https://icd.who.int/

Woodcock, R., Alvarado, C. G., Ruef, M. L., & Schrank, F. A. (2010). *The Woodcock-Muñoz Language Survey (WMLS III).*

Xie, Q. W., Sun, X., Chen, M., Qiao, D. P., & Chan, K. L. (2017). What prevents Chinese parents from reporting possible cases of child sexual abuse to authority? A holistic-interactionistic approach. *Child Abuse & Neglect, 64*, 19–31. https://doi.org/10.1016/j.chiabu.2016.12.006

Yeh, T.-C., Chou, Y.-C., Weng, J.-P., Yeh, H.-W., Kao, Y.-C., Chiang, W.-S., Chen, T.-Y., Hu, J.-M., & Tzeng, N.-S. (2019). Detection of malingering in the memory of patients with dementia: A pilot study on Coin-in-the-Hand test in a northern Taiwan memory clinic. *Journal of Medical Sciences, 39*(2), 81–89. https://doi.org/10.4103/jmedsci.jmedsci_100_18.

York, M. K., Kim, S. H., Lee, D. D., Windham, V. A., Strutt, A. M., Stinson, J. M., & McCauley, S. R. (2023). Culturally competent approaches for neuropsychological assessment for differential diagnosis of dementia of Korean-speaking patients in the United States. *Archives of Clinical Neuropsychology, 38*(3), 459–471. https://doi.org/10.1093/arclin/acac094

Yunis, F., Zoubeidi, T., Eapen, V., & Yousef, S. (2007). Psychometric properties of the Child Behavior Checklist/2–3 in an Arab population. *Psychological Reports, 100*(3), 771–776. https://doi.org/10.2466/pr0.100.3.771-776

Zapf, P. A., Roesch, R., & Viljoen, J. (2001). Assessing fitness to stand trial: The utility of the Fitness Interview Test (revised edition). *Canadian Journal of Psychiatry, 46*(5), 426–432. http://doi.org/10.1177/070674370104600508

Zeinoun, P., Iliescu, D., & El Hakim, R. (2022). Psychological tests in Arabic: A review of methodological practices and recommendations for future use. *Neuropsychology Review, 32*(1), 1–19. https://doi.org/10.1007/s11065-021-09476-6

Zhou, J., Witt, K., Cao, X., Chen, C., & Wang, X. (2017). Predicting reoffending using the Structured Assessment of Violence Risk in Youth (SAVRY): A 5-year follow-up study of male juvenile offenders in Hunan province, China. *PLOS ONE, 12*(1), e0169251. https://doi.org/10.1371/journal.pone.0169251

Index

For the benefit of digital users, indexed terms that span two pages (e.g., 52–53) may, on occasion, appear on only one of those pages.

Tables and figures are indicated by an italic *t* and *f* following the paragraph number

www.ingramcontent.com/pod-product-compliance
Lightning Source LLC
Chambersburg PA
CBHW030006020526
44271CB00015B/112